# VISIT US AT

## www.syngress.com

MW00997434

Syngress is committed to publishing high-quality books for IT Professionals and delivering those books in media and formats that fit the demands of our customers. We are also committed to extending the utility of the book you purchase via additional materials available from our Web site.

## SOLUTIONS WEB SITE

To register your book, visit www.syngress.com/solutions. Once registered, you can access our solutions@syngress.com Web pages. There you may find an assortment of value-added features such as free e-books related to the topic of this book, URLs of related Web sites, FAQs from the book, corrections, and any updates from the author(s).

## ULTIMATE CDs

Our Ultimate CD product line offers our readers budget-conscious compilations of some of our best-selling backlist titles in Adobe PDF form. These CDs are the perfect way to extend your reference library on key topics pertaining to your area of expertise, including Cisco Engineering, Microsoft Windows System Administration, CyberCrime Investigation, Open Source Security, and Firewall Configuration, to name a few.

## DOWNLOADABLE E-BOOKS

For readers who can't wait for hard copy, we offer most of our titles in downloadable Adobe PDF form. These e-books are often available weeks before hard copies, and are priced affordably.

## SYNGRESS OUTLET

Our outlet store at syngress.com features overstocked, out-of-print, or slightly hurt books at significant savings.

## SITE LICENSING

Syngress has a well-established program for site licensing our e-books onto servers in corporations, educational institutions, and large organizations. Contact us at sales@syngress.com for more information.

## CUSTOM PUBLISHING

Many organizations welcome the ability to combine parts of multiple Syngress books, as well as their own content, into a single volume for their own internal use. Contact us at sales@syngress.com for more information.

SYNGRESS®

JAY BEALE'S OPEN SOURCE SECURITY SERIES

# Wireshark &
# Ethereal
## Network Protocol
## Analyzer Toolkit

**Angela Orebaugh**

**Gilbert Ramirez**

**Josh Burke**

**Larry Pesce**

**Joshua Wright**

**Greg Morris**

SYNGRESS®
OPEN SOURCE

SECURITY TOOLS
& SCRIPTS

| KEY | SERIAL NUMBER |
| --- | --- |
| 001 | HJIRTCV764 |
| 002 | PO9873D5FG |
| 003 | 829KM8NJH2 |
| 004 | HPPPLEEEWY |
| 005 | CVPLQ6WQ23 |
| 006 | VBP965T5T5 |
| 007 | HJJJ863WD3E |
| 008 | 2987GVTWMK |
| 009 | 629MP5SDJT |
| 010 | IMWQ295T6T |

PUBLISHED BY
Syngress Publishing, Inc.
800 Hingham Street
Rockland, MA 02370

## Wireshark & Ethereal Network Protocol Analyzer Toolkit

Printed in Canada
1 2 3 4 5 6 7 8 9 0
ISBN-10: 1-59749-073-3
ISBN-13: 978-1-59749-073-3

Publisher: Andrew Williams
Acquisitions Editor: Erin Heffernan
Technical Editor: Angela Orebaugh, Gilbert Ramirez
Cover Designer: Michael Kavish

Page Layout and Art: Techne Group
Copy Editor: Judy Eby
Indexer: Richard Carlson

Distributed by O'Reilly Media, Inc. in the United States and Canada.
For information on rights, translations, and bulk sales, contact Matt Pedersen, Director of Sales and Rights, at Syngress Publishing; email matt@syngress.com or fax to 781-681-3585.

# Acknowledgments

Syngress would like to acknowledge the following people for their kindness and support in making this book possible.

A special thank you to Mike Rash and Deapesh Misra for contributing their expertise to the case studies used in Chapter 7 of this book.

Syngress books are now distributed in the United States and Canada by O'Reilly Media, Inc. The enthusiasm and work ethic at O'Reilly are incredible, and we would like to thank everyone there for their time and efforts to bring Syngress books to market: Tim O'Reilly, Laura Baldwin, Mark Brokering, Mike Leonard, Donna Selenko, Bonnie Sheehan, Cindy Davis, Grant Kikkert, Opol Matsutaro, Steve Hazelwood, Mark Wilson, Rick Brown, Tim Hinton, Kyle Hart, Sara Winge, Peter Pardo, Leslie Crandell, Regina Aggio Wilkinson, Pascal Honscher, Preston Paull, Susan Thompson, Bruce Stewart, Laura Schmier, Sue Willing, Mark Jacobsen, Betsy Waliszewski, Kathryn Barrett, John Chodacki, Rob Bullington, Kerry Beck, Karen Montgomery, and Patrick Dirden.

The incredibly hardworking team at Elsevier Science, including Jonathan Bunkell, Ian Seager, Duncan Enright, David Burton, Rosanna Ramacciotti, Robert Fairbrother, Miguel Sanchez, Klaus Beran, Emma Wyatt, Krista Leppiko, Marcel Koppes, Judy Chappell, Radek Janousek, Rosie Moss, David Lockley, Nicola Haden, Bill Kennedy, Martina Morris, Kai Wuerfl-Davidek, Christiane Leipersberger, Yvonne Grueneklee, Nadia Balavoine, and Chris Reinders for making certain that our vision remains worldwide in scope.

David Buckland, Marie Chieng, Lucy Chong, Leslie Lim, Audrey Gan, Pang Ai Hua, Joseph Chan, June Lim, and Siti Zuraidah Ahmad of Pansing Distributors for the enthusiasm with which they receive our books.

David Scott, Tricia Wilden, Marilla Burgess, Annette Scott, Andrew Swaffer, Stephen O'Donoghue, Bec Lowe, Mark Langley, and Anyo Geddes of Woodslane for distributing our books throughout Australia, New Zealand, Papua New Guinea, Fiji, Tonga, Solomon Islands, and the Cook Islands.

# About the CD

Most of the tools covered in this book are Open Source and are therefore constantly evolving. If you are deploying any of these tools to your live network, please be sure to download the most recent versions. Wherever possible, we have indicated sites where downloads are generally available. Please look for the CD Icon in the margins to indicate applications or captures contained on the CD.

For convenience, and to allow for consistency in the examples used, we have included Wireshark release 0.99.4; it is the most current stable release of Wireshark as of the printing of this book.

For installation on Win 32 systems, the "Windows Installer" folder contains the file wireshark-setup-0.99.4.exe. This Nullsoft Scriptable Install System file prompts you through the installation of Wireshark and WinPcap. Once installed, the programs are run via Start | Programs.

The Source Files folder contains the file wireshark-0.99.4.tar.gz for installation on non Windows systems.

You will also find folders containing the filters discussed in the book and folder containing captures used in the exercises in Chapters 4, 6 and 7.

Note: This CD contains packet captures of the Code Red Virus and has "strings" in it that your AntiVirus software will detect. In order to continue, you may need to disable real time protections. These files do not contain viruses, just the harmless fingerprints.

Wireshark is subject to U.S. export regulations. Take heed. Consult a lawyer if you have any questions

# Lead Author

**Angela Orebaugh** is an industry-recognized security technology visionary and scientist, with over 12 years hands-on experience. She currently performs leading-edge security consulting and works in research and development to advance the state of the art in information systems security. Angela currently participates in several security initiatives for the National Institute of Standards and Technology (NIST). She is the lead scientist for the National Vulnerability Database and author of several NIST Special Publications on security technologies. Angela has over a decade of experience in information technology, with a focus on perimeter defense, secure network design, vulnerability discovery, penetration testing, and intrusion detection systems. She has a Masters in Computer Science, and is currently pursuing her Ph.D. with a concentration in Information Security at George Mason University. Angela is the author of the Syngress best seller *Ethereal Packet Sniffing* (ISBN: 1932266828). She has also co-authored the *Snort Cookbook* and *Intrusion Prevention and Active Response: Deploying Network and Host IPS* (Syngress, ISBN: 193226647X). Angela is a researcher, writer, and speaker for SANS Institute and faculty for The Institute for Applied Network Security and George Mason University. Angela has a wealth of knowledge from industry, academia, and government from her consulting experience with prominent Fortune 500 companies, the Department of Defense, dot-com startups, and universities. She is a frequently invited speaker at a variety of conferences and security events.

Current research interests: intrusion detection, intrusion prevention, data mining, attacker profiling, user behavior analysis, network forensics

# Technical Editor
# and Contributing Author

**Gilbert Ramirez** was the first contributor to Ethereal after it was announced to the public and is known for his regular updates to the product. He has contributed protocol dissectors as well as core logic to Ethereal. He is a Technical Leader at Cisco Systems, where he works on tools and builds systems. Gilbert is a family man, a linguist, a want-to-be chef, and a student of tae kwon do. He is co-author of Syngress Publishing's popular *Ethereal Packet Sniffing* (ISBN: 1932266828).

# Contributing Authors

**Josh Burke** (CISSP) is an independent information security consultant in Seattle, Washington. He has held positions in networking, systems, and security over the past seven years in the technology, financial, and media sectors. A graduate of the business school at the University of Washington, Josh concentrates on balancing technical and business needs for companies in the many areas of information security. He also promotes an inclusive, positive security philosophy for companies, which encourages communicating the merits and reasons for security policies, rather than educating only on what the policies forbid.

Josh is an expert in open-source security applications such as Snort, Ethereal, and Nessus. His research interests include improving the security and resilience of the Domain Name System (DNS) and the Network Time Protocol (NTP). He also enjoys reading about the mathematics and history of cryptography, but afterward often knows less about the subject than when he started.

**Larry Pesce** (CCNA, GCFA Silver, GAWN Silver) is the Manager for Information Services Security at Care New England, a mid-sized health-care organization in New England. In the last 13 years in the computer industry, Larry has become a jack of all trades; PC repair, Network Engineering, Web Design, Non-Linear Audio and Video production, and Computer Security. Larry is also gainfully employed as a Penetration Tester / Ethical Hacker with Defensive Intuition, a Rhode Island-based security consulting company. A graduate of Roger Williams University in Compute Information Systems, Larry is currently exploring his options for graduate education.

In addition to his industry experience, Larry is also a Security Evangelist for the PaulDotCom Security Weekly podcast at www.pauldotcom.com. Larry is currently completing a work with his PaulDotCom Security Weekly co-host, Paul Asadoorian on hacking the Linksys WRT54G. More of Larry's writing, guides, and rants can be found on his blog at www.haxorthematrix.com.

**Greg Morris** (5-CNA, 5-CNE, 3-MCNE, Linux+, LPIC-1) is a Senior Resolution Engineer for Novell Technical Services in Provo, UT. Originally from Oklahoma, Greg has spent over 25 years in the computer industry. Although Greg has a degree in management, his passion is to be creative. This is what the software development process provides. His vast experience includes hardware and software troubleshooting on mainframe, midrange, and PC computers. Greg's early roots in software development was in database technologies, dabbling in C and assembly, but mostly working with a language called Clipper by Nantucket. Greg's work on Ethereal began in November of 2000. Since that time he has made a significant number of contributions to the Ethereal (now Wireshark) project. This would include new dissectors (NCP, NDS, NDPS) as well as new features (Extended Find capabilities). Greg has made a number of modifications to many other dissectors and is currently developing Novell Modular Authentication Services (NMAS), Novell SecretStore Services (SSS), Novell International Cryptographic Infrastructure (NICI), and a host of other Novell specific decodes. Greg has actively developed customer and internal training programs for a number of different Novell products. One of his most unique programs was developed to teach internal users the skills necessary to analyze packet traces. Greg started working with packet traces many years ago with Novell's LANalyzer product. From there Greg migrated to Network Associates Sniffer product. But, since working with Ethereal to add complete Novell NCP/NDS packet support, Greg would use nothing else. He currently develops on Windows 2000 with Microsoft's Visual C++, but has plans to move to SuSe Linux and the GNU compiler for future Wireshark development.

**Joshua Wright** is the senior security researcher for Aruba Networks, a worldwide leader in secure wireless mobility solutions. The author of several papers on wireless security and intrusion analysis, Joshua has also written open-source tools designed to highlight weaknesses in wireless networks. He is also a senior instructor for the SANS Institute, the author of the SANS Assessing and Securing Wireless Networks course, and a regular speaker at information security conferences. When not breaking wireless networks, Josh enjoys working on his house, where he usually ends up breaking things of another sort.

# Series Editor

**Jay Beale** is an information security specialist, well known for his work on mitigation technology, specifically in the form of operating system and application hardening. He's written two of the most popular tools in this space: Bastille Linux, a lockdown tool that introduced a vital security-training component, and the Center for Internet Security's Unix Scoring Tool. Both are used worldwide throughout private industry and government. Through Bastille and his work with CIS, Jay has provided leadership in the Linux system hardening space, participating in efforts to set, audit, and implement standards for Linux/Unix security within industry and government. He also focuses his energies on the OVAL project, where he works with government and industry to standardize and improve the field of vulnerability assessment. Jay is also a member of the Honeynet Project, working on tool development.

Jay has served as an invited speaker at a variety of conferences worldwide, as well as government symposia. He's written for *Information Security Magazine*, *SecurityFocus*, and the now-defunct SecurityPortal.com. He has worked on four books in the information security space. Three of these, including the best-selling *Snort 2.1 Intrusion Detection* (Syngress, ISBN: 1-9318360-43-) make up his Open Source Security Series, while one is a technical work of fiction entitled *Stealing the Network: How to Own a Continent (Syngress, ISBN: 1-931836-05-1)*."

Jay makes his living as a security consultant with the firm Intelguardians, which he co-founded with industry leaders Ed Skoudis, Eric Cole, Mike Poor, Bob Hillery and Jim Alderson, where his work in penetration testing allows him to focus on attack as well as defense.

Prior to consulting, Jay served as the Security Team Director for MandrakeSoft, helping set company strategy, design security products, and pushing security into the third largest retail Linux distribution.

# Contents

# Chapter 1

# Introducing
# Network Analysis

## Solutions in this chapter:

- What is Network Analysis and Sniffing?
- Who Uses Network Analysis?
- How Does it Work?
- Detecting Sniffers
- Protecting Against Sniffers
- Network Analysis and Policy

☑ Summary

☑ Solutions Fast Track

☑ Frequently Asked Questions

# Introduction

"Why is the network slow?" "Why can't I access my e-mail?" "Why can't I get to the shared drive?" "Why is my computer acting strange?" If you are a systems administrator, network engineer, or security engineer you have heard these questions countless times. Thus begins the tedious and sometimes painful journey of troubleshooting. You start by trying to replicate the problem from your computer, but you can't connect to the local network or the Internet either. What should you do? Go to each of the servers and make sure they are up and functioning? Check that your router is functioning? Check each computer for a malfunctioning network card?

Now consider this scenario. You go to your main network switch or border router and configure one of the unused ports for port mirroring. You plug in your laptop, fire up your network analyzer, and see thousands of Transmission Control Protocol (TCP) packets (destined for port 25) with various Internet Protocol (IP) addresses. You investigate and learn that there is a virus on the network that spreads through e-mail, and immediately apply access filters to block these packets from entering or exiting your network. Thankfully, you were able to contain the problem relatively quickly because of your knowledge and use of your network analyzer.

# What Is Network Analysis and Sniffing?

*Network analysis* (also known as traffic analysis, protocol analysis, sniffing, packet analysis, eavesdropping, and so on) is the process of capturing network traffic and inspecting it closely to determine what is happening on the network. A network analyzer decodes the data packets of common protocols and displays the network traffic in readable format. A *sniffer* is a program that monitors data traveling over a network. Unauthorized sniffers are dangerous to network security because they are difficult to detect and can be inserted almost anywhere, which makes them a favorite weapon of hackers.

A network analyzer can be a standalone hardware device with specialized software, or software that is installed on a desktop or laptop computer. The differences between network analyzers depend on features such as the number of supported protocols it can decode, the user interface, and its graphing and statistical capabilities. Other differences include inference capabilities (e.g., expert analysis features) and the quality of packet decodes. Although several network analyzers decode the same protocols, some will work better than others for your environment.

**N**OTE

The "Sniffer™" trademark, (owned by Network General) refers to the Sniffer product line. In the computer industry, "sniffer" refers to a program that captures and analyzes network traffic.

Figure 1.1 shows the Wireshark Network Analyzer display windows. A typical network analyzer displays captured traffic in three panes:

- **Summary** This pane displays a one-line summary of the capture. Fields include the date, time, source address, destination address, and the name and information about the highest-layer protocol.

- **Detail** This pane provides all of the details (in a tree-like structure) for each of the layers contained inside the captured packet.

- **Data** This pane displays the raw captured data in both hexadecimal and text format.

**Figure 1.1** Network Analyzer Display

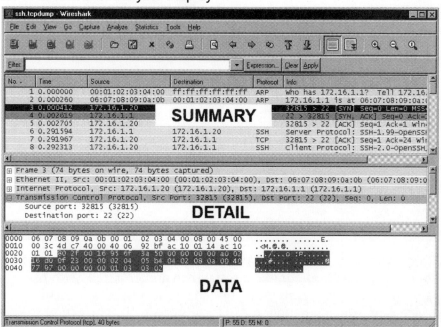

A network analyzer is a combination of hardware and software. Although there are differences in each product, a network analyzer is composed of five basic parts:

- **Hardware** Most network analyzers are software-based and work with standard operating systems (OSes) and network interface cards (NICs). However, some hardware network analyzers offer additional benefits such as analyzing hardware faults (e.g., cyclic redundancy check (CRC) errors, voltage problems, cable problems, jitter, jabber, negotiation errors, and so on). Some network analyzers only support Ethernet or wireless adapters, while others support multiple adapters and allow users to customize their configurations. Depending on the situation, you may also need a hub or a cable tap to connect to the existing cable.

- **Capture Driver** This is the part of the network analyzer that is responsible for capturing raw network traffic from the cable. It filters out the traffic that you want to keep and stores the captured data in a buffer. This is the core of a network analyzer—you cannot capture data without it.

- **Buffer** This component stores the captured data. Data can be stored in a buffer until it is full, or in a rotation method (e.g., a "round robin") where the newest data replaces the oldest data. Buffers can be disk-based or memory-based.

- **Real-time Analysis** This feature analyzes the data as it comes off the cable. Some network analyzers use it to find network performance issues, and network intrusion detection systems (IDSes) use it to look for signs of intruder activity.

- **Decode** This component displays the contents (with descriptions) of the network traffic so that it is readable. Decodes are specific to each protocol, thus network analyzers vary in the number of decodes they currently support. However, new decodes are constantly being added to network analyzers.

---

**N**OTE
_____

*Jitter* is the term that is used to describe the random variation of signal timing (e.g., electromagnetic interference and crosstalk with other signals can cause jitter). *Jabber* is the term that is used to describe when a device is improperly handling electrical signals, thus affecting the rest of the network (e.g., faulty NICs can cause jabber).

_____

# Who Uses Network Analysis?

System administrators, network engineers, security engineers, system operators, and programmers all use network analyzers, which are invaluable tools for diagnosing and troubleshooting network problems, system configuration issues, and application difficulties. Historically, network analyzers were dedicated hardware devices that were expensive and difficult to use. However, new advances in technology have allowed for the development of software-based network analyzers, which make it more convenient and affordable for administrators to effectively troubleshoot a network. It also brings the capability of network analysis.

The art of network analysis is a double-edged sword. While network, system, and security professionals use it for troubleshooting and monitoring the network, intruders use network analysis for harmful purposes. A network analyzer is a tool, and like all tools, it can be used for both good and bad purposes.

A network analyzer is used for:

- Converting the binary data in packets to readable format
- Troubleshooting problems on the network
- Analyzing the performance of a network to discover bottlenecks
- Network intrusion detection
- Logging network traffic for forensics and evidence
- Analyzing the operations of applications
- Discovering faulty network cards
- Discovering the origin of virus outbreaks or Denial of Service (DoS) attacks
- Detecting spyware
- Network programming to debug in the development stage
- Detecting a compromised computer
- Validating compliance with company policy
- As an educational resource when learning about protocols
- Reverse-engineering protocols to write clients and supporting programs

# How Are Intruders Using Sniffers?

When used by malicious individuals, sniffers can represent a significant threat to the security of a network. Network intruders use sniffing to capture confidential information, and the terms *sniffing* and *eavesdropping* are often associated with this practice. However, sniffing is becoming a non-negative term; most people use the terms sniffing and network analysis interchangeably.

Using a sniffer in an illegitimate way is considered a *passive attack*, because it does not directly interface or connect to any other systems on the network. A sniffer can also be installed as part of the compromise of a computer on a network using an *active attack*. The passive nature of sniffers is what makes detecting them difficult. (The methods used to detect sniffers are detailed later in this chapter.)

Intruders use sniffers on networks for:

- Capturing cleartext usernames and passwords
- Discovering the usage patterns of the users on a network
- Compromising proprietary information
- Capturing and replaying Voice over IP (VoIP) telephone conversations
- Mapping the layout of a network
- Passive OS fingerprinting

The above are all illegal uses of a sniffer unless you are a penetration tester whose job is to find and report these types of weaknesses.

For sniffing to occur, an intruder must first gain access to the communication cable of the systems of interest, which means being on the same shared network segment or tapping into the cable somewhere between the communication path. If the intruder is not physically present at the target system or communications access point (AP), there are still ways to sniff network traffic, including:

- Breaking into a target computer and installing remotely controlled sniffing software.
- Breaking into a communications access point (e.g., an Internet Service Provider [ISP]) and installing sniffing software.
- Locating a system at the ISP that already has sniffing software installed.
- Using social engineering to gain physical access to an ISP in order to install a packet sniffer.

- Having an inside accomplice at the target computer organization or the ISP install the sniffer.

- Redirecting or copying communications to take a path that includes the intruder's computer.

Sniffing programs are included with most *rootkits* that are typically installed on compromised systems. Rootkits are used to cover the tracks of an intruder by replacing commands and utilities and clearing log entries. Intruders also install other programs such as sniffers, key loggers, and backdoor access software. Windows sniffing can be accomplished as part of a Remote Admin Trojan (RAT) such as SubSeven or Back Orifice. Intruders often use sniffing programs that are configured to detect specific things (e.g., passwords), and then electronically send them to the intruder (or store them for later retrieval by the intruder). Vulnerable protocols for this type of activity include Telnet, File Transfer Protocol (FTP), Post Office Protocol version 3 (POP3), Internet Message Access Protocol (IMAP), Simple Mail Transfer Program (SMTP), Hypertext Transfer Protocol (HTTP), Remote Login (rlogin), and Simple Network Management Protocol (SNMP).

One example of a rootkit is "T0rnKit," which works on Solaris and Linux. The sniffer that is included with this rootkit is called "t0rns" and is installed in the hidden directory */usr/srec/.puta*. Another example of a rootkit is Linux Rootkit 5 (Lrk5), which installs with the linsniff sniffer.

Intruders may also use sniffer programs to control back doors (This practice isn't quite "common," but it isn't unheard of). One method is to install a sniffer on a target system that listens for specific information and then sends the backdoor control information to a neighboring system. This type of backdoor control is hard to detect, because of the passive nature of sniffers.

*cd00r* is an example of a backdoor sniffer that operates in non–promiscuous mode, making it even harder to detect. Using a product like Fyodor's Nmap (http://insecure.org/nmap) to send a series of TCP synchronize (SYN) packets to several predefined ports will trigger the backdoor to open up on a pre-configured port. More information about *cdoor* can be found at *www.phenoelit.de/stuff/cd00r.c*.

---

**NOTE**

A rootkit is a collection of Trojan programs that are used to replace the legitimate programs on a compromised system in order to avoid detection. Some common commands that are replaced are **ps**, **ifconfig**, and *ls*. Rootkits can also install additional software such as sniffers.

---

# What Does Sniffed Data Look Like?

The easiest way to grasp the concept of a sniffer is to watch one in action. Figure 1.2 shows a capture of a simple FTP session from a laptop to a Linux system. The two highlighted packets show how easy it is to sniff the username and password (i.e., "root" and "password").

**Figure 1.2** Sniffing a Connection

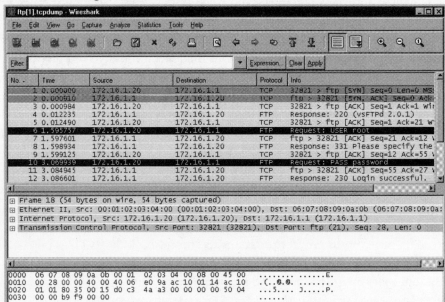

# Common Network Analyzers

A simple search on SecurityFocus (www.securityfocus.org/tools/category/4) shows the diversity and number of sniffers available. Some of the most prominent are:

■ **Wireshark** Wireshark is one of the best sniffers available and is being developed as a free, commercial-quality sniffer. It has numerous features, a nice graphical user interface (GUI), decodes over 400 protocols, and is actively being developed and maintained. It runs on UNIX-based systems, Mac OS X, and Windows. This is a great sniffer to use in a production environment, and is available at www.wireshark.org.

- **WinDump** WinDump is the Windows version of tcpdump, and is available at www.winpcap.org/windump. It uses the WinPcap library and runs on Windows 95, 98, ME, NT, 2000, and XP.

- **Network General Sniffer** A Network General Sniffer is one of the most popular commercial sniffers available. Now a suite of enterprise network capture tools, there is an entire Sniffer product line at www.networkgeneral.com.

- **Windows 2000 and 2003 Server Network Monitor** Both the Windows 2000 Server and the Windows 2003 Server have a built-in program to perform network analysis. It is located in the "Administrative Tools" folder, but is not installed by default; therefore, you have to add it from the installation CD.

- **EtherPeek** EtherPeek is a commercial network analyzer developed by WildPackets. Versions for both Windows and Mac, and other network analysis products can be found at www.wildpackets.com.

- **Tcpdump** Tcpdump is the oldest and most commonly used network sniffer, and was developed by the Network Research Group (NRG) of the Information and Computing Sciences Division (ICSD) at Lawrence Berkeley National Laboratory (LBNL). It is command line-based and runs on UNIX-based systems, including Mac OS X. It is actively developed and maintained at www.tcpdump.org.

- **Snoop** Snoop is a command-line network sniffer that is included with the Sun Solaris OS.

- **Snort** Snort is a network IDS that uses network sniffing, and is actively developed and maintained at www.snort.org. For more information, refer to *Nessus, Snort, & Ethereal Power Tools: Customizing Open Source Security Applications* (Syngress Publishing: 1597490202) and *Snort Intrusion Detection and Prevention Toolkit* (Syngress, ISBN: 1597490997).

- **Dsniff** Dsniff is a very popular network-sniffing package. It is a collection of programs that are used to specifically sniff for interesting data (e.g., passwords) and to facilitate the sniffing process (e.g., evading switches). It is actively maintained at www.monkey.org/~dugsong/dsniff.

- **Ettercap** Ettercap was specifically designed to sniff a switched network. It has built-in features such as password collecting, OS fingerprinting, and character injection, and runs on several platforms including Linux, Windows, and Solaris. It is actively maintained at ettercap.sourceforge.net.

- **Analyzer**  Analyzer is a free sniffer that is used for the Windows OS. It is being actively developed by the makers of WinPcap and WinDump at Politecnico di Torino, and can be downloaded from analyzer.polito.it.

- **Packetyzer**  Packetyzer is a free sniffer (used for the Windows OS ) that uses Wireshark's core logic. It tends to run a version or two behind the current release of Wireshark. It is actively maintained by Network Chemistry at www.networkchemistry.com/products/packetyzer.php.

- **MacSniffer**  MacSniffer is specifically designed for the Mac OS X environment. It is built as a front-end for tcpdump. The software is shareware and can be downloaded from personalpages.tds.net/~brian_hill/macsniffer.html.

# How Does It Work?

This section provides an overview of how sniffing takes place, and gives background information on how networks and protocols work. However, there are many other excellent resources available, including the most popular and undoubtedly one of the best written, Richard Stevens' "TCP/IP Illustrated, Vol. 1–3."

# Explaining Ethernet

Ethernet is the most popular protocol standard used to enable computers to communicate. A protocol is like speaking a particular language. Ethernet was built around the principle of a shared medium where all computers on the local network segment share the same cable. It is known as a *broadcast* protocol because it sends that data to all other computers on the same network segment. This information is divided up into manageable chunks called *packets*, and each packet has a header containing the addresses of both the destination and source computers. Even though this information is sent out to all computers on a segment, only the computer with the matching destination address responds. All of the other computers on the network still see the packet, but if they are not the intended receiver they disregard it, unless a computer is running a sniffer. When running a sniffer, the packet capture driver puts the computer's NIC into *promiscuous mode*. This means that the sniffing computer can see all of the traffic on the segment regardless of who it is being sent to. Normally computers run in non-promiscuous mode, listening for information designated only for themselves. However, when a NIC is in promiscuous mode, it can see conversations to and from all of its neighbors.

Ethernet addresses are also known as Media Access Control (MAC) addresses and hardware addresses. Because many computers may share a single Ethernet segment, each one must have an individual identifier hard-coded onto the NIC. A MAC address is a 48-bit number, which is also stated as a 12-digit hexadecimal number. This number is broken down into two halves; the first 24 bits identify the vendor of the Ethernet card, and the second 24 bits comprise a serial number assigned by the vendor.

The following steps allow you to view your NIC's MAC address:

- **Windows 9x/ME** Access **Start | Run** and type **winipcfg.exe**. The MAC address will be listed as the "Adapter Address."

- **Windows NT, 2000, XP, and 2003** Access the command line and type **ipconfig /all**. The MAC address will be listed as the "Physical Address."

- **Linux and Solaris** Type **ifconfig –a** at the command line. The MAC address will be listed as the "HWaddr" on Linux and as "ether" on Solaris.

- **Macintosh OS X** Type **ifconfig –a** at the Terminal application. The MAC address will be listed as the "Ether" label.

You can also view the MAC addresses of other computers that you have recently communicated with, by typing the command **arp –a**. (Discussed in more detail in the "Defeating Switches" section.)

MAC addresses are unique, and no two computers have the same one. However, occasionally a manufacturing error may occur that causes more than one NIC to have the same MAC address. Thus, most people change their MAC addresses intentionally, which can be done with a program (e.g., *ifconfig*) that allows you to fake your MAC address. Faking your MAC address (and other types of addresses) is also known as *spoofing*. Also, some adapters allow you to use a program to reconfigure the runtime MAC address. And lastly, with the right tools and skill you can physically re-burn the address into the NIC.

**NOTE**

Spoofing is the process of altering network packet information (e.g., the IP source address, the MAC address, or the e-mail address). This is often done to masquerade as another device in order to exploit a trust relationship or to make tracing the source of attacks difficult. Address spoofing is also used in DoS attacks (e.g., Smurf), where the return addresses of network requests are spoofed to be the IP address of the victim.

# Understanding the Open Systems Interconnection Model

The International Standards Organization (ISO) developed the Open Systems Interconnection (OSI) model in the early 1980s to describe how network protocols and components work together. It divides network functions into seven layers, each layer representing a group of related specifications, functions, and activities (see Figure 1.3). Although complicated at first, the terminology is used extensively in networking, systems, and development communities.

The following sections define the seven layers of the OSI model.

**Figure 1.3** Seven boxes corresponding to OSI model.

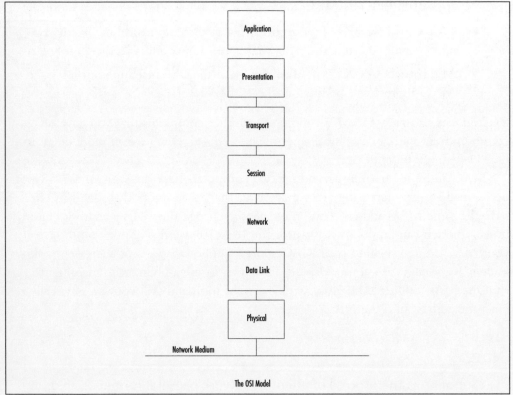

The following sections define the seven layers of the OSI model.

# Layer 1: Physical

The first layer of the OSI model is the *Physical* layer, which specifies the electrical and mechanical requirements for transmitting data bits across the transmission medium (cable or airwaves). It involves sending and receiving the data stream on the carrier, whether that carrier uses electrical (cable), light (fiber optic), radio, infrared, or laser (wireless) signals. The Physical layer specifications include:

- Voltage changes

- The timing of voltage changes

- Data rates

- Maximum transmission distances

- The physical connectors to the transmission medium (plug)

- The topology or physical layout of the network

Many complex issues are addressed at the Physical layer, including digital vs. analog signaling, baseband vs. broadband signaling, whether data is transmitted synchronously or asynchronously, and how signals are divided into channels (multiplexing).

Devices that operate at the Physical layer deal with signaling (e.g., transceivers on the NIC), repeaters, basic hubs, and simple connectors that join segments of cable). The data handled by the Physical layer is in bits of 1s (ones) and 0s (zeros), which are represented by pulses of light or voltage changes of electricity, and by the state of those pulses (*on* generally representing 1 and *off* generally representing *0*).

How these bits are arranged and managed is a function of the Data Link layer (layer 2) of the OSI model.

# Layer 2: Data Link

Layer 2 is the *Data Link* layer, which is responsible for maintaining the data link between two computers, typically called *hosts* or *nodes*. It also defines and manages the ordering of bits to and from packets. *Frames* contain data arranged in an organized manner, which provides an orderly and consistent method of sending data bits across the medium. Without such control, the data would be sent in random sizes or configurations and the data on one end could not be decoded at the other end. The Data Link layer manages the physical addressing and synchronization of the data packets. It is also responsible for flow control and error notification on the Physical layer. Flow control is the process of managing the timing of sending and receiving data so that it doesn't exceed the capacity (speed, memory, and so on) of the physical connection. Since the Physical layer is only responsible for physically moving the data onto and off of the network medium, the Data Link layer also receives and manages error messaging related to the physical delivery of packets.

Network devices that operate at this layer include layer 2 switches (switching hubs) and bridges. A layer 2 switch decreases network congestion by sending data out only on the port that the destination computer is attached to, instead of sending it out on all ports. Bridges provide a way to segment a network into two parts and filter traffic, by building tables that define which computers are located on which side of the bridge, based on their MAC addresses.

The Data Link layer is divided into two sublayers: the Logical Link Control (LLC) sublayer and the MAC sublayer.

## *The MAC Sublayer*

The MAC sublayer provides control for accessing the transmission medium. It is responsible for moving data packets from one NIC to another, across a shared transmission medium such as an Ethernet or fiber-optic cable.

Physical addressing is addressed at the MAC sublayer. Every NIC has a unique MAC address (also called the *physical address*) which identifies that specific NIC on the network. The MAC address of a NIC is usually burned into a read-only memory (ROM) chip on the NIC. Each manufacturer of network cards is provided a unique set of MAC addresses so that theoretically, every NIC that is manufactured has a unique MAC address. To avoid any confusion, MAC addresses are permanently burned into the NIC's memory, which is sometimes referred to as the Burned-in Address (BIA).

## NOTE

On Ethernet NICs, the physical or MAC address (also called the *hardware address*) is expressed as 12 hexadecimal digits arranged in pairs with colons between each pair (e.g., 12:3A:4D:66:3A:1C). The initial three sets of numbers represent the manufacturer, and the last three bits represent a unique NIC made by that manufacturer.

MAC refers to the method used to allocate network access to computers while preventing them from transmitting at the same time and causing data collisions. Common MAC methods include Carrier Sense Multiple Access/Collision Detection (CSMA/CD) used by Ethernet networks, Carrier Sense Multiple Access/Collision Avoidance (CSMA/CA) used by AppleTalk networks, and token passing used by Token Ring and Fiber Distributed Data Interface (FDDI) networks. (CSMA/CD is discussed later in this chapter.)

## The LLC Sublayer

The LLC sublayer provides the logic for the data link; thus it controls the synchronization, flow control, and error-checking functions of the Data Link layer. This layer manages connection-oriented transmissions; however, connectionless service can also be provided by this layer. Connectionless operations are known as Class I LLC, whereas Class II can handle either connectionless or connection-oriented operations. With connection-oriented communication, each LLC frame sent is acknowledged. The LLC sublayer at the receiving end keeps up with the LLC frames it receives (also called Protocol Data Units [PDUs]); therefore, if it detects that a frame has been lost during transmission, it can send a request to the sending computer to start the transmission over again, beginning with the PDU that never arrived.

The LLC sublayer sits above the MAC sublayer, and acts as a liaison between the upper layers and the protocols that operate at the MAC sublayer (e.g., Ethernet, Token Ring, and so on). The LLC sublayer is defined by Institute of Electrical & Electronics Engineers (IEEE) 802.2. Link addressing, sequencing, and definition of Service Access Points (SAPs) also take place at this layer.

# Layer 3: Network

The next layer is the *Network* layer (layer 3), which is where packets are sequenced and logical addressing is assigned. Logical addresses are nonpermanent, software-assigned addresses that can only be changed by administrators. The IP addresses used by the TCP/IP protocols on the Internet, and the Internet Package Exchange (IPX) addresses used by the IPX/Sequenced Packet Exchange (SPX) protocols on NetWare networks are examples of logical addresses. These protocol stacks are referred to as *routable* because they include addressing schemes that identify the network or subnet and the particular client on that network or subnet. Other network/transport protocols (e.g., NETBIOS Extended User Interface [NetBEUI]) do not have a sophisticated addressing scheme and thus cannot be routed between different types of networks.

> **NOTE**
>
> To understand the difference between physical and logical addresses, consider this analogy: A house has a physical address that identifies exactly where it is located. This is similar to the MAC address on a NIC.
>
> A house also has a logical address assigned to it by the post office that consists of a street name and number. The post office occasionally changes the names of streets or renumbers the houses located on them. This is similar to the IP address assigned to a network interface.

The Network layer is also responsible for creating a virtual circuit (i.e., a logical connection, not a physical connection) between points or nodes. A node is a device that has a MAC address, which typically includes computers, printers, and routers. This layer is also responsible for routing, layer 3 switching, and forwarding packets. *Routing* refers to forwarding packets from one network or subnet to another. Without routing, computers can only communicate with computers on the same network. Routing is the key to the global Internet, and is one of the most important duties of the Network layer.

Finally, the Network layer provides additional levels of flow control and error control. As mentioned earlier, from this point on, the primary methods of implementing the OSI model architecture involve software rather than hardware.

Devices that operate at this layer include routers and layer 3 switches.

# Layer 4: Transport

Layer 4 is the *Transport* layer, and is responsible for transporting the data from one node to another. It provides transparent data transfer between nodes, and manages the end-to-end flow control, error detection, and error recovery.

The Transport layer protocols initiate contact between specific ports on different host computers, and set up a virtual circuit. The transport protocols on each host computer verify that the application sending the data is authorized to access the network and that both ends are ready to initiate the data transfer. When this synchronization is complete, the data is sent. As the data is being transmitted, the transport protocol on each host monitors the data flow and watches for transport errors. If transport errors are detected, the transport protocol provides error recovery.

The functions performed by the Transport layer are very important to network communication. Just as the Data Link layer provides lower-level reliability and connection-oriented or connectionless communications, the Transport layer does the same thing but at a higher level. The two protocols most commonly associated with the Transport layer are the Transmission Control Protocol (TCP), which is connection-oriented and the User Datagram Protocol (UDP), which is connectionless.

**NOTE**

What's the difference between a connection-oriented protocol and a connectionless protocol? A connection-oriented protocol (e.g., TCP) creates a connection between two computers before sending the data, and then verifies that the data has reached its destination by using acknowledgements (ACKs) (i.e., messages sent back to the sending computer from the receiving computer that acknowledge receipt). Connectionless protocols send the data and trust that it will reach the proper destination or that the application will handle retransmission and data verification.

Consider this analogy: You need to send an important letter to a business associate that contains valuable papers. You call him before e-mailing the letter, to let him know that he or she should expect it (establishing the connection). A few days later your friend calls to let you know that he received the letter, or you receive the return receipt (ACK). This is how connection-oriented communication works. When mailing a postcard to a friend, you drop it in the mailbox and hope it gets to the addressee. You don't expect or require any acknowledgement. This is how connectionless communication works.

The Transport layer also manages the logical addressing of ports. Think of a port as a suite or apartment number within a building that defines exactly where the data should go.

**Table 1.1** Commonly Used Internet Ports

| Internet Protocol (IP) Port(s) | Protocol(s) | Description |
| --- | --- | --- |
| 80 | TCP | HTTP, commonly used for Web servers |
| 443 | TCP | Hypertext Transfer Protocol Secure sockets (HTTPS) for secure Web servers. |
| 53 | UDP and TCP | Domain Name Server/Service (DNS) for resolving names to IP addresses |
| 25 | TCP | Simple Mail Transfer Protocol(SMTP), used for sending e-mail |
| 22 | TCP | The Secure Shell (SSH) protocol |
| 23 | TCP | Telnet, an insecure administration protocol |
| 20 and 21 | TCP | An insecure Fire Transfer Protocol (FTP) |
| 135–139 and 445 | TCP and UDP | Windows file sharing, login, and Remote Procedure Call (RPC) |
| 500 | UDP | Internet Security Association and Key Management Protocol (ISAKMP) key negotiation for Secure Internet Protocol (IPSec) virtual private networks (VPNs) |
| 5060 | UDP | Session Initiation Protocol (SIP) for some VoIP uses |
| 123 | UDP | Network Time Protocol (NTP) for network time synchronization |

A computer may have several network applications running at the same time (e.g., a Web browser sending a request to a Web server for a Web page, an e-mail client sending and receiving e-mail, and a file transfer program uploading or downloading information to and from an FTP server). The mechanism for determining which incoming data packets belong to which application is the function of port numbers. The FTP protocol is assigned a particular port, whereas the Web browser and e-mail clients use different protocols (e.g., HTTP and POP3 or Internet Message Access Protocol [IMAP]) that have their own assigned ports; thus the information intended for the Web browser doesn't go to the e-mail program by mistake. Port numbers are used by TCP and UDP.

Finally, the Transport layer deals with name resolution. Most users prefer to identify computers by name instead of by IP address (i.e., *www.microsoft.com* instead of 207.46.249.222), however, computers only interpret numbers, therefore, there must be a way to match names with numerical addresses. Name resolution methods such as the DNS solve this problem.

# Layer 5: Session

After the Transport layer establishes a virtual connection, a communication session is made between two processes on two different computers. The Session layer (layer 5) is responsible for establishing, monitoring, and terminating sessions, using the virtual circuits established by the Transport layer.

The Session layer is also responsible for putting header information into data packets that indicates where a message begins and ends. Once header information is attached to the data packets, the Session layer performs synchronization between the sender's Session layer and the receiver's Session layer. The use of ACKs helps coordinate the transfer of data at the Session-layer level.

Another important function of the Session layer is controlling whether the communications within a session are sent as full-duplex or half-duplex messages. Half-duplex communication goes in both directions between the communicating computers, but information can only travel in one direction at a time (e.g., radio communications where you hold down the microphone button to transmit, but cannot hear the person on the other end). With full-duplex communication, information can be sent in both directions at the same time (e.g., a telephone conversation, where both parties can talk and hear one another at the same time).

Whereas the Transport layer establishes a connection between two machines, the Session layer establishes a connection between two processes. An application can run many processes simultaneously to accomplish the work of the application.

After the Transport layer establishes the connection between the two machines, the Session layer sets up the connection between the application process on one computer and the application process on another computer.

# Layer 6: Presentation

Data translation is the primary activity of the Presentation layer (layer 6). When data is sent from a sender to a receiver, it is translated at the Presentation layer (i.e., the sender's application passes data down to the Presentation layer, where it is changed into a common format). When the data is received on the other end, the Presentation layer changes it from the common format back into a format that is useable by the application. Protocol translation (i.e., the conversion of data from one protocol to another so that it can be exchanged between computers using different platforms or OSes) takes place here.

The Presentation layer is also where *gateway* services operate. Gateways are connection points between networks that use different platforms or applications (e.g., e-mail gateways, Systems Network Architecture (SNA) gateways, and gateways that cross platforms or file systems). Gateways are usually implemented via software such as the Gateway Services for NetWare (GSNW). Software redirectors also operate at this layer.

This layer is also where data compression takes place, which minimizes the number of bits that must be transmitted on the network media to the receiver. Data encryption and decryption also take place in the Presentation layer.

## Layer 7 Application

The *Application* layer is the point at which the user application program interacts with the network. Don't confuse the networking model with the application itself. Application processes (e.g., file transfers or e-mail) are initiated within a user application (e.g., an e-mail program). Then the data created by that process is handed to the Application layer of the networking software. Everything that occurs at this level is application-specific (e.g., file sharing, remote printer access, network monitoring and management, remote procedure calls, and all forms of electronic messaging).

Both FTP and Telnet function within the Application layer, as does the Simple Mail Transfer Protocol (SMTP), Post Office Protocol (POP), and Internet Message access Protocol (IMAP), all of which are used for sending or receiving e-mail. Other Application-layer protocols include HTTP, Network News Transfer Protocol (NNTP), and  Simple network Management Protocol (SNMP).

You have to distinguish between the protocols mentioned and the applications that might bear the same names, because there are many different FTP programs made by different software vendors that use the FTP to transfer files.

The OSI model is generic and can be used to explain all network protocols. Various protocol suites are often mapped against the OSI model for this purpose. A solid understanding of the OSI model aids in network analysis, comparison, and troubleshooting. However, it is important to remember that not all protocols map well to the OSI model (e.g., TCP/IP was designed to map to the U.S. Department of Defense (DoD) model). In the 1970s, the DoD developed its four-layer model. The core Internet protocols adhere to this model.

The DoD model is a condensed version of the OSI model. Its four layers are:

- **Process Layer** This layer defines protocols that implement user-level applications (e.g., e-mail delivery, remote login, and file transfer).

- **Host-to-host Layer** This layer manages the connection, data flow management, and retransmission of lost data.

- **Internet Layer** This layer delivers data from the source host to the destination host across a set of physical networks that connect the two machines.

- **Network Access Layer** This layer manages the delivery of data over a particular hardware media.

## Notes From the Underground…

### Writing Your Own Sniffer

There is an excellent paper titled "Basic Packet-Sniffer Construction from the Ground Up" by Chad Renfro that is located at www.packetstormsecurity.org /sniffers/Sniffer_construction.txt. In this paper, he presents a basic 28-line packet sniffer that is written in C, called *sniff.c*, which he explains line-by-line in an easy-to-understand manner. The program demonstrates how to use the *raw_socket* device to read TCP packets from the network, and how to print basic header information to *stdout*. For simplicity, the program operates in non-promiscuous mode; therefore, you first need to put your interface in promiscuous mode using the **ifconfig eth0 promisc** command.

There is also a header file that must be copied into the same directory as *sniff.c*, that provides standard structures to access the IP and TCP fields in order to identify each field in the IP and TCP header.

To run the program, copy the *sniff.c* and *headers.h* files into one directory, and enter **gcc -o sniff sniff.c**. This compiles the program and creates an executable file called *sniff*, which is run by typing ./**sniff**. The following text shows the output of the sniff program when a Telnet and FTP connection was attempted:

```
Bytes received :::    48
Source address ::: 192.168.1.1
IP header length ::: 5
```

**Continued**

```
Protocol ::: 6

Source port ::: 1372

Dest port  ::: 23

Bytes received :::    48

Source address ::: 192.168.1.1

IP header length ::: 5

Protocol ::: 6

Source port ::: 1374

Dest port  ::: 21
```

Once you are done capturing data, you can end the program by typing **Ctrl-C**. You may also want to remove your interface from promiscuous mode by typing the **ifconfig eth0 –promisc** command.

# CSMA/CD

Ethernet uses the CSMA/CD protocol in order for devices to exchange data on the network. The term *multiple access* refers to the fact that many network devices attached to the same segment have the opportunity to transmit. Each device is given an equal opportunity; no device has priority over another. *Carrier sense* describes how an Ethernet interface on a network device listens to the cable before transmitting. The network interface ensures that there are no other signals on the cable before it transmits, and listens while transmitting to ensure that no other network device transmits data at the same time. When two network devices transmit at the same time, a *collision* occurs. Because Ethernet interfaces listen to the media while they are transmitting, they can identify the presence of others through *collision detection*. If a collision occurs, the transmitting device waits for a small, random amount of time before retransmitting. This function is known as *random backoff*.

Traditionally, Ethernet operation has been half-duplex, which means that an interface can either transmit or receive data, but not at the same time. If more than one network interface on a segment tries to transmit at the same time, a collision occurs per CSMA/CD. When a crossover cable is used to connect two devices, or a single device is attached to a switch port, only two interfaces on the segment need to transmit or receive; no collisions occur. This is because the transmit (TX) of device A is connected to the receive (RX) of device B, and the TX of B is connected to the RX of device A. The collision detection method is no longer necessary, therefore, interfaces can be placed in full-duplex mode, which allows network devices to transmit and receive at the same time, thereby increasing performance.

# The Major Protocols: IP, TCP, UDP, and ICMP

The next four protocols are at the heart of how the Internet works today.

> **NOTE**
>
> Other, different protocols are used across the Internet, and new proto-cols are constantly created to fulfill specific needs. One of these is Internet Protocol version 6 (IPv6), which seeks to improve the existing Internet protocol suite by providing more IP addresses, and by improving the security of network connections across the Internet using encryption. For more information on IPv6, see http://en.wikipedia.org/wiki/IPv6.

## IP

The IP is a connectionless protocol that manages addressing data from one point to another, and fragments large amounts of data into smaller, transmittable packets. The major components of Internet Protocol datagrams are:

- **IP Identification (IPID)** Tries to uniquely identify an IP datagram.

- **Protocol** Describes the higher-level protocol contained within the datagram.

- **Time-to-live (TTL)** Attempts to keep datagrams and packets from routing in circles. When TTL reaches 0, the datagram is dropped. The TTL allows traceroute to function, identifying each router in a network by sending out datagrams with successively increasing TTLs, and tracking when those TTLs are exceeded.

- **Source IP Address** The IP address of the host where the datagram was created.

- **Destination IP Address** The destination of where the datagram should be sent.

## IP Address Source Spoofing

It is possible to spoof any part of an IP datagram; however, the most commonly spoofed IP component is the source IP address. Also, not all protocols function completely with a spoofed source IP address (e.g., connection-oriented protocols such as TCP require handshaking before data can be transmitted, thereby reducing the effectiveness of spoofing-based attacks).

Spoofing can also be used as a DoS attack. If Network A sends a datagram to Network B, with a spoofed source IP host address on Network C, Network C will see traffic going to it that originates from Network B, perhaps without any indication that Network A is involved at all.

The best practice for network administrators is to ensure that the network can only originate packets with a proper Source IP address (i.e., an IP address in the network itself).

# Internet Control Message Protocol

The Internet Control Message Protocol (ICMP) manages errors that occur between networks on the IP. The following are common types of ICMP messages:

- **Echo Request/Reply** Used by programs such as *ping* to calculate the delay in reaching another IP address.

- **Destination Unreachable: Network Unreachable and Port Unreachable** Sent to the source IP address of a packet when a network or port cannot be reached. This happens when a firewall rejects a packet or if there is a network problem. There are a number of subtypes of Destination Unreachable messages that are helpful at diagnosing communication issues.

- **Time Exceeded** Occurs when the TTL of a packet reaches 0.

# TCP

TCP packets are connection-oriented, and are used most often to transmit data. The connection-oriented nature of TCP packets makes it a poor choice for source IP address spoofing. Many applications use TCP, including the Web (HTTP), e-mail (SMTP), FTP, SSH, and the Windows Remote Desktop Protocol (RDP).

## The TCP Handshake

An important concept of the TCP is *handshaking*. Before any data can be exchanged between two hosts, they must agree to communicate. Host A sends a packet with the SYN flag set to Host B. If Host B is willing and able to communicate, it returns the SYN packet and adds an ACK flag. Host A begins sending data, and indicates to Host B that it also received the ACK. When the communication between the hosts ends, a packet with the FIN (finish) flag is sent, and a similar acknowledgement process is followed.

## TCP Sequence

Another important component of TCP is *sequence identification*, where each packet sent is part of a sequence. Through these numbers, TCP handles complex tasks such as retransmission, acknowledgement, and order.

# UDP

UDP packets are the connectionless equivalent to TCP, and are used for many purposes, the most important being that DNS uses UDP for most of its work. DNS finds out which IP address corresponds to which hostname (e.g., www.example.com is not routable as an IP address inside an IP datagram; however, through a DNS system it can find the IP address to route traffic to). Other uses of UDP include VoiP and many online games and streaming media types.

# Hardware: Cable Taps, Hubs, and Switches

*Cable taps* are hardware devices that assist in connecting to a network cable. Test access points (Taps) use this device to access any cables between computers, hubs, switches, routers, and other devices. Taps are available in full- or half-duplex for 10, 100, and 1,000 Mbps Ethernet links. They are also available in various multi-port sizes. The following is a list of some popular cable tap products:

- Net Optics carries several types of network taps for copper and fiber cables, and is available at www.netoptics.com.

- The Finisar Tap family offers a variety of taps for copper and fiber cables, and is available at www.finisar.com/nt/taps.php.

A *hub* is a device that allows you to connect multiple hosts together on a shared medium (e.g., Ethernet). When a computer sends information, it travels into the hub and the hub forwards the information to all other computers connected to it. The computer that the information was intended for will recognize its own MAC address

in the packet header and accept the data. The area that the hub forwards all information to is known as a *collision domain* (also known as *broadcast domain*). A hub has only
one collision domain for all traffic to share. Figure 1.4 shows a network architecture
with collision domains related to hubs. Large collisions make sniffing easier and
create performance issues such as bandwidth hogging or excessive traffic on the hub.

**Figure 1.4** Hub Collision Domains

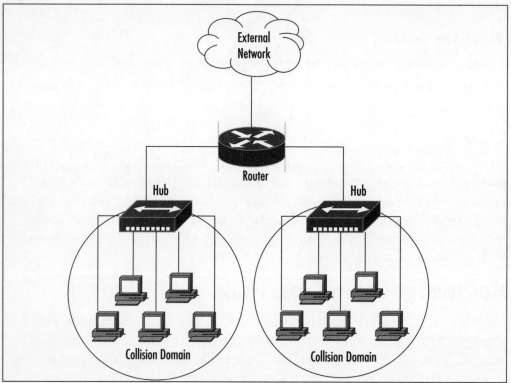

A switch is also used to connect computers together on a shared medium;
however, when a switch receives information, it doesn't blindly send it to all other
computers; it looks at the packet header to locate the destination MAC address,
and maintains a list of all MAC addresses and corresponding ports on the switch
that the computers are connected to. It then forwards the packets to the specified
port. This narrows the collision domain to a single port (see Figure 1.5). This type
of collision domain also provides a definite amount of bandwidth for each connection rather than a shared amount on a hub. Because the price of switches has
fallen dramatically in the last few years, there is no reason not to replace hubs
with switches, or to choose switches when purchasing new equipment. Also, some

of the more costly switches include better technology that makes them more resistant to sniffing attacks.

**Figure 1.5** Switch Collision Domains

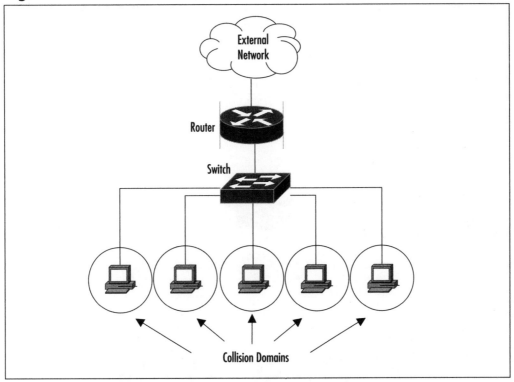

As you can see from the diagrams, hubs make sniffing easier and switches make sniffing more difficult. However, switches can be tricked, as discussed in the "Defeating Switches" section.

# Port Mirroring

If you are working on a network that uses switches and you want to perform network analysis legitimately, you are in luck; most switches and routers come with *port mirroring* (also known as *port spanning*). To mirror ports, you have to configure the switch to duplicate the traffic from the port you want to monitor to the port you are connected to.

Using port spanning does not interfere with the normal operation of switches, but you should always check the documentation of the exact switch you are configuring and periodically check the device's logs. You won't affect the switch, but you will increase the amount of traffic on a specific destination port, therefore, make sure your properly configured network analyzer is the destination port. Also, consult the documentation for your specific switch to learn the exact command to enable port mirroring (see Figure 1.6). The switch is configured to mirror all port 1 traffic to port 5, and the network analyzer sees all traffic to and from Computer A. Sometimes administrators mirror the uplink port on a switch, so that they can see all of the traffic to and from the switch and all of its ports.

**Figure 1.6** Port Mirroring

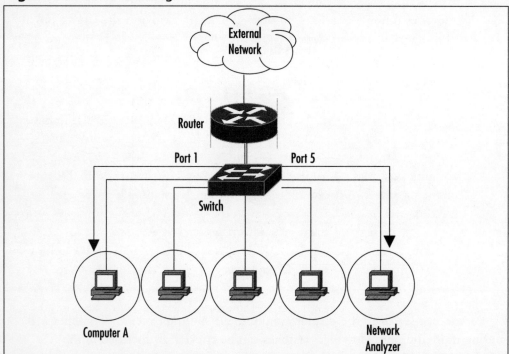

---

**NOTE**

*Span* stands for Switched Port Analyzer. Cisco uses the word *span* to describe the concept of port mirroring. In Cisco terms, spanning a port is the same as mirroring a port.

---

# Defeating Switches

As mentioned earlier, using switches on a network makes sniffing more difficult. In theory, you should only see traffic destined for you own computer on a switch; however, there are ways to circumvent its technology. The following list describes several ways in which a switch can be defeated:

- **Switch Flooding** Some switches can be made to act like a hub, where all packets are broadcast to all computers. This can be accomplished by over-flowing the switch address table with a large number of fake MAC addresses (known as a device *failing open)*, thus removing all security provisions. Devices that *fail close* incorporate some type of security measure (e.g., shutting down all communications). The Dsniff package comes with a program called *macof* that is designed to switch MAC address flooding. It can be downloaded from www.monkey.org/~dugsong/dsniff.

- **ARP Redirects** When a computer needs the MAC address of another computer, it sends an Address Resolution Protocol (ARP) request. Each computer also maintains an ARP table that stores the MAC addresses of the computers it talks to. ARPs are broadcast on a switch; therefore, all computers on that switch see the request and the response. There are several methods that use ARP to trick a switch into sending traffic somewhere it shouldn't. First, an intruder can subvert a switch by sending out an ARP claiming to be someone else. An intruder can also send an ARP claiming to be the router, in which case computers will try to send their packets through the intruder's computer. Or, an intruder will send an ARP request to just one victim, claiming to be the router, at which point the victim starts forwarding packets to the intruder.

- **ICMP Redirect** Sometimes computers are on the same physical segment and switch, but different logical segments. This means they are in different IP subnets. When Computer A wants to talk to Computer B it sends its request through a router. The router knows that they are on the same physical segment, so it sends an ICMP Redirect to Computer A letting it know that it can send its packets directly to Computer B. An intruder (Computer X) can send a fake ICMP redirect to Computer A, telling it to send Computer B's packets to Computer X.

- **ICMP Router Advertisements** These advertisements tell computers which router to use. Intruders then send out advertisements claiming to be that router, at which point the computers begin forwarding all packets through the intruder.

- **MAC Address Spoofing** An intruder can pretend to use a different computer by spoofing its MAC address. Sending out packets with the source address of the victim tricks the switch. The switch enters the spoofed information into its table and begins sending packets to the intruder. But what about the victim who is still on the switch, sending updates that are causing the switch to change the table back? This can be solved by taking the victim offline with some type of DoS attack, and then redirecting the switch and continuing communications. An intruder could also broadcast the traffic that he or she receives to ensure that the victim computer still receives the packets. Some switches have a countermeasure that allows you to statically assign a MAC address to a port. This may be difficult to manage if you have a large network, but it will eliminate MAC spoofing. Other switch configurations allow a port to be locked to the first MAC it encounters, and presents a compelling balance between manageability and security in environments where physical port access is restricted.

  To spoof your MAC on Linux or Solaris use the **ifconfig** command as follows:

```
ifconfig eth0 down
ifconfig eth0 hw ether 00:02:b3:00:00:AA
ifconfig eth0 up
```

  Register the MAC on all hosts by broadcast ping: **ping –c 1 –b 192.168.1.255**.

  Now you can sniff all traffic to the computer that owns this MAC address.

- **Reconfigure Port Spanning On the Switch** As mentioned earlier, switch ports can be configured to see traffic destined for other ports. An intruder can perform this by connecting to the switch via Telnet or some other default back door. An intruder can also use SNMP if it is not secured.

- **Cable Taps** As mentioned earlier, cable taps can be used to physically tap into the cable. Tapping into the uplink cable on a switch shows you all of the traffic entering and exiting that switch.

There are many methods for defeating switches that are contingent on how a switch operates. Not all of the methods discussed work, especially with new, more technologically savvy switches. The Dsniff Frequently Asked Questions (FAQ) helpful information for sniffing in a switched environment, and can be located at www.monkey.org/~dugsong/dsniff/faq.html.

# Detecting Sniffers

As mentioned earlier, sniffers are a form of passive attack. They don't interact with any devices or transmit any information, thus making them very difficult to detect. Although tricky, detecting sniffers is possible. The easiest method is to check your network interfaces to see if they are in promiscuous mode. On UNIX-based systems, the command **ifconfig –a** lists the network adapters on the system. Look for the PROMISC flag in the output, such as in the following example:

```
[root@localhost root]# ifconfig -a
eth0      Link encap:Ethernet  HWaddr 00:02:B3:06:5F:5A
          inet addr:192.168.1.2  Bcast:192.168.1.255  Mask:255.255.255.0
          UP BROADCAST RUNNING PROMISC MULTICAST  MTU:1500  Metric:1
          RX packets:204 errors:0 dropped:0 overruns:0 frame:0
          TX packets:92 errors:0 dropped:0 overruns:0 carrier:0
          collisions:0 txqueuelen:100
          RX bytes:46113 (45.0 Kb)  TX bytes:5836 (5.6 Kb)
          Interrupt:11 Base address:0x1800 Memory:e8120000-e8120038
```

If **ifconfig** does not detect a sniffer that you know is currently installed and in promiscuous mode, you can try using the **ip link** command, a TCP/IP interface configuration and routing utility. The following example shows the output from the IP command:

```
[root@localhost root]# ip link
1: lo: <LOOPBACK,UP> mtu 16436 qdisc noqueue
    link/loopback 00:00:00:00:00:00 brd 00:00:00:00:00:00
2: eth0: <BROADCAST,MULTICAST,PROMISC,UP> mtu 1500 qdisc pfifo_fast qlen 100
    link/ether 00:02:b3:06:5f:5a brd ff:ff:ff:ff:ff:ff
```

Detecting promiscuous mode on Windows systems is difficult because there are no standard commands that list that type of information. However, there is a free tool called PromiscDetect (developed by Arne Vidstrom), which detects promiscuous mode network adapters for Windows NT, 2000, and XP. It can be downloaded from www.ntsecurity.nu/toolbox/promiscdetect. The following example shows the output of PromiscDetect: the D-link adapter is in normal operation mode, and the Intel adapter is running Wireshark:

```
C:\>promiscdetect
PromiscDetect 1.0 - (c) 2002, Arne Vidstrom (arne.vidstrom@ntsecurity.nu)
                 - http://ntsecurity.nu/toolbox/promiscdetect/
Adapter name:
 - D-Link DWL-650 11Mbps WLAN Card
Active filter for the adapter:
 - Directed (capture packets directed to this computer)
 - Multicast (capture multicast packets for groups the computer is a member
of)
 - Broadcast (capture broadcast packets)
Adapter name:
 - Intel(R) PRO/100 SP Mobile Combo Adapter
Active filter for the adapter:
 - Directed (capture packets directed to this computer)
 - Multicast (capture multicast packets for groups the computer is a member
of)
 - Broadcast (capture broadcast packets)
 - Promiscuous (capture all packets on the network)
WARNING: Since this adapter is in promiscuous mode there could be a sniffer
         running on this computer!
```

Some sniffers cover their tracks by hiding PROMISC flags. Also, if a sniffer is installed on a compromised system using a rootkit, the intruder probably replaces commands such as **ifconfig**. The following list describes several other methods that can be used to detect sniffers on the network:

- **Monitor DNS Reverse Lookups** Some sniffers perform DNS queries to resolve IP addresses to host names. Performing a network ping scan or pinging your entire network address space can trigger this activity.

- **Send TCP/IP Packets with Fake MAC Addresses to All IP Addresses On the Same Ethernet Segment** Normally, the NIC drops packets with the wrong MAC address. However, when in promiscuous mode, some systems answer with a reset (RST) packet. This might also work in a switched environment, because switches forward broadcast packets that they don't have MAC addresses for. Many new sniffers have built-in defenses for this technique, altering the way they handle MAC addresses.

- **Carefully Monitor Hub Ports** Ideally, you have a network diagram and your cables are labeled. Then, if something unusual appears (e.g., a new device or a newly active hub port), you will recognize it. However, in reality, wiring closets and cabling can be a nightmare. If your hubs are being monitored with a protocol such as SNMP via a network management system, you may be able to use the information to detect any unusual connects and disconnects.

- **Remember How ARP is Used to Link IP Addresses to MAC Addresses** Normally, an ARP is sent out as a broadcast to everyone. However, you can also send out an ARP to a non-broadcast address, followed by a broadcast ping. No one should have your information in an ARP table except the sniffer that was listening to all of the traffic (including the non-broadcast traffic). Therefore the computer with the sniffer responds.

- **Use a Honeypot** A honeypot is a server that contains fake data and services to monitor the activity of intruders. In this case, an intruder can create fake administrator or user accounts on the honeypot, and then create connections across the network using cleartext protocols such as Telnet or FTP. If sniffers are monitoring for usernames and passwords, they will see the honeypot and the intruder will probably try to log into it. Honeypots run IDS to monitor activity, and special signatures can be added to trigger alerts when fake accounts are used.

- **Carefully Monitor Your Hosts** This includes disk space, central processing unit (CPU) utilization, and response times. Sniffers gradually consume disk space as they log traffic, and can occasionally put a noticeable load on the CPU. As the infected computer's resources become more utilized, it begins to respond slower than normal.

There are several tools that can be used to detect sniffers on a network. Many of them are outdated, no longer actively maintained, and sometimes hard to find. New sniffers have been rewritten to evade detection. The following is a list of some of those tools:

- **PromiScan Ver 0.27** This free program was developed by Security Friday, and is up-to-date and actively maintained. It runs on Windows 2000 and XP and requires the WinPcap driver. It scans the local network looking for remote promiscuous mode adapters using ARP packets, and can be downloaded from www.securityfriday.com/products/promiscan.html.

- **Sentinel** This free program performs remote promiscuous detection, and runs on various versions of Berkeley Software Distribution (BSD) and

Linux. It requires the libpcap and libnet libraries to operate, and can be downloaded from www.packetfactory.net/projects/sentinel.

- **Check Promiscuous Mode (CPM)** This is a free UNIX-based program developed by the Computer Emergency Response Team/Coordination Center (CERT/CC) in response to increased network sniffing. More information, including the program, can be obtained from www.cert.org/advisories/CA-1994-01.html.

- *Ifstatus* This is a free UNIX-based program that detects promiscuous mode interfaces on Solaris and Advanced IBM Unix (AIX) systems. It can be downloaded from ftp://ftp.cerias.purdue.edu/pub/tools/unix/sysutils/ifstatus.

- *Promisc.c* This is a free UNIX-based program that detects promiscuous mode interfaces on Linux and some SunOS systems. It can be downloaded from www.phreak.org/archives/exploits/unix/network-sniffers/promisc.c.

# Sniffing Wireless

From the airport, to the coffee shop, to the library, to your next door neighbor, wireless networks are all around us; therefore, wireless security is a serious concern. There are historical weaknesses in security protocols, because intruders no longer need to be inside a building to attack an internal network. A wireless network is still a network, however, and with a few exceptions maps well to the Ethernet and OSI models.

## Hardware Requirements

While most Ethernet cards are capable of packet sniffing in promiscuous mode, many wireless chipsets cannot use *monitor* mode, which is the wireless equivalent of promiscuous mode. Complicating the situation is that wireless card manufacturers do not generally list the chipset that they use in a readily available form. Also, chipsets can vary within model families. It is best to select the software you want to use, and then identify which chipsets and specific manufacturer's model numbers work best with the specific drivers necessary for the software to function.

Here are some general guidelines on chipset compatibility:

- **Atheros** This chipset is compatible with most software and widely available in a number of adapters.

- **Prism2** This chipset is one of the most capable used with the Host AP drivers. Not only is it supported by most software, it can also run in an AP mode.

- **Orinoco** One of the first chipsets that supported monitor mode. Supported by most software. Cannot receive 802.11g traffic.

- **Broadcom** There is no native support in Linux for this chipset. With included drivers, tools such as Kismet do not function with it. You may be able to use Windows drivers through a Network Driver Interface Specification (NDIS) compatibility wrapper such as the commercial DriverLoader, which can be downloaded from www.linuxant.com/driverloader.

# Software

The proper combination of hardware, software, and drivers will enable you to effectively sniff wireless networking traffic. The following tools may be helpful:

- **Netstumbler** Netstumbler is more of a network scanner than a network sniffing tool, but is useful for listing networks detectable from your location. Netstumbler is an active network scanner that sends out probes that are detectable by others. It can be downloaded for free from www.netstumbler.org.

- **Kismet** Kismet is an open-source, free, wireless network scanner and vulnerability detector, which keeps track of wireless clients and their network associations. Unlike other scanners, it is a completely passive network scanner, and can be downloaded from www.kismetwireless.net.

- **Wireshark** Wireshark has a number of dissectors for wireless management traffic; however, it does not track by Service Set Identifier (SSID), nor does it show signal strength.

- **CommView for WiFi** CommView for WiFi is a commercial wireless network monitor and scanner that can export in tcpdump format, which Wireshark imports and reads easily. CommView for WiFi can be downloaded from www.tamos.com/products/commwifi/.

## NOTE

### Bootable CD-ROMs

There are several bootable Linux distributions that come prepackaged with the correct drivers and software necessary for wireless and wired network sniffing. All of these include Kismet and Ethereal or Wireshark. Below are some that are available and free:

- **Backtrack** Backtrack is the result of two highly respected bootable penetration toolsets combining their efforts toward one unified bootable CDROM. For additional information, go to www.remote-exploit.org.
- **Professional Hacker's Linux Assault Kit (Phlack)** Includes many security tools and wireless auditing and scanning software. For additional information, go to www.phlak.org.
- **Knoppix Security Tools Distribution (Knoppix-STD)** A general-purpose collection of security tools on a bootable Linux image. For additional information, go to www.s-t-d.org.

# Protocol Dissection

Now that we've reviewed many of the critical portions of layers 1 through 4 of the OSI networking model, some attention should be paid to some of the protocols that you may run across while using Wireshark. The larger the network that you are sniffing, the more types of protocols (and protocol anomalies) you are likely to encounter.

# DNS

The DNS translates hostnames into IP addresses, and vice versa. Most DNS traffic is transferred over UDP port 53 in a client/server fashion. DNS can be considered *forward* or *reverse*. Forward DNS translates a hostname into an IP address, and reverse DNS translates an IP address into a hostname. On the protocol level, forward and reverse lookups are nearly identical.

To get an IP address from a given hostname, a DNS system (also known as a *resolver*) requests an address (A) record from a DNS server. In the following example, we ask the authoritative name server for the IP address of *www.example.com*. In tcpdump format, we see the following traffic:

```
IP 192.168.0.1.33141 > 192.0.34.43.53:  42827+ A? www.example.com.
IP 192.0.34.43.53 > 192.168.0.1.33141:  42827*- 1/2/2 A 192.0.34.166
```

The resolver (192.168.0.1) asked the authoritative name server (192.0.34.43) on UDP port 53 for the "A record" for www.example.com. Via UDP, the name server returned one A record for that name with IP address 192.0.34.166.

Wireshark can also be used to view more information about this DNS transaction. Wireshark would return the following information about the query and response:

```
Domain Name System (query)
    Transaction ID: 42827
    Flags: 0x0100 (Standard query)
        0... .... .... .... = Response: Message is a query
        .000 0... .... .... = Opcode: Standard query (0)
        .... ..0. .... .... = Truncated: Message is not truncated
        .... ...1 .... .... = Recursion desired: Do query recursively
        .... .... .0.. .... = Z: reserved (0)
        .... .... ...0 .... = Non-authenticated data OK
    Questions: 1
    Answer RRs: 0
    Authority RRs: 0
    Additional RRs: 0
    Queries
        www.example.com: type A, class IN
            Name: www.example.com
            Type: A (Host address)
            Class: IN (0x0001)
Domain Name System (response)
    Transaction ID: 42827
    Flags: 0x8180 (Standard query response, No error)
        1... .... .... .... = Response: Message is a response
        .000 0... .... .... = Opcode: Standard query (0)
        .... .0.. .... .... = Authoritative
        .... ..0. .... .... = Truncated: Message is not truncated
        .... ...1 .... .... = Recursion desired: Do query recursively
        .... .... 1... .... = Recursion available
        .... .... .0.. .... = Z: reserved (0)
        .... .... ..0. .... = Answer authenticated
        .... .... .... 0000 = Reply code: No error (0)
    Questions: 1
    Answer RRs: 1
    Authority RRs: 13
```

```
Additional RRs: 2
Queries
    www.example.com: type A, class IN
        Name: www.example.com
        Type: A (Host address)
        Class: IN (0x0001)
Answers
    www.example.com: type A, class IN, addr 192.0.34.166
Authoritative nameservers
    com: type NS, class IN, ns C.GTLD-SERVERS.NET
    ...
    com: type NS, class IN, ns B.GTLD-SERVERS.NET
Additional records
    A.GTLD-SERVERS.NET: type A, class IN, addr 192.5.6.30
```

## NOTE

DNS uses TCP instead of UDP for transmitting data when the data size exceeds 512 bytes. DNS also uses TCP for transferring entire DNS zones between zones. In either case, port 53 is used.

# NTP

The NTP is another helpful protocol that keeps things running smoothly in the background. In this case, NTP makes sure that all of your computer and device clocks are synchronized. NTP can use peering or client/server architecture; the network traffic will be similar either way. UDP port 123 is used for NTP.

In the following example, NTP client (192.168.0.1) asks a NTP server (192.168.0.2) for the current timestamp:

```
IP 192.168.0.1.ntp > 192.168.0.2.ntp: NTPv4, Client, length 48
IP 192.168.0.2.ntp > 192.168.0.1.ntp: NTPv4, Server, length 48


Network Time Protocol
    Flags: 0xe3
        11.. .... = Leap Indicator: alarm condition (clock not synchronized)
        ..10 0... = Version number: NTP Version 4 (4)
```

```
        .... .011 = Mode: client (3)
    Peer Clock Stratum: unspecified or unavailable (0)
    Peer Polling Interval: 6 (64 sec)
    Peer Clock Precision: 0.000008 sec
    Root Delay:    0.0000 sec
    Clock Dispersion:    0.0039 sec
    Reference Clock ID: Unindentified reference source 'INIT'
    Reference Clock Update Time: NULL
    Originate Time Stamp: Mar 29, 2006 06:09:01.6976 UTC
    Receive Time Stamp: Mar 29, 2006 06:09:01.7563 UTC
    Transmit Time Stamp: Mar 29, 2006 06:10:07.7525 UTC

Network Time Protocol
    Flags: 0x24
        00.. .... = Leap Indicator: no warning (0)
        ..10 0... = Version number: NTP Version 4 (4)
        .... .100 = Mode: server (4)
    Peer Clock Stratum: secondary reference (5)
    Peer Polling Interval: 6 (64 sec)
    Peer Clock Precision: 0.000008 sec
    Root Delay:    0.0000 sec
    Clock Dispersion:    0.0122 sec
    Reference Clock ID: 127.127.1.0
    Reference Clock Update Time: Mar 29, 2006 06:09:48.4681 UTC
    Originate Time Stamp: Mar 29, 2006 06:10:07.7525 UTC
    Receive Time Stamp: Mar 29, 2006 06:10:07.6674 UTC
    Transmit Time Stamp: Mar 29, 2006 06:10:07.6675 UTC
```

# HTTP

HTTP is the most widely used protocol that supports the Web. HTTP uses TCP to transmit data exclusively, and in a default configuration uses port 80. Each object (e.g., Web page, image, audio) fetched from a Web server is transmitted via an individual HTTP session.

To begin an HTTP session, a client establishes a regular TCP connection on port 80 and sends a packet with the SYN flag set. A packet is returned from the Web server, with an ACK flag added to the SYN flag. Finally, the client sends a packet with the ACK flag set, and then sends another packet requesting a specific HTTP object.

The following is an example of a client's request to a HTTP server:

```
GET /index.html HTTP/1.1
```

The client requests the *index.html* page using HTTP v1.1:

```
Host: www.example.com
```

The hostname that was typed in the browser allows a server to host multiple Web services on one IP address:

```
User-Agent: ELinks/0.11.0 (textmode; Linux; 80x25-2)
```

The User-Agent describes the Web browser version to the server. Some browsers allow users to change hostnames; thereby deeming it unreliable.

```
Accept-Encoding: gzip
Accept-Language: en
Connection: Keep-Alive
```

These lines tell the Web server that the client supports compression of the object requested, accepts pages in English, and the Web server doesn't have to disconnect upon completion of the object request.

The Web server sends back the following information to the client:

```
HTTP/1.1 200 OK
```

The Web server responds in HTTP/1.1 with status code "200 OK," which indicates to the browser that the object was successfully fetched. Other codes are "403 Forbidden," (the server does not have permission to send the object to the client, and "404," (the server cannot find the object that the client requested).

```
Date: Thu, 30 Mar 2006 05:23:29 GMTLast-Modified: Wed, 29 Mar 2006 16:22:05 GMT
Server: Apache/2.2.0
```

These lines allow the client to cache content efficiently. It tells the client what time the server thinks it is, and when the content was last modified. The server also identifies its product (Apache) and version (2.2.0), although this can be changed by the server administrator.

```
Accept-Ranges: bytes
Content-Length: 40Connection: close
Content-Type: text/html; charset=UTF-8<HTML><BODY>Hello, world!</BODY></HTML>
```

If needed to restart the transfer, the server tells the client in what form it can request portions of a file (in this case it accepts bytes). The server then tells the client to close the connection after the data is finished. The actual HTTP data follows, beginning with the line "Content-Type."

# SMTP

SMTP is the mechanism by which most e-mail is sent over the Internet. SMTP uses TCP to transmit data exclusively, and in most situations the server uses port 25. The entire e-mail (headers and contents) is sent in one SMTP session. It is easy to emulate a SMTP session using the Telnet program to port 25 of an e-mail server.

Think of an SMTP connection the same as sending a memo through the regular mail. On the outside of the envelope are a return address and a destination. The return address and destination might also be repeated inside the envelope, but the mail carrier doesn't care about what is inside the envelope. In an SMTP connection, the message envelope is transmitted first, followed by the letter contents inside.

The following is an example of an SMTP conversation. The client sends in normal text, and the server responds in italics:

```
220 example.org ESMTP Mail Service
HELO client.example.com
```
*250 Ok*

Upon connection, the server indicates its presence with a *banner* that includes the version of the e-mail server program, but can also be configured by the user to be an arbitrary banner, as long as it begins with the hostname of the server. The client says "HELO" to the server, and tells it what name it wants to go by. The **HELO** command is also used for clients that support advanced SMTP features such as encryption. The server acknowledges the client with an "Ok" response.

```
MAIL FROM:<person@example.com>
```
*250 Ok*

The client sends a **MAIL FROM** command, indicating the return address, which may or may not match the letter's contents. Your Mail User Agent or e–mail reader normally only show the address contained in the letter, disregarding the envelope.

```
RCPT TO:<anotherperson@example.org>
```
*250 Ok*

The client sends the destination of the envelope and the server acknowledges it.

At this point, you may see a "Relaying Denied" message, indicating that the server will not accept the e-mail. At the beginning of e-mail, systems were free to send e-mail directly to each other, or by relaying it through any other system on the Internet. However, this arrangement broke down in the 1990s when spam became a major issue on the Internet. Most systems now accept e-mail for themselves only, and relaying is generally only relevant to ISPs.

```
DATA
354 End data with <CR><LF>.<CR><LF>
From: "person" <person@example.com>
To: example@example.com
Example E-Mail subject.
Example e-mail contents.
.
250 Ok: queued as C8243B4039QUIT221
Quit 221 Bye
```

The client sends the **DATA** command, telling the server that the contents of the letter will be transmitted. The e-mail's headers are normally repeated at this point, and it is from here that e-mail is communicated. To end the e-mail, the server instructs the client to send a linefeed, followed by a dot and another linefeed. The client politely issues the *QUIT* command, and the server bids the client farewell.

# Protecting Against Sniffers

So far, you have learned what sniffing is and how it works. You have also learned some of the tricks that can be used by intruders for sniffing, and some not-so-fool-proof methods of detecting sniffers. None of this sheds a positive light on your plight to protect your network and data. However, there are some methods on your network that offer protection against sniffing.

We talked earlier about using switches instead of hubs, and we learned the methods used to defeat switches. Using switches is a network best practice that allows increased performance and security. While switches present a barrier to casual sniffing, the best method of protecting your data is to use encryption, which is the best form of protection against traffic interception on public networks and internal networks. Intruders can still sniff the traffic, but the data appears unreadable. Only the intended recipient should be able to decrypt and read the data; however, some methods of encryption leave the packet headers in cleartext, thereby allowing intruders to see the source and destination addresses and map the network. However, the data contained within the packet is protected. Other forms of encryption also mask the header portion of the packet.

A VPN uses encryption and authentication to provide secure communication over an otherwise insecure network. VPNs protect the transmission of data over the Internet and over your internal network. However, if an intruder compromises either of the end nodes of a VPN, the protection is rendered useless. Different types of VPN families are not interchangeable, but they can be combined and used in multiples. The following list describes some of the VPN methods used today that protect your data against sniffing:

- **SSH** SSH is an application-level VPN that runs over TCP to secure client-to-server transactions. This is often used for system logins and to administer servers remotely, and is typically used to replace Telnet, FTP, and the BSD **r** commands. However, any arbitrary TCP protocol can be tunneled through an SSH connection and used for numerous other applications. SSH provides authentication using Rivest, Shamir, & Adleman (RSA) or Digital Signature Algorithm (DSA) asymmetric key pairs, and many encryption options for protecting data and passwords sent over the network. The headers in an SSH session are not encrypted, so an intruder can still view the source and destination addresses.

- **Secure Sockets Layer (SSL)/Transport Layer Security (TLS)** SSL was originally developed by Netscape Communications to provide security and privacy to Internet sessions. It has been replaced by TLS, as stated in RFC 2246. TLS provides security at the transport layer and overcomes some security issues of SSL. It is used to encapsulate the network traffic of higher-level applications such as HTTP, Lightweight Directory Access Protocol (LDAP), FTP, SMTP, POP3, and IMAP. It provides authentication and integrity via digital certificates and digital signatures and the source and destination IP headers in a SSL session are not encrypted.

- **IP Security (IPSec)** IPSec is a network-level protocol that incorporates security into the IPv4 and IPv6 protocols directly at the packet level, by extending the IP packet header. This allows the ability to encrypt any higher-layer protocol. It has been incorporated into routing devices, firewalls, and clients for securing trusted networks to one another. IPSec provides several means for authentication and encryption, supporting a lot of public key authentication ciphers and symmetric key encryption ciphers. It can operate in *tunnel* mode to provide a new IP header that masks the original source and destination addresses in addition to the data being transmitted. Since IPSec uses protocols other than TCP and UDP, getting the IPSec traffic through a firewall or NAT device can be challenging.

- **OpenVPN** OpenVPN is a tunneling SSL VPN protocol, which can encrypt both the contents of a packet and its IP headers. OpenVPN uses a single TCP or UDP port; therefore, it can be easier to use in environments with challenging NAT and firewall architectures. Additionally, it can act as a virtual network bridge (a layer 2 VPN).

One-time passwords (OTP) are another method to protect against sniffing. S/key, One-time Passwords In Everything (OPIE), and other one-time password techniques protect against the collection and reuse of passwords. They operate using a challenge-response method, and a different password is transmitted each time authentication is needed. The passwords that a sniffer collects are eventually useless since they are only used once. Smart cards are a popular method of implementing one-time passwords. However, OTP technologies cannot help protect your password after you enter it.

E-mail protection is a hot topic for companies and individuals. Two methods of protecting e-mail (i.e., encrypting it in-transit and in storage) are Pretty Good Privacy (PGP) and Secure Multipurpose Internet Mail Extensions (S/MIME). Each of these methods also provides authentication and integrity using digital certificates and digital signatures.

# Network Analysis and Policy

Before cracking open your newly installed network analyzer at work, read your company policy! A properly written and comprehensive "Appropriate Use" network policy will prohibit you from running network analyzers. Usually the only exception to this is if network analysis is in your job description. Also, just because you provide security consulting services for company clients does not mean that you can use your sniffer on the company network. However, if you are an administrator and allowed to legitimately run a sniffer, you can use it to enforce your company's security policy. If the policy on using sniffers is not clear in your organization, take the time to get permission in writing from the appropriate departments before using them or any other security-related tools. On the other hand, if your security policy prohibits using file-sharing applications (e.g., KaZaA, Morpheus, BitTorrent or messaging services such as Internet Relay Chat [IRC] or Instant Messenger [IM]), you could use a sniffer to detect this type of activity.

Also, if you provide security services for clients, be sure that using a sniffer is included in your Rules of Engagement. Be very specific about how, where, and when it will be used. Also, provide clauses (e.g., Non-Disclosure Agreements) that will exempt you from the liability of learning confidential information.

Ensure that your sniffing activities do not violate any laws against wiretapping. In many countries, wiretapping laws were enacted at a time when modems were the most complicated network access device, so the clarification of laws and related regulatory requirements can be complex and differ based on the situation and the parties involved.

**CAUTION**

Many ISPs prohibit using sniffers in their "Appropriate Use" policy. If they discover that you are using one while attached to their network, they may disconnect your service. The best place to experiment with a sniffer is on your home network that is not connected to the Internet. All you need is two computers with a crossover cable between them, or a virtual machine application. You can use one as a client, and install server services on the other (e.g., Telnet, FTP, Web, and e-mail).

**NOTE**

You can download packet traces from numerous Web sites and read them with your network analyzer to get used to analyzing and interpreting packets.

The HoneyNet Project at www.project.honeynet.org has monthly challenges and other data for analysis.

The Wireshark "wiki" also has many well-described capture files that are located at www.wiki.wireshark.org/SampleCaptures.

# Summary

Network analysis is the key to maintaining an optimized network and detecting security issues. Proactive management can help find issues before they turn into serious problems and cause network downtime or compromise confidential data. In addition to identifying attacks and suspicious activity, your network analyzer can be used to identify security vulnerabilities and weaknesses and enforce your company's security policy. Sniffer logs can be correlated with IDSes, firewalls, and router logs to provide evidence for forensics and incident handling. A network analyzer allows you to capture data from the network (packet-by-packet), decode the information, and view it in an easy-to-understand format. Network analyzers are easy to find, often free, and easy to use; they are a key part of any administrator's toolbox.

This chapter covered the basics of networking, Ethernet, the OSI model, and the hardware that is used in a network architecture; however, it only scratched the surface. A good networking and protocol reference should be on every administrator's bookshelf. It will come in handy when you discover some unknown or unusual traffic on your network.

As an administrator, you should know how to detect the use of sniffers by intruders. You should keep up-to-date on the methods that intruders use to get around security measures that are meant to protect against sniffing. As always, you also need to make sure that your computer systems are up-to-date with patches and security fixes to protect against rootkits and other backdoors.

This chapter also covered a variety of methods used to protect data from eavesdropping by sniffers. It is important to remain up-to-date on the latest security technologies, encryption algorithms, and authentication processes. Intruders are constantly finding ways to defeat current security practices, thus more powerful methods are developed (e.g., cracking the Data Encryption Standard [DES] encryption scheme and its subsequent replacement with Triple Data Encryption Standard (3DES), followed by the Advanced Encryption Standard (AES).

Finally, remember the rule of network analysis—only do it if you have permission and the law is on your side. A curious, up-and-coming administrator could easily be mistaken for an intruder. Make sure you have permission, or use your own private network to experiment.

# Solutions Fast Track

## What is Network Analysis and Sniffing?

- ☑ Network analysis is capturing and decoding network data.

- ☑ Network analyzers can be hardware or software, and are available both free and commercially.

- ☑ Network analyzer interfaces usually have three panes: Summary, Detail, and Data.

- ☑ The five parts of a network analyzer are: hardware, capture driver, buffer, real-time analysis, and decode.

## Who Uses Network Analysis?

- ☑ Administrators use network analysis for troubleshooting network problems, analyzing the performance of a network, and intrusion detection.

- ☑ When intruders use sniffers, it is considered a passive attack.

- ☑ Intruders use sniffers to capture user names and passwords, collect confidential data, and map the network.

- ☑ Sniffers are a common component of a rootkit.

- ☑ Intruders use sniffers to control backdoor programs.

## How Does it Work?

- ☑ Ethernet is a shared medium that uses MAC or hardware addresses.

- ☑ The OSI model has seven layers and represents a standard for network communication.

- ☑ Hubs send out information to all hosts on the segment, creating a shared collision domain.

- ☑ Switches have one collision domain per port and keep an address table of the MAC addresses that are associated with each port.

- ☑ Port mirroring is a feature that allows you to sniff on switches.

☑ Switches make sniffing more difficult; however, the security measures in switch architectures can be overcome by a number of methods, thus allowing the sniffing of traffic designated for other computers.

☑ Sniffing wired traffic can be done with many kinds of NICs; wireless sniffing requires greater attention to hardware details such as chipset and drivers.

# Detecting Sniffers

☑ Sometimes sniffers can be detected on local systems by looking for the PROMISC flag.

☑ There are several tools available that attempt to detect promiscuous mode using various methods.

☑ Carefully monitoring hosts, hub and switch ports, and DNS reverse lookups assists in detecting sniffers.

☑ Honeypots are a good method to detect intruders on your network who are attempting to use compromised passwords.

☑ New sniffers are smart enough to hide from traditional detection techniques.

# Protocol Dissection

☑ DNS packets can use either TCP or UDP, depending on the purpose of the query and the amount of data transmitted.

☑ NTP data transmissions generally use UDP port 123 for both the client and server side ports.

☑ Multiple virtual HTTP servers can listen on one port. The Host: header indicates to the server which virtual server the client intended to connect with.

☑ A SMTP connection can be emulated with a simple network program such as Telnet. If your SMTP server is left open on the Internet, it will eventually be used to send spam.

## Protecting Against Sniffers

☑ Switches offer little protection against sniffers.

☑ Encryption is the best method of protecting your data from sniffers.

☑ SSH, SSL/TLS, and IPSec are all forms of VPNs that operate at various layers of the OSI model.

☑ IPSec tunnel mode can protect the source and destination addresses in the IP header by appending a new header.

## Network Analysis and Policy

☑ Make sure you have permission to use a sniffer on a network that is not your own.

☑ Read the appropriate use policies of your ISP before using a sniffer.

☑ If you are hired to assess a computer network and plan to use a sniffer, make sure you have a non-disclosure agreement in place, because you may have access to confidential data.

☑ One-time passwords render compromised passwords useless.

☑ E-mail should be protected while in transit, and stored with some type of data encryption method.

# Frequently Asked Questions

The following Frequently Asked Questions, answered by the authors of this book, are designed to both measure your understanding of the concepts presented in this chapter and to assist you with real-life implementation of these concepts. To have your questions about this chapter answered by the author, browse to **www.syngress.com/solutions** and click on the **"Ask the Author"** form.

**Q:** What can I do to protect my network from sniffers?

**A:** Proper network security comes by design, not just through action. Some argue that there is nothing you can do to make your network completely secure. A combination of network access controls like 802.1x, ubiquitous and oppor-tunistic encryption, and strong policies and procedures will go a long way to protecting your network from sniffers and other security issues. Using several layers of security is known as *defense-in-depth*, and is a standard best practice for secure network architectures.

**Q:** What is this opportunistic encryption that you speak of, and where can I buy it?

**A:** Opportunistic Encryption is the practice where communication between two parties becomes encrypted, even when those parties cannot be assured of each other's identity. More information on opportunistic encryption is available at www.en.wikipedia.org/wiki/Opportunistic_encryption free of charge. Ubiquitous opportunistic encryption is the theory that any network communication that *can* be encrypted, *should* be.

**Q:** How can I ensure that I am sniffing network traffic legally?

**A:** The best way to ensure that your sniffing activities are legal is to solicit expert legal counsel. In general, you should be safe if all parties to the communication that you are sniffing acknowledge that they have no expectation of privacy on your network. These acknowledgements can be in employment contracts, and should also be set as banners so that the expectation of no privacy is reinforced. It is advised that you get authorization (in writing) from your employer to use sniffing software.

**Q:** Is a sniffer running a security breach on my network?

**A:** Possibly. Check the source of the sniffing activity and verify that the interception has been authorized. Hackers and other network miscreants use sniffers to assist themselves in their work. It is best to design networks and other applications that are resilient to network sniffing and other security issues.

**Q:** Can I use a sniffer as an IDS?

**A:** While a sniffer can act similarly to an IDS, it is not designed as such. IDSes have threshold, alerting, and reporting systems that are beyond the design specifications for most sniffers.

**Q:** How do I use a sniffer to see traffic inside a VPN?

**A:** VPN traffic is normally encrypted and most sniffing software does not have the ability to read encrypted packets, even if you have the decryption key. The best place to see VPN traffic is outside of the VPN tunnel itself.

# Chapter 2

# Introducing Wireshark: Network Protocol Analyzer

## Solutions in this chapter:

- **What is Wireshark?**
- **Supporting Programs**
- **Using Wireshark in Your Network Architecture**
- **Using Wireshark for Network Troubleshooting**
- **Using Wireshark for System Administration**
- **Using Wireshark for Security Administration**
- **Securing Wireshark**
- **Optimizing Wireshark**
- **Advanced Sniffing Techniques**
- **Securing Your Network from Sniffers**

- ☑ **Summary**
- ☑ **Solutions Fast Track**
- ☑ **Frequently Asked Questions**

# Introduction

You may have picked up this book because you heard about Wireshark (or its predecessor, Ethereal) and its feature-rich graphical user interface (GUI). Or maybe you
read about it on the Internet, overheard a co-worker talking about it, or heard about
it at a security conference. No matter what the case may be, if you are looking for a
comprehensive guide to help you unleash the powers of Wireshark, you've come to
the right place.

Wireshark is the best open-source network analyzer available. It is packed
with features comparable to commercial network analyzers, and with a large,
diverse collection of authors, new enhancements are continually developed.
Wireshark is a stable and useful component for all network toolkits, and new features and bug fixes are always being developed. A lot of progress has been made
since the early days of Wireshark (when it was still called Ethereal); the application now performs comparably (and in some regards) better than commercial
sniffing software.

In this chapter, you will gain an understanding of what Wireshark is, what its
features are, and how to use it for troubleshooting on your network architecture.
Additionally, you will learn the history of Wireshark, how it came to be such a popular network analyzer, and why it remains a top pick for system and security administration. Along the way, we go over some tips for running Wireshark in a secure
manner, optimizing it so that it runs advanced techniques smoothly.

# What is Wireshark?

Wireshark is a network analyzer. It reads packets from the network, decodes them,
and presents them in an easy-to-understand format. Some of the most important
aspects of Wireshark are that it is open source, actively maintained, and free. The following are some of the other important aspects of Wireshark:

- It is distributed under the Gnu's Not UNIX (GNU) General Public
  License (GPL) open-source license.
- It works in promiscuous and non-promiscuous modes.
- It can capture data from the network or read from a capture file.
- It has an easy-to-read and configurable GUI.
- It has rich display filter capabilities.

- It supports tcpdump format capture filters. It has a feature that reconstructs a Transmission Control Protocol (TCP) session and displays it in American Standard Code for Information Interchange (ASCII), Extended Binary Coded Decimal Interchange Code (EBCDIC), hexadecimal (hex) dump, or C arrays.

- It is available in precompiled binaries and source code.

- It runs on over 20 platforms, including Uniplexed Information and Computing System (UNIX)-based operating systems (OSes) and Windows, and there are third-party packages available for Mac OS X.

- It supports over 750 protocols, and, because it is open source, new ones are contributed frequently.

- It can read capture files from over 25 different products.

- It can save capture files in a variety of formats (e.g., libpcap, Network Associates Sniffer, Microsoft Network Monitor (NetMon), and Sun snoop).

- It can capture data from a variety of media (e.g., Ethernet, Token-Ring, 802.11 Wireless, and so on).

- It includes a command-line version of the network analyzer called *tshark*.

- It includes a variety of supporting programs such as *editcap*, *mergecap*, and *text2pcap*.

- Output can be saved or printed as plaintext or PostScript.

# History of Wireshark

Gerald Combs first developed Ethereal in 1997, because he was expanding his knowledge of networking and needed a tool for network troubleshooting. The first version (v0.2.0) was released in July 1998. A development team, including Gilbert Ramirez, Guy Harris, and Richard Sharpe, quickly formed to provide patches, enhancements, and additional dissectors. Dissectors are what allow Wireshark to decode individual protocols and present them in readable format. Since then, a large number of individuals have contributed specific protocol dissectors and other enhancements to Wireshark. You can view the list of authors at www.wireshark.org/about.html#authors. Because of the overwhelming development support and the large user base, Wireshark's capabilities and popularity continue to grow every day.

## Notes From the Underground...

### The GNU GPL

The GNU Project was originally developed in 1984 to provide a free UNIX-like OS. It is argued that Linux, the "OS" should be referred to as the "GNU/Linux" system because it uses the GNU utilities with a Linux kernel.

The GNU Project is run and sponsored by the Free Software Foundation (FSF). Richard Stallman wrote the GNU GPL in 1989, for the purpose of distributing programs released as part of the GNU Project. It is a copyleft (i.e., Copyleft—all rights reserved), free software license and is based on similar licenses that were used for early versions of GNU Editor Emacs (MACroS).

Copyleft is the application of copyright law to ensure public freedom to manipulate, improve, and redistribute a work of authorship and all derivative works. This means that the copyright holder grants an irrevocable license to all recipients of a copy, permitting the redistribution and sale of possibly further modified copies under the condition that all of those copies carry the same license and are made available in a form that facilitates modification. There are legal consequences to face if a licensee fails to distribute the work under the same license. If the licensee distributes copies of the work, the source code and modification must be made available.

The text of the GPL software license itself cannot be modified. You can copy and distribute it, but you cannot change the text of the GPL. You can modify the GPL and make it your own license, but you cannot use the name "GPL." Other licenses created by the GNU project include the GNU Lesser GPL and the GNU Free Documentation License.

There remains an ongoing dispute about the GPL and whether or not non-GPL software can link to GPL libraries. Although derivative works of GPL code must abide by the license, it is not clear whether an executable that links to a GPL library is considered a derivative work. The FSF states that such executables are derivatives to the GPL work, but others in the software community disagree. To date, there have not been any court decisions to resolve this conflict.

## Compatibility

As stated, Wireshark can read and process capture files from a number of different products, including other sniffers, routers, and network utilities. Because Wireshark uses the popular Promiscuous Capture Library (libpcap)–based capture format, it interfaces easily with other products that use libpcap. It also has the ability to read captures in a variety of other formats. Wireshark can automatically determine the type of file it is reading and can uncompress GNU Zip (gzip) files. The following list shows the products from which Wireshark can read capture files:

- Tcpdump
- Sun snoop and atmsnoop
- Microsoft NetMon
- Network Associates Sniffer (compressed or uncompressed) and Sniffer Pro
- Shomiti/Finisar Surveyor
- Novell LANalyzer
- Cinco Networks NetXRay
- AG Group/WildPackets EtherPeek/TokenPeek/AiroPeek
- RADCOM's wide area network (WAN)/local area network (LAN) analyzer
- Visual Networks' Visual UpTime
- Lucent/Ascend router debug output
- Toshiba's Integrated Services Digital Network (ISDN) routers dump output
- Cisco Secure intrusion detection systems (IDS) iplog
- AIX's iptrace
- HP-UX nettl
- ISDN4BSD project's i4btrace output
- Point-To-point Protocol Daemon (PPPD) logs (pppdump-format)
- VMS's TCPIPtrace utility
- DBS Etherwatch Virtual Memory System (VMS) utility
- CoSine L2 debug
- Accellent's 5Views LAN agent output
- Endace Measurement Systems' Electronic Remote Fill (ERF) capture format
- Linux Bluez Bluetooth stack "hcidump –w" traces
- Catapult DCT2000
- Network Instruments Observer version 9
- EyeSDN Universal Serial Bus (USB) S0 traces

# Supported Protocols

When a network analyzer reads data from the network it needs to know how to interpret what it is seeing and then display the output in an easy-to-read format. This is known as *protocol decoding*. Often, the number of protocols a sniffer can read and display determines its strength, thus most commercial sniffers can support several hundred protocols. Wireshark is very competitive in this area, with its current support of over 750 protocols. New protocols are constantly being added by various contributors to the Wireshark project. Protocol decodes, also known as *dissectors*, can be added directly into the code or included as plug-ins. The following list shows the 752 protocols that are currently supported at the time of this writing:

> 3COMXNS, 3GPP2 A11, 802.11 MGT, 802.11 Radiotap, 802.3 Slow protocols, 9P, AAL1, AAL3/4, AARP, ACAP, ACN, ACSE, ACtrace, ADP, AFP, AFS (RX), AgentX, AH, AIM, AIM Administration, AIM Advertisements, AIM BOS, AIM Buddylist, AIM Chat, AIM ChatNav, AIM Directory, AIM E-mail, AIM Generic, AIM ICQ, AIM Invitation, AIM Location, AIM Messaging, AIM OFT, AIM Popup, AIM Signon, AIM SSI, AIM SST, AIM Stats, AIM Translate, AIM User Lookup, AJP13, ALC, ALCAP, AMR, ANS, ANSI BSMAP, ANSI DTAP, ANSI IS-637-A Teleservice, ANSI IS-637-A Transport, ANSI IS-683-A (OTA (Mobile)), ANSI IS-801 (Location Services (PLD)), ANSI MAP, AODV, AOE, ARCNET, Armagetronad, ARP/RARP, ARTNET, ASAP, ASF, ASN1, ASP, ATM, ATM LANE, ATP, ATSVC, Auto-RP, AVS WLANCAP, AX4000, BACapp, BACnet, Basic Format XID, BEEP, BER, BFD Control, BGP, BICC, BitTorrent, Boardwalk, BOFL, BOOTP/DHCP, BOOTPARAMS, BOSSVR, BROWSER, BSSAP, BSSGP, BUDB, BUTC, BVLC, CAMEL, CAST, CBAPDev, CCSDS, CCSRL, CDP, CDS_CLERK, cds_solicit, CDT, CFLOW, CGMP, CHDLC, CIGI, CIMD, CIP, CISCOWL-L2, CLDAP, CLEARCASE, CLNP, CLTP, CMIP, CMP, CMS, CONV, COPS, COSEVENTCOMM, CoSine, COSNAMING, COTP, CPFI, CPHA, cprpc_server, CRMF, CSM_ENCAPS, CUPS, DAAP, DAP, Data, dc, DCCP, DCE_DFS, dce_update, DCERPC, DCOM, DCP, DDP, DDTP, DEC_DNA, DEC_STP, DFS, DHCPFO, DHCPv6, DIAMETER, dicom, DIS, DISP, DISTCC, DLSw, DLT User A, DLT User B, DLT User C, DLT User D, DNP 3.0, DNS, DNSSERVER, DOCSIS, DOCSIS BPKM-ATTR, DOCSIS BPKM-REQ, DOCSIS BPKM-RSP, DOCSIS DSA-ACK, DOCSIS DSA-REQ, DOCSIS DSA-RSP, DOCSIS DSC-ACK, DOCSIS DSC-REQ, DOCSIS DSC-RSP, DOCSIS DSD-REQ, DOCSIS DSD-RSP, DOCSIS INT-RNG-REQ, DOCSIS MAC MGMT, DOCSIS MAP, DOCSIS REG-ACK, DOCSIS REG-REQ, DOCSIS REG-RSP, DOCSIS RNG-REQ,

DOCSIS RNG-RSP, DOCSIS TLVs, DOCSIS type29ucd, DOCSIS UCC-REQ, DOCSIS UCC-RSP, DOCSIS UCD, DOCSIS VSIF, DOP, DRSUAPI, DSI, DSP, DSSETUP, DTP, DTSPROVIDER, DTSSTIME_REQ, DUA, DVMRP, E.164, EAP, EAPOL, ECHO, EDONKEY, EDP, EFS, EIGRP, ENC, ENIP, ENRP, ENTTEC, EPM, EPMv4, ESIS, ESP, ESS, ETHERIC, ETHERIP, Ethernet, EVENTLOG, FC, FC ELS, FC FZS, FC-dNS, FC-FCS, FC-SB3, FC-SP, FC-SWILS, FC_CT, FCIP, FCP, FDDI, FIX, FLDB, FR, Frame, FRSAPI, FRSRPC, FTAM, FTBP, FTP, FTP-DATA, FTSERVER, FW-1, G.723, GIF image, giFT, GIOP, GMRP, GNM, GNUTELLA, GPRS NS, GPRS-LLC, GRE, Gryphon, GSM BSSMAP, GSM DTAP, GSM RP, GSM SMS, GSM SMS UD, GSM_MAP, GSM_SS, GSS-API, GTP, GVRP, H.223, H.225.0, H.235, H.245, H.261, H.263, H.263 data, H1, h221nonstd, H248, h450, HCLNFSD, HPEXT, HPSW, HSRP, HTTP, HyperSCSI, IAP, IAPP, IAX2, IB, ICAP, ICBAAccoCB, ICBAAccoCB2, ICBAAccoMgt, ICBAAccoMgt2, ICBAAccoServ, ICBAAccoServ2, ICBAAccoServSRT, ICBAAccoSync, ICBABrowse, ICBABrowse2, ICBAGErr, ICBAGErrEvent, ICBALDev, ICBALDev2, ICBAPDev, ICBAPDev2, ICBAPDevPC, ICBAPDevPCEvent, ICBAPersist, ICBAPersist2, ICBARTAuto, ICBARTAuto2, ICBAState, ICBAStateEvent, ICBASysProp, ICBATime, ICEP, ICL_RPC, ICMP, ICMPv6, ICP, ICQ, IDispatch, IDP, IEEE 802.11, IEEE802a, iFCP, IGAP, IGMP, IGRP, ILMI, IMAP, INAP, INITSHUTDOWN, IOXIDResolver, IP, IP/IEEE1394, IPComp, IPDC, IPFC, IPMI, IPP, IPv6, IPVS, IPX, IPX MSG, IPX RIP, IPX SAP, IPX WAN, IRC, IrCOMM, IRemUnknown, IRemUnknown2, IrLAP, IrLMP, ISAKMP, iSCSI, ISDN, ISIS, ISL, ISMP, iSNS, ISUP, isup_thin, ISystemActivator, itunes, IUA, IuUP, Jabber, JFIF (JPEG) image, Juniper, JXTA, JXTA Framing, JXTA Message, JXTA UDP, JXTA Welcome, K12xx, KADM5, KINK, KLM, Kpasswd, KRB4, KRB5, KRB5RPC, L2TP, LANMAN, LAPB, LAPBETHER, LAPD, Laplink, LDAP, LDP, Line-based text data, LLAP, llb, LLC, LLDP, LMI, LMP, Log, LogotypeCertExtn, LOOP, LPD, LSA, Lucent/Ascend, LWAPP, LWAPP-CNTL, LWAPP-L3, LWRES, M2PA, M2TP, M2UA, M3UA, MACC, Malformed packet, Manolito, MAP_DialoguePDU, MAPI, MDS Header, Media, MEGACO, message/http, Messenger, MGCP, MGMT, MIME multipart, MIPv6, MMS, MMSE, Mobile IP, Modbus/TCP, MOUNT, MPEG1, MPLS, MPLS Echo, MQ, MQ PCF, MRDISC, MS NLB, MS Proxy, MSDP, MSMMS, MSNIP, MSNMS, MSRP, MTP2, MTP3, MTP3MG, MySQL, NBAP, NBDS, NBIPX, NBNS, NBP, NBSS, NCP, NCS, NDMP, NDPS, NetBIOS, Netsync, nettl, NFS, NFSACL, NFSAUTH, NHRP, NIS+, NIS+ CB, NJACK, NLM, NLSP, NMAS, NMPI,

NNTP, NORM, NS_CERT_EXTS, NSIP, NSPI, NTLMSSP, NTP, Null,
NW_SERIAL, OAM AAL, OCSP, OLSR, OPSI, OSPF, P_MUL, PAGP, PAP,
PARLAY, PCLI, PCNFSD, PER, PFLOG, PFLOG-OLD, PGM, PGSQL,
PIM, PKCS-1, PKInit, PKIX Certificate, PKIX1EXPLICIT,
PKIX1IMPLICIT, PKIXPROXY, PKIXQUALIFIED, PKIXTSP, PKTC, PN-
DCP, PN-RT, PNIO, PNP, POP, Portmap, PPP, PPP BACP, PPP BAP, PPP
CBCP, PPP CCP, PPP CDPCP, PPP CHAP, PPP Comp, PPP IPCP, PPP
IPV6CP, PPP LCP, PPP MP, PPP MPLSCP, PPP OSICP, PPP PAP, PPP
PPPMux, PPP PPPMuxCP, PPP VJ, PPP-HDLC, PPPoED, PPPoES, PPTP,
PRES, Prism, PTP, PVFS, Q.2931, Q.931, Q.933, QLLC, QUAKE, QUAKE2,
QUAKE3, QUAKEWORLD, R-STP, RADIUS, RANAP, Raw,
Raw_SigComp, Raw_SIP, rdaclif, RDM, RDT, Redback, REMACT,
REP_PROC, RIP, RIPng, RLM, Rlogin, RMCP, RMI, RMP, RNSAP,
ROS, roverride, RPC, RPC_BROWSER, RPC_NETLOGON, RPL, rpriv,
RQUOTA, RRAS, RS_ACCT, RS_ATTR, rs_attr_schema, RS_BIND,
rs_misc, RS_PGO, RS_PLCY, rs_prop_acct, rs_prop_acl, rs_prop_attr,
rs_prop_pgo, rs_prop_plcy, rs_pwd_mgmt, RS_REPADM, RS_REPLIST,
rs_repmgr, RS_UNIX, rsec_login, RSH, rss, RSTAT, RSVP, RSYNC,
RTcfg, RTCP, RTmac, RTMP, RTP, RTP Event, RTPS, RTSE, RTSP,
RUDP, RWALL, RX, SADMIND, SAMR, SAP, SCCP, SCCPMG, SCSI,
SCTP, SDLC, SDP, SEBEK, SECIDMAP, Serialization, SES, sFlow, SGI
MOUNT, Short frame, SIGCOMP, SIP, SIPFRAG, SIR, SKINNY, SLARP,
SliMP3, SLL, SM, SMB, SMB Mailslot, SMB Pipe, SMB2, SMB_NETL-
OGON, smil, SMPP, SMRSE, SMTP, SMUX, SNA, SNA XID, SNAETH,
SNDCP, SNMP, Socks, SONMP, SoulSeek, SPNEGO, SPNEGO-KRB5,
SPOOLSS, SPP, SPRAY, SPX, SRP, SRVLOC, SRVSVC, SSCF-NNI,
SSCOP, SSH, SSL, SSS, STANAG 4406, STANAG 5066, STAT, STAT-CB,
STP, STUN, SUA, SVCCTL, Symantec, Synergy, Syslog, T.38, TACACS,
TACACS+, TALI, TANGO, TAPI, TCAP, TCP, TDMA, TDS, TEI_MAN-
AGEMENT, TELNET, Teredo, TFTP, TIME, TIPC, TKN4Int, TNS, Token-
Ring, TPCP, TPKT, TR MAC, TRKSVR, TSP, TTP, TUXEDO, TZSP,
UBIKDISK, UBIKVOTE, UCP, UDP, UDPENCAP, UDPlite, UMA,
Unreassembled fragmented packet, V.120, V5UA, Vines ARP, Vines Echo,
Vines FRP, Vines ICP, Vines IP, Vines IPC, Vines LLC, Vines RTP, Vines SPP,
VLAN, VNC, VRRP, VTP, WAP SIR, WBXML, WCCP, WCP, WHDLC,
WHO, WINREG, WINS-Replication, WKSSVC, WLANCERTEXTN,
WSP, WTLS, WTP, X.25, X.29, X11, X411, X420, X509AF, X509CE,
X509IF, X509SAT, XDMCP, XML, XOT, XYPLEX, YHOO, YMSG,
YPBIND, YPPASSWD, YPSERV, YPXFR ZEBRA, ZIP

# Wireshark's User Interface

Wireshark's GUI is configurable and easy to use. And like other network analyzers, Wireshark displays capture information in three main panes. Figure 2.1 shows what a typical Wireshark capture looks like. Each window is adjustable by clicking on the row of dots between the window panes and dragging up or down. The upper-most pane is the *summary* pane, which displays a one-line summary of the capture. Wireshark's default fields include:

- Packet number
- Time
- Source address
- Destination address
- Name and information about the highest-layer protocol.

These columns are easily configured, and new ones can be added under Preferences. You can also sort the columns in an ascending or descending order by field, and you can rearrange the panes.

> ## Note
>
> You will notice that the Windows Wireshark GUI resembles a UNIX appli-
> cation rather than a native Windows application. This is because
> Wireshark uses the GNU Image Manipulation Program (GIMP) Tool Kit
> (GTK) library to create the interface. So regardless of the OS you are run-
> ning it on Wireshark will look the same.

The middle pane is the *protocol detail* pane, which provides the details (in a tree-like structure) of each layer contained in the captured packet. Clicking on various parts of the protocol tree highlights corresponding hex and ASCII output in the bottom pane, and the bottom pane displays the raw captured data in both hex and ASCII format. Clicking on various parts of this data highlights their corresponding fields in the protocol tree in the protocol view pane. Figure 2.1 shows the Wireshark interface and an example of a network synchronize (SYN) scan. Notice that highlighting the source MAC address in the middle protocol view pane automatically highlights that portion of the hexdump in the bottom data pane.

**Figure 2.1** Wireshark's GUI

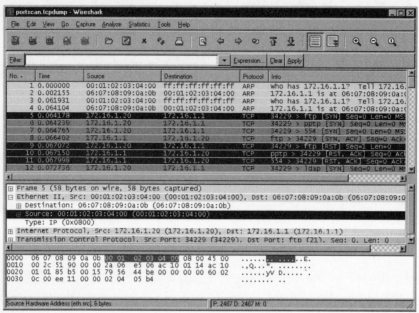

One of the best features of Wireshark is its ability to reassemble all of the packets in a TCP conversation and display the ASCII in an easy-to-read format. (It can also be viewed in EBCDIC, hexdump, and C arrays.) This data can then be saved or printed, and used to reconstruct a Web page Simple Mail Transfer Protocol (SMTP) or Telnet session. To reconstruct a Web page, follow the stream of the Hypertext Transfer Protocol (HTTP) session and save the output to a file. You should then be able to view the reconstructed Hypertext Markup Language (HTML) offline (without graphics) in a Web browser. Figure 2.2 shows the TCP stream output of a FTP session.

# Filters

Filtering packets help you find a desired packet without sifting through all of them. Wireshark has the ability to use both *capture* and *display* filters. The capture filter syntax follows the same syntax that tcpdump uses from the libpcap library. It is used on the command line or in the "Capture Filter" dialog box to capture certain types of traffic. Display filters provide a powerful syntax to sort traffic that is already captured. As the number of protocols grows, the number of protocol fields for display filters also grow. However, not all protocols currently supported by Wireshark have display filters. Also, some protocols provide display filter field names for some, but not all, of the fields. Hopefully, as the product matures and more users contribute to

**Figure 2.2** Follow the TCP Stream

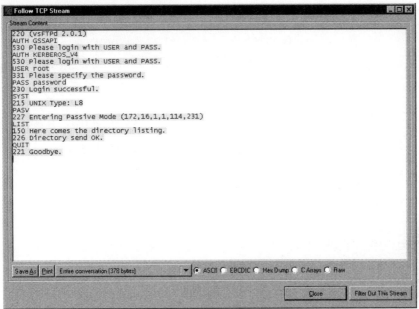

the development process, this will change. Table 2.1 shows an example of a supported protocol and its display filters:

**Table 2.1** IP Display Filters

| Internet Protocol (IP) Field | Name | Type |
|---|---|---|
| ip.addr | Source or Destination Address | IPv4 address |
| ip.checksum | Header checksum | Unsigned 16-bit integer |
| ip.checksum_bad | Bad Header checksum | Boolean |
| ip.dsfield | Differentiated Services field | Unsigned 8-bit integer |
| ip.dsfield.ce | ECN-CE, Explicit Congestion Notification: Congestion Experienced | Unsigned 8-bit integer |
| ip.dsfield.dscp | Differentiated Services Codepoint | Unsigned 8-bit integer |

**Continued**

**Table 2.1 continued** IP Display Filters

| Internet Protocol (IP) Field | Name | Type |
|---|---|---|
| ip.dsfield.ect | ECN-Capable Transport (ECT) | Unsigned 8-bit integer |
| ip.dst | Destination | IPv4 address |
| ip.flags | Flags | Unsigned 8-bit integer |
| ip.flags.df | Don't fragment | Boolean |
| ip.flags.mf | More fragments | Boolean |
| ip.frag_offset | Fragment offset | Unsigned 16-bit integer |
| ip.fragment | IP Fragment | Frame number |
| ip.fragment.error | Defragmentation error | Frame number |
| ip.fragment.multipletails | Multiple tail fragments found | Boolean |
| ip.fragment.overlap | Fragment overlap | Boolean |
| ip.fragment.overlap.conflict | Conflicting data in fragment overlap | Boolean |
| ip.fragment.toolongfragment | Fragment too long | Boolean |
| ip.fragments | IP fragments | No value |
| ip.hdr_len | Header length | Unsigned 8-bit integer |
| ip.id | Identification | Unsigned 16-bit integer |
| ip.len | Total length | Unsigned 16-bit integer |
| ip.proto | Protocol | Unsigned 8-bit integer |
| ip.reassembled_in | Reassembled IP in frame | Frame number |
| ip.src | Source | IPv4 address |
| ip.tos | Type of service | Unsigned 8-bit integer |
| ip.tos.cost | Cost | Boolean |
| ip.tos.delay | Delay | Boolean |
| ip.tos.precedence | Precedence | Unsigned 8-bit integer |
| ip.tos.reliability | Reliability | Boolean |
| ip.tos.throughput | Throughput | Boolean |
| ip.ttl | Time-to-live | Unsigned 8-bit integer |
| ip.version | Version | Unsigned 8-bit integer |

Once a display filter is implemented, all of the packets that meet the requirements are displayed in the packet listing in the summary pane. These filters can be used to compare fields within a protocol against a value such as *ip.src ==* *192.168.1.1*, to compare fields such as *ip.src == ip.dst*, or to check the existence of specified fields or protocols. Filters are also used by statistical features and to colorize the packets. To create a simple filter to search for a certain protocol or field (e.g., you want to see all of the HTTP packets), type **http**. To see just HTTP request packets (e.g., *GET POST, HEAD*, and so on) type **http.request**. Filter fields can also be compared against values such as **http.request.method==“GET”** to see only HTTP GET requests. The comparison operators can be expressed using the following abbreviations and symbols:

- **Equal:** eq, ==
- **Not equal:** ne, !=
- **Greater than:** gt, >
- **Less Than:** lt, <
- **Greater than or equal to:** ge, >=
- **Less than or equal to:** le, <=

Three operators can be expressed by name. *Is Present* allows you to test for the existence of a field (e.g., in an Address Resolution Protocol [ARP] packet, the MAC address is present but not the TCP port). *Contains* allows you to search the data of a packet for a string or phrase. *Matches* uses a regular expression (*regex*) string for more powerful pattern matching.

As you can see, filters offer a great deal of flexibility when troubleshooting network problems.

**NOTE**

Wireshark supports many different types of media (e.g., Ethernet, Token Ring, Wireless, and asynchronous transfer mode [ATM]).

To ensure that you are using a compatible OS, go to the "Supported Capture Media" table at http://wireshark.org/ CaptureSetup/NetworkMedia. As you will see, Linux supports nearly all media types, and Ethernet is supported on all OSes.

## Notes From the Underground...

## The Subversion System

Subversion (SVN) is a versioning system that allows developers to work on more than one same project simultaneously while keeping track of the changes made, who made them, and what versions were made. There are typically many versions of a project inside a SVN tree.

SVN and its predecessor Concurrent Versions Systems (CVS) are used for almost every open-source project (e.g., SourceForge [www.sourceforge.net] has CVS and SVN repositories for all of the projects it contains. Some projects allow Web-based access to SVN trees and most allow you to browse using a SVN client application.

Following are some helpful links for SVN:

- **SVN Command-line Client** The command-line client is available at www.SVN.tigris.org or in package form from many Berkeley Software Distribution (BSD) and UNIX distributions.

- **TortoiseSVN** TortioiseSVN is a shell extension for Microsoft Windows that integrates with the file explorer available from www.tortoisesvn.tigris.org.

- **RapidSVN** RapidSVN is a cross-platform GUI for SVN that is available for Windows

- **Mac OS X and Linux** are available from www.rapidsvn.tigris.org.

- **Visual Studio .NET** Developers using Microsoft Visual Studio .NET can use a AnkhSVN (www.ankhsvn.tigris.org) a third-party integration tool for SVN.

The Wireshark SVN listing is maintained at www.wireshark.org/develop.html. There are several ways to obtain the source code for Wireshark using SVN:

- **SVN Command Line** Used to anonymously download the development source.

- **Nighly Snapshots** Used to download gzipped tarballs containing nightly snapshots of the development source tree.

- **SVN Web Interface** You can download the source tree via the SVN Web Interface (http://anonsvn.wireshark.org/wireshark/trunk/) and view each file and the differences between each version file.

When using SVN versions of Wireshark or other open-source products, remember that they are considered beta code and may have bugs.

# Great Resources

Some of the best resources for Wireshark information and support include e-mail distribution lists (see www.wireshark.org/lists for the appropriate form).

> **NOTE**
>
> When filling out the application, a password is sometimes e-mailed to you in cleartext. Make sure that you don't use the same password that you use for other accounts, because anyone sniffing network traffic can see the cleartext password when it is e-mailed.

- **Wireshark-announce** includes announcements of new releases, bug fixes, and general issues about Wireshark. All Wireshark users should subscribe to this list to remain current on important topics. This list tends to be low volume. To post a message, send an e-mail to wiresharkannounce@ waireshark.org.

- **Wireshark-users** includes general information and help using Wireshark. All Wireshark users should subscribe to this list to share ideas and make suggestions. It contains moderate traffic. To post a message, send an e-mail to wireshark-users@waireshark.org.

- **Wireshark-dev** includes developer-related information about the inner workings of Wireshark, and is intended for those interested in contributing to its development. This list receives a high volume of traffic per day. To post a message, send an e-mail to wireshark-dev@wireshark.org.

- **Wireshark-commits** includes developer-related information to monitor changes to the Wireshark source tree. It informs developers when changes are made and what the changes are. The SVN repository sends e-mails to this list every time code is committed to the Wireshark SVN repository; therefore, it receives a high volume of traffic. Users do not post directly to this list. Replies to messages on this list should be sent to www.wireshark-dev@wireshark.org.

When subscribing to mailing lists, you can choose to have your e-mail batched in a *daily digest*, which is a great way to cut down on the amount of traffic and messages on high-volume lists. However, you won't get any attachments that are included with the e-mails. All of the messages from the mailing lists are archived on the Wireshark Web site and other mirror sites. Messages are categorized by month, for as far back as 1998. When troubleshooting a problem, a good strategy is to search for someone else that has the answer. Another great source of information is the Wireshark User's Guide (by Richard Sharpe) located at www.wireshark.org/docs/wsug_html/. It is also available in many other formats including PDF at www.wireshark.org/docs. And, as always, the Wireshark Web page www.wireshark.org also has a lot of good information. The sample captures page (http://wiki.wireshark.org/SampleCaptures) contains packet traces of network traffic that can be downloaded and viewed with Wireshark.

The Wireshark Wiki page is another great resource, where anyone can add their own ideas and experiences with Wireshark. There are many examples of usage references and solutions for various challenging sniffing environments. If you have found a solution, feel free to add it to the wiki at http://wiki.wireshark.org.

# Supporting Programs

Most people who are familiar with Wireshark use the Wireshark GUI. However, when Wireshark is installed, it also comes with several other support programs. The command-line version of Wireshark (called *tshark*) contains the following three programs to assist in manipulating capture files.

## Tshark

Tshark is the command-line version of Wireshark, which can be used to capture live packets from the wire or to read saved capture files. By default, tshark prints the summary line information to the screen. This is the same information contained in the top pane of the Wireshark GUI. The following shows the default tshark output:

```
1.199008 192.168.100.132 -> 192.168.100.122 TCP 1320 > telnet [SYN]
Seq=1102938967 Ack=0 Win=16384 Len=0

1.199246 192.168.100.132 -> 192.168.100.122 TCP 1320 > telnet [SYN]
Seq=1102938967 Ack=0 Win=16384 Len=0

1.202244 192.168.100.122 -> 192.168.100.132 TCP telnet > 1320 [SYN
ACK] Seq=3275138168 Ack=1102938968 Win=49640 Len=0

1.202268 192.168.100.132 -> 192.168.100.122 TCP 1320 > telnet [ACK]
Seq=1102938968 Ack=3275138169 Win=17520 Len=0

1.202349 192.168.100.132 -> 192.168.100.122 TCP 1320 > telnet [ACK]
Seq=1102938968 Ack=3275138169 Win=17520 Len=0
```

The **–V** option causes tshark to print the protocol tree view like in the middle pane in the Wireshark GUI. This shows all of the protocols in the packet and includes the data portion at the end of the list. The following shows a more detailed protocol tree tshark output:

```
Frame 5 (74 bytes on wire
74 bytes captured)
    Arrival Time: Nov  2
2003 15:22:33.469934000
    Time delta from previous packet: 0.000216000 seconds
    Time relative to first packet: 1.349439000 seconds
    Frame Number: 5
    Packet Length: 74 bytes
    Capture Length: 74 bytes
Ethernet II
Src: 00:05:5d:ee:7e:53
Dst: 08:00:20:cf:5b:39
    Destination: 08:00:20:cf:5b:39 (SunMicro_cf:5b:39)
    Source: 00:05:5d:ee:7e:53 (D-Link_ee:7e:53)
    Type: IP (0x0800)
Internet Protocol
Src Addr: 192.168.100.132 (192.168.100.132)
Dst Addr: 192.168.100.122 (192.168.100.122)
    Version: 4
    Header length: 20 bytes
    Differentiated Services Field: 0x00 (DSCP 0x00: Default; ECN: 0x00)
        0000 00.. = Differentiated Services Codepoint: Default (0x00)
        .... ..0. = ECN-Capable Transport (ECT): 0
        .... ...0 = ECN-CE: 0
    Total Length: 60
    Identification: 0x160c (5644)
    Flags: 0x00
        .0.. = Don't fragment: Not set
        ..0. = More fragments: Not set
    Fragment offset: 0
    Time to live: 128
    Protocol: ICMP (0x01)
    Header checksum: 0xda65 (correct)
    Source: 192.168.100.132 (192.168.100.132)
    Destination: 192.168.100.122 (192.168.100.122)
Internet Control Message Protocol
```

```
Type: 8 (Echo (ping) request)
Code: 0
Checksum: 0x3c5c (correct)
Identifier: 0x0500
Sequence number: 0c:00
Data (32 bytes)
0000  61 62 63 64 65 66 67 68 69 6a 6b 6c 6d 6e 6f 70   abcdefghijklmnop
0010  71 72 73 74 75 76 77 61 62 63 64 65 66 67 68 69   qrstuvwabcdefghi
```

Finally, the **–x** command causes tshark to print a hexdump and an ASCII dump of the packet data with either the summary line or the protocol tree. The following shows the hex and ASCII output with the summary line:

```
9.463261 192.168.100.122 -> 192.168.100.132 TELNET Telnet Data ...
0000  00 05 5d ee 7e 53 08 00 20 cf 5b 39 08 00 45 00   ..].~S.. .[9..E.
0010  00 9a c3 8a 40 00 3c 06 30 84 c0 a8 64 7a c0 a8   ....@.<.0...dz..
0020  64 84 00 17 05 29 cd 5d 7d 12 4c 1d ea 76 50 18   d....).]}.L..vP.
0030  c1 e8 47 ca 00 00 4c 61 73 74 20 6c 6f 67 69 6e   ..G...Last login
0040  3a 20 53 75 6e 20 4e 6f 76 20 20 32 20 31 35 3a   : Sun Nov  2 15:
0050  34 34 3a 34 35 20 66 72 6f 6d 20 31 39 32 2e 31   44:45 from 192.1
0060  36 38 2e 31 30 30 2e 31 33 32 0d 0a 53 75 6e 20   68.100.132..Sun
0070  4d 69 63 72 6f 73 79 73 74 65 6d 73 20 49 6e 63   Microsystems Inc
0080  2e 20 20 20 53 75 6e 4f 53 20 35 2e 39 20 20 20   .   SunOS 5.9
0090  20 20 20 20 47 65 6e 65 72 69 63 20 4d 61 79 20      Generic May
00a0  32 30 30 32 0d 0a 23 20                           2002..#
```

When using tshark to save packet data to a file, by default it outputs in the libpcap format. Tshark can read the same capture files and use the same display filters (also known as *read* filters) and capture filters as Wireshark. Tshark can also decode the same protocols as Wireshark. Basically, it has most of the powers of Wireshark (except those inherent to the GUI) in an easy-to-use command- line version.

# Editcap

Editcap is used to remove packets from a file, and to translate the format of capture files. It is similar to the Save As feature, but better. Editcap can read all of the same types of files that Wireshark can, and writes to the libpcap format by default. Editcap can also write captures to standard and modified versions of:

- libpcap
- Sun snoop

- Novel LANalyzer

- Network Access Identifier (NAI) Sniffer

- Microsoft NetMon

- Visual Network traffic capture

- Accellent 5Views capture

- Network Instruments Observer version 9

Editcap has the ability to specify all or some of the packets to be translated. The following is an example of using editcap to translate the first five packets from a tshark libpcap capture file (called *capture*) to a Sun snoop output file (called *capture_snoop*):

```
C:\Program Files\Wireshark>editcap -r -v -F snoop capture capture_snoop 1-5
File capture is a libpcap (tcpdump Wireshark etc.) capture file.
Add_Selected: 1-5
Inclusive ... 1
5
Record: 1
Record: 2
Record: 3
Record: 4
Record: 5
```

# Mergecap

Mergecap is used to combine multiple saved capture files into a single output file. Mergecap can read all of the same types of files that Wireshark can and writes to libpcap format by default. Mergecap can also write the output capture file to standard and modified versions of:

- libpcap

- Sun snoop

- Novel LANalyzer

- NAI Sniffer

- Microsoft NetMon

- Visual Network traffic capture

- Accellent 5Views capture

- Network Instruments Observer

By default, the packets from the input files are merged in chronological order based on each packet's timestamp. If the **–a** option is specified, packets are copied directly from each input file to the output file regardless of the timestamp. The following is an example of using mergecap to merge four capture files (*capture1*, *capture2*, *capture3*, and *capture4*) into a single Sun snoop output file called *merge_snoop* that will keep reading packets until the end of the last file is reached:

```
C:\Program Files\Wireshark>mergecap -v -F snoop -w merge_snoop capture1
capture2 capture3 capture4
mergecap: capture1 is type libpcap (tcpdump Wireshark etc.).
mergecap: capture2 is type libpcap (tcpdump Wireshark etc.).
mergecap: capture3 is type libpcap (tcpdump Wireshark etc.).
mergecap: capture4 is type libpcap (tcpdump Wireshark etc.).
mergecap: opened 4 of 4 input files
mergecap: selected frame_type Ethernet (ether)
Record: 1
Record: 2
Record: 3
Record: 4
Record: 5
Record: 6
Record: 7
Record: 8
Record: 9
Record: 10
output removed
```

# Text2pcap

Text2pcap reads in ASCII hexdump captures and writes the data into a libpcap output file. It is capable of reading hexdumps containing multiple packets and building a capture file of multiple packets. Text2pcap can also read hexdumps of application-level data by inserting dummy Ethernet IP and User Datagram Protocol (UDP) or TCP headers. The user specifies which of these headers to add. This way Wireshark and other sniffers can read the full data. The following is an example of the type of hexdump that text2pcap recognizes:

```
0000   00 05 5d ee 7e 53 08 00 20 cf 5b 39 08 00 45 00   ..].~S.. .[9..E.
0010   00 9a 13 9e 40 00 3c 06 e0 70 c0 a8 64 7a c0 a8   ....@.<..p..dz..
0020   64 84 00 17 05 49 0e a9 91 43 8e d8 e3 6a 50 18   d....I...C...jP.
0030   c1 e8 ba 7b 00 00 4c 61 73 74 20 6c 6f 67 69 6e   ...{..Last login
0040   3a 20 53 75 6e 20 4e 6f 76 20 20 32 20 31 37 3a   : Sun Nov  2 17:
0050   30 36 3a 35 33 20 66 72 6f 6d 20 31 39 32 2e 31   06:53 from 192.1
0060   36 38 2e 31 30 30 2e 31 33 32 0d 0a 53 75 6e 20   68.100.132..Sun
0070   4d 69 63 72 6f 73 79 73 74 65 6d 73 20 49 6e 63   Microsystems Inc
0080   2e 20 20 20 53 75 6e 4f 53 20 35 2e 39 20 20 20   .   SunOS 5.9
0090   20 20 20 20 47 65 6e 65 72 69 63 20 4d 61 79 20      Generic May
00a0   32 30 30 32 0d 0a 23 20                            2002..#
```

The following is an example of using text2pcap to read the previously shown hexdump *hex_sample.txt* and output it to the *libpcap_output* file:

```
C:\Program Files\Wireshark>text2pcap hex_sample.txt libpcap_output
Input from: hex_sample.txt
Output to: libpcap_output
Wrote packet of 168 bytes at 0
Read 1 potential packets
wrote 1 packets
```

# Using Wireshark in Your Network Architecture

The previous chapter discussed various cable taps, hubs, and switches that can be used to attach a sniffer to a network. This section looks at some of the network architecture and critical points of Wireshark. Network placement is critical for proper analysis and troubleshooting. Most importantly, make sure that you are on the proper network segment. When troubleshooting network issues, you may move between various wiring closets or even different buildings. For this reason, it is bene-ficial to run Wireshark on a laptop. It is also a good idea to keep a small hub and some network cables (crossover and straight-through) with your laptop for a trou-bleshooting toolkit. Figure 2.3 shows the incorrect placement of Wireshark if you want to capture communication between the external client and the server. The Wireshark laptop and the switch it is connected to will not see traffic destined for the server because it is routed to the server's switch.

**Figure 2.3** Incorrect Wireshark Placement

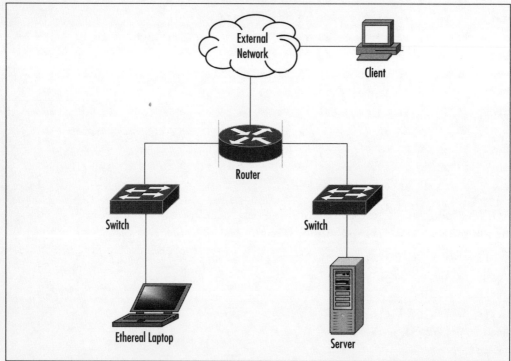

Figure 2.4 shows how to capture traffic from the external client to the server using *port spanning*. The Wireshark laptop must be connected to the same switch as the server. Next, port spanning is activated on the switch to mirror all traffic to and from the server's port to the port that Wireshark is plugged into. Using this method will not cause any disruption of traffic to and from the server.

**Figure 2.4** Correct Wireshark Placement Using Port Spanning

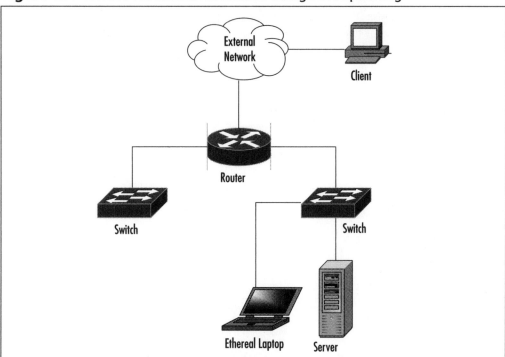

Figure 2.5 shows how to capture traffic from the external client to the server using a hub. Install a small hub between the server and the switch and connect the Wireshark laptop to it. Wireshark will then see all traffic going to and coming from the server. This method will temporarily disrupt traffic while the hub is being installed and the cables connected.

**Figure 2.5** Correct Wireshark Placement Using a Hub

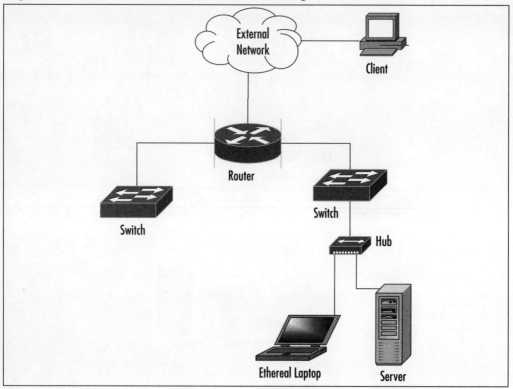

Figure 2.6 shows a network architecture that uses a permanent tap installed at the router. Some administrators use this method for a permanent connection point at critical areas. The Wireshark laptop then sees all traffic going to and from the server plus any other traffic on the segment. Using this method does not disrupt traffic to and from the server if the tap is permanently installed and the cables are already connected. Taps can also be portable and used like the hub in Figure 2.5.

**Figure 2.6** Wireshark Placement With a Cable Tap

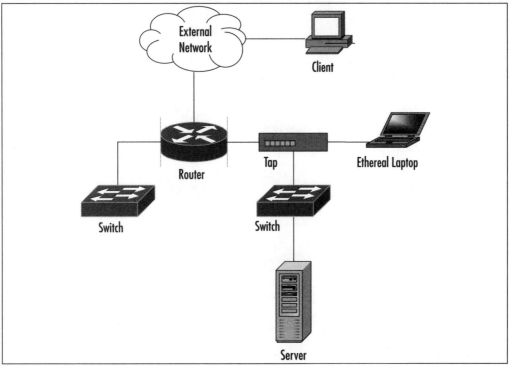

Most network architectures aren't as simple as those depicted in this section. However, these examples should give you a good idea of how to use Wireshark at various points in your network. Some architectures are complicated and can be fully meshed and include redundancy (see Figure 2.7). Also, network segments can branch out for several levels as your network is expanded to buildings and floors within buildings. You must have a good understanding of your network in order to make the most effective choices for sniffer placement.

**Figure 2.7** Fully Meshed Network

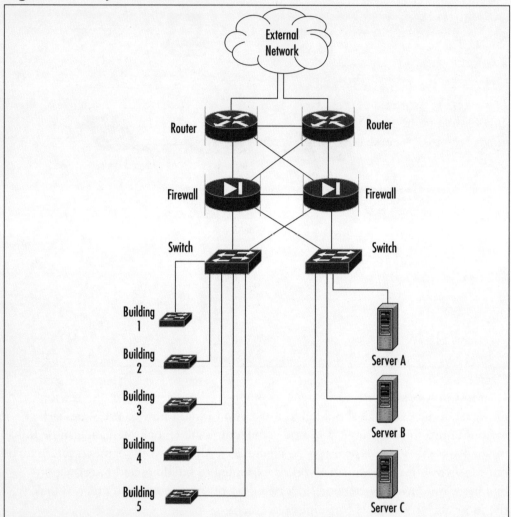

# Using Wireshark for Network Troubleshooting

Every network administrator has had the unpleasant experience of being called in the middle of the night to fix a network problem, which can often result in a surge of emotions (e.g., panic, urgency, and perhaps a sense of heroism). The key to successfully troubleshooting a problem is knowing how the network functions under normal conditions, which will allow you to quickly recognize unusual and abnormal operations. One way to know how your network normally functions is to use a sniffer at various points in the network. This will allow you to get a sense of the protocols that are running on your network, the devices on each segment, and the top talkers (computers that send and receive data most frequently).

Once you have an idea of how your network functions you can develop a strategy for network troubleshooting. This way you can approach the problem methodically and resolve it with minimum disruption to customers. With troubleshooting, a few minutes spent evaluating the symptoms can save hours of time lost tracking down the wrong problem. A good approach to network troubleshooting involves the following seven steps:

1. Recognize the symptoms

2. Define the problem

3. Analyze the problem

4. Isolate the problem

5. Identify and test the cause of the problem

6. Solve the problem

7. Verify that the problem has been solved

The first step to network troubleshooting is *recognizing* the symptoms. You can also learn about a network problem from another user network, where the management station alerts you of trouble (e.g., performance issues, connectivity issues, or other strange behaviors) accessing the network. Compare this behavior to normal network operation: Was a change made to the network or to a server right before the problem started? Did an automatic process such as a scheduled backup just begin? Is there a prescheduled maintenance window for this time period? Once you have answered these questions, the next step is to write a clear *definition* of the problem. Once the symptoms have been identified and the problem defined, the next step is to *analyze* the problem. You need to gather data for analysis and narrow down the location of the problem. Is it at the core of the network, a single building, or a remote office? Is the problem related to an entire network segment or a single computer? Can the problem be duplicated elsewhere on the network? You may need to test various parts of your network to narrow down the problem.

Now that you have analyzed and found the problem, you can move onto the next step of *isolating* the problem. There are many ways to do this, such as disconnect the computer that is causing problems, reboot a server, activate a firewall rule to stop some suspected abnormal traffic, or failover to a backup Internet connection.

The next step is to *identify* and *test* the cause of the problem. Now that you have a theory about the cause of the problem you need to test it. Your network analyzer can see what is going on behind the scenes. At this point, you may be researching the problem on the Internet, contacting various hardware or software vendors, or contacting your Internet Service Provider (ISP). You may also want to verify with www.cert.org or www.incidents.org that this is not a widespread issue. Once you have a resolution to the problem, you need to *implement* it. This could involve upgrading hardware or software, implementing a new firewall rule, reinstalling a compromised system, replacing failed hardware, or redesigning the segments of your network.

The last step of network troubleshooting is *verifying* that the problem has been resolved. Make sure that the fix for this problem did not create any new problems or that the problem you solved is not indicative of a deeper underlying problem. Part of this step of the process includes documenting the steps taken to resolve the problem, which will assist in future troubleshooting efforts. If you have not solved the problem, you must repeat the process from the beginning. The flowchart in Figure 2.8 depicts the network troubleshooting process.

**NOTE**

To be a successful network troubleshooter you need a strong understanding of network protocols. Understanding different protocols and their characteristics will help you recognize abnormal behavior as it occurs on your network.

**Figure 2.8** Network Troubleshooting Methodology

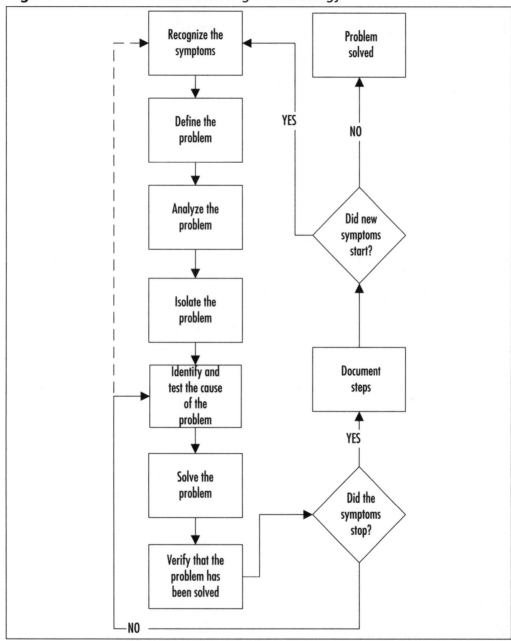

# Using Wireshark for System Administration

System administrators are notorious for asking if there is something wrong with the network, and network administrators are notorious for saying the problem is within the system. In between this chasm of blame lies the truth waiting to be discovered by Wireshark.

# Checking for Network Connectivity

At the heart of modern TCP/IP networks is Ethernet. Ethernet is a protocol that works without much fuss; however, there is a myriad of problems involving drivers, OSes, configurations, applications, network switches, and so forth, that may occur). The system administrator needs a tool that can detect whether the network is working from an OSI Layer 2 prospective or from an Ethernet prospective.

When a system administration problem occurs, the next step is to verify that the system is receiving the network packets. The most basic packet is the ARP packet.

The basics of the ARP are this: When a system needs to communicate with another system on the same subnet, and has an IP address for that system but not a MAC address, an ARP request is broadcast onto the Ethernet segment (e.g., a network with hosts 192.168.1.1 and 192.168.1.2 having MAC addresses 00:01:02:03:04:05 and 06:07:08:09:0a:0b) and issues the following command sequence through ARP:

```
00:01:02:03:04:05 to ff:ff:ff:ff:ff:ff Who has 192.168.1.2? Tell 192.168.1.1
06:07:08:09:0a:0b to 00:01:02:03:04:05 192.168.1.2 is at 06:07:08:09:0a:0b
```

Knowing that ARP traffic is a necessary precursor to normal network traffic, Ethereal can be used to check for the presence of this traffic on the network. There are several conditions of ARP that indicate specific problems. If there is no ARP traffic from the system on the network, either you are not capturing the traffic correctly or there are driver or OS issues preventing network communication. If the system is issuing ARP requests but there is no response from the host, it may not be on the network. Make sure that the system is on the correct LAN; it is no longer as easy as plugging into the correct network jack. If the system is receiving ARP requests and sending IP traffic out on the network, but not receiving a response that you have verified with your sniffer, there may be a firewall or driver issue with the system.

# Checking for Application Network Availability

After verifying that you can see the network, the next step in troubleshooting is to check that systems on the network can connect to the application. Because most network applications are TCP-based, testing is confined to applications using that protocol. For this example, we use a Web server operating on port 80.

As previously discussed, the TCP protocol relies on a three-way handshake before exchanging any data. The handshake itself is indicative of problems with an application. Because Wireshark is qualified to dissect TCP packets, we can use it to locate application problems. Following are some of the scenarios you may encounter while troubleshooting application communication on a network:

## Scenario 1: SYN no SYN+ACK

If your Wireshark capture shows that the client is sending a SYN packet, but no response is received from the server, the server is not processing the packet. It could be that a firewall between the two hosts is blocking the packet or that the server itself has a firewall running on it

## Scenario 2: SYN immediate response RST

If your Wireshark capture shows that the server is responding with the reset (RST) flag, the destination server is receiving the packet but there is no application bound to that port. Make sure that your application is bound to the correct port on the correct IP address.

## Scenario 3: SYN SYN+ACK ACK
## Connection Closed

If your Wireshark capture shows that the TCP connection is established and that it immediately closes, the destination server may be rejecting the client's IP address due to security restrictions. On UNIX systems, check the *tcpwrappers* file at */etc/hosts.allow* and */etc/hosts.deny* and verify that you haven't inadvertently blocked communication.

# Using Wireshark for Security Administration

"Is this protocol secure?" One of the most common tasks security administrators do, is verify the security of an arbitrary protocol. Wireshark is the ideal tool to use for this.

One of the most popular and useful Wireshark features is *packet reassembly*, which allows us to see the contents of exchanged data. For protocols such as Telnet and FTP, Wireshark clearly displays the username and password for the connection, without any reassembly. For unknown, custom, or otherwise obscure protocols, packet reassembly can be used. To use reassembly, capture the traffic through Wireshark or another tool and then load the capture file into Wireshark and right-click on any packet in the connection. Select the **Follow TCP Stream** option; a window will pop up with all of the communication that occurred in that session. It may help to select the ASCII option, and if the protocol is noisy you can select that sender, receiver, or *Entire Conversation* be displayed.

## Detecting Internet Relay Chat Activity

Besides the policy implications of chat rooms, IRC is frequented by hackers and used as a command and control mechanism. IRC normally uses TCP port 6667. If you set Wireshark to detect traffic with destination port 6667, you will see IRC traffic that looks like the following:

```
Local client to IRC server
port 6667:
USER username localsystem.example.com irc.example.net :gaim
Remote IRC server to local client:
NOTICE AUTH :*** Looking up your hostname...
Local client to IRC server
port 6667:
NICK clever-nick-name


Remote IRC server to local client:
NOTICE AUTH :*** Checking identNOTICE AUTH :*** Found your hostname
```

At this point, you can be reasonably assured that you are seeing an IRC connection. Make sure that you know who is using it

# Wireshark As a Network Intrusion Detection System

Although there are specialized open-source tools for Network Intrusion Detection Systems (NIDSes) such as Sourcefire's Snort (www.snort.org), if you had nothing except Wireshark to use as an IDS system, it would be able to alert you on any criteria. Consider the following Wireshark "rules" for intrusion detection:

- Database connections to your database from systems other than your Web servers

- Attempts to send e-mail to external e-mail servers on TCP port 25 from servers other than your e-mail relays

- Attempts to use Remote Desktop Connection (RDC) from outside your network or use Wireshark as a honeypot, listening for connections to an unused IP address.

# Wireshark as a Detector for Proprietary Information Transmission

If your company marks its confidential and proprietary information with a consistent phrase, there is no reason why you cannot use Wireshark to detect the transmission of information. You could use Wireshark to capture all outbound traffic on a span port and then use Wireshark's *Find Packet* function. However, this could create a lot of traffic to sort through. To reduce the amount of traffic captured, you can use capture filters to exclude traffic where you don't expect proprietary information to be transferred through (e.g., DNS queries and internal network traffic).

# Securing Ethereal

Although Wireshark is considered a security tool, it is not without its own occasional security issues. According to www.Securityfocus.com, between 2002 and 2006 there were 44 security advisories regarding Ethereal and Wireshark. Most of these were in obscure or rarely used protocol decoders. Still, there are a few things you can do to minimize the effects of any Wireshark bugs.

The primary step to running a more secure Wireshark installation is to update the software and the OS. Updates to Wireshark normally come out every few months and many people use binary versions of Wireshark that are easy to upgrade. The next step for securing Wireshark is to separate the capture process from the analysis process, and run both with the least amount of OS privilege that will work. Normally, all capture libraries require Local Administrator privilege access in Windows or root access in UNIX. Since many of the historical issues with Wireshark were in protocol decoders, if you run your analysis console as a non-privileged or non-root user, it may reduce the risk of security issues impeding your sniffing efforts. You can also use tshark or dumpcap (both included with Wireshark) to capture the network traffic to a file and then view the results later in Wireshark using a non-privileged account.

# Optimizing Wireshark

Optimizing the system that you are running your sniffer on will go a long way towards speeding up Wireshark or any other sniffing application that you run. Your network card drivers and Wireshark will do their best to capture all the traffic that you throw at it, but to make sure that you are seeing the full picture of your network, some system-related issues should be considered.

## Network Link Speed

Wireshark cannot capture packets any faster than the slowest point between you and the data you are sniffing. Careful attention must be paid so that the slowest link is not the one that Wireshark is on if the network is heavily loaded (e.g., if you are trying to sniff the connection between two computers that are exchanging data at 75 mbit/second, using a 10 mbit/second port span may cause you to not receive all of the data onto the sniffer.

## Minimizing Wireshark Extras

Wireshark is an efficient packet sniffer, and not only due to its cost. While Ethereal has the capability to capture data efficiently, some of the more advanced options can slow it down.

In the "Capture Options" dialog box, the following options can slow down the capture: Update list of packets in real-time, Automatic scrolling in live capture, and any of the Name Resolution options. The "Enable network name" resolution option can particularly slow down the capture of a busy network, because DNS lookups need to be made for each source and destination. Using capture filters can speed up Wireshark if you know what type of packet data you are looking for. (Hint: If you separate the capture functions from the analysis functions of Wireshark, you may be able to capture more data.) Use tcpdump, tshark, or the specific tool for your OS, and use it to save the capture data to a file. After the capture is done, load the capture file into Wireshark.

## CPU

A fast computer is not strictly necessary to run Wireshark, but tasks such as finding strings in large packet captures will complete faster with a speedier processor. The Wireshark application tries to be as optimized as possible, but faster processors allow more operations per second, which decreases the amount of time you spend waiting for it to process packets or to find certain bits of text in a packet capture.

# Memory

The most effective way to make Wireshark run faster is to give it more random-access memory (RAM). This becomes especially important when working with captures that contain many packets. As with most applications, Wireshark needs memory to hold data. When an OS does not have enough memory to hold an application, the OS will *swap* memory from the RAM to the hard drive. The hard drive is much slower than the system memory, and moving data back and forth between the drive and RAM takes time. When Wireshark is short on memory, swapping will slow down the system and applications precipitously.

# Advanced Sniffing Techniques

There are alternatives to using Wireshark with port spanning or using a network tap. Unfortunately, attackers can use these techniques to steal passwords and other data from your network.

## Dsniff

Dsniff is a sniffing toolkit provided by Dug Song. Dsniff and many mirrors are available on Web site www.monkey.org/~dugsong/dsniff. Dsniff is most famous for its authentication (i.e., usernames and passwords) and sniffing capabilities. The current version of dsniff decodes authentication information for the following protocols:

- America Online (AOL) Instant Messenger (IM) (Citrix Winframe)
- CVS
- File Transfer Protocol (FTP)
- HTTP
- I Seek You (ICQ)
- IMAP
- IRC
- Lightweight Directory Access Protocol (LDAP)
- Remote Procedure Call (RPC) mount requests
- Napster
- Network News Transfer Protocol (NNTP)
- Oracle SQL*Net

- Open Shortest Path First (OSPF)
- PC Anywhere
- Post Office Protocol (POP)
- PostgreSQL
- Routing Information Protocol (RIP)
- Remote Login (rlogin)
- Windows NT plaintext Server Message Block (SMB)
- Network Associates Sniffer Pro (remote)
- Simple Network Management Protocol (SNMP)
- Socks
- Telnet
- X11
- RPC yppasswd

With today's switched networks and encrypted protocols, password sniffing doesn't always work as well as we want it to. Dsniff contains several redirect and man-in-the-middle (MITM) utilities to redirect the flow of traffic and decrypt sessions.

The first utility is *arpspoof* (formerly known as *arpredirect*), which is used by hosts to find the local router's Media Access Control (MAC) address. By spoofing ARP packets, you can convince other nearby computers that you are the router, which means that your machine has to forward the packets on to the legitimate router after receiving them; however, in the meantime, the dsniff password sniffer has a chance to process the packets. This runs well on local switched networks and cable-modem networks. However, this tool isn't completely foolproof; you are essentially trying to convince other machines of the local MAC address. As a result, traffic flows through your machine are sometimes intermittent. This technique is easily detected by network-based intrusion detection systems (IDSes). Sniffer Pro also has an expert diagnostic mode that will flag these as "duplicate IP addresses" (i.e., multiple machines claiming to have the IP address of the router).

The *dnsspoof* utility redirects traffic by spoofing responses from the local Domain Name System (DNS) server. When you go a Web site such as www.example.com, your machine sends a request to your local DNS server asking for the IP address of www.example.com. This usually takes a while to resolve; however, DNS spoofs quickly send their own response. The victim takes the first response and ignores the second one. The spoofed response contains a different IP address than the legitimate response, usually the IP address of the attacker's machine. The attacker is probably using one of the other dsniff MITM utilities. The name MITM comes from cryptography, and describes the situation when somebody intercepts communications, alters it, and then forwards it. The dsniff utilities for these attacks are called *webmitm* for HTTP traffic (including Secure Sockets Layer [SSL]) and *sshmitm* (for Secure Shell [SSH]). Normally, SSH and SSL are thought to be secure encrypted protocols that cannot be sniffed. MITM utilities work by presenting their own encryption keys to the SSL/SSH clients. This allows them to decrypt the traffic sniff passwords and then reencrypt with the original server keys. In theory, you can protect yourself against this by checking the validity of the server certificate, but in practice, nobody does this. Dsniff can sniff passwords and other cleartext traffic.

The *mailsnarf* utility sniffs e-mails (e.g., the FBI's Carnivore), and reassembles them into an *mbox* format that can be read by most e-mail readers.

The *msgsnarf* utility sniffs messages from ICQ, IRC, Yahoo!, Messenger, and AOL IM.

The *filesnarf* utility sniffs files transferred via Network File System (NFS).

The *urlsnarf* utility saves all Universal Resource Locators (URLs) going across the wire.

The *webspy* utility sends those URLs to a Netscape Web browser in real time, essentially allowing you to watch in real-time what a victim sees on his or her Web browser.

The *macof* utility sends out a flood of MAC addresses, which is intended as another way of attacking Ethernet switches. Most switches have limited tables that can only hold 4,000 MAC addresses. When the switch overloads, it "fails open" and starts repeating every packet out every port, thereby allowing everyone's traffic to be sniffed.

The *tcpkill* utility kills TCP connections, and can be used as a Denial of Service (DoS) attack (e.g., you can configure it to kill every TCP connection your neighbor makes). It can also be integrated with tools like network-based IDSes to kill connections from hackers. The *tcpnice* utility is similar to tcpkill, but instead of killing connections, it slows them down (e.g., you could spoof Internet Control Message Protocol (ICMP) Source Quenches from your neighbor's cable modems so that you can get a higher percentage of bandwidth for your downloads).

# Ettercap

Ettercap is similar to dsniff. It has many of the same capabilities (e.g., MITM attacks against SSL and SSH and password sniffing). It also has additional features for MITM attacks against normal TCP connections such as inserting commands into the stream. Ettercap was written by Alberto Ornaghi and Marco Valleri, and is available at http://ettercap.sourceforge.net.

# MITM Attacks

The most effective defense against sniffing is using encrypted protocols such as SSL and SSH. However, the latest dsniff and Ettercap packages contain techniques for fooling encryption, known as a MITM attack. The same technique can be applied to encrypted protocols, when an attacker sets up a server that answers requests from clients (e.g., the server answers a request for https://www.amazon.com. A user contacting this machine will falsely believe they have established an encrypted session to Amazon.com. At the same time, the attacker contacts the real Amazon.com and pretends to be the user. The attacker plays both roles, decrypting the incoming data from the user and re-encrypting it for transmission to the original destination. In theory, encryption protocols have defenses against this. A server claiming to be Example.com needs to prove that it is indeed Example.com. In practice, most users ignore this. MITM attacks have proven very effective when used in the field.

# Cracking

Tools such as dsniff and Ettercap capture unencrypted passwords and encrypted passwords. In theory, capturing encrypted passwords is useless. However, people sometimes choose weak passwords (e.g., words from the dictionary) and it only takes a few seconds for an attacker to go through a 100,000-word dictionary, comparing the encrypted form of each dictionary word against the encrypted password. If a match is found, the attacker has discovered the password. These password cracking programs already exist. Tools like dsniff and Ettercap simply output the encrypted passwords in a form that these tools can read.

# Switch Tricks

A lot of people think that if they have a switched network it is impossible for an attacker to use a sniffer successfully to capture information. The following section discusses methods of successfully sniffing on a switched network.

## ARP Spoofing

When attempting to monitor traffic on a switched network, you will run into a serious problem: The switch will limit the traffic that is passed over your section of the network. Switches keep an internal list of the MAC addresses of hosts that are on each port. Traffic is only sent to a port if the destination host is recorded as being present on that port. It is possible to overwrite the ARP cache on many OSes, which would allow you to associate your MAC address with the default gateway's IP address. This would cause all outgoing traffic from the target host to be transmitted to you. You would have to be sure to manually add an ARP table entry for the real default gateway, to ensure that the traffic will be sent to the real target and to ensure that you have IP forwarding enabled. Many cable modem networks are vulnerable to this type of attack, because the cable modem network is essentially an Ethernet network with cable modems acting as bridges. In short, there is no solution to this attack and new generations of cable modem networks will use alternate mechanisms to connect a user to the network. The dsniff sniffer (developed by Dug Song) includes a program named *arpspoof* (formerly *arpredirect*) for exactly this purpose. arpspoof redirects packets from a target host (or all hosts) on the LAN intended for another host on the LAN, by forging ARP replies. This is an extremely effective way of sniffing traffic on a switch.

## MAC Flooding

To serve its purpose, a switch must keep a table of all MAC (Ethernet) addresses of the hosts that appear on each port. If a large number of addresses appear on a single port thereby filling the address table on the switch, the switch no longer has a record of which port the victim MAC address is connected to. This is the same situation as when a new machine first attaches to a switch and the switch must learn where that address is. Until it learns which port it is on, the switch must send copies of frames for that MAC address to all switch ports, a practice known as *flooding*.

The dsniff sniffer includes a program named *macof* that facilitates flooding a switch with random MAC addresses to accomplish this. macof floods the local network with random MAC addresses (causing some switches to fail open in repeating mode facilitating sniffing). A straight C port of the original Perl Net::RawIP macof program by Ian Vitek <ian.vitek@infosec.se>.—dsniff FAQ

## Routing Games

One method to ensure that all traffic on a network passes through your host is to change the routing table of the host you wish to monitor. This may be possible by sending a fake route advertisement message via the RIP, declaring yourself as the default gateway. If successful, all traffic will be routed through your host. Make sure that you have enabled IP forwarding so that all outbound traffic from the host will pass through your host and onto the real network gateway. You may not receive return traffic unless you have the ability to modify the routing table on the default gateway in order to reroute all return traffic back to you.

# Securing Your Network from Sniffers

At this point, you might be considering unplugging the network completely so that sniffers like Wireshark (or other more nefarious applications) cannot be used against you. Hold on to those wire cutters: there are other, more function-friendly ways to help secure your network from a determined eavesdropper.

## Using Encryption

Fortunately for the state of network security, when used properly, encryption is the silver bullet that will render a packet sniffer useless. Using encryption (assuming its mechanism is valid) will thwart any attacker attempting to passively monitor your network.

Many existing network protocols have counterparts that rely on strong encryption and all-encompassing mechanisms (e.g., IPSec and OpenVPN) provide this for all protocols. Unfortunately, IP Security (IPSec) is not widely used on the Internet outside of large enterprise companies.

## SSH

SSH is a cryptographically secure replacement for the standard UNIX Telnet rlogin, Remote Shell (RSH), and Remote Copy Protocol (RCP) commands. It consists of a client and server that use public key cryptography to provide session encryption. It also provides the ability to forward arbitrary TCP ports over an encrypted connection, which comes in handy for forwarding X11 Windows and other connections.

SSH has received wide acceptance as the secure mechanism to access a remote system interactively. SSH was conceived and initially developed by Finnish developer Tatu Ylönen. The original version of SSH turned into a commercial venture and, although the original version is still freely available, the license has become more restrictive. A public specification has been created, resulting in the development of a number of different versions of SSH-compliant client and server software that do not contain these restrictions (most significantly those that restrict commercial use). A free version of SSH-compatible software (OpenSSH) developed by the OpenBSD OS project, can be obtained from www.openssh.com. The new commercialized SSH can be purchased from SSH Communications Security (www.ssh.com) who have made the commercial version free to recognized universities. Mac OS X already contains OpenSSH software. PuTTY is a free alternative for the commercial SSH software for Windows. Originally developed for cleartext protocols such as Telnet, PuTTY is very popular among system administrators and can be downloaded at www.chiark.greenend.org.uk/~sgtatham/putty/.

# SSL

SSL provides authentication and encryption services and can also be used as a virtual private network (VPN). From a sniffing perspective, SSL can be vulnerable to a MITM attack. An attacker can set up a transparent proxy between you and the Web server. This transparent proxy can be configured to decrypt the SSL connection, sniff it, and then re-encrypt it. When this happens, the user is prompted with a dialog box indicating that the SSL certificate was not issued by a trusted authority. The problem is, most users ignore the warnings and proceed anyway.

# Pretty Good Protection and Secure/Multipurpose Internet Mail Extensions

Pretty Good Protection (PGP) and Secure/Multipurpose Internet Mail Extensions (S/MIME) are standards for encrypting e-mail. When used correctly, these standards prevent e-mail sniffers (e.g., dsniff and Carnivore) from being able to interpret intercepted e-mail. The sender and receiver must both use the software in order to encrypt and decrypt the communication. In the United States, the FBI has designed a Trojan horse called "Magic Lantern" that is designed to log keystrokes, hopefully capturing a user's passphrase. When the FBI gets a passphrase, they can decrypt the e-mail messages. In the United Kingdom, users are required by law to give their encryption keys to law enforcement when requested.

# Switching

Network switches make it more difficult for attackers to monitor your network, but not by much. Switches are sometimes recommended as a solution to the sniffing problem; however, their real purpose is to improve network performance, not provide security. As explained in the "Advanced Sniffing Techniques" section, any attacker with the right tools can monitor a switched host if they are on the same switch or segment as that system.

# Employing Detection Techniques

But what if you can't use encryption on your network for some reason? What do you do then? If this is the case then you must rely on detecting any network interface card (NIC) that may be operating in a manner that could be invoked by a sniffer.

# Local Detection

Many OSes provide a mechanism to determine whether a network interface is running in promiscuous mode. This is usually represented by the type of status flag that is associated with each network interface and maintained in the kernel. This can be obtained by using the **ifconfig** command on UNIX-based systems.

The following example shows an interface on the Linux OS when it isn't in promiscuous mode:

```
eth0      Link encap:Ethernet  HWaddr 00:60:08:C5:93:6B
inet addr:10.0.0.21  Bcast:10.0.0.255  Mask:255.255.255.0
UP BROADCAST RUNNING MULTICAST  MTU:1500  Metric:1
RX packets:1492448 errors:2779 dropped:0 overruns:2779 frame:2779
TX packets:1282868 errors:0 dropped:0 overruns:0 carrier:0
collisions:10575 txqueuelen:100
Interrupt:10 Base address:0x300
```

Note that the attributes of this interface mention nothing about promiscuous mode. When the interface is placed into promiscuous mode (as shown next) the **PROMISC** keyword appears in the attributes section:

```
eth0      Link encap:Ethernet  HWaddr 00:60:08:C5:93:6B
inet addr:10.0.0.21  Bcast:10.0.0.255  Mask:255.255.255.0
UP BROADCAST RUNNING PROMISC MULTICAST  MTU:1500  Metric:1
RX packets:1492330 errors:2779 dropped:0 overruns:2779 frame:2779
TX packets:1282769 errors:0 dropped:0 overruns:0 carrier:0
collisions:10575 txqueuelen:100
Interrupt:10 Base address:0x300
```

It is important to note that if an attacker has compromised the security of the host on which you run this command, he or she can easily affect the output. An important part of an attacker's toolkit is a replacement **ifconfig** command that does not report interfaces in promiscuous mode.

# Network Detection

There are a number of techniques of varying degrees of accuracy available to detect whether a host is monitoring a network for all traffic. There is no guaranteed method to detect the presence of a network sniffer.

# DNS Lookups

Most programs that are written to monitor networks, perform reverse DNS lookups when they produce output that consists of the source and destination hosts involved in a network connection. In the process of performing this lookup, additional network traffic is generated; mainly the DNS query looking up the network address. It is possible to monitor the network for hosts that are performing a large number of address lookups alone; however, this may be coincidental and may not lead to a sniffing host. An easier way that would result in 100 percent accuracy would be to generate a false network connection from an address that has no business on the local network. You could then monitor the network for DNS queries that attempt to resolve the faked address giving away the sniffing host.

# Latency

A second technique that can be used to detect a host that is monitoring the network is to detect latency variations in the host's response to network traffic (i.e., ping). Although this technique is prone to a number of errors (e.g., the host's latency being affected by normal operation) it can assist in determining whether a host is monitoring the network. The method that can be used is to probe the host initially and sample the response times. Next, a large amount of network traffic is generated that is specifically crafted to interest a host that is monitoring the network for authentication information. Finally, the latency of the host is sampled again to determine whether it has changed significantly.

# Driver Bugs

Sometimes an OS driver bug assists in determining whether a host is running in promiscuous mode. In one case, CORE-SDI (an Argentine security research company) discovered a bug in a common Linux Ethernet driver. They found that when the host was running in promiscuous mode, the OS failed to perform Ethernet address checks to ensure that the packet was targeted toward one of its interfaces. Instead, this validation was performed at the IP level and the packet was accepted if it was destined to one of the host's interfaces. Normally, packets that do not correspond to a host's Ethernet address are dropped at the hardware level; however, in promiscuous mode this doesn't happen. You can determine whether the host was in promiscuous mode by sending an ICMP ping packet to it with a valid IP address and an invalid Ethernet address. If the host responds to this ping request, it is determined to be running in promiscuous mode.

## NetMon

NetMon, available on Windows NT-based systems, has the ability to monitor who is actively running NetMon on a network. It also maintains a history of who has NetMon installed on their system. It only detects other copies of NetMon; therefore, if the attacker is using another sniffer, you must detect it using one of the previous methods discussed. Most network-based IDSes also detect these instances of NetMon.

# Summary

In this chapter, we have given you a high-level overview of Wireshark and its various features and supporting programs. We covered the history of Wireshark, its compatibility with other sniffers, and its supported protocols. We took a brief look into the Wireshark GUI and the filter capabilities, because these areas are covered in detail in later chapters. We also covered the programs that come with Wireshark, that add additional functionality by manipulating capture files.

We explored several scenarios for using Wireshark in your network architecture. Spend time getting to know your network and the way it is connected. Knowing how your network is segmented will help with placing Wireshark to capture the information you need.

We also explored how Wireshark can be used by a wide range of people, including network system and security administrators. Wireshark can also be used by anyone on their own network. We touched on securing and optimizing Wireshark as part of your workflow. Although the application is robust and stable, there are some simple, cost-effective things you can do to improve your Wireshark experience.

Finally, we covered an example network troubleshooting methodology. It is good practice to use this methodology every time you troubleshoot a problem. Once again, spending time getting to know your network and the protocols running on it will help make troubleshooting a lot easier.

# Solutions Fast Track

## What is Wireshark?

- ☑ Wireshark is a free and feature-rich network analyzer that rivals commercial counterparts

- ☑ Wireshark can decode more than 750 protocols

- ☑ Wireshark is compatible with more than 25 other sniffers and capture utilities

- ☑ Display and capture filters can be used to sort through network traffic

- ☑ Wireshark mailing lists are a great resource for information and support

- ☑ Wireshark is free of charge and free to distribute, and you are free to modify it

# Supporting Programs

☑ Wireshark installs with supporting programs (e.g., tshark)

☑ editcap

☑ mergecap

☑ and text2pcap

☑ Tshark is a command line version of Wireshark

☑ Editcap is used to remove packets from a file and to translate the format of capture files

☑ Mergecap is used to merge multiple capture files into one

☑ Text2pcap is used to translate ASCII hexdump captures into libpcap output files

# Using Wireshark in Your Network Architecture

☑ The correct placement of Wireshark in your network architecture is critical to capture the data you need.

☑ Taps, hubs, and switches with port spanning enabled can all be used to connect Wireshark to your network.

☑ You can create a troubleshooting toolkit consisting of a small hub, a small network tap, and extra straight-through and crossover cables.

☑ Installing Wireshark on a laptop makes troubleshooting at various locations easier.

# System and Security Troubleshooting

☑ Following a methodical troubleshooting process can minimize the time it takes to solve a problem.

☑ Identifying and testing the cause of a problem often involves research on the Internet or support calls to hardware or software vendors.

☑ Sometimes solving one problem could create another.

☑ Keeping detailed notes on how you solved a problem will assist in future troubleshooting efforts.

# Securing and Optimizing Wireshark

☑  Capture packets using the appropriate security privileges; analyze packets with the least privilege possible.

☑  Update Wireshark when security vulnerabilities are found.

☑  Adding system memory will improve application responsiveness when analyzing large numbers of packets.

# Advanced Sniffing Techniques

☑  MAC and ARP manipulation techniques can be used to sniff switched traffic without changing your physical network architecture.

☑  MITM attacks can be used to intercept traffic.

☑  Tools are available that sniff traffic and capture and crack passwords at the same time.

# Securing Your Network from Sniffers

☑  If those hosts are also authenticated, host-to-host VPN encryption effectively hides data within packets from sniffers. Depending on the method used, the ports and protocols can also be hidden.

☑  Application-level encryption such as SSL also protects the data within the packets.

☑  Switched networks are slightly more difficult to sniff than networks using hubs.

# Employing Detection Techniques

☑  Promiscuous mode interfaces on hosts may show the presence of a sniffer.

☑  You can detect the presence of some sniffers by their effects on the network such as extra DNS lookups, network latency, driver issues, and the applications themselves.

☑  No detection tool is effective in an organization without a strong policy that contains the guidelines for the appropriate use of sniffing technologies.

# Frequently Asked Questions

The following Frequently Asked Questions, answered by the authors of this book, are designed to both measure your understanding of the concepts presented in this chapter and to assist you with real-life implementation of these concepts. To have your questions about this chapter answered by the author, browse to **www.syngress.com/solutions** and click on the **"Ask the Author"** form.

**Q:** Many open-source security tools have recently become commercialized. If the Wireshark team converted to a commercial product, would the open-source Wireshark still be free to use?

**A:** Wireshark was released using the GNU GPL; the source code will remain available and free for any version of software released using the GPL.

**Q:** With all the other commercial software out there that my company prefers, why should I use Wireshark?

**A:** Wireshark doesn't require you to decide on it; however, keep it in your toolkit in case you ever need it.

**Q:** I think I have found an intruder on my network and I would like to save my data. Can Wireshark help?

**A:** The best response is to use your company's predefined incident response plan. If your company doesn't have an incident response policy, the best time to create one is before you need one.

**Q:** How can I verify that the version of Wireshark I downloaded doesn't contain a virus or other unwanted software?

**A:** Downloading from a reputable place is a good start. However, no matter where you downloaded the software from, run **md5sum** and **sha1sum** against the file you downloaded. Check the results of those programs against the hashes in the SIGNA-TURE file in the Wireshark release directory. To verify that the hashes are correct, use GnuPG (www.gnupg.org) to verify that the hashes were signed correctly.

**Q:** How can I create packets for Wireshark to sniff?

**A:** Using the ping utility or going to a Web page will create traffic on your network. If you are looking for an example of a specific type of traffic, creating an environment where that traffic is likely to happen is the best bet. In other words, if you're looking to sniff Web traffic, create a Web server and use a Web browser. If your goal is to create specifically crafted packets, a Perl module named **Raw::IP** should do the trick and is downloadable from CPAN or www.ic.al.lg.ua/~ksv/index.shtml.

**Q:** How can I sniff all the traffic on my network if my switch doesn't support sniffing or is unmanaged?

**A:** One way or another you'll need to get into the network path. You can either run a sniffer on the host that sees the most traffic, replace the switch with a hub or another sniffable switch, or use ARP trickery such as dsniff.

**Q:** Is there a way to use Wireshark without installing it?

**A:** Using a bootable CD or DVD-ROM is a good option. After downloading and burning a bootable image such as Backtrack (www.remote-exploit.org) or Helix (www.e-fense.com/helix/), you can use Wireshark and other security tools without any installation. However, these bootable disks should not be used to violate your organization's security policies regarding the use of third-party software.

PV27

# Chapter 3

# Getting and Installing Wireshark

## Solutions in this chapter:

- **Getting Wireshark**

- **Packet Capture Drivers**

- **Installing Wireshark on Windows**

- **Installing Wireshark on Linux**

- **Installing Wireshark on Mac OS X**

- **Installing Wireshark from Source**

☑ **Summary**

☑ **Solutions Fast Track**

☑ **Frequently Asked Questions**

# Introduction

In this chapter, we will cover all of the steps necessary to complete a functioning installation of the Wireshark network analyzer. Due to the overwhelming amount of Unix-based distributions available today, installation instructions can vary from distribution to distribution, and are beyond the scope of this chapter. For this reason, we will be focusing on information specific to installation on the Fedora Core 6 platform. We have chosen Fedora Core because it is the most commonly used Linux distribution in the world, and serves as a good starting point on which to base further installations. Most of what we cover here should apply to most other popular distributions without a large amount of modification. If the instructions do vary, however, the difference should be minimal. For the Windows side, we will be focusing on Windows XP, due to its common use. Lastly, we have included several installation options for Mac OS X.

For this chapter, we started with fresh installations of Fedora Core 6, Windows XP, and Mac OS X. We accepted the default installation parameters for each of the operating systems (OSs). These types of installations often install needless software, and leave many security vulnerabilities wide open. You should follow security best practices when installing new systems and also when subsequently applying operating system security procedures. These methods are beyond the scope of this book, but you should pick up a good reference for securing your particular operating system. Please make sure your operating system is current, patched, and secured. You will also need to verify that your networking is set up and functioning properly, or you might not be able to see any packets to analyze!

Let's take a moment to introduce you to the way we approached this chapter. When it comes to computers, networking, and security, some of you are beginners and some are pros. Based on the varying technical abilities of the target audience of this book, we tried to approach almost every subject as if we were learning it for the first time. Our only assumption was that you do have a basic understanding of the operating system and how to use it. For the beginners, we made the step-by-step instructions for each installation easy to find and read. This chapter will serve as an excellent *skimming* reference for the more experienced reader. The only time we will have a lengthier explanation with the procedures is when there is possibly some pitfall to watch for, or during description of certain side notes that might be helpful. We keep all of our longer descriptions and discussions *outside* of the chapter installation instructions. So, let's start installing Wireshark!

# Getting Wireshark

Wireshark is readily available, in both source and binary form, for download from a variety of sources. The CD that accompanies this book contains Version 0.99.4. You may browse to the "Windows Installer" folder to install a Win32 system, or you may install using the source files. The most authoritative source for downloads is the Wireshark download Web site at www.wireshark.org/download.html. This Web page contains a list of locations around the world where users can download binary distributions and ready-to-install packages for several platforms. It also contains the source code in zipped archive (tar.gz) format. Another source for obtaining Wireshark may be your OS CD-ROM. However, these tend to be older versions, and it is worth the time to download the latest versions. Several requirements and dependencies surround the proper installation of Wireshark. These requirements depend on a variety of factors, including the operating system platform and whether you are installing a precompiled binary, or compiling from source. We will address these issues for several platforms throughout this chapter.

The packages needed for installing Wireshark are available free of charge on the Internet at their respective Web sites. You may want to download the latest version of the software before beginning. Feel free to do so; just make sure to substitute package names when necessary. For example, if we reference the file wireshark-0.99.4.tar.gz and you have wireshark-0.99.5.tar.gz, use *your* filename because it's newer.

# Platforms and System Requirements

So, on what operating system platforms can you install Wireshark? The following list shows a number of platforms that have readily available Wireshark binaries:

- Mac OS X
- Debian GNU/Linux
- FreeBSD
- Gentoo Linux
- HP-UX
- Mandriva Linux
- Windows
- NetBSD
- OpenPKG
- Red Hat Fedora/Enterprise Linux

- rPath Linux

- Sun Solaris/i386

- Sun Solaris/Sparc

This list is constantly expanding as developers *port* the Wireshark source to new platforms. If your operating system is not listed, and you are feeling brave, go ahead and download the source code and begin building it for your system!

## NOTE

Several Wireshark binary packages are available through The Written Word at www.thewrittenword.com. The Written Word provides precompiled binaries of open-source software, specifically for AIX, HP-UX, IRIX, Red Hat Linux, Solaris, and Tru64 Unix. Releases can be purchased on a one-time basis, or as a subscription service.

# Packet Capture Drivers

When a computer is placed on a network, the network card is responsible for receiving and transmitting data to other hosts. Network applications use methods, like sockets, to establish and maintain connections, while the underlying operating system handles the low-level details and provides protocol stacks for communications. Some programs, however, need direct access to handle the raw network data, without interference from protocol stacks. A packet capture driver provides exactly this; it has the ability capture raw network packets. Better than that, a packet capture driver can capture *all* data on a shared network architecture, regardless of the intended recipient. This is what allows a program like Wireshark to passively monitor network traffic.

Two very famous and widely used packet capture drivers are libpcap, and its Windows counterpart, WinPcap. Libpcap is a free, open-source packet capture library originally developed at the Lawrence Berkeley National Laboratory in California. It is now maintained by a variety of authors at www.tcpdump.org. Not only does libpcap allow data to be captured, it also provides a mechanism for filtering the data based on user specifications before passing it to the application. WinPcap is maintained by a group of developers at www.winpcap.org. It uses some of the code of libpcap as well as some newly added code. Many other programs use the libpcap and WinPcap libraries, including TCPDump, WinDump, Snort, Ettercap,

Dsniff, Nmap, tcpflow, and TCPstat. Programs that use libpcap tend to be network monitors, protocol analyzers, traffic loggers, network intrusion detection systems, and various other security tools.

> **NOTE**
>
> TCPDump is another protocol analyzer, like Wireshark, that can be used to monitor network traffic. It is a command-line application that runs on Unix-based systems. The Windows version is called Windump.

## Notes from the Underground...

### Compression Utilities

As you are downloading software packages from the Internet, you will encounter numerous compression utilities. Many people are already familiar with the zip compression format used on both Windows and UNIX systems. In this chapter, we discuss the tar format used for archiving files. The tar format does not provide compression. Instead, it merely packages files together into one single file. This single tar file will still take up the same amount of space, plus a little more, as the sum of all of the individual files. Tar files are typically compressed with other utilities such as gzip or bzip2.

Gzip is used to reduce the size of files, thus making it a great tool for compressing large packet captures. Gzip files are recognized by the .gz extension. Wireshark can automatically uncompress and read Gzip compressed files, even if they don't have the .gz extension. Files can be compressed by typing the command **gzip** *filename*. Files can be *uncompressed* by using the commands **gzip –d** *filename* or **gunzip** *filename*.

Bzip2 is a newer file compression utility and is capable of greater compression ratios than gzip. Bzip2 files are recognized by the .bz2 extension. Files can be compressed by typing the command **bzip2** *filename*. Files can be *uncompressed* by using the commands **bzip2 –d** *filename* or **bunzip2** *filename*. At this time, Wireshark can not read bzip2 compressed files.

## Installing libpcap

A lot of Linux systems already have libpcap preinstalled, including Fedora Core 6. However, this section addresses two methods of installing libpcap: the Red Hat

Package Manager (RPM), and building from source—for those of you who may still need to install it. Once you install libpcap (or WinPcap), you won't have to do anything else with it unless you are a developer. Wireshark will use the libpcap libraries to passively capture network data. So let's get started installing libpcap!

If you used the Windows Installer on the CD that accompanies this book, WinPcap was also installed into **Start | Programs**. Also if you use Yellow dog Updater, Modified (YUM) to install Wireshark, it will install libpcap for you.

## Installing libpcap Using the RPMs

Installing software from the RPM can be a very tricky process. See the "Notes from the Underground" sidebar in this chapter for more details on RPMs. Luckily, the libpcap installation poses no problems. Remember, there might be newer versions that have been released since the writing of this book; you can download the latest libpcap RPM from www.rpmfind.net. Make sure you are getting the proper RPM for your system. Before you begin, you will need to have root privileges to install an RPM. Make sure you are logged in as root, or switch to root by typing **su root**, pressing **Enter**, and typing the appropriate root password.

1. Install the libpcap RPM by typing **rpm –ivh libpcap-0.9.4-8.1.i386.rpm** and pressing **Enter**.

2. Verify the installation by typing **rpm –q libpcap** and pressing **Enter**. If you see libpcap-0.9.4-8.1 listed, it is installed!

The following output shows how to install the libpcap RPM and then verify it is installed:

```
[root@localhost]# rpm -ivh libpcap-0.9.4-8.1.i386.rpm
Preparing...                ########################################### [100%]
   1:libpcap               ########################################### [100%]
[root@localhost root]# rpm -q libpcap
libpcap-0.9.4-8.1
```

Not too bad! Now that you have libpcap installed, feel free to move on to the "Installing Wireshark on Linux" or "Installing Wireshark from Source" sections in this chapter.

## Notes from the Underground…

## A Word about RPMs

The Red Hat Package Manager (RPM) is a powerful package management system capable of installing, uninstalling, verifying, querying, and updating Linux software packages. Finding RPMs is relatively easy, and www.rpmfind.net has a well-designed search and download system. However, since RPMs tend to be contributed by various individuals, they are often times a version or two behind the current source-code release. They are created on systems with varying file structures and environments, which can lead to difficulties if your system does not match those parameters. Installing an RPM can sometimes be easier than compiling from source—provided there are no dependency problems.

The RPM system, while an excellent package management tool, is fraught with problems regarding dependencies. It understands and reports which specific files the package requires that you install, but is not yet capable of acquiring and installing the packages necessary to fulfill its requirements. If you are not familiar with the term, *dependencies* are packages and/or libraries required by other packages. The Red Hat Linux OS is built on dependencies, which you can visualize as an upside-down tree structure. At the top of the tree are your basic user-installed programs, such as Wireshark. Wireshark depends on libpcap to operate, and libpcap requires other libraries to function. This tree structure is nice, but it adds to the dependency problem. For example, you may want to install a new software package and receive an error stating that another library on the system needs to be updated first. OK, so you download that library and attempt to update it. But, now, that library has dependencies too that need to be updated! This can be a never-ending and stressful adventure.

You can get information about RPMs in several ways:

- *rpm –q* (query) can be used to find out the version of a package installed—for example, *rpm –q wireshark*.

- *rpm –qa* (query all) can be used to show a very long list of all of the packages on the system. To make this list shorter, you can *pipe* the query into a *grep* to find what you are looking for: *rpm –qa | grep wireshark*.

- *rpm –ql* (query list) shows all of the files that were installed on the system with a particular package—for example, *rpm –ql wireshark*.

- *rpm –qf* (query file) can be used to find out which RPM a particular file belongs to—for example, *rpm –qf /usr/bin/wireshark*.

**Continued**

When using the RPM utility, you can install software three ways:

- *rpm –i* (install) installs a new RPM file, and leaves any previously installed versions alone.

- *rpm –u* (update) installs new software and removes any existing older versions.

- *rpm –f* (freshen) installs new software, but only if a previous version already exists. This is typically used for installing patches.

You can uninstall an RPM from your system by using the following:

- *rpm –e* (erase) removes an RPM from the system—for example, *rpm –e wireshark*.

Sometimes you can be successful by installing a package with the *--nodeps* option (notice it includes two hyphens). This causes the package to install regardless of the dependencies it calls for. This may, or may not, work, depending on whether the package you are installing really does need all of the dependencies to function.

## Installing libpcap from the Source Files

Installing libpcap from the source *tarball* is a relatively simple process. A tarball is a single file that can contain many other files, like a zip file. The tar format by itself does not provide compression like the zip format does, so it is customary to compress the tar file with either gzip or bzip2. See the sidebar for more information on using the gzip and bzip2 compression utilities. We will be extracting the contents of the tar file as well as compiling the source code by following the common **configure | make | make install** format for building the package into the system. It is standard practice NOT to build software as root, but to change to root to do the *make install* step. Perform the following steps to install libpcap from the source files.

1. Unzip and extract the tarball by typing **tar –zxvf libpcap–0.9.5.tar.gz** and pressing **Enter**. This will create a new directory called **libpcap–0.9.5**. Notice the extracted output displayed on the screen.

2. Change directories by typing **cd libpcap–0.9.5** and pressing **Enter**.

3. Run the configure script by typing **./configure** and pressing **Enter**. The configure script will analyze your system to make sure that dependencies, environment variables, and other parameters are acceptable. Note the question-and-answer type of analysis displayed on the screen.

4.  When the *configure* process is complete, and the command prompt is displayed, make sure there are no errors. If everything appears trouble-free, run the *make* utility simply by typing **make** and pressing **Enter**. This utility will compile the actual source code. The output of the compilation should appear on the screen.

5.  The last step of the process is to distribute the executables and other files to their proper locations in the systems directories. Switch to the root user to perform this step. If the *make* utility completes without errors, type **sudo make install** and press **Enter**. Enter the password for root and press **Enter**. Once again, the output of this process should appear on the screen.

6.  After the *make install* process completes, the command prompt will be displayed once again. If everything looks error free, you are done!

If at any time during the installation process you receive errors, you will need to investigate the problem and resolve it before continuing. Most of the time, dependency issues, software versions, or environment settings cause compiling errors. Compiling software from the source files offers the benefit of providing highly customized and optimized software for your system. Now that you have libpcap installed, move on to the "Installing Wireshark from Source" section where you can continue compiling Wireshark from the source code or choose one of the other processes.

## NOTE

Let's take a moment to define the typical variables used for the tar command: *-z, -x, -v*, and *-f* options.

The *-z* option specifies that the file must be processed through the *gzip* filter. You can tell if an archive was created with gzip by the *.gz* extension. The *-z* option is only available in the GNU version of tar. If you are not using the GNU version, you will have to unzip the tar file with a command such as *gunzip* or *gzip –dc filename.tar.gz | tar xvf -*.

The *-x* option indicates you want the contents of the archive to be extracted. By default, this action will extract the contents into the current working directory unless otherwise specified.

The *-v* option stands for verbose, which means that tar will display all files it processes on the screen. This is a personal preference and is not critical to the extraction operation.

The *-f* option specifies the file that tar will process. For example, this could be libpcap-0.9.5.tar.gz. Sometimes it might be necessary to specify a full path if the file you want to work with is located in another directory.

NOTE

Some Linux distributions have software like libpcap and others prein-stalled. It is worth the time and effort to install the latest versions of these packages. You will benefit from the increased stability, features, bug fixes, and speed of updated software.

# Installing WinPcap

The Windows version of Wireshark now includes WinPcap, which you can choose to install as you are installing Wireshark. However, we wanted to include instructions for those of you who wish to install WinPcap separately. The latest WinPcap installation executable can be downloaded from www.winpcap.org. To install WinPcap, you need to have the right to install new drivers to your system, and you will need to be logged in as Administrator or have Administrator rights. Perform the following steps to install WinPcap 3.1 on a Windows XP system:

1. Download the WinPcap executable from www.winpcap.org.

2. Begin the installation process by double-clicking the installer, **WinPcap_3_1.exe**. The first screen is a general welcome screen for the installation wizard. Click **Next** to continue.

3. The next screen displays information on the WinPcap license. Once you have read and accepted the terms of the agreement, click **I Agree** to accept the license and continue.

4. The Setup Status window appears, showing the files being copied and dis-playing a progress bar. Once the installation is complete, click **Finish** to exit the setup.

NOTE

If you do not have WinPcap installed, you will be able to open saved capture files, but you won't be able to capture live network traffic.

**WARNING**

If you have an older version of WinPcap and would like to install a new one, you must uninstall the old version and reboot. This ensures the new version of WinPcap installs properly. At the time of this writing, version 3.1 was recommended.

**NOTE**

To make sure WinPcap is installed on your system, check by choosing **Start | Control Panel | Add or Remove Programs**. You should see WinPcap listed under the currently installed programs list.

WinPcap installs by default in C:\Program Files\WinPcap. If you need to uninstall WinPcap, use the provided uninstall executable located in this directory. See how easy that was! Now let's move on to the Wireshark installation.

# Installing Wireshark on Windows

The latest Wireshark Windows executable can be downloaded from www.wireshark.org/download.html, and installs on a variety of Windows platforms. Note that you don't need Administrator rights to install Wireshark. Now that WinPcap is installed, perform the following to install Wireshark 0.99.4 on a Windows XP system.

1. Download the Wireshark executable from www.wireshark.org/download.html.

2. Begin the installation process by double-clicking the installer: **wireshark-setup-0.99.4.exe**. The first screen is a general welcome screen for the setup wizard. Click **Next** to continue.

3. The next screen is the Wireshark GNU General Public License Agreement. After reading and accepting the terms of the license, click **I Agree** to accept the license and continue.

4. The next screen allows you to choose which Wireshark components to install. The Appendix discusses other programs packaged with Wireshark. The default components require 65.2MB of free space. Of course, you should have adequate free space for storing your capture files as well. Click **Next** to continue.

5.   The screen that appears allows you to select shortcuts to create and asso-
     ciate file extensions with Wireshark. Click **Next** to continue.

6.   The next screen allows you to choose the folder where you would like to
     install Wireshark. Accept the default of C:\Program Files\Wireshark and
     click **Next**.

7.   The screen that next appears allows you to install WinPcap if it is not
     already installed. If you have not installed WinPcap already, you may choose
     to do so by clicking the Install WinPcap 3.1 box. Click **Install** to begin the
     installation process.

8.   A screen showing the status of the installation process should appear. It
     gives line-by-line details of what is happening behind the scenes, as well as
     an overall progress bar. If Wireshark is installing WinPcap for you, you will
     need to click **Next** through the WinPcap installation screens and accept
     the WinPcap license agreement. Once the Wireshark installation is com-
     plete, click **Next** to continue.

9.   All done! Wireshark is now installed and ready to go. It even puts a nice
     shortcut icon right on the desktop. You may click the boxes to run
     Wireshark and to show the Wireshark news file. Click **Finish** to close the
     dialog box. You can now double-click the Wireshark desktop icon to open
     the Wireshark network analyzer GUI.

## NOTE

A nice feature of the completed installation box is the ability to save the
installation log to a file. Simply right-click one of the lines in the box and
a small window pops up that says "Copy Details To Clipboard." Select this
option and paste the results into Notepad or your favorite text editor.

By default, Wireshark is installed in C:\Program Files\Wireshark. As you saw
during the installation process, this can be changed. Several files are placed within
the Wireshark directory, including the uninstall.exe file. You can use this executable
to uninstall Wireshark if necessary. Other important files to note are the seven executables and their associated manual pages in HTML format: wireshark.exe,
tshark.exe, capinfos.exe, dumpcap.exe, editcap.exe, mergecap.exe, and text2pcap.exe.
These supporting programs are discussed in detail in Chapter 9.

**NOTE**

If you are having trouble capturing packets with Wireshark, ensure that WinPcap is working properly by using Windump to try capturing packets. Windump can be downloaded from http://www.winpcap.org/windump/install/default.htm. The command *windump –D* will display a list of valid adapters that WinPcap is able to detect.

# Installing Wireshark on Linux

In this section, we will cover the Yellow dog Updater, Modified (YUM) method of installing Wireshark. YUM is an open-source, command-line package management utility for RPM-compatible Linux systems. It is an automated method of installing, updating, and removing RPM packages. The next section will focus on building Wireshark from source. Each example performs the process of installing Wireshark 0.99.4 on Fedora Core 6. So let's get started installing Wireshark!

## Installing Wireshark from the RPMs

Installing software from the RPMs can be a very tricky process because of dependencies. Luckily, YUM takes care of dependencies and does all the work for us. For example, you don't need to worry about installing libpcap because YUM downloads and installs it as part of the Wireshark package. The following step-by-step process can be used to install Wireshark on Fedora Core 6. Remember, newer versions may have been released since the writing of this book. Before beginning, you must have root privileges to install Wireshark. Make sure you are logged in as root, or switch to root by typing **su root**, pressing **Enter**, and typing the appropriate root password. Let's begin the Wireshark installation process:

1. Install the Wireshark package by typing **yum install wireshark-gnome** and pressing **Enter**.

That's it! YUM downloads Wireshark and its dependencies and installs them for you. Verify the installation by typing **wireshark** and pressing **Enter**. You should see the Wireshark GUI appear on your screen.

> **NOTE**
>
> When using YUM, you must install the wireshark-gnome package to get the Wireshark GUI.

The following output shows how to install the Wireshark RPMs and their dependencies using YUM:

```
[root@localhost]# yum install wireshark-gnome
Loading "installonlyn" plugin
Setting up Install Process
Setting up repositories
Reading repository metadata in from local files
Parsing package install arguments
Resolving Dependencies
--> Populating transaction set with selected packages. Please wait.
---> Downloading header for wireshark-gnome to pack into transaction set.
wireshark-gnome-0.99.4-1. 100% |=========================| 4.9 kB    00:00
---> Package wireshark-gnome.i386 0:0.99.4-1.fc6 set to be updated
--> Running transaction check
--> Processing Dependency: libwiretap.so.0 for package: wireshark-gnome
--> Processing Dependency: wireshark = 0.99.4-1.fc6 for package: wireshark-gnome
--> Processing Dependency: libwireshark.so.0 for package: wireshark-gnome
--> Restarting Dependency Resolution with new changes.
--> Populating transaction set with selected packages. Please wait.
---> Downloading header for wireshark to pack into transaction set.
Wireshark-0.99.4-1.fc6.i3 100% |=========================| 27 kB    00:00
---> Package wireshark.i386 0:0.99.4-1.fc6 set to be updated
--> Running transaction check
Dependencies Resolved
```

| Package | Arch | Version | Repository | Size |
|---|---|---|---|---|
| Installing: | | | | |
| wireshark-gnome | i386 | 0.99.4-1.fc6 | updates | 542 k |
| Installing for dependencies: | | | | |
| wireshark | i386 | 0.99.4-1.fc6 | updates | 7.8 M |

```
Transaction Summary
==========================================================================
Install       2 Package(s)
Update        0 Package(s)
Remove        0 Package(s)
Total download size: 8.4 M
Is this ok [y/N]: y
Downloading Packages:
(1/2): wireshark-gnome-0. 100% |=========================| 542 kB     00:03
(2/2): wireshark-0.99.4-1 100% |=========================| 7.8 MB     00:45
warning: rpmts_HdrFromFdno: Header V3 DSA signature: NOKEY, key ID 4f2a6fd2
Importing GPG key 0x4F2A6FD2 "Fedora Project <fedora@redhat.com>"
Is this ok [y/N]: y
Running Transaction Test
Finished Transaction Test
Transaction Test Succeeded
Running Transaction
  Installing: wireshark                    ######################### [1/2]
  Installing: wireshark-gnome              ######################### [2/2]
Installed: wireshark-gnome.i386 0:0.99.4-1.fc6
Dependency Installed: wireshark.i386 0:0.99.4-1.fc6
Complete!
```

# Installing Wireshark on Mac OS X

## Installing Wireshark on Mac OS X from Source

Building Wireshark from the source code on Mac OS X is a lengthy, and sometimes tricky, process. However, many people prefer this method because of the control they have over the packages installed. We performed the source-code method of installing Wireshark on Mac OS X Tiger. If you have some free time and are feeling ambitious, you may try this method of installation; otherwise, use one of the ported methods such as DarwinPorts or Fink. If you downloaded newer versions of the software, make sure you change the names accordingly as you proceed through the installation steps.

1. Prepare your Mac by installing Xcode Tools, which is located on your Mac OS X CD. This installs the gcc compiler and other development tools needed to compile source code, such as the X11 environment. If you are running Tiger, find the **Xcode Tools** folder on the Mac OS X Install Disc 1.

Double-click the **XcodeTools.mpkg** in this folder and follow the onscreen instructions to install **Xcode Tools**.

2. Install the X11 user environment, which is also located on your Mac OS X Install Disc 1. The package is located in **System | Installation | Packages | X11User.pkg**. Double-click the **X11User.pkg** and follow the onscreen instructions. This installs the X11 application in the Utilities folder.

3. Download the following packages and save them to your user folder, typically /Users/*username*:

   - **Pkg-config** pkgconfig.freedesktop.org

   - **Gettext** www.gnu.org/software/gettext

   - **Glib** www.gtk.org/download

   - **ATK** ftp.gtk.org/pub/gtk/v2.10/dependencies

   - **Libpng** libpng.sourceforge.net

   - **Libxml** ftp://xmlsoft.org/libxml2

   - **Freetype** freetype.sourceforge.net

   - **Fontconfig** fontconfig.org

   - **Cairo** ftp.gtk.org/pub/gtk/v2.10/dependencies

   - **Pango** www.gtk.org/download

   - **Jpgsrc** ftp.gtk.org/pub/gtk/v2.10/dependencies

   - **Tiff** ftp.gtk.org/pub/gtk/v2.10/dependencies

   - **GTK+** www.gtk.org/download

   - **Libpcap** www.tcpdump.org

   - **Wireshark** www.wireshark.org

4. Run the X11 application in the Utilities folder by double-clicking it. This will open an Xterminal window. By default, Xterminal should put you into the /Users/*username* directory and you should be able to see all of the packages you just downloaded by typing **ls** and pressing **Enter**.

5. Ensure that /usr/local/bin is in your $PATH. If not, add it by typing **PATH=$PATH:/usr/local/bin** and pressing **Enter**.

6. Extract pkg-config by typing **tar zxvf pkg-config-0.21.tar.gz** and pressing **Enter**. Next, change into the pkg-config directory by typing **cd**

**pkgconfig-0.21** and pressing **Enter**. Run the configure script by typing **./configure** and pressing **Enter**. Compile the source code by typing **make** and pressing **Enter**. Next, install the files in their appropriate locations by typing **sudo make install** and pressing **Enter**. To install the software, you must enter the root password when prompted. When the software install is complete, change back to the original directory by typing **cd ..** and pressing **Enter**.

7.  Extract gettext by typing **tar zxvf gettext-0.12.1.tar.gz** and pressing **Enter**. Next, change to the gettext directory by typing **cd gettext-0.12.1** and pressing **Enter**. Run the configure script by typing **./configure** and pressing **Enter**. Then, compile the source code by typing **make** and pressing **Enter**. Next, install the files in their appropriate locations by typing **sudo make install** and pressing **Enter**. To install the software, you must enter the root password when prompted. When the software install is complete, change back to the original directory by typing **cd ..** and pressing **Enter**.

8.  Extract Glib by typing **tar zxvf glib-2.12.4.tar.gz** and pressing **Enter**. Next, change to the glib directory by typing **cd glib-2.12.4** and pressing **Enter**. Run the configure script by typing **./configure** and pressing **Enter**. Then, compile the source code by typing **make** and pressing **Enter**. Next, install the files in their appropriate locations by typing **sudo make install** and pressing **Enter**. To install the software, you must enter the root password when prompted. When the software install is complete, change back to the original directory by typing **cd ..** and pressing **Enter**.

9.  Extract ATK by typing **tar zxvf atk-1.12.3.tar.gz** and pressing **Enter**. Next, change into the ATK directory by typing **cd atk-1.12.3** and pressing **Enter**. Run the configure script by typing **./configure** and pressing **Enter**. Then, compile the source code by typing **make** and pressing **Enter**. Next, install the files in their appropriate locations by typing **sudo make install** and pressing **Enter**. To install the software, enter the root password when prompted. When the software install is complete, change back to the original directory by typing **cd ..** and pressing **Enter**.

10. Extract libpng by typing **tar zxvf libpng-1.2.12.tar.gz** and pressing **Enter**. Next, change to the libpng directory by typing **cd libpng-1.2.12** and pressing **Enter**. Run the configure script by typing **./configure** and pressing **Enter**. Compile the source code by typing **make** and pressing **Enter**. Next, install the files in their appropriate locations by typing **sudo**

**make install** and pressing **Enter**. To install the software, you must enter the root password when prompted. When the software install is complete, change back to the original directory by typing **cd ..** and pressing **Enter**.

11. Extract libxml by typing **tar zxvf libxml2-2.6.27.tar.gz** and pressing **Enter**. Next, change to the libxml directory by typing **cd libxml2-2.6.27** and pressing **Enter**. Run the configure script by typing **./configure** and pressing **Enter**. Compile the source code by typing **make** and pressing **Enter**. Next, install the files in their appropriate locations by typing **sudo make install** and pressing **Enter**. To install the software, you must enter the root password when prompted. When the software install is complete, change back to the original directory by typing **cd ..** and pressing **Enter**.

12. Extract Freetype by typing **tar zxvf freetype-2.2.1.tar.gz** and pressing **Enter**. Next, change to the freetype directory by typing **cd freetype-2.2.1** and pressing **Enter**. Run the configure script by typing **./configure** and pressing **Enter**. Then, compile the source code by typing **make** and pressing **Enter**. Next, install the files in their appropriate locations by typing **sudo make install** and pressing **Enter**. To install the software, you must enter the root password when prompted. When the software install is completed, change back to the original directory by typing **cd ..** and pressing **Enter**.

13. Extract Fontconfig by typing **tar zxvf fontconfig-2.4.1.tar.gz** and pressing **Enter**. Next, change to the fontconfig directory by typing **cd fontconfig-2.4.1** and pressing **Enter**. Run the configure script by typing **./configure** and pressing **Enter**. Then, compile the source code by typing **make** and pressing **Enter**. Next, install the files in their appropriate locations by typing **sudo make install** and pressing **Enter**. To install the software, you must enter the root password when prompted. When the software install is complete, change back to the original directory by typing **cd ..** and pressing **Enter**.

14. Extract Cairo by typing **tar zxvf cairo-1.2.4.tar.gz** and pressing **Enter**. Next, change to the cairo directory by typing **cd cairo-1.2.4** and pressing **Enter**. Run the configure script by typing **./configure** and pressing **Enter**. Then, compile the source code by typing **make** and pressing **Enter**. Next, install the files in their appropriate locations by typing **sudo make install** and pressing **Enter**. To install the software, enter the root password when prompted. When the software install is complete, change back to the original directory by typing **cd ..** and pressing **Enter**.

15. Extract Pango by typing **tar zxvf pango-1.14.7.tar.gz** and pressing **Enter**. Next, change to the pango directory by typing **cd pango-1.14.7** and pressing **Enter**. Run the configure script by typing **./configure** and pressing **Enter**. Compile the source code by typing **make** and pressing **Enter**. Next, install the files in their appropriate locations by typing **sudo make install** and pressing **Enter**. To install the software, enter the root password when prompted. When the software install is complete, change back to the original directory by typing **cd ..** and pressing **Enter**.

16. Extract jpgsrc by typing **tar zxvf jpgsrc.v6b.tar.gz** and pressing **Enter**. Next, change to the jpgsrc directory by typing **cd jpgsrc-6b** and pressing **Enter**. Run the configure script by typing **./configure** and pressing **Enter**. Then, compile the source code by typing **make** and pressing **Enter**. Next, install the files in their appropriate locations by typing **sudo make install** and pressing **Enter**. To install the software, enter the root password when prompted. When the software install is complete, change back to the original directory by typing **cd ..** and pressing **Enter**.

17. Extract tiff by typing **tar zxvf tiff-3.7.4.tar.gz** and pressing **Enter**. Next, change to the tiff directory by typing **cd tiff-3.7.4** and pressing **Enter**. Run the configure script by typing **./configure** and pressing **Enter**. Compile the source code by typing **make** and press **Enter**. Next, install the files in their appropriate locations by typing **sudo make install** and pressing **Enter**. To install the software, enter the root password when prompted. When the software install is complete, change back to the original directory by typing **cd ..** and pressing **Enter**.

18. Extract GTK+ by typing **tar zxvf gtk+-2.10.6.tar.gz** and pressing **Enter**. Next, change to the gtk+ directory by typing **cd gtk+-2.10.6** and pressing **Enter**. Run the configure script by typing **./configure** and pressing **Enter**. Compile the source code by typing **make** and pressing **Enter**. Next, install the files in their appropriate locations by typing **sudo make install** and pressing **Enter**. To install the software, enter the root password when prompted. When the software install is complete, change back to the original directory by typing **cd ..** and pressing **Enter**.

19. Extract libpcap by typing **tar zxvf libpcap-0.9.5.tar.gz** and pressing **Enter**. Next, change to the libpcap directory by typing **cd libpcap-0.9.5** and pressing **Enter**. Run the configure script by typing **./configure** and pressing **Enter**. Compile the source code by typing **make** and pressing **Enter**. Next, install the files in their appropriate locations by typing **sudo**

**make install** and pressing **Enter**. To install the software, enter the root password when prompted. When the software install is complete, change back to the original directory by typing **cd ..** and pressing **Enter**.

20. Finally the moment we have been waiting for. Extract Wireshark by typing **tar zxvf wireshark-0.99.4.tar.gz** and pressing **Enter**. Next, change to the wireshark directory by typing **cd wireshark-0.99.4** and pressing **Enter**. Run the configure script by typing **./configure** and pressing **Enter**. Then, compile the source code by typing **make** and pressing **Enter**. Next, install the files in their appropriate locations by typing **sudo make install** and pressing **Enter**. To install the software, enter the root password when prompted. When the software install is complete, change back to the original directory by typing **cd ..** and pressing **Enter**.

21. To run Wireshark, type **wireshark** and press **Enter**. The GUI should open.

Now you have successfully built Wireshark from the source code! Each time you wish to run Wireshark, make sure to run the X11 application and run Wireshark from the Xterminal window that opens. The Wireshark binary installs in /usr/local/bin, so if you don't have that directory in your permanent $PATH, you will need to add it. Once everything is installed, you may also remove the *.tar.gz files from your /User/*username* folder.

> **NOTE**
>
> SharkLauncher is a helpful tool that will launch the X11 environment and the Wireshark binary. It may be downloaded from sourceforge.net/projects/aquaethereal.

# Installing Wireshark on Mac OS X Using DarwinPorts

DarwinPorts contains Unix-based software that has been modified to run on Mac OS X, known as *porting*. DarwinPorts automates the process of building third-party software for Mac OS X and other operating systems. It also tracks all dependency information for a given software tool. It knows what to build and install and in what order. After you download and install DarwinPorts, you can use it to easily install all kinds of other software—in our case, Wireshark.

1.  Prepare your Mac by installing Xcode Tools, which is located on your Mac OS X CD. This will install the gcc compiler and other development tools needed to compile source code, such as the X11 environment. If you are running Tiger, find the **Xcode Tools** folder on the Mac OS X Install Disc 1. Double-click the **XcodeTools.mpkg** in this folder and follow the onscreen instructions to install **Xcode Tools**.

2.  Install the X11 user environment located on your Mac OS X Install Disc 1 as well. The package is located in **System | Installation | Packages | X11User.pkg**. Double-click the **X11User.pkg** and follow the onscreen instructions. This installs the X11 application in the Utilities folder.

3.  Download **DarwinPorts** from **macports.com**. Copy the file to the **/Users/***username* folder.

4.  Run the **X11** application in the **Utilities** folder by double-clicking it. This will open an Xterminal window. By default, Xterminal should put you into the **/Users/***username* directory and you should be able to see the package you just downloaded by typing **ls** and pressing **Enter**.

5.  Extract **DarwinPorts** by typing **tar zxvf DarwinPorts-1.3.2.tar.gz** and pressing **Enter**. Next, change into the DarwinPorts base directory by typing **cd DarwinPorts-1.3.2/base** and pressing **Enter**. Run the configure script by typing **./configure** and pressing **Enter**. Compile the source code by typing **make** and pressing **Enter**. Install the files in their appropriate locations by typing **sudo make install** and pressing **Enter**. To install the software, enter the root password when prompted. When the software install is complete, change back to the original directory by typing **cd ../..** and pressing **Enter**.

6.  DarwinPorts installs the binary in the /opt/local/bin directory, so you may need to add that to your PATH by typing **PATH=$PATH:/opt/local/bin** and pressing **Enter**.

7.  Update the ports to make sure they are current by typing **sudo port –d selfupdate** and pressing **Enter**.

8.  Install Wireshark by typing **sudo port install wireshark** and pressing **Enter**. DarwinPorts will then start fetching and installing the appropriate software dependencies and the Wireshark binary. This may take a while to complete.

9.  Once the installation is complete, run Wireshark by typing **wireshark** and pressing **Enter**. The GUI will now open.

Now you have successfully installed Wireshark using DarwinPorts! Each time you wish to run Wireshark, make sure you run the X11 application and run Wireshark from the Xterminal window that opens. The Wireshark binary installs in /usr/local/bin, so if you don't have that directory in your permanent $PATH, you will need to add it. Once everything is installed, you may also remove the DarwinPorts-1.3.2.tar.gz file from your /User/*username* folder.

# Installing Wireshark on Mac OS X Using Fink

The Fink Project modifies UNIX software so it compiles and runs on Mac OS X. This is known as *porting*. The distribution is then built with the package management tools **dpkg** and **apt-get**.

1. The first thing you need to do is prepare your Mac by installing Xcode Tools, which are located on your Mac OS X CD. This installs the gcc compiler and other development tools needed to compile source code, such as the X11 environment. If you are running Tiger, an **Xcode Tools** folder can be found on the Mac OS X Install Disc 1. Double-click the **XcodeTools.mpkg** in this folder and follow the onscreen instructions to install **Xcode Tools**.

2. Install the X11 user environment, which is located on your Mac OS X Install Disc 1 as well. The package can be found by choosing **System | Installation | Packages | X11User.pkg**. Double-click the **X11User.pkg** and follow the onscreen instructions. This installs the X11 application in the Utilities folder.

3. Download the Fink installer image from **fink.sourceforge.net**. Double-click the image to uncompress it, then double-click the **Fink pkg file** to launch the installer. Follow the onscreen instructions to walk through the Fink installer.

4. Open the **FinkCommander** file on the installer image and drag the **FinkCommander** binary to the **Applications** folder.

5. Double-click the **FinkCommand** application to open the GUI.

6. Perform an update by clicking the **Source** menu and choosing **Selfupdate-rsync**. This will ensure that all of the packages are current.

7. Now you are ready to install Wireshark. Scroll down through the list of packages and choose the **Wireshark** package. Click the icon in the upper-left corner of the window to install the binary package.

8. Once the installation is complete, you must open an Xterminal windows to run Wireshark. Run Wireshark by typing **wireshark** and pressing **Enter**. The GUI will open.

Now you have successfully installed Wireshark using Fink. Each time you wish to run Wireshark, make sure you run both the X11 application and Wireshark from the Xterminal window that opens. The Wireshark binary installs in /sw/bin, so if you don't have that directory in your permanent $PATH, you should add it.

# Installing Wireshark from Source

Installing Wireshark from the source code is very beneficial in a number of ways. Not only will you have all of the source code, additional documentation, and miscellaneous files to peruse, you will also have the ability to control numerous aspects of the build process. Wireshark can be built from sources on both the Windows and Unix/Linux OS. We will only focus on the Unix-based build in this book, however. Building software from source will give you a better feel for how the whole process works and what goes on behind the scenes. What you will take away is a wealth of knowledge about the software package, programming, and operating system management.

The first thing we need to do to install Wireshark software from source code is install all of the required dependencies. Remember that we earlier stated we need certain files for Wireshark to operate smoothly and effectively? In addition to libpcap, Wireshark requires the following prerequisites: GTK+ and Glib. However, depending on your version of Unix/Linux you may also have the following additional prerequisites:

- **Pkg-config** pkgconfig.freedesktop.org
- **Gettext** www.gnu.org/software/gettext
- **ATK** ftp.gtk.org/pub/gtk/v2.10/dependencies
- **Libpng** libpng.sourceforge.net
- **Libxml** ftp://xmlsoft.org/libxml2
- **Freetype** freetype.sourceforge.net
- **Fontconfig** fontconfig.org
- **Cairo** ftp.gtk.org/pub/gtk/v2.10/dependencies
- **Pango** www.gtk.org/download
- **Jpgsrc** ftp.gtk.org/pub/gtk/v2.10/dependencies

■  **Tiff** ftp.gtk.org/pub/gtk/v2.10/dependencies

For more information on installing these packages, see the section "Installing Wireshark on Mac OS X from Source."

---

**NOTE**

As we stated previously, most installations follow the **configure | make | make install** format. However, in some instances, there may be other steps. Once the tar file has been extracted, there is usually an INSTALL text file included in the software subdirectory. Take a look at this file by typing **more INSTALL** to verify the installation process.

---

After the required dependencies are installed, we are ready to install Wireshark. There may be newer versions that have been released since the writing of this book, and you can download the latest versions from www.wireshark.org. Remember, it is standard practice NOT to build software as root, but to change to root to do the *make install* step.

1. Uncompress and extract the Wireshark tarball by typing **tar zxvf wireshark-0.99.4.tar.gz** and pressing **Enter**. This will create a new directory called **wireshark-0.99.4**.

2. Change to the wireshark directory by typing **cd wireshark-0.99.4** and pressing **Enter**.

3. Run the configure script by typing **./configure** and pressing **Enter**. At the end of the configure script output, you will see a summary of the options. These can be changed by using specific parameters with the configure script, something which is discussed in the section "Enabling and Disabling Features via *configure*."

4. When the *configure* process is complete and the command prompt is displayed, make sure there are no errors. If everything appears trouble-free, run the make utility simply by typing **make** and pressing **Enter**.

5. If the *make* utility completed without errors, type **su root** and press **Enter**. Enter the password for root and press **Enter**. Next, install the files in their appropriate locations by typing **make install** and pressing **Enter**. When

the software install is completed, change back to the original directory by typing **cd ..** and pressing **Enter**.

6. After the *make install* process completes, the command prompt will be displayed once again. To run Wireshark, type **wireshark** and press **Enter**. The GUI will open.

Now you have successfully built Wireshark from the source code! The Wireshark binary installs in /usr/local/bin, so if you don't have that directory in your permanent $PATH, you must add it. Once everything is installed, you may also remove the *.tar.gz files.

**NOTE**

Other programs are listed in the configure output that you may not be familiar with. They are each very useful when you are developing for Wireshark. The idl2wrs program is used by developers to convert a CORBA Interface Definition Language (IDL) file to C source code for a Wireshark plug-in. The randpkt program is used to generate random packet capture files. It can generate different types of packets with a user-specified maximum byte count and the number of packets to create. Finally, the dftest program is a display filter compiler test program. It is used to display filter byte-code for debugging filter routines.

Once the installation is complete, the following programs should now be installed in /usr/local/bin: wireshark, tshark, editcap, mergecap, dumpcap, text2pcap, and idl2wrs. Plugins are installed in /usr/local/lib/wireshark/plugins/0.99.4. Some important resources to note are the files in the wireshark-0.99.4/doc directory. They contain several good README files about the inner workings of Wireshark. Several helpful README files can also be found in the wireshark-0.99.4 directory. Finally, the INSTALL and INSTALL.configure files located in the wireshark-0.99.4 directory are also a good resource.

**NOTE**

The *manuf* file is a text document, located in the /usr/local/share/wireshark directory, that contains a very large listing of well-known vendor MAC addresses. This can come in handy when troubleshooting network problems.

> **NOTE**
>
> The absolute latest version of Wireshark can be downloaded from the automated build section at www.wireshark.org/download/automated. This is the version of Wireshark that the developers are currently working on, so you must be aware that this is a beta version that may contain bugs.

## Enabling and Disabling Features via *configure*

During the *configure* script portion of the build process, you can pass options to the installer to customize the application to your specific needs. The following options were harvested from the INSTALL file in the Wireshark tarball.

> **NOTE**
>
> Running *./configure—help* will give you information on the optional parameters, plus a whole lot more!

- **--sysconfdir=DIR**  Wireshark installs a support file (manuf) in ${PREFIX}/etc by default, where ${PREFIX} comes from --prefix=DIR. If you do not specify any *--prefix* option, ${PREFIX} is "/usr/local". You can change the location of the manuf file with the *—sysconfdir* option.

- **--disable-usr-local**  By default, *configure* will look in /usr/local/{include,lib} for additional header files and libraries. Using this switch keeps configure from looking there.

- **--disable-wireshark**  By default, if *configure* finds the GTK+ libraries, the Makefile builds Wireshark, the GUI packet analyzer. You can disable the build of the GUI version of Wireshark with this switch.

- **--disable-gtk2**  Build Glib/Gtk+ 1.2[.x]–based Wireshark.

- **--disable-tshark**  By default, the line-mode packet analyzer, Tshark, is built. Use this switch to avoid building it.

- **--disable-editcap**  By default, the capture-file editing program is built. Use this switch to avoid building it.

- **--disable-mergecap**  By default, the capture-file merging program is built. Use this switch to avoid building it.

- **--disable-text2pcap**  By default, the hex-dump-to-capture file conversion program is built. Use this switch to avoid building it.

- **--disable-idl2wrs**  By default, the IDL-to-wireshark-dissector-source-code converter is built. Use this switch to avoid building it.

- **--enable-dftest**  By default, the display-filter-compiler test program is not built. Use this switch to build it.

- **--enable-randpkt**  By default, the program that creates random packet-capture files is not built. Use this switch to build it.

- **--without-pcap**  If you choose to build a packet analyzer that can analyze capture files but cannot capture packets on its own, but you *do* have libpcap installed, or if you are trying to build Wireshark on a system that doesn't have libpcap installed (in which case you have no choice but to build a version that can analyze capture files but cannot capture packets on its own), use this option to avoid using libpcap.

- **--with-pcap=DIR**  Use this to tell Wireshark where you have libpcap installed (if it is installed in a nonstandard location).

- **--without-zlib**  By default, if *configure* finds zlib (a.k.a., libz), the wiretap library will be built so that it can read compressed capture files. If you have zlib but do not wish to build it into the wiretap library used by Wireshark, Tshark, and the capture-file utilities that come in this package, use this switch.

- **--with-zlib=DIR**  Use this to tell Wireshark where you have zlib installed, if it is installed in a nonstandard location.

- **--disable-ipv6**  If *configure* finds support for IPv6 name resolution on your system, the packet analyzers will make use of it. To avoid using IPv6 name resolution if you have the support for it, use this switch.

- **--enable-setuid-install**  Use this switch to install the packet analyzers as setuid. Installing Wireshark and Tshark as setuid root is dangerous. Repeat: IT'S DANGEROUS. Don't do it.

- **--with-ssl=DIR**  If your SNMP library requires the SSL library, and your SSL library is installed in a nonstandard location, you can specify where your SSL library is with this switch.

- **--without-net-snmp**  If configure finds a supported version of the Net SNMP library on your system, the SNMP dissector will be enhanced to use routines from that SNMP library. Employ this switch to avoid using the Net SNMP library even if you have it installed.

- **--with-net-snmp=PATH**  Tell the configure script where your net-snmp-config shell script that comes with the Net-SNMP package is located, if not in a standard location.

- **--without-ucd-snmp**  If configure finds a supported version of the UCD SNMP library on your system, the SNMP dissector will be enhanced to use routines from that SNMP library. Use this switch to avoid using the UCD SNMP library even if you have it installed.

- **--with-ucd-snmp=DIR**  Tell the configure script where your UCD SNMP library is located, if not in a standard location.

- **--without-plugins**  By default, if your system can support run-time loadable modules, the packet analyzers are built with support for plug-ins. Use this switch to build packet analyzers without plug-in support.

- **--with-plugins=DIR**  By default, plug-ins are installed in ${LIBDIR}/wireshark/plugins/${VERSION}. ${LIBDIR} can be set with —*libdir*, or they default to ${EPREFIX/lib}. ${EPREFIX} can be set with —*exec-prefix*, or iy can default to ${PREFIX}. ${VERSION} is the Wireshark version. Use this switch to change the location where plug-ins are installed.

# Summary

In this chapter, we covered the basics of Wireshark installation, including RPM and source-code packages. We also covered complete installations of the libpcap and WinPcap libraries, as well as Wireshark for Windows, Mac OS X, and UNIX-based and Windows systems. We also learned how to install the necessary prerequisite software, and troubleshoot dependency issues. You are now armed with the knowledge and software necessary to continue with this book.

As stated previously in this chapter, it is important to keep your Wireshark installation up-to-date. This includes the packet capture libraries, the supporting prerequisite software, and the Wireshark software itself. You should also visit the Wireshark site frequently to keep up on the latest announcements, as well as subscribe to some of the mailing lists. We also strongly recommend you keep your OS up-to-date as well, especially when it comes to security updates and patches. Computer security is an ever-changing technology, and it is necessary to keep up with things to avoid system compromises.

All of these parts will come together to form a solid network analysis system that will assist your network troubleshooting and security efforts for years to come.

# Solutions Fast Track

## Getting Wireshark

- ☑ Wireshark can be downloaded as binaries or source code.
- ☑ Wireshark binaries are available for a number of platforms.
- ☑ The packages you will need for installing Wireshark are available for free on the Internet at their respective Web sites.

## Packet Capture Drivers

- ☑ Packet capture drivers are responsible for capturing the raw network packets.
- ☑ libpcap is a packet capture library for Unix systems; Windows uses WinPcap.
- ☑ Sometimes RPMs are a version or two behind the current source-code release.
- ☑ Wireshark must have libpcap (or WinPcap) installed to capture packets.
- ☑ Libpcap can be installed from a binary or source code.

☑ Uninstall older versions of WinPcap before installing newer ones.

# Installing Wireshark on Windows

☑ Wireshark installs WinPcap for you if selected.

☑ Uninstall Wireshark by using the uninstall.exe program.

☑ Wireshark for Windows also installs tshark, editcap, mergcap, and text2pcap.

# Installing Wireshark on Linux

☑ Yellow dog Updater, Modified (YUM) installs Wireshark and all its dependencies automatically.

☑ When using YUM, you must install the Wireshark-gnome package to get the Wireshark GUI.

☑ You may also install the individual Wireshark RPMs for your Linux system, but this can be a tricky process due to dependencies.

# Installing Wireshark on Mac OS X

☑ You may install Wireshark on Mac OS X using DarwinPorts, Fink, or by compiling from source code.

☑ You must have Xcode Tools and the X11 user environment installed on your Mac OS to run Wireshark.

☑ DarwinPorts and Fink will install Wireshark and its dependencies for you automatically.

# Installing Wireshark from Source

☑ Wireshark source-compiling prerequisites include libpcap, GTK+, and Glib.

☑ Source code installs are accomplished with the configure | make | make install process.

☑ Installing from source code gives you more control over the installation process.

☑ Installing from source gives you access to the source code and additional documentation.

☑ Wireshark installs by default in the /usr/local/bin directory.

☑ Many options to the configure script are available to customize your install.

# Frequently Asked Questions

The following Frequently Asked Questions, answered by the authors of this book, are designed to both measure your understanding of the concepts presented in this chapter and to assist you with real-life implementation of these concepts. To have your questions about this chapter answered by the author, browse to **www.syngress.com/solutions** and click on the **"Ask the Author"** form.

**Q:** Can I mix methods of installation? For example, can I install libpcap with the RPM and then build Wireshark from source, or vice-versa?

**A:** Yes, you can, as long as your OS supports the methods you are trying to use. Depending on the method, you may have to adjust your $PATH variable for the install to find the necessary dependencies.

**Q:** What if I installed Wireshark and then later upgraded to GTK+2?

**A:** No problem, just re-run the *configure* script for Wireshark and then run *make* and *make install* again. Wireshark will automatically detect GTK+2 and use that version.

**Q:** A new version of Wireshark was released and I want to upgrade. How do I do that?

**A:** For Linux, you would use the *rpm −Uvh* command or *yum*. For Windows, simply run the new executable and it will upgrade your current version. For Mac OS X using DarwinPorts, you may use the *port upgrade wireshark* command. If you have compiled the code from source, you will need to perform the *configure | make | make install* process again for the new version

**Q:** A new version of WinPcap was released. How do I upgrade to it?

**A:** First, go to the directory with your current version of WinPcap (usually C:\Program Files\WinPcap) and run the uninstall.exe program. Reboot and proceed with installing the executable for the new version.

**Q:** I installed everything and it looks like it worked okay, but when I try to run Wireshark it says it can't find it?

**A:** Make sure the Wireshark directory is in the proper path—for example, */usr/local/bin*.

**Q:** Why do I have to install all this other stuff just to compile Wireshark?

**A:** Wireshark is a feature-rich, multifaceted software program. It relies on the details of some previously written libraries to take care of the low-level functions.

# Chapter 4

# Using Wireshark

## Solutions in this chapter:

- **Getting Started with Wireshark**
- **Exploring the Main Window**
- **Other Window Components**
- **Exploring the Menus**
- **Using Command-line Options**

☑ **Summary**

☑ **Solutions Fast Track**

☑ **Frequently Asked Questions**

# Introduction

Wireshark provides insight into what is occurring on a network, which is useful when implementing protocols, debugging network applications, testing networks, and debugging live networks. In situations involving interaction with a network at a technical level, most problems can be resolved using Wireshark.

Wireshark is an excellent educational aid. Being able to see and analyze network traffic is very instructive. This chapter covers the main components of the Wireshark Graphical User Interface (GUI), including:

- Main window
- Menu bar
- Tool bar
- Summary window
- Protocol Tree window
- Data View window
- Filter bar
- Information field
- Display information

This chapter also covers the context-sensitive pop-up windows available in the Summary window, the Protocol Tree window, and the Data View window. It also explains the various dialog boxes that are launched by the menus and toolbars.

You will learn how to perform basic tasks in Wireshark (e.g., capturing network traffic, loading and saving capture files, performing basic filtering, printing packets) using the advanced tools provided by Wireshark. Examples have been provided to show you step-by-step how some of the less obvious areas of Wireshark work.

# Getting Started with Wireshark

You can download binary packages for Wireshark from the Wireshark Web site at www.wireshark.com. If there are no binary packages available for your platform, or if they are not up-to-date, or if they are compiled without the options you need, you can download the source code from the Wireshark Web site and compile Wireshark using the following command:

```
wireshark
```

To launch Wireshark on Windows, select **Start | Programs | Wireshark | Wireshark**. The Main window of the Wireshark application will now be displayed. Select **File | Open** and browse to the captures/chap-04 folder on the CD, then open bgp.pcap.

# Exploring the Main Window

It is important to define a common set of labels for the different components of the Main window. Figure 4.1 shows the Main window of Wireshark with its major components labeled.

**Figure 4.1** Main Window

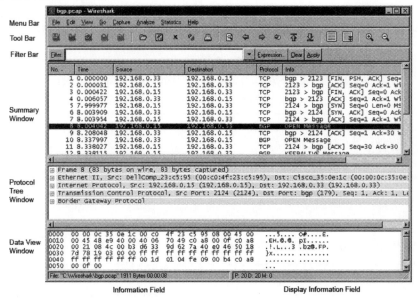

The Main window components are described in Table 4.1.

**Table 4.1** Main Window Components

| Window Component | Description |
| --- | --- |
| Menu Bar | A typical application menu bar containing drop-down menu items. |
| Tool Bar | Contains buttons for some commonly used functions of Wireshark. The Tool Bar icons have tool tips that are displayed when you pause the mouse pointer over them. |

**Continued**

**Table 4.1** Main Window Components

| Window Component | Description |
|---|---|
| Filter Bar | Applies filters to the Summary window to restrict which packets in the capture are displayed, based on their attributes. |
| Summary Window | Provides a one-line summary for each packet in the capture. |
| Protocol Tree Window | Provides a detailed decode of the packet selected in the Summary window. |
| Data View Window | Provides a view of the raw data in the packet selected in the Summary window. |
| Information Field | A display area that provides information about the capture or field selected in the Protocol Tree window. |
| Display Information Field | A display area that provides information about the packet count in the current capture |

## Summary Window

The Summary window displays a summary of each packet (one per line) in a capture. One or more columns of summary data are displayed for each packet. Typical columns are shown in Table 4.2.

**Table 4.2** Summary Window Columns

| Column Name | Description |
|---|---|
| No. | The frame number within the capture. |
| Time | The time from the beginning of the capture to the time when the packet was captured (in seconds). |
| Source | This is the highest level source address, (frequently the Internet Protocol (IP) address); however, it can also be the Media Access Control (MAC) address for layer 2 Ethernet protocols, or other address types for other protocols (e.g., Internetwork Packet Exchange [IPX], Appletalk, and so forth). (See the Wireshark "Name Resolution" sidebar for a discussion of MAC addresses.) |

**Continued**

**Table 4.2 continued** Summary Window Columns

| Column Name | Description |
| --- | --- |
| Destination | This is the highest level destination address (frequently the IP destination address); however, it can also be the MAC address for layer 2 Ethernet protocols, or other address types for other protocols (IPX, Appletalk, and so forth). |
| Protocol | Typically the highest level protocol that is decoded. Examples include user-level protocols such as Hypertext Transfer Protocol (HTTP), File Transfer Protocol (FTP), and Simple Mail Transfer Protocol (SMTP). |
| Info | This field contains information that was determined by the highest level decode to be useful or informative as part of a summary for this packet. |

The "Preferences" feature can be used to select which columns are displayed in the Summary window. Go to **Edit | Preferences** from the Menu bar.

The summary information for the packet selected in the Summary window in Figure 4.1, is shown in Table 4.3.

**Table 4.3** Summary Window Column

| Column Name | Value |
| --- | --- |
| No. | 8 |
| Time | 8.004042 seconds since the capture started |
| Source | IP number *192.168.0.15* |
| Destination | IP number *192.168.0.33* |
| Protocol | Border Gateway Protocol (BGP) |
| Info | OPEN Message |

We immediately see that this packet is carrying a message for opening a BGP session between *192.168.0.15* and *192.168.0.33*. (More information on BGP is available in Request for Comment (RFC) 1771 at www.ietf.org/rfc/rfc1771.txt?number=1771.) Select packets in the Summary window by clicking on the row summarizing a given packet. The information for the selected packet is then displayed in the Protocol Tree window and the Data View window. Once you have selected a packet in the Summary window, you can use the Protocol Tree window to go into greater detail.

# Protocol Tree Window

Conceptualize a packet as a tree of fields and subtrees. For each protocol, there is a tree node that can be expanded to provide the values in that protocol's fields. Within some protocols, there may be tree nodes summarizing more complicated data structures in the protocol. These tree nodes can be expanded to show those data structures. For any given node that has a subtree, you can expand its subtree to reveal more information, or collapse it to only show the summary. The Protocol Tree window allows you to examine the tree created by Wireshark from decoding a packet.

Now we'll examine the Protocol Tree window in the packet that was selected in the previous example (see Figure 4.2).

**Figure 4.2** Protocol Tree Window Collapsed

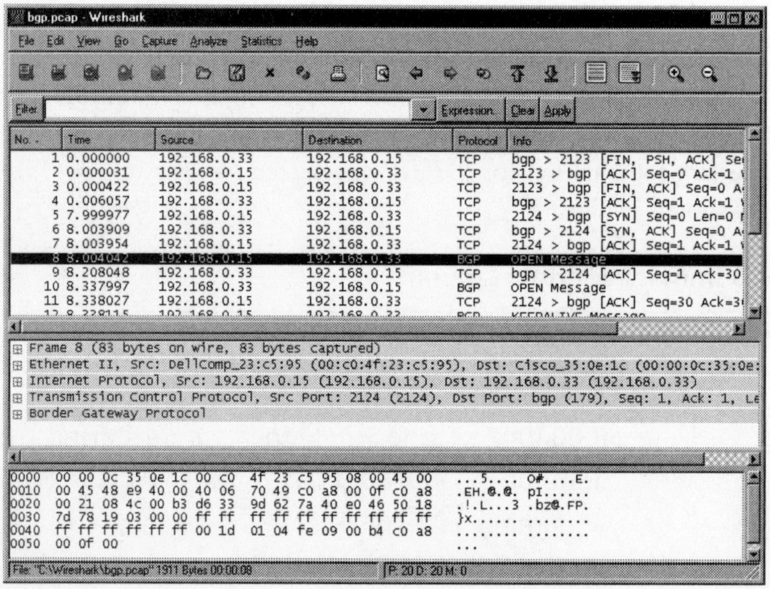

In the Protocol Tree window, each layer in the protocol stack for this packet contains a one-line summary of that layer (see Table 4.4).

**Table 4.4** Protocol Layer Example

| Layer | Protocol | Description |
|---|---|---|
| Packet Meta Data | Frame | 83 bytes on wire, 83 bytes captured |
| Data Link ( Layer 2/L2 ) | Ethernet II | Src Addr: 00:c0:4f:23:c5:95, Dst Addr: 00:00:0c:35:0e:1c |

**Continued**

**Table 4.4 continued** Protocol Layer Example

| Layer | Protocol | Description |
|---|---|---|
| Network ( Layer 3/L3 ) | IP | Src Addr: 192.168.0.15, Dst Addr: 192.168.0.33 |
| Transport ( Layer 4/L4) | Transmission Control Protocol (TCP) | Src Port: 2124, Dst Port: bgp(179), Seq: 2593706850, Ack … |
| Application Layer ( Layer 7/L7) | BGP | |

Each of these layers have plus (+) signs next to them, which indicate that there is a subtree that can be expanded to provide more information about that particular protocol.

In Figure 4.3, the BGP tree was expanded to reveal one OPEN message, and then the OPEN message was expanded to reveal the fields contained within.

**Figure 4.3** Protocol Tree Window Expanded

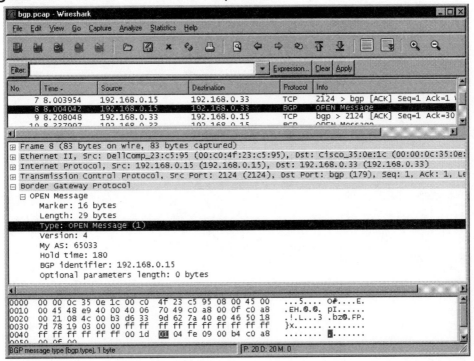

Selecting the Type field in the Protocol Tree window displayed the message, "BGP message type (*bgp.type*), 1byte." This indicates the long name of this field (BGP message type), the display filter field name used to identify this field for filtering and colorization (*bgp.type*), and the size of this field in the packet (1 byte).

# Data View Window

The Data View window contains a series of rows that each begin with a four-digit number that represents the number of bytes in an octet. (An octet is comprised of either 8 bits, 1 byte, or 2 hexadecimal digits). The first octet in that row is offset from the beginning of the packet (see Figure 4.4). This offset is then followed by 16 two-character hexadecimal bytes. The last item in each row is a series of 16 American Standard Code for Information Interchange (ASCII) characters representing the same 16 bytes from the packet. Not all bytes can be displayed in ASCII. For those bytes, a period (.) is substituted as a placeholder.

**Figure 4.4** Data View Window

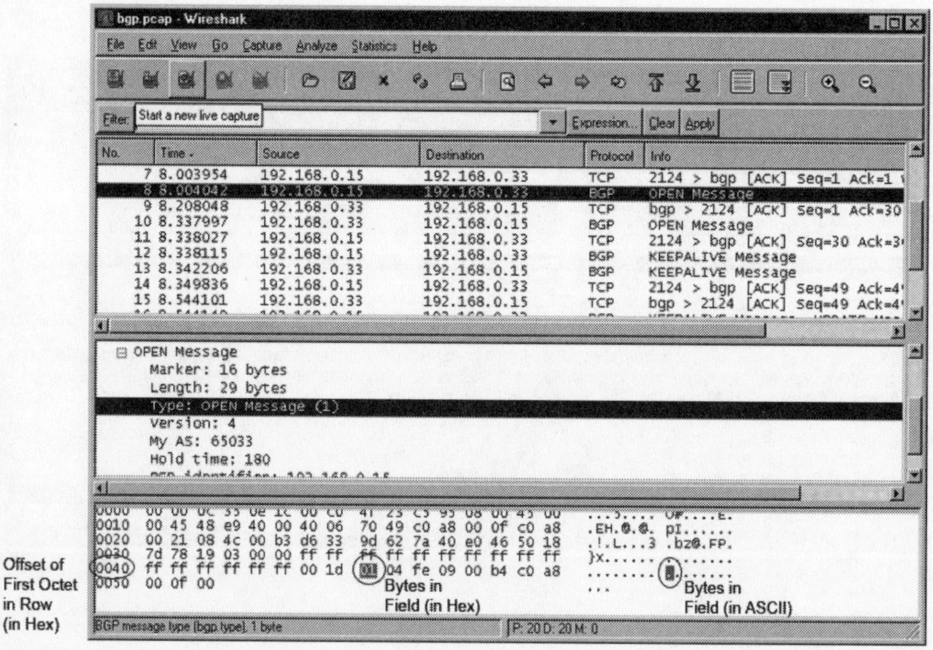

When a field in the Protocol Tree window is selected, the bytes corresponding to that field are highlighted in the Data View window. In Figure 4.4 we selected the BGP Message Type field in the Protocol Tree window. In the Data View window, that byte is highlighted in the row with offset *0040* representing *0×40* hexadecimal or 64 bytes into the packet. The ninth byte in the row is highlighted, and has a value of *01* hexadecimal. In the ASCII representation, there is a period (.), because the value *0×01* is not represented in ASCII.

When you click on a hexadecimal byte or ASCII character in the Data View window, Wireshark highlights the field in the Protocol Tree window that corresponds to the selected byte and to all of the bytes in the Data View window associated with that Protocol field.

In Figure 4.5, we clicked on the beginning of row 0030 (note that the 48th byte [0030 or hexadecimal *0×30*] is the first byte of the 2-byte TCP Window Size field). As a result, the TCP Protocol Tree was automatically expanded and the Window Size field was highlighted. Additionally, the second byte (78 hexadecimal) in the 0030 row was also selected, because the TCP Window Size field is a 2-byte field.

This feature makes it easy to use the Protocol Tree window and the Data View window together, in order to obtain a solid grasp of the relationships between the fields in a protocol and the actual bits on the wire.

**Figure 4.5** Data View Window Byte Selection

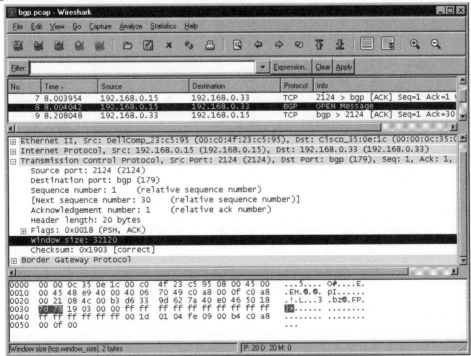

# Other Window Components

The following are additional various components of the Wireshark window that you will find useful when examining packets.

## Filter Bar

The Filter Bar (see Figure 4.6) allows you to enter a filter string that restricts which packets are displayed in the Summary window. Only packets that match the display filter string are displayed in the Summary window. A display filter string defines the conditions on a packet that may or may not match the packet (e.g., the display filter string *(ip.addr == 10.15.162.1 && bgp)* would match all packets with an IP address [source or destination] of *10.15.162.1* that are BGP protocol packets).

**Figure 4.6** Filter Bar

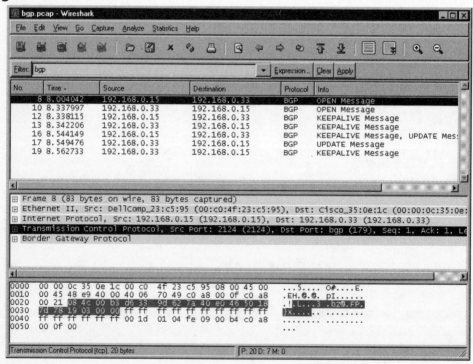

In Figure 4.6, a bgp filter has been applied. To apply a filter, enter the desired string into the Filter: text field and press **Enter** (or click the **Apply** button). Note that filter strings are case-sensitive; therefore, filter string BGP (uppercase) will not work. (Traditionally, filter string labels such as bgp are entirely in lowercase.) Also note that the Filter Bar text field has three different background colors, which indicate the status of the current filter. When the Filter Bar text field changes color, white indicates that there is no current filter, green indicates that a filter has valid syntax, and red indicates that the filter is incomplete or the syntax is invalid.

> **NOTE**
>
> Even though the Filter Bar text field is green (indicating a valid filter), it may not have been applied. When the field is red, Wireshark does not allow an invalid filter to be applied, and provides a warning message if you attempt to apply it.

Once the display filter string bgp is applied, only BGP packets are displayed in the Summary window. The No. column displays jumps between the frame numbers of the displayed packets, because there are packets in the capture that are being suppressed by the bgp filter string. Previously used filters can be easily recalled (see Figure 4.7).

**Figure 4.7** Filter Bar Drop-down List

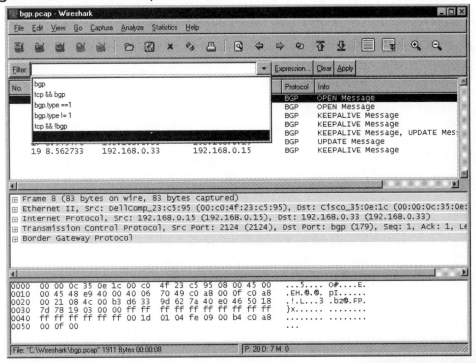

By clicking the drop-down arrow at the end of the Filter field, you can access a list of previously applied filters. To use one of these filters, select it from the list and press **Enter** or click the **Apply** button. To remove the currently displayed filter string and redisplay all packets, click the **Reset** button. If you click the **Filter:** button, the Display Filter dialog box will be displayed.

---

**NOTE**

To remove items from the Filter drop-down list, edit the *RECENT* file under the user's profile under *C:\Documents and Settings\<user>\Application Data\Wireshark*. Remove the appropriate lines from the RECENT file located in the "Recent Display Filters" section.

---

# Information Field

The Information field displays the name of the capture file, or information about the protocol field selected in the Protocol Tree window.

# Display Information Field

The Display Information field displays the number of packets displayed in or filtered from the Summary window. $P$ indicates the number of total packets, $D$ indicates the total displayed packets, and $M$ indicates the total marked packets.

# Exploring the Menus

All of the functionality available within Wireshark is accessible from the Menu bar. In this section, we systematically explore that functionality and provide examples of its use.

## File

The File menu provides access to loading, saving, and printing capture files (see Figure 4.8). The File menu options are defined in Table 4.5.

**Figure 4.8** File Menu

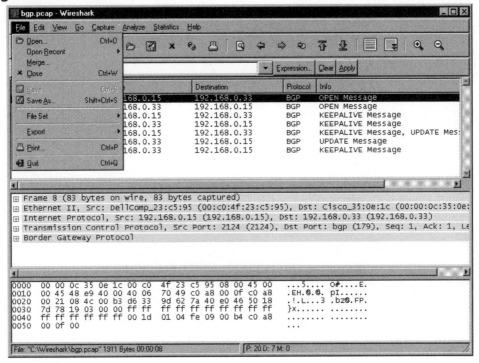

**Table 4.5** File Menu Options

| Menu Option | Description |
| --- | --- |
| Open... | Opens a capture file. |
| Open Recent | Displays the Open Recent submenu to open a capture file from a list of recently used capture files. |
| Merge | Merges one or more capture files with the current capture file. |
| Close | Closes the current capture file. |
| Save | Saves the current capture file. |
| Save As... | Saves the current capture file with a different filename/format. |
| File Set | Displays the File Set submenu for file set information and navigation |
| Export | Displays the Export submenu, allowing the portion of the packet highlighted in the Data View window to be exported as a hexadecimal dump. |
| Print... | Prints the current capture file. |
| Quit | Quits the Wireshark application. |

# Open

To open a file select **File | Open** (see Figure 4.9).

**Figure 4.9** Open Dialog Box

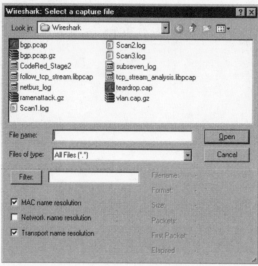

The Open dialog box provides normal mechanisms for navigation in selecting a file. Additionally, it provides a Filter: field where a Wireshark display filter string can be entered to filter out which packets are read from the capture file. Clicking the **Filter:** button opens the Display Filter dialog box (described in the "Analyze" section).

The Open dialog box also has checkboxes to enable name resolution for MAC addresses, network names, and transport names. To open a file, browse to the correct location and select the desired file, optionally provide a filter string, and enable or disable the name resolutions you want to use. Finally, click the **OK** button.

## Notes from the Underground...

### Wireshark Name Resolution

Wireshark provides three kinds of name resolution to make the numbers found in network protocols more comprehensible. You can choose to enable or disable MAC name resolution, network name resolution, and transport name resolution,

**Continued**

when opening a file, starting a capture, or while a capture is running. It is useful to understand what the different name resolutions mean.

Every host on a LAN is identified by a 6-byte MAC address, which is used in Ethernet frames to provide source and destination addresses at the Data Link layer. MAC addresses are globally unique. To achieve this, the Institute of Electrical and Electronic Engineers (IEEE) assigns blocks of MAC addresses to manufacturers. The first 3 bytes of every MAC address designate the manufacturer who produced the device. When you select the **Enable MAC name resolution** checkbox in the Open dialog box, Wireshark resolves the first 3 bytes of the MAC address to a manufacturer and displays that information for each MAC address (e.g. the prefix *00:00:0c* has been assigned to Cisco Systems). When MAC address resolution is enabled, Wireshark displays the MAC address *00:00:0c:35:0e 1c* as *00:00:0c:35:0e:1c (Cisco_35:0e:1c)*.

Every node on an IP network has an IP address. When you select the **Enable network name resolution** checkbox, Wireshark performs a reverse Domain Name System (DNS) lookup when it encounters an IP address, to determine its associated domain name (e.g., www.syngress.com). Wireshark then displays this domain name with the IP address (e.g., IP address *66.35.250.150* can be resolved via reverse DNS to the domain name *slashdot.org* If network name resolution is enabled, Wireshark displays it as *slashdot.org (66.35.250.150)*.

Transport layer protocols like TCP and User Datagram Protocol (UDP) typically provide some form of multiplexing by allowing a source and destination port to be specified. As a result, two hosts can have multiple clearly delineated conversations at the same time, as long as they have unique source port and destination port pairs for each conversation. Many protocols that use TCP or UDP for their Transport layer have well-known ports that servers listen in on. When you select the **Enable transport name resolution** checkbox, Wireshark displays the name of the service that traditionally runs over each port. This behavior can be seen in many of the examples in this chapter, where port 179 was labeled by the protocol that is known to run over that port: *bgp*. It's important to note that most ports have no protocols associated with them.

# Save As

The Save As dialog box is displayed by selecting **File | Save As** (or by selecting **File | Save** for a capture that was previously saved). (See Figure 4.10.)

The Save As dialog box allows you to perform normal tasks for saving a capture file in the desired location and with the desired name. You can save various subsets of the packets by selecting different radio options in the Packet Range section (e.g., only the packets that pass the currently active display filter) by enabling the **All packets** radio button while selecting the **Displayed** column radio button. To save only marked packets that pass the currently active display filter, select the **Marked Packets** radio button while selecting the **Displayed** column radio button.

**Figure 4.10** The Save As Dialog Box

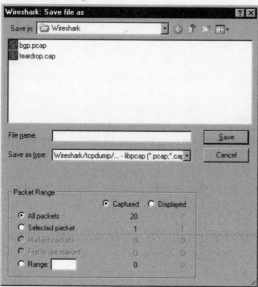

Finally, save the file in one of the supported capture file formats (see Figure 4.11).

**Figure 4.11** File Formats

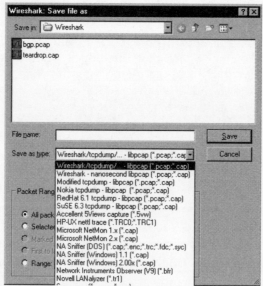

# Print

The Print dialog box is displayed by selecting **File | Print** (see Figure 4.12).

**Figure 4.12** Print Dialog Box

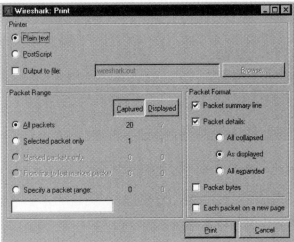

The Print dialog box helps answer the relevant questions regarding printing in Wireshark:

- How am I going to print?
- Which packets am I going to print?
- What information am I going to print for each packet?

The Printer section allows you to choose which packets you are going to print. You can choose your output format to be either Plaintext or Postscript. Once you have selected your output format, you may choose to print the output to a file by enabling the **Output to File:** checkbox and providing a filename in the **Output to File:** text box. If you do not choose to print to file, you can provide a command to be executed to print in the **Print command:** text box. This option is not available on Windows.

The Print Range section allows you to choose which packets you are going to print. You may choose to print only the packet currently selected in the Summary window, only packets that are marked in the Summary window, all packets displayed in the Summary window by the currently applied filter, or all packets captured. You can choose to print only the packet currently selected in the Summary window by selecting the **Selected packet only** radio button and the **Captured** column button. To print only the packets that have been marked in the Summary window, select the **Marked packets only** radio button and the **Captured** column button. To print all of the packets between the first and last marked packets, select the **From first to last marked packet** radio button and the **Captured** column button. If you want the current filter to apply, select the **Displayed** column button. By selecting the **Specify a packet range** radio button, Wireshark allows you to specify a packet range entered in a comma separated list (e.g., *1-12,15,17,17-19*). To print all packets displayed in the Summary window by the currently applied display filter, select the **All packets displayed** radio button and the **Displayed** column button. Printing all packets displayed or captured means that all of the packets that pass the currently applied filter will print. When you scroll up and down to a packet in the Summary window, it is considered to be "displayed" for the purposes of this print range option. You can print all packets in the capture by selecting the **All packets** radio button and the **Captured** column button.

The Packet Format section allows you to choose which information you want to print for each packet. If you do not enable the **Print packet details** checkbox, a one-line summary consisting of the columns currently being displayed in the Summary window, will be printed for each packet If the **Print packet details** checkbox is not selected, the result of just printing the selected packet ( packet 8 ) would be:

```
No. Time        Source        Destination    Protocol Info
  8 8.004042   192.168.0.15   192.168.0.33   BGP      OPEN Message
```

The Packet Details section allows you to choose which details are printed for a packet when you enable the **Print packet details** checkbox. You may choose to print the protocol tree with all subtrees collapsed, with subtrees expanded in the Protocol Tree window, or with all subtrees in the protocol tree expanded. If you select the **All collapsed** option, the protocol tree prints with all subtrees collapsed. When printing only the selected packet, the output would look like:

```
Frame 8 (83 bytes on wire, 83 bytes captured)
Ethernet II, Src: 00:c0:4f:23:c5:95, Dst: 00:00:0c:35:0e:1c
Internet Protocol, Src Addr: 192.168.0.15 (192.168.0.15), Dst Addr:
192.168.0.33 (192.168.0.33)
Transmission Control Protocol, Src Port: 2124 (2124), Dst Port: bgp (179),
Seq: 3593706850, Ack: 2051072070, Len: 29
Border Gateway Protocol
```

If you select the **As displayed** option, the protocol tree is printed with the subtrees that would be expanded in the Protocol Tree window if that packet was selected in the Summary window. Using this option to print only the selected packet would produce output like:

```
Frame 8 (83 bytes on wire, 83 bytes captured)

Ethernet II, Src: 00:c0:4f:23:c5:95, Dst: 00:00:0c:35:0e:1c

Internet Protocol, Src Addr: 192.168.0.15 (192.168.0.15), Dst Addr:
192.168.0.33 (192.168.0.33)

Transmission Control Protocol, Src Port: 2124 (2124), Dst Port: bgp (179),
Seq: 3593706850, Ack: 2051072070, Len: 29

Border Gateway Protocol

    OPEN Message

        Marker: 16 bytes

        Length: 29 bytes

        Type: OPEN Message (1)

        Version: 4

        My AS: 65033

        Hold time: 180

        BGP identifier: 192.168.0.15

        Optional parameters length: 0 bytes
```

If you select the **All expanded** option, the protocol tree will be printed with all subtrees expanded. Printing just the selected packet would produce the output:

```
Frame 8 (83 bytes on wire, 83 bytes captured)

    Arrival Time: Mar 29, 2000 23:56:56.957322000

    Time delta from previous packet: 0.000088000 seconds

    Time since reference or first frame: 8.004042000 seconds

    Frame Number: 8

    Packet Length: 83 bytes

    Capture Length: 83 bytes

Ethernet II, Src: 00:c0:4f:23:c5:95, Dst: 00:00:0c:35:0e:1c

    Destination: 00:00:0c:35:0e:1c (Cisco_35:0e:1c)

    Source: 00:c0:4f:23:c5:95 (DellComp_23:c5:95)

    Type: IP (0x0800)

Internet Protocol, Src Addr: 192.168.0.15 (192.168.0.15), Dst Addr:
192.168.0.33 (192.168.0.33)

    Version: 4

    Header length: 20 bytes
```

    Differentiated Services Field: 0x00 (DSCP 0x00: Default; ECN: 0x00)

        0000 00.. = Differentiated Services Codepoint: Default (0x00)

        .... ..0. = ECN-Capable Transport (ECT): 0

        .... ...0 = ECN-CE: 0

    Total Length: 69

    Identification: 0x48e9 (18665)

    Flags: 0x04

        .1.. = Don't fragment: Set

        ..0. = More fragments: Not set

    Fragment offset: 0

    Time to live: 64

    Protocol: TCP (0x06)

    Header checksum: 0x7049 (correct)

    Source: 192.168.0.15 (192.168.0.15)

    Destination: 192.168.0.33 (192.168.0.33)

Transmission Control Protocol, Src Port: 2124 (2124), Dst Port: bgp (179), Seq: 3593706850, Ack: 2051072070, Len: 29

    Source port: 2124 (2124)

    Destination port: bgp (179)

    Sequence number: 3593706850

    Next sequence number: 3593706879

    Acknowledgement number: 2051072070

    Header length: 20 bytes

    Flags: 0x0018 (PSH, ACK)

        0... .... = Congestion Window Reduced (CWR): Not set

        .0.. .... = ECN-Echo: Not set

        ..0. .... = Urgent: Not set

        ...1 .... = Acknowledgment: Set

        .... 1... = Push: Set

        .... .0.. = Reset: Not set

        .... ..0. = Syn: Not set

        .... ...0 = Fin: Not set

    Window size: 32120

    Checksum: 0x1903 (correct)

Border Gateway Protocol

    OPEN Message

        Marker: 16 bytes

        Length: 29 bytes

```
Type: OPEN Message (1)
Version: 4
My AS: 65033
Hold time: 180
BGP identifier: 192.168.0.15
Optional parameters length: 0 bytes
```

Regardless of the option you choose for expanding protocol tree subtrees, if you enable the **Packet bytes** checkbox, following the protocol tree for each packet will be a hexadecimal dump of that packet. Printing only the packet with the **All dissections collapsed** checkbox enabled and the **Packet bytes** checkbox enabled would produce this output:

```
Frame 8 (83 bytes on wire, 83 bytes captured)
Ethernet II, Src: 00:c0:4f:23:c5:95, Dst: 00:00:0c:35:0e:1c
Internet Protocol, Src Addr: 192.168.0.15 (192.168.0.15), Dst Addr:
192.168.0.33 (192.168.0.33)
Transmission Control Protocol, Src Port: 2124 (2124), Dst Port: bgp (179),
Seq: 3593706850, Ack: 2051072070, Len: 29
Border Gateway Protocol


0000  00 00 0c 35 0e 1c 00 c0 4f 23 c5 95 08 00 45 00   ...5....O#....E.
0010  00 45 48 e9 40 00 40 06 70 49 c0 a8 00 0f c0 a8   .EH.@.@.pI......
0020  00 21 08 4c 00 b3 d6 33 9d 62 7a 40 e0 46 50 18   .!.L...3.bz@.FP.
0030  7d 78 19 03 00 00 ff ff ff ff ff ff ff ff ff ff   }x.............
0040  ff ff ff ff ff ff 00 1d 01 04 fe 09 00 b4 c0 a8   ...............
0050  00 0f 00                                          ...
```

If the **Each Packet on a new page** checkbox is selected, each new packet that is printed starts on a new page.

# Edit

The Edit menu (see Figure 4.13) allows you to find and mark packets and set user preferences. Descriptions of the Edit menu options are given in Table 4.6.

**Figure 4.13** Edit Menu

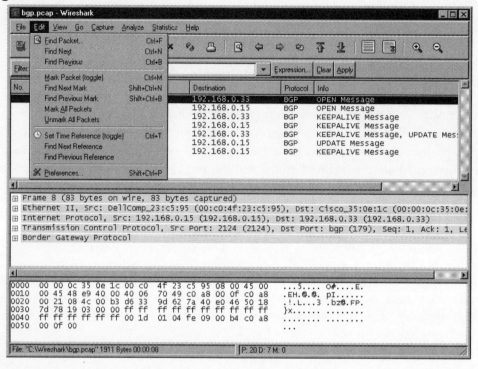

**Table 4.6** Edit Menu Options

| Menu Option | Description |
|---|---|
| Find Packet... | Searches for a packet using a display filter or by searching for a matching hexadecimal string or character string. |
| Find Next | Finds the next packet that matches the search defined in the Find Packet dialog box. |
| Find Previous | Finds the previous packet that matches the search defined in the Find Packet dialog box. |
| Mark Packet | Marks the packet currently selected in the Summary window. Marking provides a mechanism for manually selecting a packet or group of packets to be subsequently printed or saved. |
| Find Next Mark | Finds and highlights the next marked packet in the capture. |

**Continued**

**Table 4.6** Edit Menu Options

| Menu Option | Description |
| --- | --- |
| Find Previous Mark | Finds and highlights the previously marked packet in the capture. |
| Mark All Packets | Marks all packets that match the currently applied display filter. |
| Unmark All Packets | Unmarks all packets that match the currently applied display filter. |
| Set Time Reference (toggle) | Toggles the Time Reference flag for the currently selected packet. |
| Find Next Reference | Finds and highlights the next marked time reference packet in the capture. |
| Find Previous Reference | Finds and highlights the previous marked time reference packet in the capture. |
| Preferences... | Change user preferences, including preferences for packet decodes. |

# Find Packet

The Find Packet dialog box is displayed when you select **Edit | Find Packet...**
(see Figure 4.14).

**Figure 4.14** Find Packet Dialog Box

The Find Packet dialog box helps answer relevant questions regarding finding a
packet in Wireshark:

- What am I trying to find?
- Which direction should I search in?

The **Filter:** text box allows you to define a search criterion by entering a string such as a display filter or hexadecimal or ASCII string. If you need assistance constructing a filter string, click the **Filter:** button to display the Display Filter dialog box.

The **Direction** section allows you to choose which direction you want to search in: *forward* from the packet currently selected in the Summary window, or *backward* from the packet currently selected in the Summary window.

The **Find Syntax** section allows you to define your search criteria. You can choose to search for packets that match a display filter string, a hexadecimal string, or a character string. If you select the **Display Filter** option, the string in the **Filter:** text box will be interpreted as a display filter string and you will search for matches to that display filter string. If you select the **Hex** option, the string in the **Filter:** text box will be interpreted as a hexadecimal string and will search for packets that contain that string.

If you select the **String** option, the string in the **Filter:** will be interpreted as a character string and you will search for packets that contain that character string.

The search for character strings is handled differently than the search for hexadecimal strings. Hexadecimal string searches attempt to search for a packet containing a particular sequence of bytes anywhere in the raw data of that packet. The search for character strings will not look for a packet that contains a string anywhere in the packet. Instead, you can use the **Search In** section to specify whether to look for the string in the **Packet data** left over after decoding all possible fields, look for the character string in the **Decoded packet** displayed in the Protocol Tree window, or look for the character string in the one-line **Packet summary** in the Summary window. If you select the **Packet data** option, Wireshark will search for the character string in the packet data. By packet data, we mean the data in the packet that is left over after decoding the protocol fields. Selecting the **Find Decoded packet** will cause Wireshark to search for the character string in the protocol field strings that are displayed in the Protocol Tree window. It does not matter if the subtree of the protocol tree containing the character string is collapsed or expanded. If you use the **Decoded packet** option, you must also use the **Character Set** drop-down list to select the character set for the character string you are trying to find. To make your character string search case-insensitive, enable the **Case Insensitive Search** checkbox.

# Set Time Reference (toggle)

The **Set Time Reference (toggle)** menu option will toggle the time reference flag in the Summary window so that we may perform some time calculation based upon the marked packet. When the **Time** column in the Summary window is configured to display the time that has elapsed since the beginning of the capture, then the time displayed is the number of seconds since the beginning of the capture or the last time reference packet.

In Figure 4.15 below, we have set packets 5 and 10 as time reference packets. This is indicated by their **Time** column value (*REF*). Packets 1-4 are marked with the time since the beginning of the capture in which they were captured. Packets 6-9 are marked with the time since the time reference packet 5. Packets 11 and greater are marked with the time since the time reference packet 10.

**Figure 4.15** Set Time Reference (toggle) Example

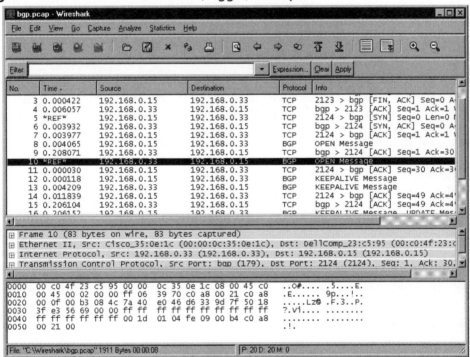

## Preferences

The Preferences dialog box, shown in Figure 4.16, is displayed when you select **Edit | Preferences...**.

The Preferences dialog box allows you to set preferences for various subsystems of Wireshark, including setting preferences for decodes of various protocols. To edit preferences for an area of Wireshark, like **Columns** in Figure 4.16, select that area

www.syngress.com

**Figure 4.16** Preferences Dialog Box

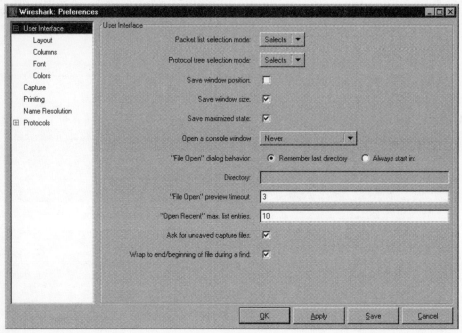

from the box on the left and change the settings displayed in the box on the right. It is strongly recommended that you browse through the protocol preferences for any protocol you use frequently, as protocol preferences can change the way a protocol is decoded or displayed.

When you have made your changes to Wireshark's preferences you can choose to apply them without closing the Preference dialog box by clicking the **Apply** button. To apply your settings and close the Preferences dialog box, click the **OK** button. To save your preferences for use in a different Wireshark session, click the **Save** button.

**NOTE**

The **Columns** preference, selected in Figure 4.18, is subtly broken in Wireshark. You can add, delete, or reorder columns in the Preferences dialog box, but your changes will not take effect unless you save them, then exit and restart Wireshark. As an upgrade to previous versions, this note is mentioned in the **Preferences** dialog box.

# View

The **View** menu, shown in Figure 4.17, allows you to control GUI toolbar elements as well as how packets are displayed in the Summary window and the Protocol Tree window. You can also set up color filters to color the packets in the Summary window. The **View** menu options are described in Table 4.8.

**Figure 4.17** View Menu

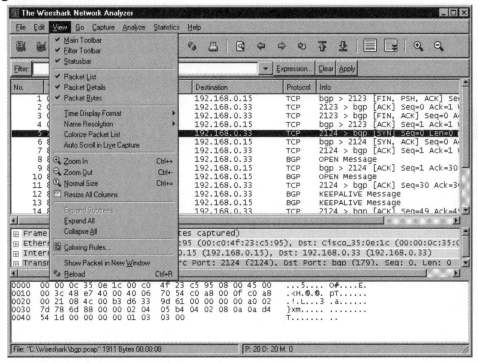

**Table 4.8** View Menu Options

## View Submenu Options

| Menu Option | Description |
| --- | --- |
| Main Toolbar | Display or remove the Main Toolbar |
| Filter Toolbar | Display or remove the Filter Toolbar |
| Status Bar | Display or remove the Information Field and the Display Information Field |
| Packet List | Display or remove the Summary window |

*Continued*

**Table 4.8 continued** View Menu Options

**View Submenu Options**

| Menu Option | Description |
| --- | --- |
| Packet Details | Display or remove the Protocol Tree window |
| Packet Bytes | Display or remove the Data View window |
| Time Display Format | A submenu for modifying the time displayed in the Summary window |
| Name Resolution | A submenu for selecting the name resolution options to perform during capture. |
| Colorize Packet List | Apply or remove the coloring defined in **Coloring Rules** to the Summary window |
| Auto Scroll in Live Capture | Sets the option to automatically scroll and update the Summary window list while capturing packets. |
| Zoom In | Proportionally increases the font and column size in the Summary window |
| Zoom Out | Proportionally decreases the font and column size in the Summary window |
| Normal Size | Returns the Summary window font and column size to the default setting. |
| Resize All Columns | Automatically resizes column width in the Summary window to eliminate white space. |
| Expand Subtrees | Expands the entire selected subtree in the Protocol Tree window |
| Expand All | Expand all subtrees in the Protocol Tree window |
| Collapse All | Collapse all subtrees in the Protocol Tree window |
| Coloring Rules... | Create and edit color filters to colorize the packets in the Summary window that match a given display filter string. |
| Show Packet In New window | For the packet currently selected in the Summary window display it's Protocol Tree window and Data View window in a new window. |
| Reload | Reload the current capture file. |

# Time Display Information

For a given packet, you may choose to have the **Time** column in the Summary window display the **Time of day** when that packet was captured, **Date and time of day** when that packet was captured, **Seconds since beginning of capture** (or the last time reference packet) that packet was captured, or the **Seconds since the previous frame** that matched the current display filter.

**Figure 4.18** Time of Day Display

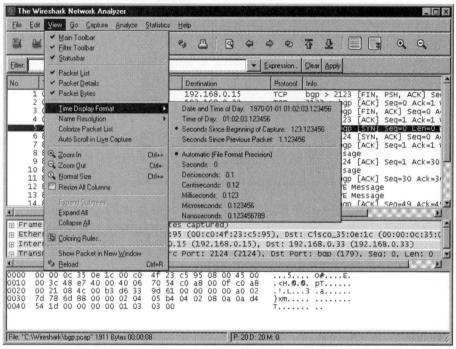

# Auto Scroll in Live Capture

In a live capture, you can choose to have old packets scroll up and out of view as new packets are captured and appended to the end of the Summary window. To do so, enable the **Automatic scrolling in live capture** menu option. This option is particularly helpful while performing a packet capture in which you need to watch for a particular even in real time.

# Apply Color Filters

The Apply Color Filters dialog box, shown in Figure 4.19, can be displayed by selecting **View | Coloring Rules...**.

**Figure 4.19** Apply Color Filters Dialog Box

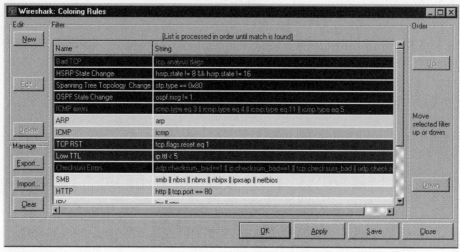

Wireshark has the ability to color packets in the Summary window that match a given display filter string, making patterns in the capture data more visible. This can be hugely useful when trying to follow request response protocols where variations in the order of requests or responses may be interesting. You can color such traffic into as many categories as you'd like and will be able to see at a glance what is going on from the Summary window instead of having to go through the Protocol Tree window for each packet.

To create a color filter click the **New** button in the Apply Color Filters dialog box. The Edit Color Filter dialog box will be displayed (Figure 4.20).

**Figure 4.20** Edit Color Filter Dialog Box

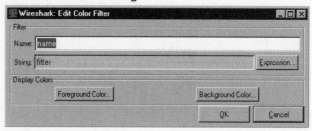

When the Edit Color Filter dialog box is first opened, the **Name** text box will have the string *name* in it, and the **String** field will contain the string *filter*. To create a color filter you should first fill in a name for it in the **Name** text box. Then, you should enter a filter string in the **String** text box. You may use the **Add Expression** button to display the Filter Expression dialog box to assist you in constructing a filter string. The Filter Expression dialog box is described in the section entitled "Analyze". Once you have a name and filter string you are happy with, you need to select the foreground and background color to colorize the packets matching your filter string. Click the **Background Color…** button to set the foreground color, as shown in Figure 4.21.

**Figure 4.21** Background Color Dialog box

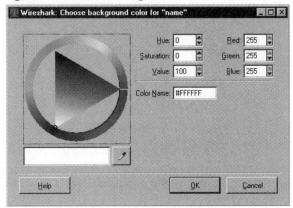

When you are happy with the color you have selected click the **OK** button. The Edit Color Filter dialog box (Figure 4.25) will be displayed.

In Figure 4.22 we have created a filter named *BGP Update* with a filter string *bgp.type == 2*. The name and filter string will be colored to match our background color choice. Click the **Foreground Color…** button to set the foreground color and proceed as you did with the background color. When you are happy with your name, filter string, and text coloring click the **OK** to close the Edit Color Filter dialog box.

**Figure 4.22** Edit Color Filter

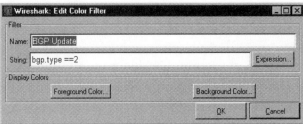

Figure 4.23 shows the Apply Color Filters dialog box now populated with the new *BGP Update* entry and a *BGP* filter.

**Figure 4.23** Apply Color Filters Dialog Box

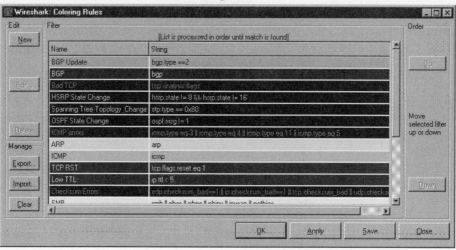

Click the **OK** button to apply the changes and close the dialog box. Click **Apply** to apply the changes and leave the dialog box open. If you wish to use your color filters with another Wireshark session, click **Save**.

If you click the **Revert** button, all coloring will be removed from the Summary window, the color filters will be removed from the **Filter** list, and the saved color file will be deleted. Use the **Export** or **Import** buttons to export your color filters to another file or import the color filters from a file of your choice. This is very useful for sharing color filters with coworkers or between different machines on which you have Wireshark installed. Notice the order of the color filters in the **Filter** list in Figure 4.23. For every packet in the Summary View the color filters strings will be tried in order until one is matched. At that point, its associated color will be applied. The filters in the **Filter** list are applied from the top down, so the *BGP Update* color filter will be tried first. Only if the *BGP Update* color filter does not match a packet will Wireshark proceed to try the *BGP* color filter to that packet. An example of the application of these color filters can be seen in Figure 4.24.

In Figure 4.24, the *BGP Update* messages (lines 16 and 17) are black text on light blue, not white text on dark blue, even though they would also match the white text on dark blue *BGP* color filter. This is because the black text on light blue *BGP Update* filter is applied first, and since it matches, no further color filter is tried.

# Show Packet in New Window

You can display a packet's Protocol Tree window and Data View window in a new window by selecting a packet in the Summary window and selecting **View | Show**

**Figure 4.24** Application of Color Filters

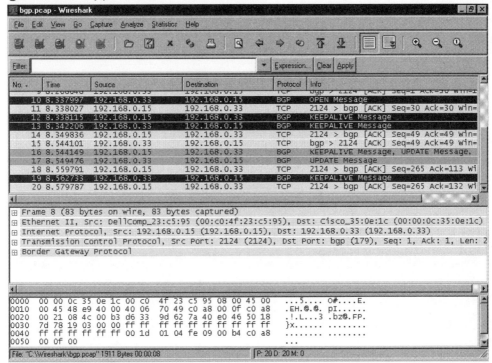

**Packet in New Window** (see Figure 4.25). This is useful when you would like to be able to see detailed information about more than one packet at once. Note that the title bar shows the same information as the summary line for this packet in the Summary window.

**Figure 4.25** Show Packet in New Window

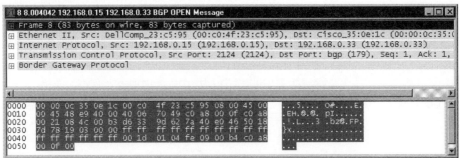

# Go

The Go menu is shown in Figure 4.26, and the menu entries are explained in Table 4.9.

**Figure 4.26** Go Menu

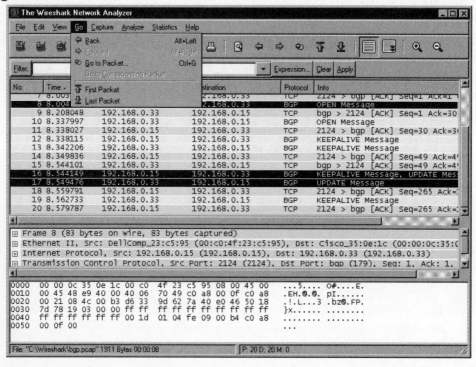

**Table 4.9** Go Menu Options

| | |
|---|---|
| Back | Moves to the previous packet displayed in the current capture. |
| Forward | Moves to the next packet displayed in the current capture. |
| Go To Packet... | Go to a packet by frame number. |
| Go To Corresponding Packet | When a field that refers to another frame is selected in the Protocol Tree window, select the packet being referred to in the Summary window. |
| First Packet | Moves to the first displayed packet |
| Last Packet | Moves to the last displayed packet |

# Go To Packet

The Go To Packet dialog box, shown in Figure 4.27, can be displayed by selecting **Edit | Go To Packet Dialog**.

**Figure 4.27** Go To Packet Dialog Box

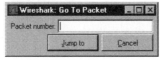

Enter a packet number in the **Packet Number** text box and click **OK**. The packet with that packet number will be selected in the Summary window.

# Capture

The **Capture** menu is shown in Figure 4.28, and the menu entries are explained in Table 4.10.

**Figure 4.28** Capture Menu

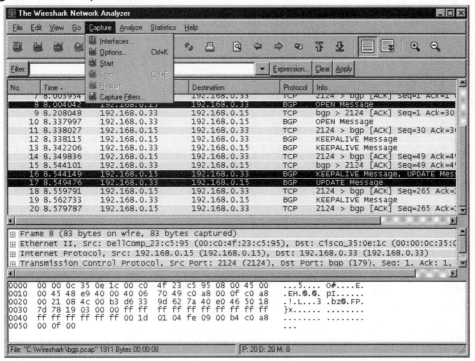

**Table 4.10** Capture Menu Options

| Menu Option | Description |
| --- | --- |
| Interfaces… | Opens the **Interfaces** dialog box |
| Options… | Opens the **Capture Options** |
| Start | Start a capture. |
| Stop | Stop a running packet capture. |
| Restart | Restart a stopped packet capture |
| Capture Filters… | Edit the capture filters. |

# Capture Interfaces

The Capture Interfaces dialog box, shown in Figure 4.29, can be displayed by selecting **Capture | Interfaces…**.

**Figure 4.29** Capture Interfaces Dialog

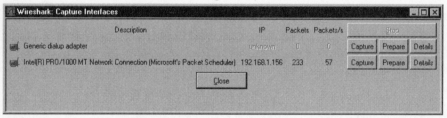

This dialog box gives us a wealth of information about the current interfaces in the system. With this dialog box we are presented a list and description of the current interfaces, the IP address assigned to each interface, the number of packets seen by the interface, and the rate at which they are seen (in packets per second). We are also presented with a number of options that can be performed on each interface.

> **NOTE**
>
> The packet count and packets per second displayed in the Capture Interfaces dialog box are not the total seen by the interfaces, but are the total count and rate seen by the interface from the time the Capture Interface dialog box was opened.

The **Capture** button immediately starts capturing packets in the selected interface with the options previously defined in the **Capture Options** dialog box. By utilizing the **Prepare** we are able to display the **Capture Options** dialog box to allow us to change options for the capture session before beginning to capture packets. Please refer to the Capture Options section later in this chapter for more information on the Capture Options dialog box.

If we need to know more information about the interface itself, we can select the **Details** button for the desired interface.

## Notes from the Underground…

### Where Did My Loopback Go?

You may notice in the screenshots for this section, there is no option for a loopback (or lo) interface, as these screen captures were taken under Windows. Due to the way Windows implements its loopback, it is not possible for us to capture traffic on the true loopback under Windows.

Wireshark relies on winpcap to provide an interface to the network devices on the system. Winpcap is only able to discover actual physical devices installed on the system through discovery of the actual network drivers. Unfortunately the Windows loopback adapter is not considered a physical device, and Windows does not install drivers. As a result, winpcap is unable to bind to non-existent drivers to capture the loopback traffic.

It is possible to install a loopback adapter under Windows, but again it is not a true loopback adapter, and does not get an address assigned out of the 127.0.0.0 subnet. Microsoft designed the special loopback adapter to provide a dummy interface for certain applications that require a network interface to function, and that may be installed in instances where a real network adapter is not needed, for example in a standalone demo system.

In the Interface Details dialog box, we are presented with five tabs that provide extremely detailed information about the selected interface, as queried from the underlying system driver. This information can prove invaluable in determining capabilities of the selected interface, as well some vital statistics including packet counts and driver information

**Figure 4.30** Capture Interfaces Details

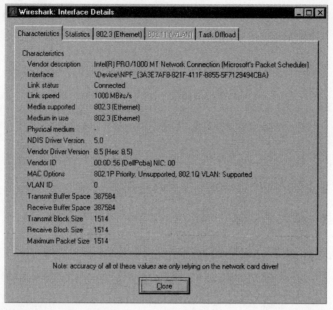

## Capture Options

The Capture Options dialog box, shown in Figure 4.31, can be displayed by selecting **Capture | Start...**.

This dialog box helps answer basic questions about capturing data:

- What traffic am I capturing?
- Where am I saving it?
- How am I displaying it?
- When do I stop capturing?

The **Capture** section allows you to choose which traffic you are capturing. When choosing what traffic to capture ask:

- Which interface am I capturing from?
- How much of each packet am I capturing?
- Which packets arriving at the interface am I capturing?

The **Interface** drop-down list allows you to choose the interface you want to capture from. You can choose from the interfaces listed in the drop-down list, or you can enter one manually into the text box. If both libpcap and the interface you

**Figure 4.31** Capture Options Dialog

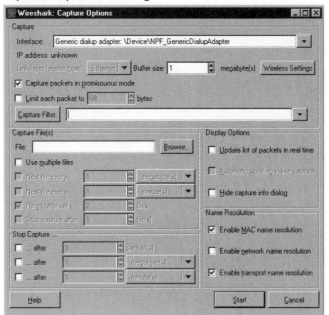

select support multiple link layers for that interface, you can choose the link layer header type to capture using the **Link–layer header type:** selector.

The Limit Each Packet To field lets you choose to capture a piece of an entire packet. When the **Limit each packet to** checkbox is enabled and a number is provided in the **Limit each packet to** text box, only the first number of bytes are captured from each packet. Be aware that if you choose to capture less than the full packet, Wireshark may mark your packets as fragments.

The **Capture packets in promiscuous mode** checkbox and the **Filter:** text box allow you to choose which packets arriving at the interface will be captured. If you enable the **Capture packets in promiscuous mode** checkbox, Wireshark puts the interface into promiscuous mode before capturing data. Normally, an interface only passes on the operating system packets that are destined for the MAC address of the interfaces. When an interface is in promiscuous mode, it passes on all packets arriving at the interface to the operating system. So, if you choose not to capture in promiscuous mode, you will only capture packets addressed to or being sent by the interface on which you are capturing. If you choose to capture in promiscuous mode you will capture all packets arriving at the interface. Entering a tcpdump-style capture filter in the **Filter** text box will cause Wireshark to only capture packets matching that capture filter. When you click on the **Filter** button, the Edit Capture Filter List dialog box will be displayed to allow you to choose among previously defined capture filters. (See the section entitled "Edit Capture Filter List" for more details.)

## Notes from the Underground...

## Promiscuous Mode Detection

There are many instances in which you may want to perform packet captures with Wireshark in promiscuous mode, and go undetected using an Intrusion detection System (IDS)/Intrusion Prevention System (IPS). Promiscuous mode captures all of the traffic seen by an interface, as well as traffic for other devices.

Assume that an attacker has installed Wireshark on a computer that is attached to your network, and is actively capturing traffic on your network in promiscuous mode with Network Name Resolution enabled. You monitor the uplink for this particular network segment with your installation of Wireshark, so that you can detect the attacker. If a user on the same network segment as the attacker opens a Web browser and directs it to the www.syngress.com Web site, both the attacker's installation and your installation will capture the request to DNS. (In this instance, you were able to detect the malicious individual, because Network Name Resolution was enabled in the attacker's copy of Wireshark.) Under normal circumstances, you should only see one DNS request for the www.syngress.com domain; however, because the attacker's copy of Wireshark has Network Name Resolution enabled, his or her copy attempts to resolve the www.syngress.com domain. As a result, there is a second DNS lookup for www.syngress.com that did not originate from the original computer.

With this information, you can discern that there is a computer on this network segment that is capturing packets in promiscuous mode.

The Capture File(s) section allows you to choose where to save a capture. If this section is left blank, Wireshark saves the capture to a temporary file until it is saved by selecting **File | SaveAs**. If you enter a filename in the **File** text box, Wireshark saves the capture to that file. Clicking the **File** button opens the Save As dialog box. If the **Use ring buffer** checkbox is enabled, you can save your capture to a ring buffer.

The **Display options** section allows you to choose how you are going to display packets as they are captured. By default, Wireshark does not update the list of packets in the Summary window during capture; only once the capture is stopped. If the **Update list of packets in real time** checkbox is enabled, Wireshark updates the Summary window as soon as a packet is captured and processed. By default, when Wireshark updates the Summary window during live capture, new packets are appended to the end of the Summary window. Consequently, the Summary window does not reveal new packets. To enable the Summary window to display the most recent packets, enable the **Automatic scrolling in live capture** checkbox. If you decide that you want automatic scrolling once a capture has started, select **View | Options** to disable this feature.

The **Capture limits** section allows you to choose when to stop capturing. You can manually stop a capture by selecting **Capture | Stop**; however, some-times it's convenient to set conditions under which a capture will automatically stop. There are three types of automatic limits to a capture that are supported by Wireshark:

- Capture a specified number of packets.

- Capture a specified number of kilobytes of traffic.

- Capture for a specified number of seconds.

Wireshark allows you to set up any combination of these three limits simultane-ously (i.e., it is possible to limit the number of packets, kilobytes, and seconds at the same time. Whenever one of the limits is satisfied, the capture stops.

When you enable the **Stop capture after... packet(s) captured** checkbox and enter a number of packets in the **Stop capture after... packet(s) captured** text box, the capture stops when it has reached the specified number of packets. When you enable the **Stop capture after... kilobyte(s) captured** checkbox and enter a number of kilobytes in the **Stop capture after... kilobytes(s) captured** text box, the capture stops once it has reached the specified number of kilobytes. When you enable the **Stop capture after... seconds(s)** checkbox and enter a number of packets in the **Stop capture after... seconds(s)** text box, the capture stops when the specified number of seconds have elapsed since the beginning of the capture. The **Name resolution** section allows you to choose the name resolution options for the capture.

When you have specified your capture choices via the Capture Options dialog box, start the capture by clicking the **OK** button. The **Capture Dialog** dialog box will be displayed (see Figure 4.32).

The Capture dialog box displays the number of packets of the various protocols that have been captured, and the percentage of all captured traffic consisting of those protocols. In Figure 4.32, a total of 12 packets have been captured, of which seven (58.3 percent) are TCP packets, four (33.3 percent) are UDP packets, and one (8.3 percent) is an Other (miscellaneous) packet. The capture can be stopped at any time by clicking the **Stop** button.

**Figure 4.32** Capture Dialog Box

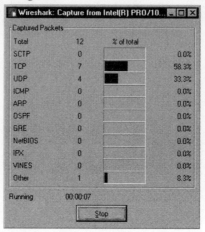

## Ring Buffer Captures

There are applications where it makes sense to capture network traffic to a series of smaller files. At times, you may want to limit the number of small files and delete the oldest when starting a new one. This structure is called a *ring buffer*, because conceptually the data fills up a buffer and loops back to the beginning when it reaches the end.

There are certain questions that must be answered regarding ring buffer files:

- How many capture files in the ring buffer?
- What are the capture files named?
- When do I rotate to the next capture file?

To enable ring buffer captures, access the Capture Options dialog box and enable the **Use ring buffer** checkbox. The appearance of the Capture Options dialog box changes (see Figure 4.33).

The **Rotate capture file every... second(s)** checkbox becomes available and the **Stop capture after... kilobytes captured** checkbox is renamed **Rotate capture file very... kilobyte(s)** and becomes unavailable.

The **Number of files** text box allows you to choose how many files are in the ring buffer. If you choose zero, the number of ring buffer files is assumed to be infinite (i.e., no old files are deleted to make room for new files).

The **File** text box provides the base name for the filenames in the capture ring buffer. The base name is broken up into a prefix and a suffix. The filename of a ring buffer capture file is *prefix_NNNNN_YYYYMMDDhhmmss.suffix*, where *NNNNN* is

## Figure 4.33 Capture Options Dialog Box - Use Ring Buffer Selected

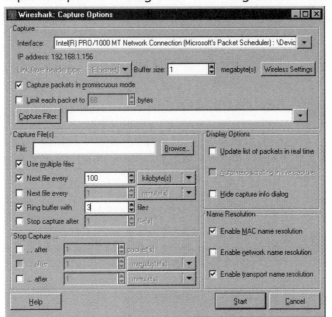

a 5-digit 0-padded count indicating the sequence number of the ring buffer file; *YYYY* is a 4-digit year; *MM* is the 2-digit 0-padded month; *DD* is a 2-digit zero-padded date; *hh* is a 3-digit 0-padded hour; *mm* is a 2-digit 0-padded minute; and *ss* is a 2-digit 0-padded second. (e.g., if the *foo.bar.libpcap* file is the fifth capture file in the ring buffer created at *23:21:01* on January 8, 2004, it would be named *foo.bar_00005_20040108232101.libpcap*). It is important to note that the sequence numbers in the filenames increase monotonically. If a ring buffer contains three files, when the fourth capture file is started it has sequence number 00004, and the file with sequence number *00001* is deleted. The sequence numbers are not recycled as you loop through the ring.

The **Rotate capture file every... kilobyte(s)** text box and the optional **Rotate capture file every... second(s)** text box allow you to choose when the capture files are rotated. Provide a kilobyte limit to the size of a capture file in the ring buffer, by entering a number (or accepting the default value) in the **Rotate capture file every... kilobyte(s)** text box. When a capture file reaches the number of kilobytes you have specified, a new capture file is created to store any new packets, and the oldest capture file in the ring buffer is deleted if the new capture file exceeds the limit specified in the **Number of files** text box. If you enable the **Rotate capture file every... second(s)** checkbox and enter a number of seconds in the **Rotate capture file every... second(s)** text box, if a capture file is open for that number of seconds, a new capture file is created to store any new packets captured. The oldest capture file in the ring buffer may then be deleted if the new capture file exceeds the limit specified in the **Number of files** text box.

## NOTE

The **Use ring buffer** checkbox and the **Update list of packets in real time** checkbox are incompatible; therefore, Wireshark will not enable **Use ring buffer** if the **Update list of packets in real time** is already enabled. However, Wireshark will allow you to select **Update list of packets in real time** if **Use ring buffer** has *already been selected*. When this occurs, the **Use Ring buffer** checkbox is automatically (and without warning) disabled, which, in turn, causes the **Rotate capture file every... kilobyte(s)** checkbox to revert to **Stop capture after... kilobyte(s)**.

## Tools & Traps...

### Handling Large Captures

Eventually, everyone encounters a problem that involves enormous amounts of network data to analyze. Maybe it's an intermittent problem that happens every couple of days, where you need to see the message exchange that led up to the problem, or maybe it's a problem on a fairly active network. Whatever the reason, the issue of capturing and analyzing large captures is common. As captures become larger, Wireshark uses up memory; thus, filtering and finding packets takes a long time.

In these situations, it is best to use Tshark (the console-based version of Wireshark) to do the actual capture and initial processing of the data. To capture from an interface *<interface>* to a file *<savefile>*, use this command:

```
tshark -i <interface> -w <savefile>
```

If you have a limited amount of space and/or want to limit the size of your capture files, you can use the ring buffer functionality with Tshark to capture from interface *<interface>* to *<num_capture_files>* capture files with a maximum size each *<filesize>* and a base filename *<savefile>* by executing the following at the command line:

```
tshark -i <interface> -w <savefile> -b <num_capture_files> -a
filesize:<filesize>
```

**Continued**

Once you have captured the data you need, you can use Tshark to reduce the capture to a more manageable size. To use a display filter string *<filter string>* to filter a capture file *<savefile>* and save the results to a new capture file *<newsavefile>*, execute the following at the command line:

```
tshark -r <savefile> -w <newsavefile> -R <filter string>
```

If you need to extract all packets from the capture file that were captured between Jan 8, 2004 22:00 and Jan 8, 2004 23:00, execute the following command:

```
tshark -r <savefile> -w <newsavefile> -R '(frame.time >= "Jan 8, 2004
22:00:00.00" ) && (frame.time <= "Jan 8, 2004 23:00:00.00")'
```

Once you have reduced the data down to a size where Wireshark's performance is workable, open the Capture file in Wireshark to perform more involved analysis.

## Edit Capture Filter List

The Edit Capture Filter List dialog box is displayed by selecting **Capture | Capture Filters...** (see Figure 4.34).

**Figure 4.34** Edit Capture Filter List Dialog Box

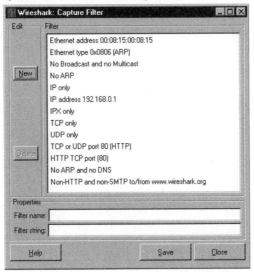

This dialog box allows you to create new tcpdump-style capture filters and save them for later use. To create a new capture filter, provide a name for your filter in the **Filter name** text box, provide a tcpdump-style capture filter string in the **Filter string** text box, and then click the **New** button (see Figure 4.35).

**Figure 4.35** Edit Capture Filter List Dialog Box

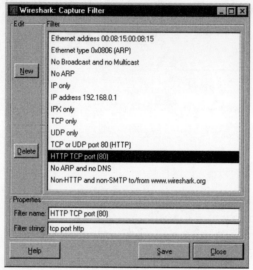

You can select an existing capture filter from the **Capture Filters** list to create a new capture filter, change an existing filter, or delete a filter. To change an existing capture filter, select it from the **Capture Filters** list and double-click on its name in the **Filter name** text box, and/or change its tcpdump-style capture filter string in the **Filter string** text box and then click **Save**. To create a new capture filter, enter a new Filter name and a new Filter string in the appropriate fields and select **New**.

You can delete a capture filter by selecting it from the **Capture Filters** list and clicking the **Delete** button. If you want your list of capture filters to be available in a subsequent Wireshark session, click the **Save** button to save them to disk.

# Analyze

The Analyze Menu is shown in Figure 4.36, and its options are explained in Table 4.11.

**Figure 4.36** Analyze Menu

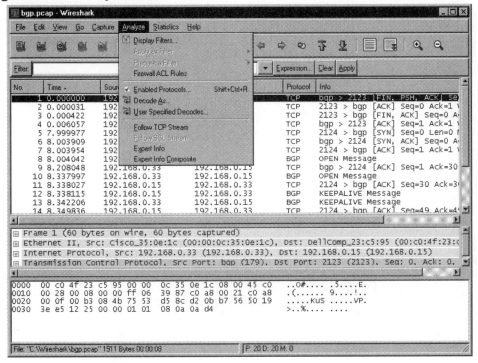

**Table 4.11** Analyze Menu Options

| Menu Option | Description |
| --- | --- |
| Display Filters... | Edits the display filters. |
| Apply as Filter | A submenu for preparing and automatically applying a display filter based on any field selected in the Protocol Tree window. |
| Prepare a Filter | A submenu for preparing a display filter based on any field selected in the Protocol Tree window. |
| Firewall ACL Rules | Creates a filter for several standard firewall types based on the current selected packet in the Summary Window. |
| Enabled Protocols... | Enables and disables the decoding of individual protocols. |
| Decode As... | Specifies decoding certain packets as being part of a particular protocol. |
| User Specified Decodes | Reports which user-specified decodes are currently in force. |

*Continued*

**Table 4.11 continued** Analyze Menu Options

| Menu Option | Description |
|---|---|
| Follow TCP Stream | Displays an entire TCP stream at once. |
| Follow SSL Stream | Displays an entire SSL stream at once. |
| Expert Info | Displays a summary of the capture file. |
| Expert Info Composite | Displays statistics in a Protocol Tree view for the protocols in the capture. |

# Edit Display Filter List

The Edit Display Filter List dialog box can be displayed by selecting **Analyze | Display Filter...** (see Figure 4.37).

**Figure 4.37** Edit Display Filter List Dialog Box

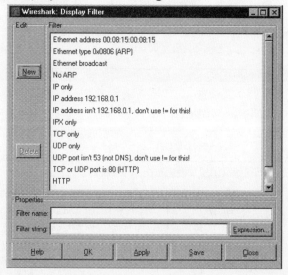

This dialog box is designed to help you construct a filter string. To create a new filter string, click the **Add Expression** button. The Filter Expression dialog box is displayed (see Figure 4.38).

Select the protocol you want for your filter expression and expand it to show which of its fields can be filtered. Select the desired filter field. When you pick a relation other than **is present**, the Filter Expression dialog box changes to show your options for that field (see Figure 4.39).

**Figure 4.38** Filter Expression Dialog Box

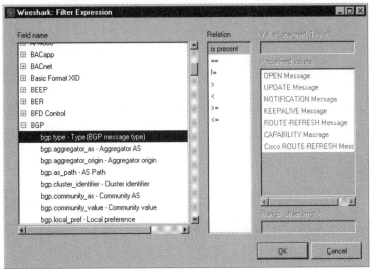

**Figure 4.39** Filter Expression Dialog - Equality

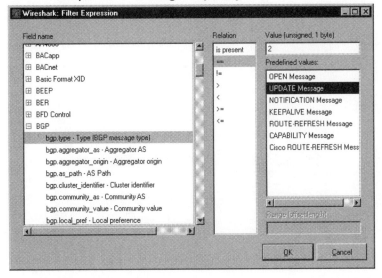

In this case, we have chosen the equality (==) relation. Choose the value you want to match and click the **Accept** button, which will insert the filter expression you just constructed into the **Filter string:** text box (see Figure 4.40).

If you want to save the filter string you have just created, type a name in the **Filter name** text box and click the **New** button. The filter string will be added to the Display Filters List dialog box (see Figure 4.41).

**Figure 4.40** Edit Display Filter List Dialog Box - Filter String

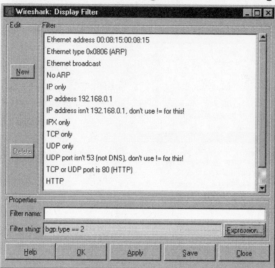

**Figure 4.41** Edit Display Filter List Dialog Box - Filter Name

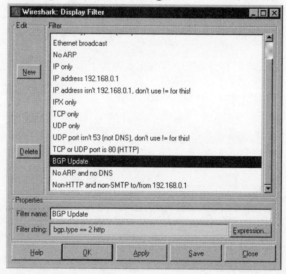

Select an existing display filter from the list and choose to either change, delete, or copy it. To change an existing display filter, select it from the list, change its name in the **Filter name** text box (or change its display filter string in the **Filter string** text box), and click the **Change** button. To copy an existing display filter, select it from the list and click the **Copy** button. Save the list by clicking the **Save** Button.

When you have accessed the Edit Display Filter List dialog box from the filter bar, click **OK** to apply the filter and close the dialog box. Use the **Apply** button to apply the filter and leave the dialog box open (see Figure 4.42).

**Figure 4.42** Display Filter Dialog Box - OK and Apply Buttons

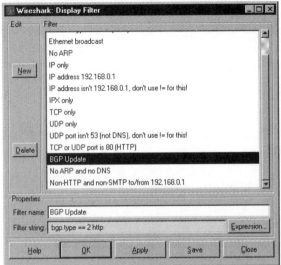

# "Apply as Filter" and "Prepare a Filter" Submenus

The Apply as Filter and Prepare a Filter submenus have the same options and behave in the same way with one exception: the Prepare a Filter submenu items prepare a display filter string and place it in the **Filter** text box. The Apply as Filter submenu items prepare a display filter string, place it in the **Filter** text box, and apply it to the capture. Because of their close similarity, we will only discuss the Apply as Filter submenu.

The Apply as Filter submenu becomes available when a field in the Protocol Tree window is selected with an associated filter name that can be used in a display filter string (see Figure 4.43).

In Table 4.12, the filter string has been put into the **Filter:** text box for each of the **Apply as Filter** submenu options (see Figure 4.43). Note that the *ip.addr ==
192.168.0.15* filter changes the initial behavior of **And Selected**, **Or Selected**, **And Not Selected**, and **Or Not Selected** (see Table 4.12).

**Figure 4.43** Apply as Filter Submenu

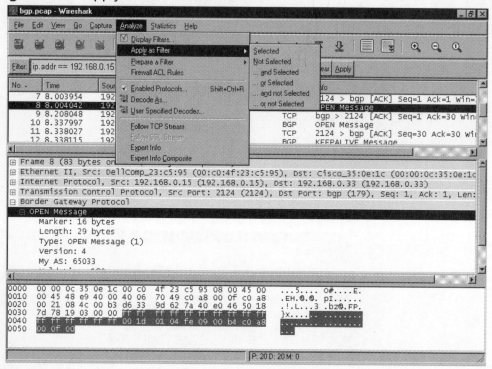

**Table 4.12** Apply as Filter Submenu Option Examples

| Menu Option | Display Filter String |
| --- | --- |
| Selected | bgp.type == 1 |
| Not Selected | !(bgp.type == 1) |
| And Selected | (ip.addr == 192.168.0.15) && ( bgp.type == 1 ) |
| Or Selected | (ip.addr == 192.168.0.15) \|\| ( bgp.type == 1) |
| And Not Selected | (ip.addr == 192.168.0.15) && !( bgp.type == 1 ) |
| Or Not Selected | (ip.addr == 192.168.0.15) \|\| !( bgp.type == 1 ) |

# Enabled Protocols

The Enabled Protocols dialog box is displayed by selecting **Analyze | Enabled Protocols...** (see Figure 4.44).

This dialog box allows you to enable or disable the decoding of one or more protocols. This can be done by clicking the Status column to toggle the status between

**Figure 4.44** Enabled Protocols Dialog Box

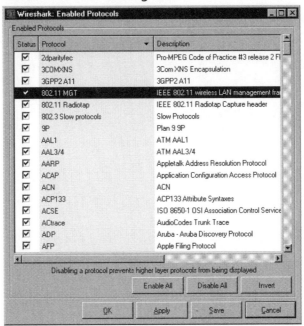

*Enabled* and *Disabled.* Additionally, you can enable all protocols by clicking the **Enable All** button, disable all protocols by clicking the **Disable All** button, or enable all disabled protocols and disable all enabled protocols by clicking the **Invert** button. These settings can be applied to all Wireshark sessions by clicking the **Save** button.

# Decode As

To force the decode of a packet as a particular protocol, select it in the Summary window and then select **Analyze | Decode As...**. The Decode As dialog box will be displayed (see Figure 4.45).

When Wireshark is decoding a packet, it uses *magic numbers* in each protocol to decide which dissector to use to decode subsequent parts of the packet. Magic numbers are values that specify a higher-level protocol (e.g., Ethertype *0×0800* specifies that an Ethernet packet contains an IP packet; IP protocol 6 specifies that an IP packet contains a TCP payload; TCP port 179 specifies that a TCP packet is carrying a BGP payload). There are occasions when you want to override Wireshark's choices of how to decode subsequent parts of a packet based on the magic numbers. The most common examples involve TCP ports; Wireshark frequently decides which dissector to call for a TCP packet, based on the source or destination port. You may be running a protocol over a non-standard port (e.g.,

**Figure 4.45** Decode As Dialog Box - Link Tab

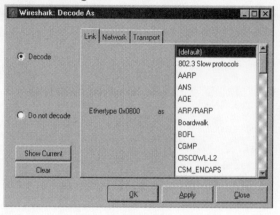

running HTTP over port 7000 ). The **Decode As** feature allows you to tell Wireshark about these non-standard cases.

Wireshark allows you to force decodes based on the magic numbers in the Link, Network, and Transport layers. For the transport layer, you have the option of decoding based on source, destination, or both (see Figure 4.46).

**Figure 4.46** Decode As Dialog Box - Transport Tab

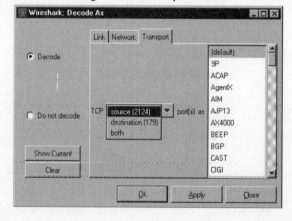

To force a particular decode, you need to answer these questions:

- After which layer do I want to start forcing my custom decode?
- Which magic number do I want to key off of to determine whether to decode a packet with my custom decode?
- Which protocol do I want the remaining traffic in the packet decoded as?

To choose the layer where you want to start forcing your custom decode, select the appropriate tab (Link, Network, or Transport), and choose which magic numbers to pick for the Transport layer (by source port, destination port, or both). Then, select from the list of protocols as to how you want the remaining traffic in the packet decoded.

Click the **Show Current** button to open the **Decode As: Show** dialog box, in order to see which decodes are currently being forced.

## Decode As: Show

The **Decode As: Show** dialog box can also be displayed by selecting **Analyze | User Specified Decodes** from the menu bar (see Figure 4.47).

**Figure 4.47** Decode As: Show

This dialog box displays the decodes specified through the **Decode As** dialog box (one per line). The Table column shows the magic number of the alternate decode (in this case, the TCP port). The Port column shows the magic number of the alternate decode (in this case 179). The Initial column shows the dissector that would normally be used to decode the payload of a packet with this magic number and magic number type (in this case, BGP). And, finally, the Current column shows the dissector currently being used to decode the payload of packets having this magic number and magic number type (in this case HTTP).

## Follow TCP Stream and Follow SSL Stream

The Follow TCP Stream and Follow SSL Stream windows have the same options and behave in the same way with one exception; the Follow TCP Stream window follows any TCP stream, while the Follow SSL Stream only follows the selected Secure Sockets Layer (SSL) stream. Because of their close similarity, we will only discuss the Follow TCP Stream submenu.

The Follow TCP Stream window can be displayed by selecting a TCP packet in the Summary window and then selecting **Analyze | Follow TCP Stream** from the menu bar (see Figure 4.48).

**Figure 4.48** Follow TCP Stream Window

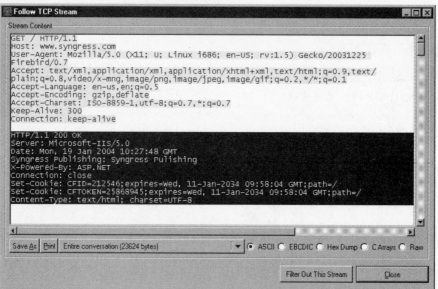

In this example, a TCP packet that was part of an HTTP conversation with the Web server for www.syngress.com, is shown. By default, one side of the conversation is shown in red (the upper portion), and the other portion is shown in blue (the lower portion). For readability purposes, the side of the conversation that is usually highlighted blue is shown as white text on a dark blue background. By scrolling down in this window, you can see all of the data exchanged during this TCP conversation. Click the **Entire conversation** selector to choose between displaying the entire conversation or one of the directions (see Figure 4.49).

Clicking the **Save As** button brings up a Save As dialog box where you can save the stream contents as a text file. Clicking the **Print** button prints the capture as text. (Note that there is no dialog box associated with the **Print** button.) The **Filter out this stream** button appends the necessary filter string to the one in the filter bar and closes the Contents of the TCP Stream window. This can be useful when going through a large capture. As you look at the possible TCP streams of interest one by one and exclude them from the Summary window, you are left with only the unconsidered data.

**Figure 4.49** Follow TCP Stream: Direction Selector

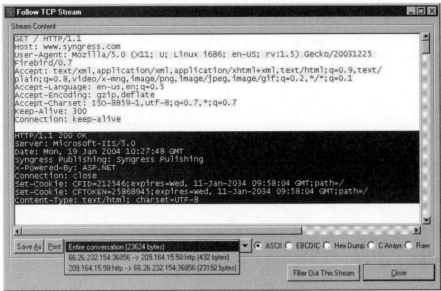

You also have the option of choosing how the TCP stream is presented. In Figure 4.49, the **ASCII** option is selected. By choosing the **EBCDIC** option, you can cause the stream to be presented with Extended Binary Coded Decimal Interchange Code (EBCDIC). If you choose the **Hex Dump** option, there will be a hexadecimal dump of the TCP stream. And, if you choose the **C Arrays** option, the TCP stream will appear as a series of C arrays.

# Expert Info and Expert Info Composite

The Expert Info and Expert Info Composite menu options provide identical information in similar layouts. Both options provide a breakdown of the current capture, and display summary information about current conversations, errors, and warnings that can be derived from the traffic patterns. These options are a great method to use to begin troubleshooting traffic-related issues, as they provide some simple error-related information without having to analyze each packet by hand.

# Statistics

The Statistics Menu provides a variety of specialized tools to analyze network traffic (see Figure 4.50). These statistics are reported for certain protocol features. Many of the tools in the Statistics Menu are specialized and beyond the scope of this book;

however, we will discuss some of the more generalized items, including graphing. The menu items are described in Table 4.13

**Figure 4.50** Statistics Menu

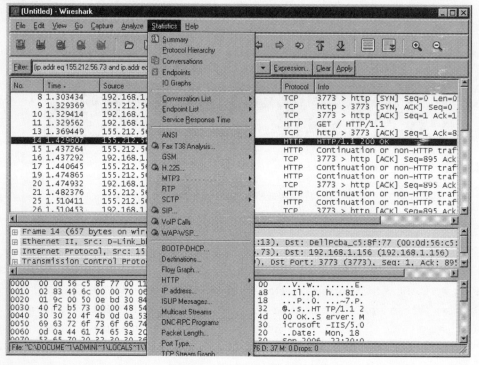

**Table 4.13** Statistics Menu Options

| Menu Option | Description |
| --- | --- |
| Summary | Provides basic statistics about the current capture. |
| Protocol Hierarchy | Displays a hierarchical breakdown of the protocols in the current capture |
| Conversations | Provides basic information on all of the conversations in the current capture. |
| Endpoints | Provides basic information on all endpoint counts in the current capture. |
| IO Graphs | Displays basic time sequence graphs. |
| Conversation List | A submenu for displaying conversation counts and basic statistics for 13 different layer 2 and layer 3 protocols and transport methods |

**Continued**

**Table 4.13 continued** Statistics Menu Options

| Menu Option | Description |
| --- | --- |
| Endpoint List | A submenu for displaying endpoint counts and basic statistics for 12 different layer 2 and layer 3 protocols and transport methods |
| Service Response Time | A submenu for displaying the service response time for 11 different protocols. |
| ANSI | A submenu for displaying breakdown counts of three different American National Standards Institute (ANSI) protocols. |
| Fax T38 Analysis… | Displays basic information on Fax T.38. This feature is currently implemented in the Voice Over Internet Protocol (VoIP) Calls menu. |
| Global System for Mobile Com-munications (GSM) | A submenu for displaying breakdown counts for GSM ANSI protocols. |
| H.225… | Displays counts of H.225 messages. |
| MTP3 | A submenu for displaying basic MTP3 count A submenu. |
| RTP | A submenu for displaying Real-Time Protocol (RTP) stream sessions and analysis of selected RTP streams. |
| SCTP | A submenu for analyzing and providing statistics on Stream Control Transmission Protocol (SCTP) associations. |
| SIP | Provides basic analysis of Session Initiation Protocol (SIP) code volumes. |
| VoiP Calls | Displays session information on Voice over Internet Protocol (VoIP) calls. |
| Wireless Application Protocol—Wireless Session Protocol (WAP-WSP…) | Provides basic analysis of WAP-WSP. |
| BOOTP-DHCP… | Displays a count of Dynamic Host Configuration Protocol (DHCP) and Bootstrap Protocol (BOOTP) mes-sages broken down by message type. |
| Destinations… | Provides a hierarchical view of all conversations in the current capture. |
| Flow Graph… | Provides a detailed graphical display of protocol flow information. |

*Continued*

**Table 4.13 continued** Statistics Menu Options

| Menu Option | Description |
| --- | --- |
| HTTP | A submenu for displaying HTTP request information. |
| IP Address... | Provides a hierarchical view of all IP conversations in the current capture. |
| ISUP Messages... | Displays a count of ISUP message types for the current captures. |
| Multicast Streams | Displays a detailed breakdown of multicast streams, and allow for Summary window filter preparation. |
| ONC-RPC Programs | Provides summary information on Open Network Computing (ONC)-Remote Procedure Call (RPC) conversations. |
| Packet Length... | Calculates packet length statistics by ranges for the current capture. |
| Port Type... | Provides a hierarchical view of all port usage for conversations in the current capture. |
| TCP Streams Graph | A submenu for calculating and displaying robust graphs. |

# Summary

The Summary dialog box can be displayed by selecting **Statistics | Summary** from the menu bar (see Figure 4.51).

This Summary dialog box provides information about the capture file, basic statistics about the capture data, and basic information about the capture.

# Protocol Hierarchy

The Protocol Hierarchy dialog box can be displayed by selecting **Statistics | Protocol Hierarchy** from the menu bar (see Figure 4.52).

**Figure 4.51** Summary Dialog Box

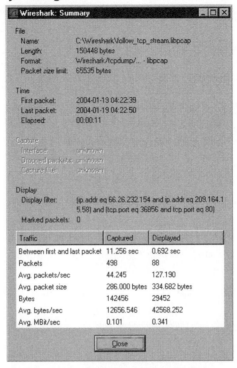

**Figure 4.52** Protocol Hierarchy Statistics Dialog Box

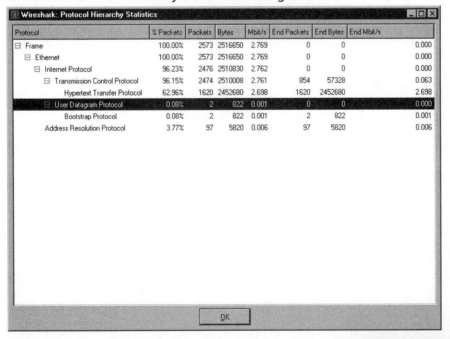

This dialog box provides a tree representation of protocols and statistics associated with them. Table 4.14 provides a description of what each columns means.

**Table 4.14** Protocol Hierarchy Statistics Columns

| Column | Description |
| --- | --- |
| Protocol | The protocol on which statistics are being reported. The protocol may have subitems on the tree representing the protocols it contains (e.g., the IP contains TCP and UDP). |
| % Packets | Percentage of all packets in the capture that are of this protocol. |
| Packets | The number of packets in the capture that are of this protocol. |
| Bytes | The number of bytes in this capture containing this protocol. |
| End Packets | The number of packets for which this protocol is the last protocol in the decode (e.g., a TCP synchronize [SYN] packet containing no data would be an end packet for TCP and counted in TCP's end packets count). |
| End Bytes | The number of bytes for which this protocol is the last protocol in the decode. |

## TCP Stream Graph Submenu

The **TCP Stream Analysis** submenucan be displayed by selecting a TCP packet in the Summary window and selecting **Statistics | TCP Stream Graph** from the menu bar (see Figure 4.53). the **TCP Stream Graph** submenu options are shown in Table 4.15.

**Table 4.15** TCP Stream Graph Submenu Options

| Menu Option | Description |
| --- | --- |
| Round Trip Time Graph | Displays a graph of the round trip time (RTT) vs. the sequence number. |
| Throughput Graph | Displays a graph of throughput vs. time. |
| Time-Sequence Graph (Stevens) | Displays a time-sequence graph in the style used by W. Richard Stevens' TCP/IP Illustrated book. |
| Time-Sequence Graph (tcptrace) | Displays a time-sequence graph in the style used by the tcptrace program, which can be found at www.tcptrace.org. |

**Figure 4.53** TCP Stream Graph Submenu

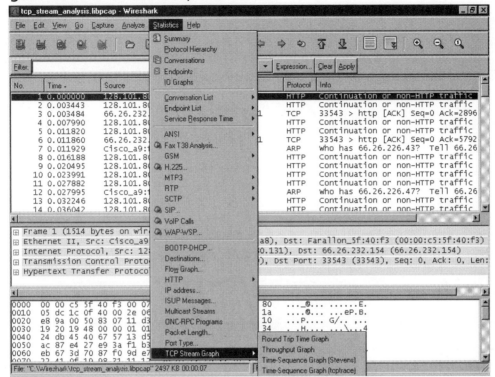

## RTT Graph

The RTT graph shows the RTT vs. the sequence number (see Figure 4.54).

You can see the RTT spike around sequence number 1000000, which is roughly the same sequence number where you will see discontinuity in the time-sequence graphs.

## Throughput Graph

The throughput graph shows the throughput of the TCP stream vs. time (see Figure 4.55).

In Figure 4.58, the throughput fell off dramatically during the retransmit sequence seen in the time-sequence graphs.

**Figure 4.54** RTT Graph

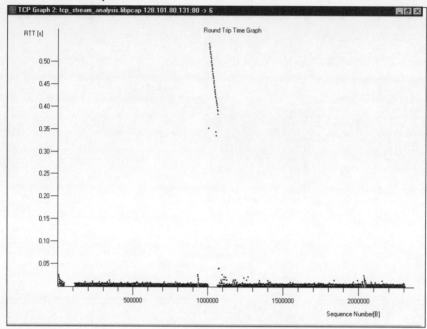

**Figure 4.55** Throughput Graph

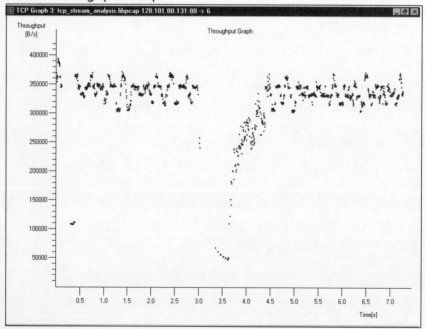

## Time-sequence Graph (Stevens)

The time-sequence graph (Stevens) produces a simple graph of TCP sequence numbers vs. time for the TCP stream containing the packet that was selected in the Summary window. The first derivative of this graph is the TCP traffic throughput. In an ideal situation where there is a constant throughput, the graph would be a straight rising line with its slope equaling the throughput. Unfortunately, things are seldom ideal, and you can learn a lot about where the source of throughput issues is coming from by looking at the time-sequence graph. In Figure 4.56, there is a graph showing a throughput problem. You can reproduce this graph by selecting the first packet of the *tcp_stream_analysis.libpcap* capture file, and selecting **Statistics | TCP Stream Graph | Time-Sequence Graph (Stevens)**. The captured file used in this graph is a classic example of TCP retransmit and the kind of issues you use the TCP Stream Analysis tool to debug. The full network capture can be found on the accompanying CD, and has been added to the collection of network captures on the Wireshark Web site.

After about 0.3 seconds, the traffic has an even slope (constant throughput) for approximately 3 seconds, when there is a major disruption, as shown by the discontinuity in the graph. This gap suggests TCP retransmissions. The Steven's style time-sequence graph is simple, but you can see where the problems are.

**Figure 4.56** Time-sequence Graph (Stevens)

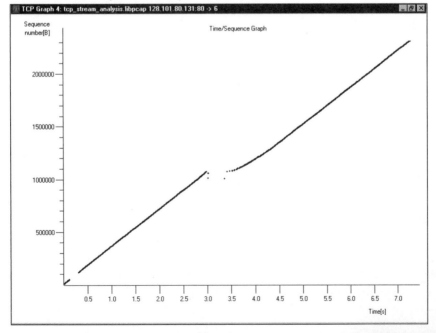

## *Time-Sequence Graph (tcptrace)*

The time-sequence graph (tcptrace) is also primarily a graph of TCP sequence numbers vs. time. Unlike the Stevens' style time-sequence graph, however, it conveys a lot more information about the TCP stream. Figure 4.57 shows that the tcptrace style time-sequence graph of this stream looks very similar to the Stevens' style time-sequence graph.

**Figure 4.57** Time-sequence Graph (tcptrace)

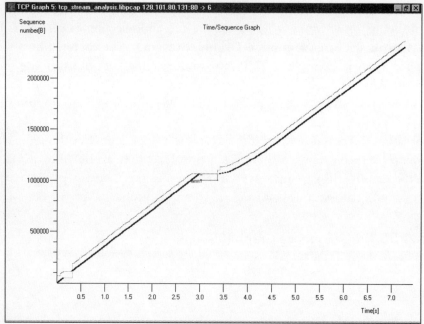

Explaining the elements shown in the tcptrace style time-sequence graph is easy using some of the graph manipulation tools that are available in all of the TCP stream analysis graphs. You can magnify a portion of the graph by pressing **Ctrl+right-click** on the graph (see Figure 4.58).

The box in the middle of the graph in Figure 4.58 is magnifying the region of discontinuity where packet loss has occurred. To get an even better view of it, use the zoom feature. Clicking on the graph with the middle mouse button allows you to zoom in on the part of the graph you are clicking on. Pressing **Shift+middle-click** zooms out. Whether you have zoomed in or out, clicking and dragging with the right mouse button on the graph allows you to move around in the zoomed graph. A zoom-in on the region of discontinuity in Figure 4.58, is shown in Figure 4.59.

**Figure 4.58** Time-sequence Graph (tcptrace) - Magnify

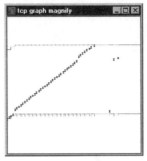

**Figure 4.59** Time-sequence Graph (tcptrace) - Zoom

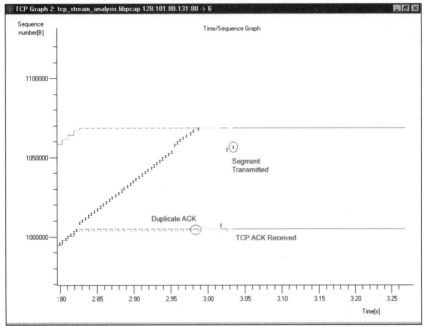

Figure 4.59 is a zoom-in on the section of the graph right before the discontinuity. The beginning of the discontinuity can be seen on the far right of the graph. There are the different elements of the tcptrace style time-sequence graph. The lower line represents the sequence number of the last Acknowledgement (ACK) (TCP acknowledgement) seen. The top line represents the TCP window and consists of the sequence number of the last observed TCP ACK plus the previously seen TCP window size. The hash marks on the lower line represent duplicate ACKs, and the "I" bars represent transmitted segments.

Figure 4.59 is the same graph as Figure 4.60, but with different annotations to magnify what went wrong for this TCP stream. The capture behind this graph was taken from the receiver of a large transmission over TCP. Therefore, we only see the segments that we are receiving from the far end. What is seen in this graph is that early on the receiver missed two segments. The receiver continued to ACK the last segment received, and to receive subsequent segments until the segments received filled the TCP window. A couple of other segments were lost along the way. Finally, we receive the second missed segment, the third missed segment, and then the fourth missed segment. However, because the first missed segment has not yet turned up, the receiver continues sending the same duplicate ACK.

**Figure 4.60** Time-sequence Graph (tcptrace) - Diagnosis

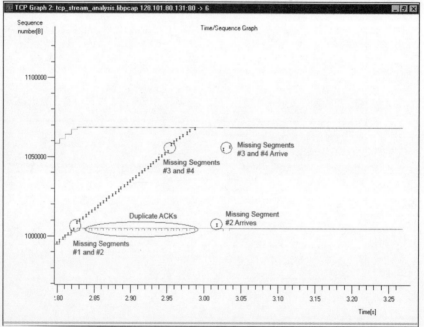

Figure 4.61 shows how this logjam is resolved.

In Figure 4.61, you can see the missing segment (presumed to be a retransmit) arrive. At this point, an ACK is transmitted acknowledging the last received segment, the TCP window increases, and the receiver begins to receive segments again.

## Throughput Graph

The throughput graph shows the throughput of the TCP stream vs. time (see Figure 4.62).

**Figure 4.61** Time-sequence Graph (tcptrace) - Zoom in on Retransmit

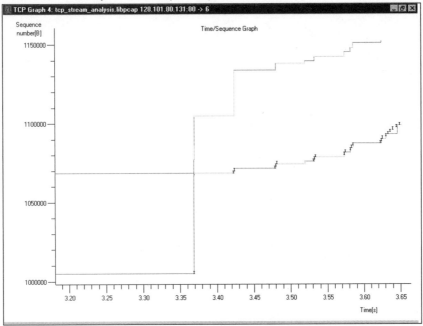

**Figure 4.62** Throughput Graph

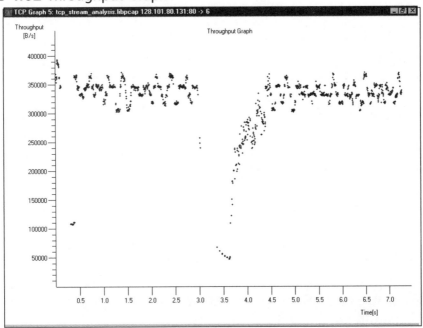

As seen in Figure 4.62, the throughput fell off dramatically during the retransmit sequence seen in the time-sequence graphs.

## Graph Control

Throughout this section, we refer to any window containing a TCP stream analysis graph as a *graph window*. The term graph window refers to a Stevens' or tcptrace style time-sequence graph, a throughput graph, or an RTT graph. Whenever a graph window is created, a Graph Control dialog box is also created (see Figure 4.63).

**Figure 4.63** Graph Control Dialog Box: Zoom Tab

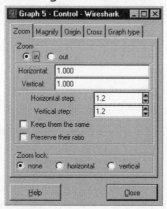

Notice that the number on the dialog box (*1*) matches the number on the graph window in Figure 4.59 (*1*). In the event that multiple graph windows are opened, you can use the index number to associate a Graph Control dialog box with its graph window.

The **Zoom** tab allows you to set the parameters related to the zoom functionality of the graph function (see Figure 4.63). The **Horizontal** and **Vertical** text boxes show the amount of zoom currently employed in the graph window.

The **Horizontal step** and **Vertical step** text boxes allow you to set the horizontal and vertical zoom factors applied to the graph when you press **Shift+middle-click** in the graph window. If you enable the **Keep them the same** checkbox, whenever you change either the horizontal step or the vertical step, the other will be changed to the same value. The **Preserve their ratio** checkbox causes the ratio between the horizontal step and the vertical step to be preserved. If the horizontal step is 1.2 and the vertical step is 2.4, when you change the horizontal step to 1.3, the vertical step will automatically change to 2.6.

The **Zoom lock** section allows you to lock the horizontal or vertical steps so that zoom is not applied to them. If the **horizontal** option is enabled, no matter what the value is for the horizontal step, zooming will not change the horizontal scale. If the **vertical** option is enabled, no matter what the value is for a vertical step, zooming will not change the vertical scale.

The **Magnify** tab allows you to control the parameters associated with the magnify functionality (see Figure 4.64).

**Figure 4.64** Graph Control Dialog Box - Magnify Tab

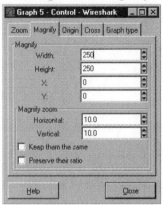

The **Width** and **Height** text boxes allow you to set the width and height of the magnification box that is displayed when you press **Ctrl+right-click** in the graph window. The **X:** and **Y:** text boxes allow you to set the x and y offset of the magnification box from the location of the mouse pointer. This can be useful for offsetting the magnification box to where it won't occlude the graph. The **Horizontal:** and **Vertical:** text boxes allow you to set the zoom factor used to blow up the graph in the magnification box. The **Keep them the same** checkbox causes the horizontal and vertical zoom factors to change in accordance with one another, and the **Preserve their ratio** checkbox causes the ratio between the horizontal and vertical zoom factors to remain constant.

The **Origin** tab allows you to change the various origins of the graph (see Figure 4.65).

The **Time origin** section allows you to choose the zero of time for your graph. If you select the **beginning of this TCP connection** option, you establish the beginning of the TCP connection as being graphed as your zero of time. If you select the **beginning of capture** option, you establish the beginning of the capture as your zero of time.

The **Sequence number origin** section allows you to choose whether your actual TCP sequence numbers or the relative TCP sequence numbers (the TCP sequence numbers minus your initial TCP sequence number) are shown on the

**Figure 4.65** Graph Control Dialog Box - Origin Tab

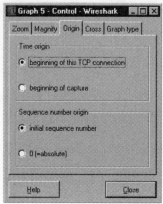

graph. It is often convenient to use the relative sequence number, because it gives you an idea of how much data has been transmitted. If you select the **initial sequence number** option, the relative TCP sequence numbers will be used. If you select the **0 (=absolute)** option, the actual TCP sequence numbers will be used in the graph.

The **Cross** tab allows you to control whether crosshairs follow the mouse pointer in the graph window (see Figure 4.66).

**Figure 4.66** Graph Control Dialog Box - Cross Tab

If you select the **off** radio button, there will be no crosshairs following the mouse pointer in the graph window. If you select the **on** option, there will be crosshairs following the mouse pointer in the graph window.

Once the graph window is displayed, use the **Graph type** tab to change which type of graph is being displayed (see Figure 4.67).

**Figure 4.67** Graph Control Dialog Box - Graph Type Tab

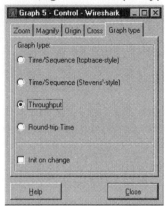

If you select the **Time/Sequence (tcptrace-style)** option, the Time-sequence (tcptrace-style) window will be displayed. If you select the **Time/Sequence (**Stevens'-style**)** option, the time-sequence (Stevens'-style) window will be displayed. If you select the **Throughput** option, the throughput graph window will be displayed. If you select the **Round-trip Time** option, the RTT graph window will be displayed.

By default, if you have applied a zoom to the graph window for one graph type, it will persist if you change graph types. If the **Init on change** checkbox is enabled, each time you change graph types the zoom will be reset.

# Help

The **Help** menu is shown in Figure 4.68, and the **Help** options are explained in Table 4.16.

**Table 4.16** Help Menu Options

| Menu Option | Description |
| --- | --- |
| Contents | Displays the contents for the Wireshark online help. |
| Supported Protocols | Displays a list of the supported protocols and the display filter fields they provide. |
| Manual Pages | A submenu for accessing traditional UNIX-style manual pages for Wireshark, Wireshark filters, and command line utilities. |
| Wireshark Online | A submenu for accessing online Wireshark resources. |
| About Wireshark | Displays information about Wireshark version and compile information. |

**Figure 4.68** Help Menu

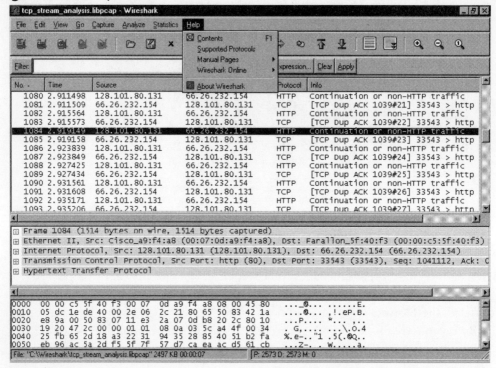

## Contents

The Contents dialog box can be displayed by selecting **Help | Contents** from the menu bar (see Figure 4.69).

This dialog box provides an overview of Wireshark information, including Getting Started, Capturing, Capture Filters, Display Filters, and answers to Frequently Asked Questions (FAQs).

## Supported Protocols

The Supported Protocols dialog box can be displayed by selecting **Help | Supported Protocols** from the menu bar (see Figure 4.70).

This dialog box provides a list of the protocols supported by the current version of Wireshark, and a list of the display filter fields provided in the current version of Wireshark.

**Figure 4.69** Help Contents Dialog Box

**Figure 4.70** Supported Protocols Dialog Box

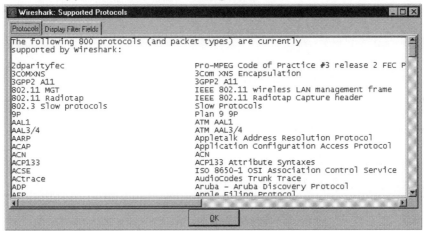

# Manual Pages Submenu

The Manual Pages submenu can be displayed by selecting **Help | Manual Pages** from the menu bar (see Figure 4.71). The Manual Pages submenu options are described in Table 4.17.

**Figure 4.71** Manual Pages Submenu

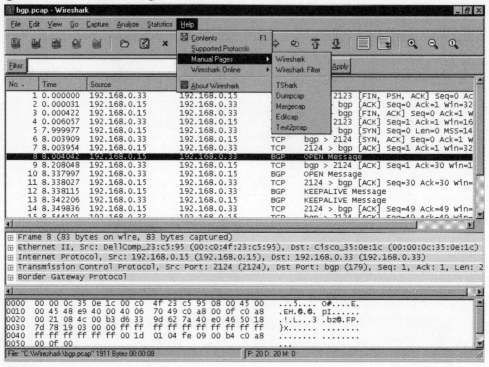

**Table 4.17** Manual Pages Submenu Options

| Menu Option | Description |
| --- | --- |
| Wireshark | Opens the manual page (manpage) for Wireshark. |
| Wireshark Filter | Opens the manpage for creating Wireshark filters. |
| TShark | Opens the manpage for TShark, the command-line version of Wireshark. |
| Dumpcap | Opens the manpage for Dumpcap, a command-line packet capture utility. |
| Mergecap | Opens the manpage for Mergecap, a command-line utility for merging two or more libpcap capture files |
| Editcap | Opens the manpage for Mergecap, a command-line utility for editing and translating libpcap files. |
| Text2pcap | Opens the manpage for text2pcap, a command-line utility for generating capture files from a text hexdump of packets |

All of the Manual Pages submenu options display a Hypertext Markup Language (HTML)-formatted UNIX-style manpage with the default system Web browser. All of the command-line tools support libpcap files, (as indicated by the manpages), which is the default format used by Wireshark.

## Wireshark Online Submenu

The Wireshark Online submenu can be displayed by selecting **Help | Wireshark Online** from the menu bar (see Figure 4.72). The Wireshark Online submenu options are described in Table 4.18.

**Figure 4.72** Wireshark Online Submenu

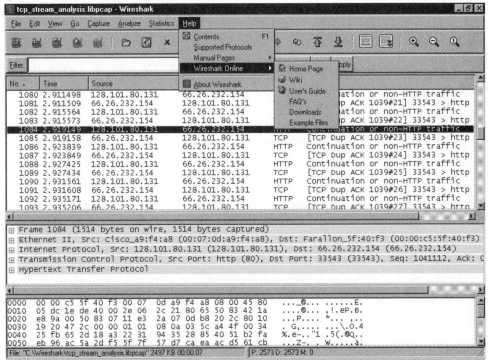

**Table 4.18** Wireshark Online Options

| Menu Option | Description |
| --- | --- |
| Home Page | Opens the Wireshark homepage, www.wireshark.org. |
| Wiki | Opens the Wireshark Wiki, http://wiki.wireshark.org. |
| User's Guide | Opens the online Wireshark User's Guide. |

**Continued**

**Table 4.18 continued** Wireshark Online Options

| Menu Option | Description |
| --- | --- |
| FAQ's | Opens the FAQ section of the Wireshark Web site. |
| Downloads | Opens the Downloads section of the Wireshark Web site. |
| Example Files | Opens the Sample captures section of the Wireshark Wiki. Here you can find the *bgp.pcap.gz* capture used in this chapter, as well as other real-world captures. |

The Wireshark Online Options submenu provides instant access to more online content than we can cover in this book. The items and information available online are a great supplement to this book.

# About Wireshark

The About Wireshark dialog box can be displayed by selecting **Help | About Plugins** from the menu bar (see Figure 4.73).

**Figure 4.73** About Wireshark Dialog Box

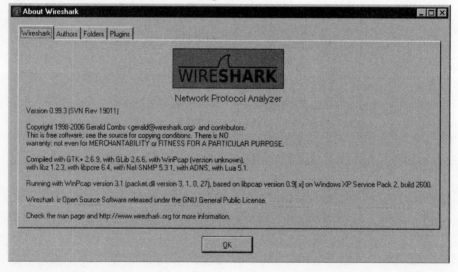

This dialog box contains information about the version of Wireshark you are running and the options it was compiled with. This information is important to know when you report a bug to the Wireshark developers.

# Pop-up Menus

Wireshark has context-sensitive pop-up menus to assist you in performing tasks. None of these menus provide any additional functionality beyond what is available through the menu bar, but they are easier and quicker to use in some circumstances.

## Summary Window Pop-up Menu

The Summary window pop-up menu can be displayed by right-clicking on the Summary window (see Figure 4.74).

**Figure 4.74** Summary Window Pop-up Menu

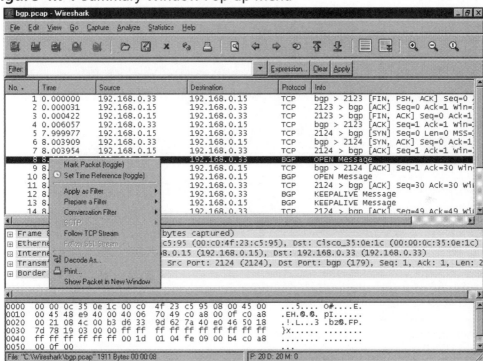

Table 4.19 indicates where to find more information in this chapter on the Summary window pop-up menu options.

**Table 4.19** Summary Window Pop-up Menu References

| Menu Option | Reference |
|---|---|
| Mark Packet (toggle) | See "Edit: Mark Packet" |
| Set Time Reference (toggle) | See "Edit: Time Reference" |
| Apply as Filter | See "Analyze: Apply as Filter" |
| Prepare a Filter | See "Analyze: Prepare a Filter" |
| Conversation Filter | Opens the Conversation Filter submenu for filtering based on Ethernet, IP, TCP, UDP or PN-CBA Server |
| SCTP Submenu | Opens the SCTP submenu for following SCTP streams for Public Switched Telephone Network (PSTN) over IP |
| Follow TCP Stream | See "Analyze: Follow TCP Stream" |
| Follow SSL Stream | See "Analyze: Follow SSL Stream" |
| Decode As... | See "Analyze: Decode As" |
| Print... | See "File: Print" |
| Show Packet in New Window | See "View: Show Packet in New Window" |

# Protocol Tree Window Pop-up Menu

The Protocol Tree pop-up menu can be displayed by right-clicking on the Protocol Tree window (see Figure 4.75).

Table 4.20 includes descriptions for some items and indicates where to find more information in this chapter for other items.

**Table 4.20** Protocol Tree Window Pop-up Menu References/Descriptions

| Menu Option | Reference/Description |
|---|---|
| Copy | Copies the contents of the selected line to the clipboard |
| Expand Subtrees | See "View: Expand Subtrees" |
| Expand All | See "View: Expand All" |
| Collapse All | See "View: Collapse All" |
| Apply as Filter | See "Analyze: Apply as Filter" |
| Prepare a Filter | See "Analyze: Prepare a Filter" |
| Follow TCP Stream | See "Analyze: Follow TCP Stream" |

**Continued**

**Table 4.20 continued** Protocol Tree Window Pop-up Menu
References/Descriptions

| Menu Option | Reference/Description |
|---|---|
| Follow SSL Stream | See "Analyze: Follow SSL Stream" |
| Wiki Protocol Page | Opens the Wireshark Wiki at http://wiki.wireshark.org with the default system Web browser to the page for the selected protocol in the tree. |
| Filter Field Reference | Opens the Wireshark Documentation Web site on creating filters for the selected protocol with the default system Web browser. |
| Protocol Preferences | See "Edit: Preferences" |
| Decode As... | See "Analyze: Decode As" |
| Resolve Name | Forces resolution of all names for this packet. See the Wireshark Name Resolution sidebar for more information about Wireshark name resolution. Note that this option is only available if all name resolution is disabled. |
| Go to Corresponding Packet | See "Edit: Go To Corresponding Packet" |

**Figure 4.75** Protocol Tree Window Pop-up Menu

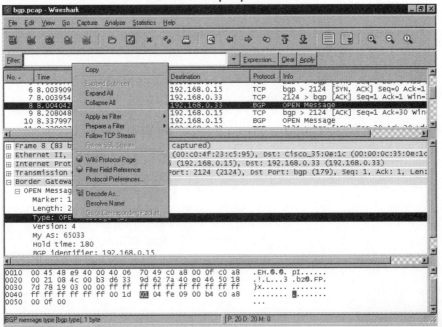

# Data View Window Pop-up Menu

The Data View window pop-up menu can be displayed by right-clicking in the Data View window (see Figure 4.76).

**Figure 4.76** Data View Window Pop-up Menu

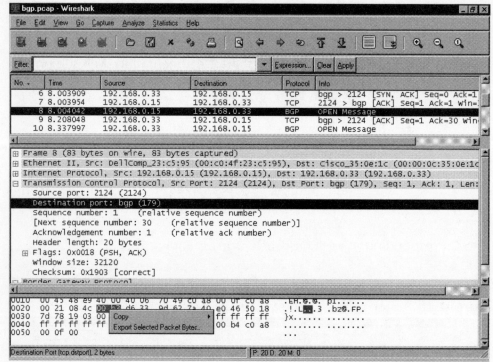

Table 4.22 indicates where to find more information in this chapter on the Data View window pop-up menu options.

**Table 4.22** Data View Window Pop-up Menu References

| Menu Option | Reference |
| --- | --- |
| Copy Submenu | Displays the Copy submenu in order to copy the entire contents of the decoded packet, as either the entire data block or just the ASCII reproducible characters. |
| Export Selected Packet Bytes | Allows the currently selected bytes to be exported in raw data format. |

# Using Command-line Options

Wireshark supports a large number of command-line options. This section documents some of the most commonly used options.

## Capture and File Options

The most commonly used Wireshark options are those related to captures and files. Table 4.23 lists some of the most common command-line options related to these tasks.

**Table 4.23** Capture and File Command Line Options

| Command Line Option | Description |
|---|---|
| *-i <interface>* | Sets the name of the interface used for live captures to *<interface>*. |
| *-k* | Starts capture immediately; requires the *–i* option. |
| *-a <test>:<value>* | Sets an autostop condition for the capture. *<test>* may be one of duration or filesize. If the *<test>* is duration, *<value>* must be the number of seconds the capture should run before it stops. If *<test>* is the filesize, *<value>* is the number of kilobytes that should be captured before the capture stops. |
| *-c <count>* | Sets the number of packets to read before stopping the capture. After *<count>* packets have been read the capture stops. |
| *-r <filename>* | Reads the capture saved in *<filename>*. |
| *-w <filename>* | Writes the capture to *<filename>*. |
| *-b <count>* | Enables the use of *<count>* files in a ring buffer for captures. A maximum capture size must be specified with the *–a filesize:<value>* option. |

To capture on interface *eth0* immediately and write the results to a ring buffer with three files of maximum size *100* kilobytes with base filename *foo.bar.libpcap*, execute the following at the command line:

```
Wireshark -i eth0 -k -w foo.bar.libpcap -b 3 -a filesize:100
```

# Filter Options

Wireshark also allows you to specify filter information from the command line. Table 4.24 lists some of the most commonly used filter-related command-line options.

**Table 4.24** Filter Command Line Options

| Command Line Option | Description |
| --- | --- |
| *-f <capture filter >* | Set the tcpdump style capture filter string to *<filter string>*. |
| *-R <display filter>* | Only applicable when reading a capture from a file with the *–r* option. Applies the display filter *<display filter>* to all packets in the capture file and discards those that do not match. |

To extract all packets from capture file *bgp.pcap.gz* with *bgp.type == 2*, execute the following at the command line:

```
Wireshark -r bgp.pcap.gz -R "bgp.type == 2"
```

# Other Options

Other commonly used options are shown in Table 4.25.

**Table 4.25** Other Command-line Options

| Command Line Option | Description |
| --- | --- |
| *-N <flags>* | Turns on name resolution. Depending on which letters follow *–N*, various names will be resolved by Wireshark. *n* will cause network name resolution to be turned on, *t* will enable transport name resolution, *m* will enable MAC address resolution, and *C* will enable asynchronous DNS lookups for network name resolution. |
| *-v* | Prints the Wireshark version information. |
| *-h* | Prints Wireshark's help information. |

# Summary

In this chapter, you learned about the major components of the Wireshark GUI. You also learned about the major functionality of the Wireshark application and how to access it.

You should now be able to perform network captures, open saved network captures, and print captures. You are also equipped to use display filters to filter the packets displayed in the Summary window, color the packets in the Summary window for easier readability, or find a packet in the capture with particular characteristics.

We've shown you how to navigate the protocol tree in the Protocol Tree window to examine the contents of a packet, and to use the Protocol Tree fields to prepare new display filter strings.

Finally, we showed you how to force a packet or group of packets to be decoded by a particular dissector. You also learned how to enable and disable decoding of particular protocols, and should have some understanding of how to use some of the more commonly used tools in Wireshark to gain better visibility into TCP Streams.

# Solutions Fast Track

## Getting started with Wireshark

☑ Binary Wireshark packages for Windows, Linux, and various UNIX programs can be downloaded from www.wireshark.org.

☑ Source code can be downloaded and compiled from www.wireshark.org if the binary packages available don't meet your needs.

☑ Wireshark can be launched by typing **wireshark** at the command line.

## Exploring the Main Windows

☑ The Summary window provides a one-line summary for each packet.

☑ The Protocol Tree window provides a detailed decode of the packet selected in the Summary window.

☑ The Data View window provides the hexadecimal dump of a packet's actual bytes.

# Other Window Components

☑ The filter bar provides a quick mechanism for filtering the packets displayed in the Summary window.

☑ Clicking the filter bar's **Filter:** button displays the Display Filter dialog box to help you construct a display filter string.

☑ The **Information** field shows the display filter field name of the field selected in the Protocol Tree window.

# Exploring the Menus

☑ Most preferences can be set in the Preferences dialog box.

☑ There are context-sensitive pop-up menus available by right-clicking on the Summary window, Protocol Tree window, or Data View window.

☑ Packets in the Summary window can be color-coded for easy reading using the Apply Color Filters dialog box.

# Using Command-line Options

☑ Wireshark can apply display filters to packets read from a file with the *−R* flag, discarding packets that don't match the filter.

☑ Wireshark uses *−r* to indicate a file to read from and *−w* to indicate a file to write to.

☑ Wireshark can be made to start capturing from an interface immediately on startup by using the *−i* and *-k* options.

# Frequently Asked Questions

The following Frequently Asked Questions, answered by the authors of this book, are designed to both measure your understanding of the concepts presented in this chapter and to assist you with real-life implementation of these concepts. To have your questions about this chapter answered by the author, browse to **www.syngress.com/solutions** and click on the **"Ask the Author"** form.

**Q:** Why is Wireshark so slow displaying data during capture? It seems to lock up.

**A:** Your version of Wireshark may have been compiled without the Asynchronous DNS (ADNS) library. If so, Wireshark is stopping to do a DNS lookup for the source and destination IP address in each packet it decodes. It can take a long time for DNS queries to time out if they fail, and during this time, Wireshark may lock up while waiting for those failures. To solve this problem, get a version of Wireshark with ADNS compiled in. To work around this problem, deselect **Enable Network Name Resolution** in the Capture Options dialog box when starting a capture, or in the File dialog box when opening a capture file.

**Q:** Why is it that when I select some fields in the Protocol Tree window I don't see the field name in the Information field? How can I filter on the field if I can't find out its name?

**A:** Wireshark has been developed over many years by a team of volunteer programmers. Many different people have written the dissectors, which decode the protocols in Wireshark, at many different times. Not all dissector authors associated a filterable field with each field they display in the Protocol Tree. You will not be able to filter on such fields. If such filtering is important to you for a particular protocol, you are encouraged to alter the source code for that dissector to include the capacity, and submit it to the Wireshark team for inclusion.

**Q:** Why do I sometimes see an IP address or a TCP/UDP port number or a MAC address twice, once in parenthesis and once not?

**A:** When name resolution is turned off for an address type, or when no name is found for a given address, Wireshark inserts the actual address into the place where the name would have gone. As a result, the place where you would have seen the name with the address in parentheses (or vice versa) will show two copies of the address.

**Q:** I need more complicated capture filtering than tcpdump-style capture filters provide. Can I use Wireshark's display filters to restrict what I capture?

**A:** The short answer is no. Wireshark will not allow you to use display filters to filter on capture. However, there is a workaround to achieve this. While Wireshark will not allow you to use display filters on capture, Tshark will. To capture from an interface *<interface>* to a file *<savefile>* filtering with a display filter string *<filter string>* execute the following at the command line:

```
tshark -i <interface> -w <savefile> -R <filter string>
```

Tshark will capture from *<interface>* and only save to *<savefile>* those packets that match <filter string>. In many cases, display filter strings will not be as fast as the tcpdump-style capture filters.

**Q:** Does Wireshark really capture all the traffic arriving at an interface when capturing in promiscuous mode?

**A:** That depends. Wireshark gets whatever is captured by libpcap. Sometimes, due to a high load on the system you are capturing from, or just due to trying to capture from too-high bandwidth an interface, packets may be lost for a number of reasons, including being dropped by the kernel.

**Q:** Why am I seeing packets that aren't addressed to or being sent by my local interface even though I've turned off capturing in promiscuous mode?

**A:** There may be other applications running (e.g., Snort) on the system you are capturing from that have put the interface into promiscuous mode. Whether Wireshark or some other application puts the interface in promiscuous mode, if the interface is in promiscuous mode, you will see all traffic that arrives at it, not just the traffic addressed to or sent from the interface.

# Chapter 5

# Filters

## Solutions in this chapter:

- **Writing Capture Filters**
- **Writing Display Filters**

☑ **Summary**

☑ **Solutions Fast Track**

☑ **Frequently Asked Questions**

# Introduction

When capturing packets from a network interface, Wireshark's default behavior is to capture all of the packets provided by the operating system's (OSes) device driver. On a lightly loaded home network this is not a problem; however, on a busy network at a large enterprise, the deluge of packets would be too much to handle. Wireshark provides *capture filters*, which allow you to capture only the packets that you are interested in. By using capture filters, the OS sends only selected packets to Wireshark for processing.

Once the packets are loaded into Wireshark, there may still be too many. For this situation, Wireshark provides *display filters,* which allow you to specify which packets are shown in Wireshark's Graphical User Interface (GUI). Because all of the packets are still in memory, they become visible when you reset your display filter.

The difference between *capture filters* and *display filters* is in how they are implemented in Wireshark. The Wireshark program relies on a program library to capture packets. On UNIX, the library is *pcap* (also known as *libpcap*), and is maintained by the same group that developed *tcpdump*, the UNIX Command Line Interface (CLI) sniffer (available at www.tcpdump.org). On Windows, the library is *WinPcap*, which is a device driver and dynamic link library (DLL) that provides a *pcap* interface for Windows programs. For convenience, we refer to *pcap* and *WinPcap* as *pcap*, because for our purposes they are operationally equivalent.

The *pcap* library provides a capture-filtering mechanism and a fast filtering engine to Wireshark. The packet data must be analyzed to determine if it passes the filter condition. If the analysis takes a long time, your OS may not have time to address the next incoming packet, thus resulting in a dropped packet.

*pcap*'s filter language is not powerful or expressive enough for many sniffing and analysis needs. To overcome this deficiency, display filters were introduced to Wireshark that enable you to use the protocol and field names to filter packets for display. Display filters rely on a complete dissection of the packet by Wireshark, and thus are much slower than capture filters. Each type of filter has its place; capture filters are good for quickly discarding packets from a live network interface, and display filters are good for fine-tuning which packets you see after they have been loaded into Wireshark.

# Writing Capture Filters

Wireshark's capture filters (often called *tcpdump* filters) use the *pcap* library's filter mechanism. The filter syntax is documented in the *tcpdump* manual page (man page). Any program that uses *pcap* (e.g., *tcpdump* or Wireshark) can use this filter syntax.

While *tcpdump* can *decode* protocols, it cannot directly *address* many of them. The keywords defined in the *tcpdump* filter language are oriented toward Link layer (layer 2) and Transmission Control Protocol/Internet Protocol (TCP/IP) filtering.

---

**NOTE**

The man page is the documentation that comes with UNIX programs. Man pages can be read using the UNIX *man* command (e.g., you would type **man tcpdump** to read the *tcpdump* man page). The Wireshark man page can be read by typing **man wireshark**. Many man pages are available on the Web as Hypertext Markup Language (HTML). See the *tcpdump* man page at www.tcpdump.org/tcpdump_man.html.

---

## *tcpdump* Syntax Explained

The *tcpdump* filter language provides keywords that are used to match the values of host addresses, hardware addresses, and ports. It also allows to you look for specific protocols or at arbitrary bytes in the packet data.

### Host Names and Addresses

*tcpdump* filters are commonly used to capture network traffic that is originating from or destined for a particular Internet Protocol (IP) address. An Internet Protocol version 4 (IPv4) address, Internet Protocol version 6 (IPv6) address, or a hostname can be identified using the *host* command; e.g., to capture all IPv4 packets that have a source or destination address of 192.168.1.1, you would use:

```
host 192.168.1.1
```

You can use an IPv6 address to capture IPv6 packets:

```
host 2::8100:2:30a:c392:fc5a
```

You can also use a hostname that resolves to either an IPv4 or IPv6 address:

```
host www.wireshark.org
```

The above codes return any IP packets (e.g., Transmission Control Protocol [TCP] and User Datagram Protocol [UDP]) that have an IP source or destination address that matches the given IP address or hostname. Furthermore, if the hostname resolves to more than one IP address, all of the resolved IP addresses are used in the match.

To narrow the filter to capture packets that only originate from an IP address, use the *src* (source) command:

```
src host 192.168.1.1
```

Similarly, to match a destination IP address, use the *dst* (destination) command:

```
dst host 192.168.255.255
```

You can also use a shorthand notation to check host addresses without using *host*:

```
src 192.168.1.1
dst 192.168.255.255
```

The *host* command allows you to check for an IP address, and the *net* command allows you to check for an IP network. Use the *net* keyword in combination with an address formatted in Classless Inter-domain Routing (CIDR) notation. CIDR notation is made up of an IPv4 address and a number, separated by a slash (/). The number after the slash specifies the number of bits (out of 32) in the IPv4 address that make up the network portion of the address. To look at packets coming from any host on the 192.168.100.0 network, i.e. which uses 24 bits for the network number (255.255.255.0 netmask), you would use this capture filter:

```
src net 192.168.100.0/24
```

# Hardware Addresses

Use the *ether* (Ethernet) modifier to capture packets based on the hardware address of the network card. For example, to find all broadcast packets (i.e., packets destined for the hardware address *ff:ff:ff:ff:ff:ff*) use:

```
ether host ff:ff:ff:ff:ff:ff
```

There are also Fiber Distributed Data Interface (*fddi*) and Token Ring (*tr*) keywords that match the hardware addresses of Network Interface Cards (NICs). However, because *ether*, *fddi*, and *tr* all contain 6-byte hardware addresses in their protocol headers, the *tcpdump* filter language treats them as synonyms. Any of the three keywords can be used, no matter which topology is on your NIC; however, in practice, ether is most commonly used.

The *ether* modifier is placed before the *dst* and *src* modifiers. To capture packets destined for a particular hardware address enter:

```
ether dst host ff:ff:ff:ff:ff:ff
```

You can also use shorthand:

```
ether dst ff:ff:ff:ff:ff:ff
```

The *src* modifier is used to filter packets based on the source hardware address:

```
ether src host 00:f9:06:aa:01:03
ether src 00:f9:06:aa:01:03
```

# Ports

The *port* keyword can be used to capture packets that are destined for certain applications. For example, to capture only Hypertext Transfer Protocol (HTTP) packets (commonly sent on TCP port 80), use:

```
port 80
```

This checks for packets on both UDP port 80 and TCP port 80. To narrow it down to TCP, use *tcp* as the qualifier:

```
tcp port 80
```

If HTTP is defined for a port number in the */etc/services* file on UNIX, use:

```
tcp port http
```

The *udp* keyword can be used to capture UDP packets on a certain port. If you are sniffing for UDP requests being sent to a Domain Name Server (DNS), you want to capture UDP packets destined for port 53:

```
udp dst port 53
```

If you want replies, look for UDP packets with a port 53 source:

```
udp src port 53
```

# Logical Operations

The *tcpdump* filter language allows you to combine several statements with logical operators to create complicated filters. The logic operator *not* reverses the value of a test, while *and* and *or* let you join multiple tests. These three logic keywords have alternate representations that are used in the C programming language:

- **not** is equivalent to **!**
- **and** is equivalent to **&&**
- **or** is equivalent to **||**

You can also use parentheses when you need to group multiple statements with logical operations. Parentheses are not always needed, but can be used to make a filter easier to understand.

To capture everything except DNS lookups, use:

```
not port 53
```

Normally, *port 53* captures any TCP or UDP packets with a source or destination port of 53. The logical keyword *not* reverses the sense of the filter so that everything is captured *except* for TCP and UDP packets with a source or destination port of 53.

The logical operator *and* is used to require that multiple conditions in a test be true. For example, to look at Telnet packets to or from the host www.wireshark.org, use:

```
host www.wireshark.org and port telnet
```

If you want either Telnet packets or Secure Shell (SSH) packets, use:

```
port telnet or port ssh
```

To combine the *port telnet or port ssh* test with a test for the www.wireshark.org host, use *and* and parentheses:

```
host www.wireshark.org and ( port telnet or port ssh )
```

The logical operators *and* and *or* have the same precedence, which means that they are analyzed in the order in which they are listed in the capture filter. If parentheses are not used, the capture filter will test for Telnet packets to or from the host www.wireshark.org, or SSH packets to and from any IP address:

```
host www.wireshark.org and port telnet or port ssh
```

# Protocols

The *tcpdump* filter syntax provides some protocol names as keywords, allowing you to test for the existence of those protocols. These protocol keywords are:

- *aarp* AppleTalk Address Resolution Protocol
- *ah* Authentication Header
- *arp* Address Resolution Protocol
- *atalk* AppleTalk
- *clnp* Connectionless Network Protocol
- *decnet* Digital Equipment Corporation Network protocol suite
- *esis* (or *es-is*) End System-to-Intermediate System
- *esp* Encapsulating Security Payload

- *icmp* Internet Control Message Protocol
- *icmp6* Internet Control Message Protocol, for IPv6
- *igmp* Internet Group Management Protocol
- *igrp* Interior Gateway Routing Protocol
- *ip* Internet Protocol
- *ip6* Internet Protocol version 6
- *ipx* Internetwork Packet Exchange
- *isis* (or *is-is*) Intermediate System-to-Intermediate System
- *iso* International Organization for Standardization
- *lat* Local Area Transport
- *mopdl* Maintenance Operation Protocol
- *moprc* Maintenance Operation Protocol
- *netbeui* NetBIOS Extended User Interface
- *pim* Protocol Independent Multicast
- *rarp* Reverse Address Resolution Protocol
- *sca* Systems Communication Architecture
- *sctp* Stream Control Transmission Protocol
- *stp* Spanning Tree Protocol
- *tcp* Transmission Control Protocol
- *udp* User Datagram Protocol
- *vrrp* Virtual Router Redundancy Protocol

For example, to capture all ICMP packets the capture filter use:

```
icmp
```

To capture everything that is not an Internetwork Packet Exchange (IPX) packet, use negation and the protocol keyword:

```
not ipx
```

Some protocols indicate the type of payload a packet is carrying (e.g., the IP header contains a *protocol* field whose numeric value indicates the type of payload it is carrying). Possible values for this protocol field are 1 (ICMP), 5 (TCP), and 17 (UDP). On UNIX systems, there is a list of IP protocol numbers in the */etc/protocols* file.

The *tcpdump* filter syntax allows you to test the *proto* (protocol) field. You can also use the *proto* keyword with the *ether, fddi, tr, ppp, ip, ip6,* and *iso* protocol keywords. For example, while you can test for the presence of the TCP protocol via the *tcp* keyword, you can also check for 5 as the value of the IP protocol field, as "5" designates TCP:

```
ip proto 5
```

# Protocol Fields

While *tcpdump* can decode many protocols, the *tcpdump* filter syntax does not allow you to easily test for the values of all fields that *tcpdump* knows how to parse. Many protocol names are provided as keywords, but very few fields within these protocols have names in the *tcpdump* filter syntax.

*tcpdump* filters allow you to compare values out of a packet, so that if the offset of a field within a protocol is known, its value can be checked. This method is not as good as using a field name, but it works.

To retrieve a single byte from a packet, use square brackets to indicate the offset of that byte from the beginning of a particular protocol. Offsets start at zero (e.g., *tcp[0]* gives the first byte in the TCP header and *tcp[1]* gives the second byte). Figure 5.1 shows the bit layout of the TCP header, as defined by Request For Comment (RFC) 793 (available at www.ibiblio.org/pub/docs/rfc/rfc793.txt).

**Figure 5.1** TCP Header Layout

| 0 1 2 3 4 5 6 7 8 9 10 11 12 13 14 15 | 16 17 18 19 20 21 22 23 24 26 27 28 29 30 31 32 |
|---|---|
| Source Port | Destination Port |
| Sequence Number | |
| Acknowledgment Number | |
| Data Offset / Reserved / URG ACK PSH RST SYN FIN | Windows |
| Checksum | Urgent Pointer |
| Options | Padding |
| Data | |

You can also retrieve a 2-byte integer (*tcp[0:2]*) or a 4-byte integer (*tcp[0:4]*) by using a colon inside the square brackets. Multi-byte integers are always extracted in *network* order (also known as *big-endian* order). To compute the value of multi-byte network-order integers, use these formulas:

- **2-byte** *value = byte0* \* *0×100 + byte1*
- **4-byte** *value = byte0* \* *0×1000000 + byte1* \* *0×10000 + byte2* \* *0×100 + byte3*

The numbers preceded by *0×* in the formulas are hexadecimal.

Unfortunately, only some protocols allow you to retrieve bytes from their data. Interestingly, some protocols whose names cannot be used as keywords, allow you to retrieve their data by using square brackets. Square brackets can be used to retrieve bytes from these protocols:

- *arp* Address Resolution Protocol
- *atalk* Appletalk
- *decnet* Digital Equipment Corporation Network protocol suite
- *ether* Ethernet
- *fddi* Fiber Distributed Data Interface
- *icmp* Internet Control Message Protocol
- *igmp* Internet Group Management Protocol
- *igrp* Interior Gateway Routing Protocol
- *ip* Internet Protocol
- *lat* Local Area Transport
- *link* Link layer
- *mopdl* Maintenance Operation Protocol
- *moprc* Maintenance Operation Protocol
- *pim* Protocol Independent Multicast
- *ppp* Point-to-Point Protocol
- *rarp* Reverse Address Resolution Protocol
- *sca* Systems Communication Architecture
- *sctp* Stream Control Transmission Protocol
- *tcp* Transmission Control Protocol
- *tr* Token-Ring
- *udp* User Datagram Protocol
- *vrrp* Virtual Router Redundancy Protocol

The value that is retrieved from the packet data is an *integer*, which can be compared with any of the numeric relations shown in Table 5.1.

**Table 5.1** Numeric Relations

| Numeric Relation | Meaning |
| --- | --- |
| > | Greater Than |
| >= | Greater Than or Equal To |
| < | Less Than |
| <= | Less Than or Equal To |
| = or == | Equal To |
| != | Not Equal To |

Additionally, the arithmetic operators +, -, *, and / are provided, as are the bitwise operators & and |. The bitwise operator & allows you to logically *AND* the bits of integers, while the bitwise operator | allows you to logically *OR* the bits.

For example, the *icmp* keyword lets you filter for any ICMP packet; however, there are different types of ICMP packets, depending on their function. What if you want to look only for ICMP ping packets? The ICMP ping, or echo request/reply packet layout is shown in Figure 5.2, and comes from RFC 792 (available at www.ibiblio.org/pub/docs/rfc/rfc792.txt).

**Figure 5.2** ICMP Echo Request/Reply Header Layout

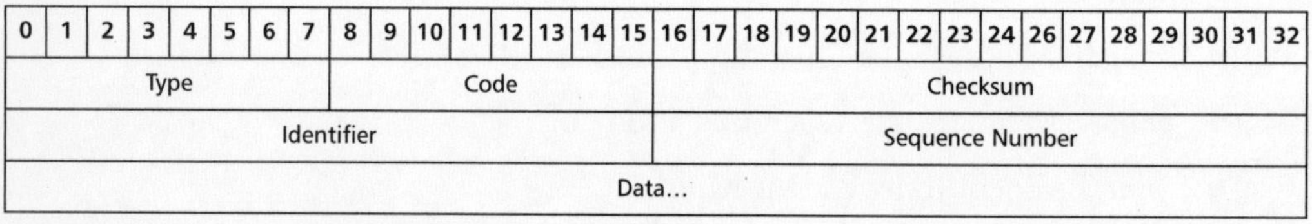

| 0 | 1 | 2 | 3 | 4 | 5 | 6 | 7 | 8 | 9 | 10 | 11 | 12 | 13 | 14 | 15 | 16 | 17 | 18 | 19 | 20 | 21 | 22 | 23 | 24 | 26 | 27 | 28 | 29 | 30 | 31 | 32 |
| --- | --- | --- | --- | --- | --- | --- | --- | --- | --- | --- | --- | --- | --- | --- | --- | --- | --- | --- | --- | --- | --- | --- | --- | --- | --- | --- | --- | --- | --- | --- | --- |
| Type | | | | | | | | Code | | | | | | | | Checksum | | | | | | | | | | | | | | | |
| Identifier | | | | | | | | | | | | | | | | Sequence Number | | | | | | | | | | | | | | | |
| Data... | | | | | | | | | | | | | | | | | | | | | | | | | | | | | | | |

The *type* ICMP protocol field, which is a 1-byte field at the very beginning of the ICMP protocol header, indicates the type of an ICMP packet. If the *type* field is 8, the packet is an ICMP *echo (ping) request*. If the *type* field is 0, the packet is an ICMP *echo (ping) reply*. This capture filter tests for packets that are either ICMP ping requests or ICMP ping replies by retrieving the first byte:

```
icmp[0] == 8 or icmp[0] == 0
```

*libpcap* has some constant value keywords (named after ICMP fields) that give the offset and the possible values of those fields. The value keywords can be used so that the numbers they stand for do not need to be remembered. For example, the *icmptype* is equal to the offset of the ICMP *type* field (which is 0), the *icmp-echo* variable is equal to 8, which means that the ICMP packet is an echo request, and *icmp-echoreply* is equal to 0, which means that the ICMP packet is an echo reply. The test for ICMP ping requests and replies can be written as:

```
icmp[icmptype] == icmp-echo or icmp[icmptype] == icmp-echoreply
```

The keywords that define constant values for field offsets are listed in Table 5.2.

**Table 5.2** Constant Value Keywords

| Keyword | Value | Used in Protocol |
| --- | --- | --- |
| *icmptype* | 0 | ICMP |
| *icmpcode* | 1 | ICMP |
| *tcpflags* | 13 | TCP |

Table 5.3 lists the keywords that provide names for the ICMP *type* values.

**Table 5.3** ICMP *type* Constant Value Keywords

| Keyword | Value |
| --- | --- |
| *icmp-echoreply* | 0 |
| *icmp-unreach* | 3 |
| *icmp-sourcequench* | 4 |
| *icmp-redirect* | 5 |
| *icmp-echo* | 8 |
| *icmp-routeradvert* | 9 |
| *icmp-routersolicit* | 10 |
| *icmp-timxceed* | 11 |
| *icmp-paramprob* | 12 |
| *icmp-tstamp* | 13 |
| *icmp-tstampreply* | 14 |
| *icmp-ireq* | 15 |
| *icmp-ireqreply* | 16 |
| *icmp-maskreq* | 17 |
| *icmp-maskreply* | 18 |

# Bitwise Operators

The TCP *flags* field is a bit field, which is an integer where the individual bits are used as separate fields. For example, the TCP *flags* field is an 8-bit integer field, but the bits in that integer represent independent fields that are either true or false (or 1 or 0). In the *tcpdump* filter language, the fields for TCP flags have keywords with constant values, as shown in Table 5.4.

**Table 5.4** TCP Flags Constant Value Keywords

| Keyword | Value |
| --- | --- |
| *tcp-fin* | 0x01 |
| *tcp-syn* | 0x02 |
| *tcp-rst* | 0x04 |
| *tcp-push* | 0x08 |
| *tcp-ack* | 0x10 |
| *tcp-urg* | 0x20 |

The *tcpdump* filter language defines keywords with constant values for the TCP *flags* field, because it is common to test for the values of this field when looking at TCP problems, especially when related to firewalls or Network Address Translation (NAT). It is important to know how to use bit–field operators properly, because complications arise when multiple bits can be set in the *bit* field. The TCP *flags* field can have multiple bits set. Table 5.5 shows the *flags* field of a TCP packet with its SYN bit (*tcp-syn*) set.

**Table 5.5** TCP SYN Packet Flags Bit Field

| URG | ACK | PUSH | RST | SYN | FIN |
| --- | --- | --- | --- | --- | --- |
| 0 | 0 | 0 | 0 | 1 | 0 |

In this case, only the *tcp-syn* bit is set; therefore, the value $0\times02$ can be tested, which is the value of *tcp-syn*:

```
tcp[tcpflag] == 0x02
```

or:

```
tcp[tcpflag] == tcp-syn
```

However, in the case of the second packet in a TCP handshake (a Synchronize (SYN)/Acknowledge (ACK) packet), both the *tcp-syn* and *tcp-ack* bits are set, as shown in Table 5.6.

**Table 5.6** TCP SYN/ACK Packet Flags Bit Field

| URG | ACK | PUSH | RST | SYN | FIN |
|-----|-----|------|-----|-----|-----|
| 0   | 1   | 0    | 0   | 1   | 0   |

When SYN and ACK are both set, the TCP *flags* field equals $0 \times 02 + 0 \times 10$, or $0 \times 12$. Thus, the filter *tcp[tcpflag] == tcp-syn* will fail to show the packets that have SYN plus any other field set; the filter will give you packets that have only SYN set. To write a filter to test for the SYN bit, use the bitwise *&* operator to mask out all of the bits except for the SYN bit.

```
tcp[tcpflag] & tcp-syn == 0x02
```

or:

```
tcp[tcpflag] & tcp-syn == tcp-syn
```

The bitwise arithmetic using *&* (bitwise AND) when comparing a TCP flags field that has SYN and ACK set, is shown in Table 5.7.

**Table 5.7** TCP SYN/ACK Packet Bitwise &Against *tcp-syn*

|      | URG | ACK | PUSH | RST | SYN | FIN | Value | Meaning |
|------|-----|-----|------|-----|-----|-----|-------|---------|
|      | 0   | 1   | 0    | 0   | 1   | 0   | 0x12  | SYN/ACK |
| AND  | 0   | 0   | 0    | 0   | 1   | 0   | 0x02  | tcp-syn |
|      | 0   | 0   | 0    | 0   | 1   | 0   | 0x02  | tcp-syn |

In this case, the bitwise *&* produces a result of $0 \times 02$, which is equal to *tcp-syn*; therefore, we have determined that the SYN bit is indeed set. By using bitwise *&*, you can tell if any particular bit in the bit field is set. Table 5.8 shows the bitwise arithmetic when the TCP packet is an ACK packet, and the TCP *flags* field has only ACK set.

**Table 5.8** TCP ACK Packet Bitwise & Against *tcp-syn*

|      | URG | ACK | PUSH | RST | SYN | FIN | Value | Meaning |
|------|-----|-----|------|-----|-----|-----|-------|---------|
|      | 0   | 1   | 0    | 0   | 0   | 0   | 0x10  | ACK     |
| AND  | 0   | 0   | 0    | 0   | 1   | 0   | 0x02  | tcp-syn |
|      | 0   | 0   | 0    | 0   | 0   | 0   | 0x00  | 0       |

The result is $0 \times 00$, which does not equal *tcp-syn*; therefore, a TCP ACK packet does not pass the *tcp[tcpflag] & tcp-syn == tcp-syn* test.

# Packet Size

The *tcpdump* filter language allows you to test metadata about a packet instead of data from a packet itself. The packet size is available in a variable named *len*, and can be tested with the standard arithmetic operators. To test for packets smaller than 100 bytes, use:

```
len < 100
```

The **less** and **greater** operators are built-in shorthand keywords for testing the **len** veriable against a number.

---

## Tools & Traps...

### Testing Capture Filters

Would you like to test your capture filter without actually loading Wireshark? Capture filters are the same filters that *tcpdump* uses, therefore, you can supply the capture filter on *tcpdump's* command line to see if *tcpdump* can understand your capture filter:

```
$ tcpdump less 100
```

If your capture filter uses punctuation that is normally special to the UNIX shell, you must enclose your capture filter in single quotes:

```
$ tcpdump 'len > 1500'
```

*Tcpdump* has a *–d* option, which shows you the Berkeley Packet Filter (BPF) code used to operate the capture filter. BPF is the mechanism that many OSes provide for packet capture filters. You can read about BPF, "The BSD Packet Filter: A New Architecture for User-Level Packet Capture," by Steven McCanne and Van Jacobson, at www.tcpdump.org/papers/bpf-usenix93.pdf. Here's an example of BPF code:

```
$ tcpdump -d  'len > 0xff'
(000) ld       #pktlen
(001) jgt      #0xff              jt 2     jf 3
(002) ret      #96
(003) ret      #0
```

# Examples

The following list includes some examples of capture filters.

- **All HTTP Packets** *tcp port 80*

- **Non-HTTP Packets** not *tcp port 80*, *!tcp port 80*, *tcp port not 80*, or *tcp port !80*

- **HTTP Browsing to www.wireshark.org** *tcp port 80* and *dst www.wireshark.org*

- **HTTP Browsing to Hosts Other Than www.wireshark.org** *tcp port 80 and not dst www.wireshark.org*

- **IPX Packets** *ipx*

- **IPX Packets Destined for IPX Network 00:01:F0:EE** Not possible, because you cannot retrieve bytes using the *ipx* keyword

- **TCP Packets** *tcp* or *ip proto 5*

- **TCP SYN Packets** *tcp[tcpflag] & tcp-syn == tcp-syn*

- **IP Packets with Total Length > 255** *ip[2:2] > 0xff*

- **IP or IPX Packets** *ip* or *ipx*

# Using Capture Filters

TShark accepts capture filters on the command-line with the *-f* option, as shown in this example.

```
# tshark -i eth1 -f icmp
Capturing on eth1
  0.000000    10.0.0.5 -> 10.0.0.1      ICMP Echo (ping) request
  0.000062    10.0.0.1 -> 10.0.0.5      ICMP Echo (ping) reply
  1.010753    10.0.0.5 -> 10.0.0.1      ICMP Echo (ping) request
  1.010814    10.0.0.1 -> 10.0.0.5      ICMP Echo (ping) reply
```

Remember that the argument to *-f* is a single argument. If your capture filter has spaces in it, you must surround the capture filter in quotes so that it is passed as a single argument of the *-f* option:

```
# tshark -i eth1 -f 'icmp[0] == 0 or icmp[0] == 8'
```

Conveniently, like *tcpdump*, *tshark* also accepts any leftover arguments on the command line and uses them as a capture filter:

```
# tshark -i eth1 icmp[0] == 8
```

When using this facility, you cannot use the *-f* option.

```
# tshark -f icmp -i eth1 icmp[0] == 8
tshark: Capture filters were specified both with "-f" and with additional
command-line arguments
```

When using capture filters on the command line, be aware of characters that are special to the UNIX shell. This filter should be picking up echo requests and echo replies, however, only echo replies are seen.

```
# tshark  -i eth1 icmp[0] == 0 || icmp[0] == 8
Capturing on eth1
  0.000000    10.0.0.1 -> 10.0.0.5      ICMP Echo (ping) reply
  1.009672    10.0.0.1 -> 10.0.0.5      ICMP Echo (ping) reply
  2.016646    10.0.0.1 -> 10.0.0.5      ICMP Echo (ping) reply
```

The problem is that the two vertical bars (||) are interpreted by the UNIX shell and the two vertical bars and the rest of the command line are never seen by *tshark*. To avoid this behavior, use quotes around the capture filter:

```
# tshark  -i eth1  'icmp[0] == 0 || icmp[0] == 8'
Capturing on eth1
  0.000000    10.0.0.5 -> 10.0.0.1      ICMP Echo (ping) request
  0.000057    10.0.0.1 -> 10.0.0.5      ICMP Echo (ping) reply
  1.010248    10.0.0.5 -> 10.0.0.1      ICMP Echo (ping) request
  1.010299    10.0.0.1 -> 10.0.0.5      ICMP Echo (ping) reply
```

Like TShark, Wireshark accepts capture filters with the *-f* option. If you use Wireshark's *-k* option, Wireshark will immediately begin capturing packets. You can use the *-k* option to start a capture and the *-f* option to supply a capture filter. Besides *-k* and *-f*, Wireshark and TShark share many of the same capture-related command-line options. However, Wireshark does not treat leftover arguments on the command line, as a capture filter.

Being a graphical application, Wireshark also accepts capture filters in its GUI. Before starting to capture packets, the "Capture Options" dialog box provides a **Capture Filter** text entry box where you can type a capture filter (see Figure 5.3).

**Figure 5.3** Capture Options Dialog Box

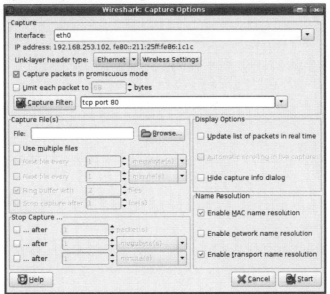

# Writing Display Filters

Wireshark's display filter mechanism is designed differently than *tcpdump's* filters. *Tcpdump* is a packet analyzer that knows how to decode many protocols, but relies on *libpcap's* filtering engine. *Libpcap* is a separate library that does not know how to parse many protocols.

In Wireshark, the protocol dissection mechanism is intertwined with the display filter mechanism. For almost every item you see in the protocol tree in the middle pane of Wireshark's GUI, Wireshark has a field name that you can use in a display filter. The CD-ROM that accompanies this book lists some commonly used display filter field names that Wireshark defines, and the CD-ROM that accompanies this book provides HTML pages that show all of the display filter field names for Wireshark version 0.99.4. These HTML pages are in the */filters* directory on the CD-ROM). You can also go to the **Help | Supported Protocols | Display Filter Fields** option in Wireshark to see a similar list. Perhaps the easiest way to find the display-filter name of a field that you're interested in is to highlight that field in the Wireshark GUI. When highlighted, Wireshark provides the display filter field name on the left-hand side of the status bar at the bottom of the GUI. Figure 5.4 shows that *ip.len* is the name of the IP Total Length field. The *ip.len* field name is shown in parentheses in the status bar on the bottom left side of the Wireshark window. Be aware that the status bar can be hidden by toggling **View | Statusbar**; therefore, be sure it is enabled if you want to see the field name.

**Figure 5.4** Display Filter Name for IP Total Length

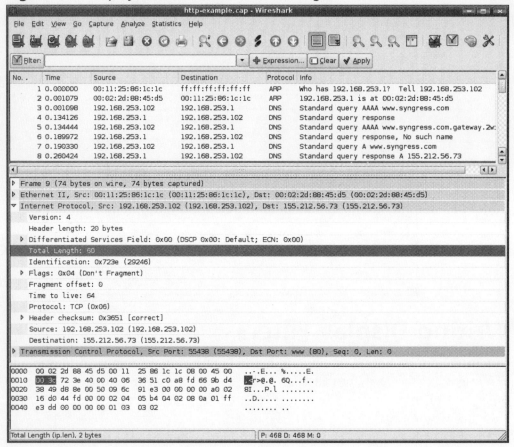

The protocol names also have display-filter names. Figure 5.5 shows that the *ip* field name represents the IP protocol.

# Writing Expressions

To test for the existence of a protocol or a field, the display filter is simply the display filter field name of that protocol or field. To show all IP packets use:

```
ip
```

This shows all of the packets where the IP protocol is present. You can also show all of the packets where a field is present:

```
ip.len
```

**Figure 5.5** Display Filter Name for IP

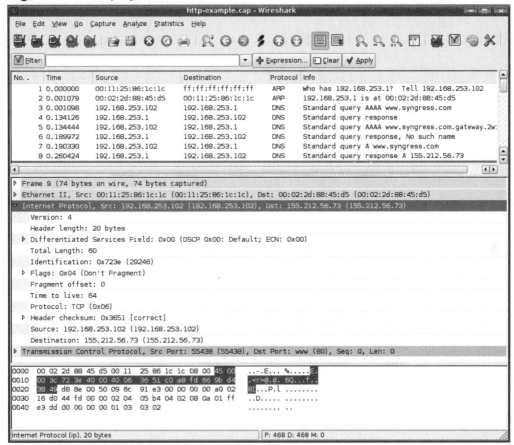

Because IP packets always have a *total length* (*ip.len*) field, this is functionally equivalent to testing for an *ip*. However, some protocols (e.g., TCP) can vary the fields that are present in a protocol header. TCP has optional fields such as *MSS*, which is represented by the *tcp.options.mss_val* field name. To find all packets that have the *tcp.options.mss_val* field, name the field in the display filter:

```
tcp.options.mss_val
```

The values of display filter fields in Wireshark belong to specific types, which means that depending on its type, a field can hold only certain values. The types in the display filter language are shown in Table 5.9.

**Table 5.9** Display Filter Field Types

| Display Filter Field Types | Possible Values | Example Values |
|---|---|---|
| Unsigned Integer | Non-negative integers: can be 8-, 16-, 24-, 32-, or 64-bits wide | 80 |
| Signed Integer | Integers: can be 8-, 16-, 24-, 32-, or 64-bits wide | -1 |
| Boolean | True or False | true |
| Frame Number | Like a 32-bit Unsigned Integer, but with special behaviors | 55 |
| Floating Point | A decimal number (i.e., real numbers) | 2.3 |
| Double-precision Floating Point | A floating point number that can store more digits | 82.390923033 |
| String | A sequence of characters | "hello" |
| Byte String | A sequence of hexadecimal digits | 12:23:2c |
| Hardware Address | A 6-byte long byte string with name-lookup capabilities | 14:0a:ff:3c:42:9a |
| IPv4 Address | An IPv4 address with name-lookup capabilities | 192.168.1.200 |
| IPv6 Address | An IPv6 address with name-lookup capabilities | 2::8100:2:30a:c392:fc5a |
| IPX Network | A 4-byte IPX network number with name-lookup capabilities | 0xc08022aa |
| Absolute Time | A date/time stamp | "Oct 31, 2006 15:00:00" |
| Relative Time | The number of seconds between two absolute times | 180 |
| None | A field that holds no value and is used only as a label or placeholder | |
| Protocol | The protocol keywords | http |

The operators that can be used to compare values are shown in Table 5.10.

**Table 5.10** Operators Used to Compare Values

| Operators | Meanings |
|---|---|
| > or gt | Greater Than |
| >= or ge | Greater Than or Equal To |
| < or lt | Less Than |
| <= or le | Less Than or Equal To |
| == or eq | Equal To |
| != or ne | Not Equal To |
| contains | A string or byte string is found within another |
| matches | A regular expression matches a string |
| & or bitwise_and | "Bitwise AND" to test specific bits |

Multiple relations can be combined with the logical operators *and* and *or*. You can negate the logical meanings with *not*. Parenthesis can be used to group logical operations correctly.

**NOTE**

The *matches* operator only works if your copy of Wireshark was compiled with support for the Perl Compatible Regular Expressions (PCRE) library. Select **Help | About Wireshark** from Wireshark's menu to check if Wireshark was compiled with or without *libpcre*. If you have *libpcre*, the *matches* operator works in your copy of Wireshark.

# Integers

Integer fields hold numeric values, which are integers (or whole numbers) without fractional parts. Integers can be expressed in decimal, octal, or hexadecimal notation. The octal notation requires an initial *0*, while hexadecimal notation requires an initial *0×*. Table 5.11 shows examples of how to write the same integer in decimal, octal, and hexadecimal representations.

**Table 5.11** Different Representations for the Same Integer

| Display Filter | Integer Notation |
|---|---|
| *eth.len > 1500* | Decimal |
| *eth.len > 02734* | Octal |
| *eth.len > 0x5dc* | Hexadecimal |

Integer fields are categorized as either signed or unsigned, and as 8, 16, 24, 32, or 64 bits wide. These two categories describe how the integers are stored in a computer's memory, and the categories determine the range of values that the integer can be (see Table 5.12).

**Table 5.12** Range of Values According to Integer

| Bit Width | Signed Range | Unsigned Range |
|---|---|---|
| 8-bit | $-2^7$ to $2^7-1$ <br> −128 to 127 | 0 to $2^8-1$ <br> −128 to 127 |
| 16-bit | $-2^{15}$ to $2^{15}-1$ <br> −32,768 to 32,767 | 0 to $2^{16}-1$ <br> 0 to 65,535 |
| 24-bit | $-2^{23}$ to $2^{23}-1$ <br> −8,388,608 to 8,388,607 | 0 to $2^{24}-1$ <br> 0 to 16,777,215 |
| 32-bit | $-2^{31}$ to $2^{31}-1$ <br> −2,147,483,648 to <br> 2,147,483,647 | 0 to $2^{32}-1$ <br> to 4,294,967,295 |
| 64-bit | $-2^{63}$ to $-2^{63}-1$ <br> -9,223,372,036,854,775,008 <br> to <br> 9,223,372,036,854,775,807 | 0 to $2^{64}-1$ <br> 0 to 18,446,744,073,709,551,615 |

Some integer fields also have labels representing the specific values of fields. For example, the Systems Network Architecture (SNA) Transmission Group Segmenting Field (or *sna.th.tgsf*) can have four distinct values, as shown in Table 5.13.

**Table 5.13** SNA Transmission Group Segmenting Field

| Integer Field/Value | Label |
|---|---|
| 0 | Not Segmented |
| 1 | Last segment |
| 2 | First segment |
| 3 | Middle segment |

In these cases, either the integer value or the label can be used when testing for values of *sna.th.tgsf*. These display filters are equivalent to:

```
sna.th.tgsf == 2
sna.th.tgsf == "First segment"
```

This example also shows how text (or *strings*) can be represented in a display filter. Note that the label is enclosed by double quotes.

---

**NOTE**

You can use the "Filter Expression" dialog box to look at the possible values for fields with label values. You can also use the HTML pages in the */filters* directory on the accompanying CD-ROM to find the same information.

---

Some integer fields are of a type called *frame number*, which is a special integer type within Wireshark that acts like a 32-bit unsigned integer type. By right-clicking on this field in the GUI, the pop-up menu has the option "Go to Corresponding Frame" that brings you to the frame indicated in the field. This is used for protocols that use request/response packet pairs (e.g., the Server Message Block [SMB] protocol and the NetWare Core Protocol [NCP] use frame number fields). Figure 5.6 shows an SMB response packet with a field *smb.response_to*, which gives the frame number of the request packet. Being able to jump to the request packet by clicking on a field in the reply packet can be handy when debugging network problems.

# Booleans

Boolean fields are fields that have a *true* or *false* value. In some cases, boolean fields, like integer fields, have labels that better describe the *1* or *0* value. For example, the *sna.rh.sdi* field is a boolean field that has the labels *Included* and *Not Included*, which describe its values more accurately than *True* or *False*. These display filters are equivalent:

```
sna.rh.sdi == 0
sna.rh.sdi == "Not Included"
sna.rh.sdi == false
```

**Figure 5.6** SMB Response

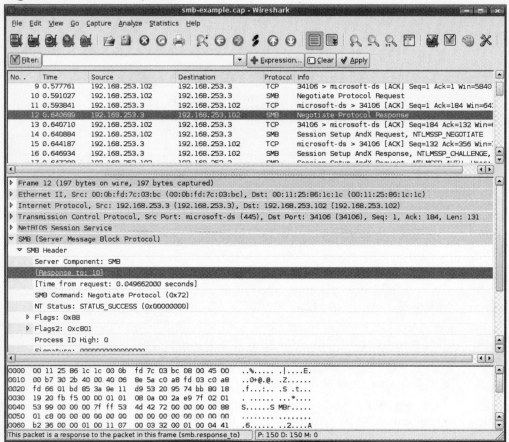

## Floating Point Numbers

Floating point numbers are different from integer numbers in that they contain fractional parts. Wireshark provides two types of floating point numbers: *regular* and *double-precision*. Double-precision floating point numbers more accurately represent numbers than regular floating point numbers, because more digits can be stored. In practice, all of Wireshark's floating point numbers are double-precision.

Whether regular or double-precision, floating point numbers are not usually found in protocols, but they do exist. For example, the *who* protocol (i.e., the format of the messages sent by the *rwhod* program on UNIX systems announcing load averages and current logins) has floating point numbers. Some example display filters include:

```
who.loadav_5 > 3.5
who.loadav_10 <= 10
who.loadav_10 <= 10.0
```

# Strings

Some fields hold text files, text values, or sequence of characters, are called strings. If the string you want to represent does not contain spaces and does not have the same name as one of the fields, you can use the string directly in your display filter:

```
sna.rh.csi == ASCII
```

However, if the string has a space in it, or has the same name as a field, the string must be enclosed in double quotes:

```
sna.rh.sdi == "Not included"
```

If the string you're providing contains a double quote, use a backspace followed by a double quote to embed that double quote into the string. The following display filter looks for a double-quote, followed by *YES,* followed by another double-quote.

```
http contains "\"YES\""
```

The backslash also allows you to embed 8-bit unsigned integers (i.e., single bytes) inside the string by using either hexadecimal or octal notation:

```
frame contains "\0777"
frame contains "\xff"
```

To look for a backslash, use a backslash followed by another backslash. To look for \*begin***,** the display filter would look like:

```
http contains "\\begin"
```

Wireshark's display filter syntax currently only allows you to look for American Standard Code for Information Interchange (ASCII) strings. While the **Edit | Find Packet** GUI option allows you to search for ASCII and Unicode strings, the display filter language doesn't allow you to search for any other string encoding, including Unicode or Extended Binary Coded Decimal Interchange Code (EBCDIC) strings. Similarly, be aware that all string comparisons are case-sensitive. The information in the display filter language is case-sensitive. A new facility called "display filter functions" has been provided to overcome this deficit.

The *matches* operator lets you search for text in string fields (and byte sequences) using a regular expression. The *matches* operator and the regular expressions supported by Wireshark are the same expressions that Perl uses. Wireshark does this by using the

PCRE library, which is helpful because you can leverage existing knowledge of regular expressions from Perl, Python, Apache, Exim, or many other applications.

## Regular Expressions

The best documentation for Perl regular expressions comes from the Perl regular expression manual page, available online at http://perldoc.perl.org/perlre.html. The Python documentation at www.python.org/doc/current/lib/re-syntax.html also provides a useful summary of regular expression syntax. In short, by using a special syntax, you can search for patterns of strings instead of just simple strings, in a *string* field. A regular expression (or *regex*) lets you cope with variability in your search pattern. You can vary the content of substrings and the number of instances of the substrings.

To accomplish this, the *regex* syntax gives meaning to certain punctuation marks e.g., the * character means match the preceding item zero or more times. In other words, the preceding item might not occur, might occur once, or might occur many times. If we search with this regular expression, the preceding item (the letter *s*) can occur zero or more times.

```
files*
```

The *regex* would match these strings:

```
file
files
filessss
filessssssss
```

but would not match these strings:

```
Files
filed
file search
```

An item can be a character, a class of characters, or a string of characters. A class of characters means a group from which any character can be chosen. A string of characters is a sequence of specific characters. Square brackets denote classes, while parentheses denote strings.

If you want to find a string starting with *eth* followed by any numerical digit, you can use a character class by listing the characters inside square brackets:

```
eth[0123456789]
```

or, you can use a character range:

```
eth[0-9]
```

Both of those *regexes* would match these strings:

```
eth0
eth1
eth2
eth3
eth4
eth5
eth6
eth7
eth8
eth9
```

But, neither *regex* would match *eth10*, because the character class matches only one character in the text that is being searched. However, the * quantifier applies to a character class, so you could use this *regex* to match *eth10* or *eth* followed by any number of digits:

```
eth[0-9]*
```

Because the * matches zero or more times, the *regex* would also match *eth*. You want to use the + quantifier, which matches one or more items:

```
eth[0-9]+
```

There are three quantifiers, as shown in Table 5.14.

**Table 5.14** Regular Expression Quantifiers

| Character | Meaning |
| --- | --- |
| * | The preceding item occurs zero or more times |
| + | The preceding item occurs one or more times |
| ? | The preceding item either occurs once, or not at all |

Furthermore, you can indicate that an item occurs a specific number of times using curly brackets. The three varieties are shown in Table 5.15.

**Table 5.15** Specific Regular Expression Quantifiers

| Syntax | Meaning |
|--------|---------|
| {m} | The preceding item occurs exactly *m* times |
| {m,} | The preceding item occurs at least *m* times |
| {m,n} | The preceding item occurs a minimum of *m* times, and a maximum of *n* times. |

For example, to find *eth* followed by 2 or 3 digits, the *regex* would be:

```
eth[0-9]{2,3}
```

If you want to search for a substring that occurs one or more times, put the substring in parentheses:

```
file(\.txt)+
```

The period (.) has a special meaning in *regex* syntax; it matches any character except new line characters. Thus, to find the period itself, we have to prepend a backslash. The *regex* would match these strings:

```
file.txt
file.txt.txt
file.txt.txt.txt
```

Parentheses also allow you to match on alternatives. If you want to find an interface name that is *eth* or *tr* followed by one or more numerical digits, use:

```
(eth|tr)[0-9]+
```

The Perl regular expression syntax that Wireshark uses also has pre-defined character classes that are listed in Table 5.16.

**Table 5.16** Regular Expression Character Classes

| Syntax | Character Class |
|--------|-----------------|
| \d | Any numerical digit |
| \D | Any non-digit character |
| \s | Any whitespace character (e.g., space, tab) |
| \S | Any non-whitespace character |

Knowing this, the previous example of finding *eth* followed by one or more digits could be written in shorthand form:

```
eth\d+
```

Some other punctuation marks also have special meaning, as shown in Table 5.17.

**Table 5.17** Special Regular Expression Punctuation

| Character | Meaning |
|-----------|---------|
| ^ | Match the beginning of a string |
| $ | Match the end of a string |
| . | Match any character except the new line character |

For example, to find *.doc* at the end of a string, use *$*:

```
\.doc$
```

As mentioned earlier, use the backslash character (\) to find a punctuation mark that normally would have a special *regex* meaning. That is, to find the word *eth* followed by any number of digits in square brackets, use the backslash in front of the square brackets:

```
eth\[\d+\]
```

# Byte Sequences

A sequence of bytes, including Ethernet addresses, is represented by a sequence of hexadecimal digits in uppercase or lowercase letters and separated by colons, periods, or dashes. For example, the broadcast Ethernet address *ff:ff:ff:ff:ff:ff* can be also be represented as *ff.ff.ff.ff.ff.ff* or as *ff-ff-ff-ff-ff-ff*.

Ethernet addresses are byte sequences that have names assigned to them via an *ethers* file. On UNIX, the global file is */etc/ethers* and the personal file is *$HOME/.wireshark/ethers*. On Windows, the global *ethers* file would be placed in the Wireshark installation directory, and the personal file would be created as *%APPDATA%\Wireshark\ethers*, or if *%APPDATA%* doesn't exist, *%USERPRO-FILE%\Application Data\Wireshark\ethers*. The *ethers* file format is one hardware address and one name per line, separated by any amount of spaces or tabs:

```
00:09:f6:01:cc:b3    picard
01:1a:e3:01:fe:37    worf
```

When a name exists for an Ethernet address, it can be used in the display filter:

```
eth.src == 00:09:f6:01:cc:b3
eth.src == picard
```

Internally, Wireshark treats protocols as a special field type; however, in one aspect, protocols act like byte sequence fields. The *contains* and *matches* operators can be used to search through the bytes that belong to each protocol in the packet. The bytes in a packet that are specific to a protocol are treated as belonging to that protocol in the display filter language. The exception is the special *frame* pseudo-protocol. At the top of every protocol tree, Wireshark places a pseudo protocol that contains metadata about the packet, including the arrival time and the length of packet. These fields don't actually appear in the packet data, but are relevant to the packet. Wireshark regards all the bytes in the packet as belonging to the *frame* pseudo-protocol. Therefore, you can use the *contains* operator to search for any bytes or ASCII text within the entire packet by checking if the *frame* protocol contains the bytes or text:

```
frame contains "POST"
frame contains 50:4f:53:54
```

You can limit your search to a more specific protocol. For example, to search for GET in the *http* protocol, use:

```
http contains "GET"
```

# Addresses

Address fields have the distinction of being represented by either a numeric value or a name. The Ethernet address field is both an address field and a byte sequence field. The other address fields are the IPv4 address, IPv6 address, and IPX network fields.

IPv4 address fields can be compared against the dotted-quad format of IPv4 addresses, hostnames, and DNS names. The dotted-quad notation is four numbers separated by periods (or *dots*). In this example, the source IP address field name is *ip.src* and the destination IP address field name is *ip.dst*:

```
ip.src == 192.168.1.1
ip.dst == wizard
ip.dst == www.wireshark.org
```

To test if either the source IP address or the destination IP address is *wizard*, can use the logic *or* operator to combine two tests:

```
ip.src == wizard or ip.dst == wizard
```

Wireshark provides another field, *ip.addr*, which stands for either *ip.src* or *ip.dst*:

```
ip.addr == wizard
```

Most of the fields with a concept of source and destination, provide a third field that tests for either source or destination, to help you write display filters that test both addresses.

To test if an IPv4 address is within a certain subnet, the == operator and CIDR notation can be used. In CIDR notation, the IPv4 address, hostname, or DNS name is followed by a slash and the number of bits that make up the network portion of the IPv4 address:

```
ip.addr == 192.168.1.0/24
ip.addr == wizard/24
```

IPv6 address fields are similar to their IPv4 counterparts: *ipv6.src* for the source address, *ipv6.dst* for the destination address, and *ipv6.addr* to test either source or destination address. For example:

```
ipv6.dst == 2::8100:2:30a:c392:fc5a or ipv6.dst == 2::8100:2:30a:c392:fc5a
ipv6.addr == 2::8100:2:30a:c392:fc5a
```

IPX addresses are comprised of two parts, the *network address* and the *node address*. This is comparable to an IPv4 address, where part of the 32-bit IPv4 address is the network portion, and the other part refers to a specific host on that IPv4 network. In IPX, however, the network and node (i.e., the host) are separate fields instead of being combined into a single value.

The IPX node fields are hardware address-type fields, but the IPX network fields are unsigned 32-bit integer fields. Wireshark treats IPX network fields differently than normal integer fields, in that Wireshark allows you to give names to IPX network numbers. This is useful if you need to analyze IPX packets in an environment where there are many different IPX networks; names are easier to remember than numbers. To define the IPX network names, create a file called *ipxnets*. On UNIX, you can create a global *ipxnets* file in */etc/ipxnets*, and a personal file whose values override the global values in *$HOME/.wireshark/ipxnets*. On Windows, the global file is the *ipxnets* file in the Wireshark installation directory, while the personal file is *%APPDATA%\Wireshark\ipxnets*, or if *%APPDATA%* doesn't exist, then *%USERPROFILE%\Application Data\Wireshark\ipxnets*. The format of the *ipxnets* file is the same as the *ethers* file, except that the hexadecimal bytes representing the IPX network number can be separated by periods, dashes, colons, or nothing. Following is an example from the Wireshark man page:

```
C0.A8.2C.00              HR
c0-a8-1c-00              CEO
00:00:BE:EF              IT_Server1
110f                     FileServer3
```

Given this *ipxnets* file, these two display filters are equivalent:

```
ipx.src.net == 0xc0a82c00
ipx.src.net == HR
```

> **NOTE**
>
> Storing hardware addresses in an */etc/ethers* file used to be common practice on UNIX systems; however, the UNIX systems used today no longer come with an */etc/ethers* file. The */etc/ipxnets* file is a file that is unique to Wireshark.

# Time Fields

There are two types of time fields in Wireshark that are represented very differently. An *absolute time* is a timestamp that combines a date and a time in order to specify a specific moment in time. A *relative time* is a floating point number (i.e., the number of seconds [including fractional seconds] between two absolute times).

Absolute times are represented as strings of the format:

```
Month Day, Year Hour:Minute:Seconds
```

and can include fractions of a second, with nanosecond resolution:

```
Month Day, Year Hour:Minute:Seconds.Nsecs
```

To look at packets that arrived before December 31st, 2003, at 5:03AM, the display filter would be:

```
frame.time < "Dec 31, 2003 05:03:00"
```

Wireshark provides the *frame.time_delta* field to record the difference in arrival times between a packet and its immediate predecessor. Currently, the only way to represent this relative time is with a floating point number that indicates seconds with nanosecond resolution:

```
frame.time_delta > 0.02
```

# Other Field Types

Some fields have no values associated with them (e.g., an integer value, string value, or any other value). You can test for the existence of these fields, but they don't have a value that can be checked with ==, <, >, or any other relation. These no-value fields are generally used by the protocol dissector to place text or a branch in a protocol tree.

If you inspect the protocol trees in your packet captures, you'll eventually discover that some of the items in the protocol tree don't have any display filter field associated with them. In some cases, protocol dissectors merely add text to the protocol tree, without labeling the text as belonging to a field. Figure 5.7 shows how the HTTP protocol dissector does this for the HTTP headers. It places the *Keep-Alive* field in the protocol tree without giving it a display filter field name.

**Figure 5.7** HTTP Headers as Text

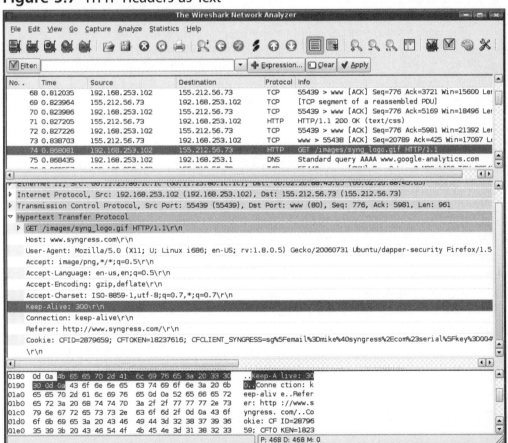

You cannot create a display filter to search for these types of text labels. However, if the text is found in the packet data, the *contains* operator can be used to search for the text in a protocol or the entire packet by using the *frame* pseudo-protocol. To find HTTP packets where the *Keep-Alive* is "300," use the *contains* operator:

```
http contains "Keep-Alive: 300"
```

## Notes from the Underground…

### Exchanging Filters With Your Friends

Do you need an easy way to exchange your extensive collection of capture filters or display filters with your friends? Wireshark saves capture filters in a file named *cfilters*, and saves display filters in a file name *dfilters*. On a UNIX system, those files are in the *$HOME/.wireshark* directory, while on a Windows system those files are in *%APPDATA%\Wireshark*, or if *%APPDATA%* isn't defined, in *%USERPROFILE%\Application Data\Wireshark*. *cfilter* and *dfilte* are simple text files with one record per line. You can paste new entries into these files and the next time you start Wireshark, the new filters will be available.

# Ranges

The string, byte sequence, and protocol field types have something in common besides being searchable by the *contains* and *matches* operators: they are all sequences of bytes. Strings are sequences of characters, and characters are bytes. The other field types (e.g., integers, floating points, times, and so forth) can be thought of as single values rather than sequences. Sometimes it is useful to take a portion of a string, byte sequence, or protocol and slice the data into smaller sections and compare it against a value. A sequence can be sliced using the *ranges* functionality of Wireshark's display filter language. The *ranges* syntax uses square brackets: *[* and *]*.

To obtain a single byte from a sequence, use the offset of that byte in square brackets. The offset is the position of the byte starting at the beginning of the named field. Wireshark's display filter language offsets begin at *0*. To compare the very first byte in an Ethernet address to the hexadecimal value *0xaa*, use:

```
eth.addr[0] == aa
```

The value that is compared against a range is always treated as a sequence of bytes. The hexadecimal byte value *aa* is not interpreted as the string *aa*, nor can you provide a integer value by typing *0xaa*.

Since *0* is the offset of the first byte, *1* is the offset of the second byte. To compare the second byte of the bytes in the *telnet* portion of the packet to the hexadecimal value *0xff*, use:

```
telnet[1] == ff
```

A sample of a full hexadecimal table can be found at: www.cookwood.com/cookwood/html4_examples/4files/colorhex/hexchart.html.

Ranges can do more than extract single bytes; they can also extract actual ranges of bytes from the fields. Use a colon to separate the offset from the number of bytes in the brackets. To compare the first 3 bytes of a *tr* address to 00:06:29, type the length of the slice after the colon. The length is 3 because we are comparing three bytes:

```
tr.addr[0:3] == 00:06:29
```

If you would rather provide ranges of offsets rather than offset/length pairs, a hyphen in the brackets can be used. This display filter also compares the first 3 bytes of a *tr* address to 00:06:29, but by slicing the *tr.addr* field from offset *0* up to and including byte 2:

```
tr.addr[0-2] == 00:06:29
```

When using the colon notation to give byte offset and range length, you can choose not to provide either the offset or the length, yet keep the colon.

```
eth[:2] == ff:ff
http[10:] contains 00:01:02
```

When the offset is not provided, as in the *eth[:2]* case, the offset is assumed to be *0*. When the length is not provided, as in the *http[10:]*, the range includes all of the bytes until the end of the field or protocol mentioned.

Within the brackets, you can use commas to concatenate multiple ranges of the same field. For example, if you want to look at the first byte (offset = *0*) and the third byte (offset = *2*) of the *tr* protocol, you can either create two ranges combining them with the *and* logical operator, or combine the ranges into one range using a comma inside the square brackets:

```
tr[0] == ff and tr[2] == ee
tr[0,2] == ff:ee
```

The comma operator can combine any number of ranges, therefore, the following is entirely legal:

```
tr[0-2,4:3,7,9] == 01:02:03:04:05:06:07:08
```

Table 5.18 is a summary of the range syntax options.

**Table 5.18** Range Syntax

| Range Syntax | Meaning |
|---|---|
| [ offset ] | Slice a single byte at "offset" |
| [ offset : length ] | Slice "length" bytes starting at "offset" |
| [ offset$_1$ – offset$_2$ ] | Slice bytes from "offset$_1$" to "offset$_2$", inclusive |
| [ : length ] | Slice "length" bytes starting at offset 0 |
| [ offset : ] | Slice bytes from "offset" to end of field |
| [ range , range ] | Combine any range syntax with another |

**NOTE**

The Wireshark documentation states that you are supposed to be able to use negative numbers as offsets. Negative offsets indicate the offset counting *backwards* from the end of the field. However, in our testing, this doesn't work as advertised. It is likely that this will be fixed in a future version of Wireshark.

# Logical Operators

The *and* logical operator tests whether the two relations it combines are true. To filter for a specific source IP address and a specific destination IP address, use *and*:

```
ip.src == 192.168.1.1 and ip.dst == 192.168.2.2
```

The *or* logical operator tests if either, or both, of the two relations that it joins is true. If you want to test an IP address to see if it was one of two values, use *or*:

```
ip.addr == 192.168.3.3 or ip.addr == 192.168.4.4
```

The *not* logical operator reverses the sense of the relation. To find NetWare Core Protocol packets that have an *ncp.directory_name* field that does not contain the string "System," use this display filter:

```
not ncp.directory_name contains "System"
```

Parentheses are used to group relations according to how *not*, *and*, and *or*, should combine them. These two display filters are not the same, due to the presence of parenthesis:

```
not eth.dst eq ff:ff:ff:ff:ff:ff and ip.len gt 1000
not (eth.dst eq ff:ff:ff:ff:ff:ff and ip.len gt 1000)
```

In the first example, *not* negates the meaning of the **eq**. In the second example, *not* negates the meaning of the grouped expression, which is an *and* expression.

# Functions

A new feature called "display filter functions" (or functions) is available in Wireshark. These functions operate on field data and return new values.

The only two functions currently defined in Wireshark are *upper* and *lower*, which convert a string field to either uppercase or lowercase. This is useful if you need to perform a case-insensitive search. For example, if the hostname can be "angel" or "Angel" or any combination of upper- and lowercase letters, you want to do a case-insensitive search:

```
upper(mount.dump.hostname) == "ANGEL"
lower(mount.dump.hostname) == "angel"
```

Ensure that if you use *upper*, the string you're matching against is in uppercase. If you use *lower*, the string you're matching against should be in lowercase. It doesn't matter which function you use, because either allow you perform a case-insensitive search.

# Multiple Occurrences of Fields

Some protocols occur more than once per packet. This can happen when you're looking at encapsulated or tunneled protocols. For example, Protocol Independent Multicast (PIM) can run on top of IPv6 and at the same time send other IPv6 data. Thus, you can have two instances of IPv6 in a single packet by using PIM. More commonly, the same field can occur more than once in a single protocol. Some protocols have repeated fields (e.g., the ring/bridge pairs in source-routed token-ring packets).

In cases where the protocol does not normally have multiple occurrences of fields, Wireshark can create multiple occurrences of fields to enhance the filtering. As mentioned in the discussion about address fields, there are many fields that have a source version and a destination version. In those cases, the protocol dissector adds two generic (non-source, non-destination) versions of the field so that a display filter

can test both the source and destination fields in one statement. Table 5.19 shows
some examples of those fields.

**Table 5.19** Generic Versions of Source and Destination Fields

| Source Field | Destination Field | Generic Version |
| --- | --- | --- |
| eth.src | eth.dst | eth.addr |
| fddi.src | fddi.dst | fddi.addr |
| ip.src | ip.dst | ip.addr |
| ipx.src.net | ipx.dst.net | ipx.net |
| ipx.src.node | ipx.dst.node | ipx.node |
| tcp.srcport | tcp.dstport | tcp.port |
| tr.src | tr.dst | tr.addr |
| udp.srcport | udp.dstport | udp.port |

Care must be given when testing fields that occur more than once in a packet.
For example, if you have a packet capture that has a lot of HTTP traffic in it and
you want to use a display filter to hide the HTTP traffic, you might be tempted to
use the following display filter, where 80 is the TCP port for HTTP:

```
tcp.port != 80
```

Unfortunately, this doesn't work, because this display filter is saying "show me all
the packets that have a *tcp.port* that does not equal 80." Look at Figure 5.8; one
*tcp.port* (the destination port) is 80, while the other *tcp.port* (the source port) is
55,438. This packet passes the *tcp.port != 80* filter, because it has one *tcp.port* that is
not equal to 80.

What you want to say is "show me all of the packets where none of the *tcp.port*
values are equal to 80." Or equivalently, "show me the packets which do not have at
least one *tcp.port* equal to 80." In the correct display filter language, this is:

```
not tcp.port == 80
```

It takes some getting used to, but once you understand what the display filter
language is doing, you will become more comfortable with it.

**Figure 5.8** TCP Ports for HTTP Traffic

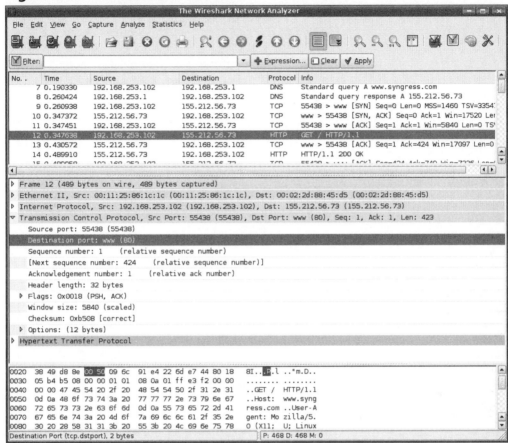

## Other Uses of Display Filters

Display filters are used in Wireshark for other reasons besides limiting which packets are shown in Wireshark's main window. Wireshark allows you to use display filters any time you want to select packets. The **View | Coloring Rules** facility for colorizing packet summaries lets you use display filters to select which packets to colorize. The **Statistics | IO Graphs** report, as well as many other reports, allow you to select packets with display filters. And the **File | Open**

Continued

dialog box allows you to supply a display filter for use when reading a capture file from disk. This facility is unique among the various uses of display filters. While reading a capture file, if a packet does not match the display filter, the packet is skipped and is not loaded into Wireshark's memory. In this way, the *read* display filter acts like a capture filter, in that it limits the packets that are loaded into Wireshark's memory. But of course, it uses the display filter syntax, not the capture filter syntax.

# Hidden Fields

By looking closely at some protocols in the protocol dissection tree, you will notice that some fields that should be present are not visible. For example, if you look at the Ethernet portion of a protocol tree in Figure 5.9, you'll find the Ethernet source address (*eth.src*) and the Ethernet destination address (*eth.dst*), but you'll never find a

**Figure 5.9** Ethernet Source and Destination Address Fields

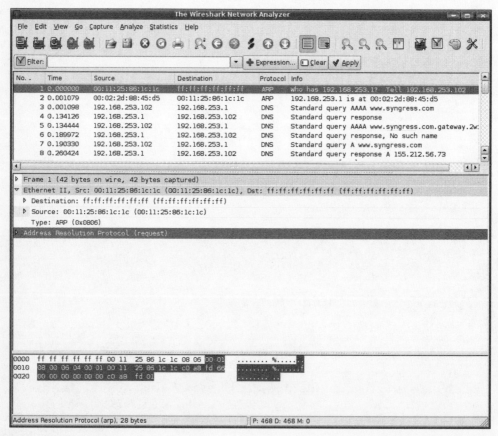

field labeled "Source or Destination Address," which is the description for the *eth.addr* field. This is because *eth.addr* was placed in the protocol tree as a hidden field to aid in writing display filters. You can use the hidden fields in display filters, but you never see them in the protocol tree. Wireshark does this for convenience, and to keep the protocol tree from having duplicate information. Unfortunately, there is no option to make Wireshark display hidden fields.

## Notes from the Underground…

### Undocumented Glossary Option

TShark has an undocumented command-line switch that produces a glossary of protocol and field names. The -*G* switch causes the program to output the glossary, then quit. Even the format of the output is undocumented, but you can look at the *epan/proto.c* file in the Wireshark source code. Search for *proto_registrar_dump_fields*, which is the function that documents the format.

```
/* Dumps the contents of the registration database

 * to stdout. An indepedent

 * program can take this output and format it into

 * nice tables or HTML or

 * whatever.

 *

 * There is one record per line. Each is either a

 * protocol or a header

 * field, differentiated by the first field.

 * The fields are tab-delimited.

 *

 * Protocols

 * ---------

 * Field 1 = 'P'

 * Field 2 = protocol name

 * Field 3 = protocol abbreviation

 *

 * Header Fields

 * -------------
```

**Continued**

```
* Field 1 = 'F'
* Field 2 = field name
* Field 3 = field abbreviation
* Field 4 = type ( text representation of the ftenum type )
* Field 5 = parent protocol abbreviation
*/
```

You can see this glossary by running *tshark -G*. The *-G* option can also take a parameter, which can cause tshark to produce a different type of glossary. The *-G protocols* option makes tshark show the glossary only for protocols. The *-G fields* option shows both protocol and non-protocol fields, just like the *-G* option with no additional parameters. The *tshark.c* source file shows the various parameters of *-G*: *fields*, *fields2*, *fields3*, *protocols*, *values*, *decodes*, *defaultprefs*, and *currentprefs*. You can also look at *doc/Makefile.am* (or *doc/Makefile.nmake* for Windows) and *doc/dfilter2pod.pl* in the Wireshark source distribution to see how the Wireshark build system uses the *-G* switch to produce the *wireshark-filter* man page.

# Summary

If you're trying to pinpoint a network problem or understand how a particular network operation works, the amount of extraneous traffic on the network can overwhelm you. Filters are the way to manage this huge amount of information. Capture filters allow you to limit the amount of packets that Wireshark receives from the OS. Display filters allow you to limit the packets that are shown in Wireshark's main window, giving you the opportunity to concentrate on the problem at hand.

Wireshark's capture filter syntax is the same as *tcpdump's* filter syntax. This is because both Wireshark and *tcpdump* use a library called *libpcap*, which is the library that provides the filter engine. The filter engine provided by *libpcap*, while fast, does not provide many protocol or field names in its language. To find data for fields whose names are not provided in the filter language, you must extract bytes from the packet by using offsets within specific protocols.

Wireshark's display filter syntax is unique to Wireshark. It is part of Wireshark's protocol dissection engine, and provides names for almost all protocols and fields that Wireshark can dissect. Display filters are slower at processing packets than capture filters, but the trade-off is ease of use.

To find the names of all of the available fields and protocols in the display filter language, Wireshark provides some information in its GUI and manual pages. The wireshark Web site has a reference, and this book provides a reference on the included CD-ROM.

# Solutions Fast Track

## Writing Capture Filters

☑ Capture filters operate quickly and are good for limiting the number of packets captured by Wireshark.

☑ The capture filter language has keywords for comparing host names and addresses, hardware addresses, ports, and protocols.

☑ *Tcpdump* can dissect many protocols and fields, but only a handful of those protocols and fields are available in the *tcpdump* filter (or "capture filter") language.

☑ To test individual fields in a bit-field correctly, you must use the bitwise *AND* operator: &.

## Writing Display Filters

☑ Display filters are slower than capture filters, but allow you to test almost any field or protocol that Wireshark knows how to dissect.

☑ Display filter fields have values of certain types, which means each field can hold only certain values.

☑ The *contains* operator searches for text; the *matches* operator searches using regular expressions.

☑ Take care when testing fields that occur multiple times in a packet; you might be testing these fields may be the wrong way.

☑ The *upper()* and *lower()* display filter functions let you test strings, regardless of case.

☑ Display filters are important to understand because they are used throughout Wireshark for selecting packets (i.e., for viewing, colorization, graphing, and reporting).

# Frequently Asked Questions

The following Frequently Asked Questions, answered by the authors of this book, are designed to both measure your understanding of the concepts presented in this chapter and to assist you with real-life implementation of these concepts. To have your questions about this chapter answered by the author, browse to **www.syngress.com/solutions** and click on the **"Ask the Author"** form.

**Q:** My capture filter or display filter that uses multiple *ands* and *ors* doesn't work the way I intended it to work.

**A:** The precedence of the operations may not be what you're expecting it to be. This means that the parts of your filter are being run in an order that you didn't expect. Use parentheses to group the parts properly.

**Q:** I'm using *contains* to look for a certain string that I know should be there, but Wireshark can't find it.

**A:** When you have the field that you're interested in selected, look closely at the hex dump; the encoding of the string may be Unicode or EBCDIC, which won't work with the *contains* operator. Only ASCII strings are currently compatible with *contains*.

**Q:** I want to find all packets that do not have an IP address of 1.2.3.4. Why does *ip.addr != 1.2.3.4* show all packets instead of limiting the packets to what I want?

**A:** The *ip.addr* field occurs more than once in a packet. Your display filter is running correctly; it shows you all of the packets that have at least one *ip.addr* that is not equal to *1.2.3.4*. You want *not ip.addr == 1.2.3.4*.

**Q:** How can I search a packet for strings that can be in either uppercase or lower-case?

**A:** You can use the display filter function *upper()* to convert a string entirely to uppercase, and test against an uppercase version of the matching string. For example, you can use *upper(mount.dump.hostname)* == *"ANGEL."* Note that you can use *lower()* in a similar way.

**Q:** My filter can be expressed very easily in both the capture filter and display filter languages. Which should I choose?

**A:** If you have little traffic on your network, it's easier to use only display filters. However, if you have a lot of traffic on the network, especially extraneous traffic, and you're sure that your filter will provide all the packets that you need, then use a capture filter. If you're not sure where to find the clues that will help you solve your problem, capture everything and use a display filter to look for packets that might help you.

**Q:** Wireshark comes with a manual for its display filter language. Where's the manual for the capture filter language?

**A:** It's provided by the *tcpdump* manual page. It's also on-line at www.tcpdump.org/tcpdump_man.html.

# Chapter 6

# Wireless Sniffing with Wireshark

## Solutions in this chapter:

- **Techniques for Effective Wireless Sniffing**
- **Understanding Wireless Card Operating Modes**
- **Configuring Linux for Wireless Sniffing**
- **Configuring Windows for Wireless Sniffing**
- **Using Wireless Protocol Dissectors**
- **Useful Wireless Display Filters**
- **Leveraging Wireshark Wireless Analysis Features**

☑ Summary

☑ Solutions Fast Track

☑ Frequently Asked Questions

# Introduction

Wireless networking is a complex field. With countless standards, protocols, and implementations, it is not uncommon for administrators to encounter configuration issues that require sophisticated troubleshooting and analysis mechanisms.

Fortunately, Wireshark has sophisticated wireless protocol analysis support to help administrators troubleshoot wireless networks. With the appropriate driver support, Wireshark can capture traffic "from the air" and decode it into a format that helps administrators track down issues that are causing poor performance, intermittent connectivity, and other common problems.

Wireshark is also a powerful wireless security analysis tool. Using Wireshark's display filtering and protocol decoders, you can easily sift through large amounts of wireless traffic to identify security vulnerabilities in the wireless network, including weak encryption or authentication mechanisms, and information disclosure risks. You can also perform intrusion detection analysis to identify common attacks against wireless networks while performing signal strength analysis to identify the location of a station or access point (AP).

This chapter introduces the unique challenges and recommendations for traffic sniffing on wireless networks. We examine the different operating modes supported by wireless cards, and configure Linux and Windows systems to support wireless traffic capture and analysis using Wireshark and third-party tools. Once you have mastered the task of capturing wireless traffic, you will learn how to leverage Wireshark's powerful wireless analysis features, and learn how to apply your new skills.

All of the files used in this chapter's exercises can be found in the /captures directory on the CD-ROM, accompaying this book. A wireless card is required.

# Challenges of Sniffing Wireless

Traditional network sniffing on an Ethernet network is fairly easy to set up. In a *shared environment*, an analysis workstation running Wireshark starts a new packet capture, which configures the card in promiscuous mode and waits until the desired amount of traffic has been captured. In a *switched environment*, you need to configure a span port that mirrors the traffic sent to other stations, before initiating the packet capture.

In both of these cases, it is easy to initiate a packet capture and start collecting traffic for analysis. When you switch to wireless analysis, however, the process of traffic sniffing becomes more complicated and requires additional decisions up front to best support the analysis you want to perform.

# Selecting a Static Channel

Where a wired network offers a single medium mechanism for packet capture (i.e., the wire), wireless networks can operate on multiple wireless channels using different frequencies in the same location. A table of wireless channel numbers and the corresponding frequencies is listed in Table 6.1. Even if two wireless users are sitting side-by-side, their computers may be operating on different wireless channels.

**Table 6.1** Wireless Frequencies and Channels

| Frequency | Channel Number | Frequency | Channel Number |
|---|---|---|---|
| 2.412 GHz | 1 | 2.484 GHz | 14 |
| 2.417 GHz | 2 | 5.180 GHz | 36 |
| 2.422 GHz | 3 | 5.200 GHz | 40 |
| 2.427 GHz | 4 | 5.220 GHz | 44 |
| 2.432 GHz | 5 | 5.240 GHz | 48 |
| 2.437 GHz | 6 | 5.260 GHz | 52 |
| 2.442 GHz | 7 | 5.280 GHz | 56 |
| 2.447 GHz | 8 | 5.300 GHz | 60 |
| 2.452 GHz | 9 | 5.320 GHz | 64 |
| 2.457 GHz | 10 | 5.745 GHz | 149 |
| 2.462 GHz | 11 | 5.765 GHz | 153 |
| 2.467 GHz | 12 | 5.785 GHz | 157 |
| 2.472 GHz | 13 | 5.805 GHz | 161 |

If you want to analyze the traffic for a specific wireless AP or station, you must identify the channel or frequency used by the target device, and configure your wireless card to use the same channel before initiating your packet capture. This is because wireless cards can only operate on a single frequency at any given time. If you wanted to capture traffic from multiple channels simultaneously, you would need an additional wireless card for every channel you wanted to monitor.

# Using Channel Hopping

If you want to capture traffic for a specific station, how do you locate the channel number that it is operating on? One technique is to use *channel hopping* to rapidly scan through all available wireless channels until the appropriate channel number is identified. With channel hopping, the wireless card is still only operating on a single frequency at any given time, but is rapidly switching between different channels, thus allowing Wireshark to capture any traffic that is present on the current channel. Fortunately, Wireshark operates independently of the current channel selection; therefore, it is not necessary to stop and restart the packet capture before each channel hop. Change to the desired channel while Wireshark is running and Wireshark will continue to collect traffic.

Unfortunately, you cannot rely on channel hopping for all of your wireless traffic sniffing needs. Channel hopping will cause you to lose traffic, because you are rapidly switching channels. If your wireless card is configured to operate on channel 11 and you hop to another channel, you will not be able to "hear" any traffic that is occurring on channel 11 until you return as part of the channel-hopping pattern. As a result, channel hopping is not a useful technique for analyzing traffic for a specific AP or station, but it can be useful to identify the channel the network is operating on, which can be used to set a static channel assignment.

# Range in Wireless Networks

Another unique characteristic of Wireshark is the range between the capture station and the transmitting device(s). When capturing wireless traffic, the range between the capture station and the transmitter is significant, and must be accounted for to provide the most reliable traffic collection.

If the capture station is too far away from one or more transmitters, it is unable to "hear" the wireless traffic. If the capture station is too close to another transmitting station, the radio interface may become overwhelmed with too much signal, thus resulting in corrupted traffic. Placing the station near the transmitter no closer than 3 feet is the most desirable location for achieving optimal traffic capture. You can achieve satisfactory results for a wireless packet capture from further away, but you will lose traffic from the capture if there is a significant distance between the capture station and the transmitter(s).

# Interference and Collisions

Another challenge of sniffing wireless networks is the risk of interference and lost packets. Unlike an Ethernet network that can transmit and monitor the network simultaneously, wireless cards can only receive or transmit asynchronously. As a result, wireless networks must take special precautions to prevent multiple stations from transmitting at the same time. While these collision-avoidance mechanisms work well, it is still possible to experience collisions between multiple transmitters on the same channel, or to experience collisions with wireless local area networks (LANs) and other devices using the same frequency (e.g., cordless phones, baby monitors, microwave ovens, and so on).

When two devices transmit simultaneously within range of the sniffing station, the transmission becomes corrupted and is rejected by the receiver as an invalid packet.

After waiting random back-off intervals, the two stations repeat their transmission, thus indicating they are attempting to transmit the same information again. This is normal activity in a wireless LAN, but presents a challenge to the sniffing station.

When capturing traffic on a wireless network, there is no guarantee that you captured 100 percent of the traffic. Some traffic may have become corrupted in transit. In other cases, your capture station may be positioned such that it receives valid frames before they become corrupt en-route to the destination host. This forces the transmitting station to re-transmit the corrupted packets, which causes the capture station to have multiple copies of the same packet in the capture.

# Recommendations for Sniffing Wireless

Now that you understand some of the limitations and challenges in sniffing wireless networks, you can apply some recommendations to achieve the best fidelity in wireless packet captures:

- **Locate the Capture Station Near the Source** When initiating a packet capture, locate the capture station close to the source of the wireless activity you are interested in (i.e., an AP or a wireless station).

- **Disable Other Nearby Transmitters** If you are using an external wireless card for sniffing traffic, and you have a built-in card in your laptop, it is common to experience lost traffic on the sniffing card due to interference from the built-in card. To eliminate this factor and achieve a more accurate packet capture, disable any built-in wireless transmitters on the capture station during the packet capture, including Institute of Electrical & Electronics Engineers (IEEE) 802.11 interfaces and Bluetooth devices.

- **Reduce CPU Utilization While Capturing** If your host experiences excessive central processing unit (CPU) utilization during a packet capture, you may experience packet loss in the wireless capture (e.g., it is not a good idea to burn a DVD while capturing wireless traffic). To prevent packet loss, try to reduce your CPU utilization when capturing traffic with any sniffer software.

- **Match Channel Selection** If you take a comprehensive packet capture of a wireless network, make sure your wireless card is sniffing on the same channel as the target network. If you are channel hopping during a packet capture, you will inevitably lose traffic from your target network. Only use channel hopping to discover the available networks; focus your capture on a single channel. Note that while you may capture some traffic from a nearby channel (e.g., you see traffic from channels 1 and 6 when listening on channel 3), the captured traffic will be sporadic and incomplete.

- **Match Modulation Type** With the progression of different IEEE 802.11 Physical layer standards, different modulation mechanisms have been developed to accommodate faster data rates. Ensure the supported modulation mechanism for your wireless card matches the target network you are targeting. For example, an IEEE 802.11b wireless card sniffing an IEEE 802.11g network will capture some backward-compatible modulated traffic, but may miss other traffic modulated for an 802.11g network. If in doubt, ensure the card you are using for traffic capture supports all the standard modulation mechanisms. Currently, this includes an IEEE 802.11a/b/g card, but will also include IEEE 802.11n cards with MIMO (multiple input, multiple output) technology in the future.

# Understanding Wireless Card Modes

Before we start wireless sniffing using Wireshark, it is helpful to understand the different operating modes supported by wireless cards. Most wireless users only use their wireless cards as a station to an AP. In *managed mode*, the wireless card and driver software rely on a local AP to provide connectivity to the wireless network.

Another common mode for wireless cards is *ad-hoc mode* (or Independent Basic Service Set [IBSS] mode. Two wireless stations that want to communicate with each other directly can do so by sharing the responsibilities of an AP for a limited subset of wireless LAN services. Ad-hoc mode is used for short-term connectivity between stations, when an AP is not available to provide connectivity.

Many wireless cards also support *master mode*, where the wireless card provides the services of an AP when paired with the appropriate software. Managed mode allows you to configure your laptop or desktop system as an AP for providing connectivity to other wireless stations.

Finally, wireless cards support *monitor mode* functionality. When configured in monitor mode, the wireless card stops transmitting data and sniffs the currently configured channel, reporting the contents of any observed packets to the host operating system. This is the most useful mode of operation for analysis when using Wireshark, because a wireless card configured in monitor mode reports the entire contents of wireless packets, including header information and the encrypted or unencrypted data contents. When in monitor mode, the wireless card and driver reports the wireless frames "as-is," giving the most accurate view of the wireless activity for the selected channel.

In order to analyze a wireless network effectively using Wireshark, you need to configure your wireless card to operate in monitor mode on the appropriate channel, and then start a packet capture. Unfortunately, this is easier said than done. Because the majority of wireless card users use their wireless cards in managed or ad-hoc mode, wireless driver developers may not include support for monitor mode access. In the case of Linux, many drivers support monitor mode. Those Linux drivers that do not natively support monitor mode are often "patched" by other interested users or developers in order to access monitor mode functionality. However, in the case of Windows, drivers are closed-source, which prevents anyone except the driver developer from supplying monitor mode functionality. However, some commercial options exist for Windows that allow you to leverage the monitor mode support in your wireless card with custom driver software.

Next, we examine the steps necessary to configure your wireless card to support monitor mode access on Linux and Windows systems.

# Getting Support for Monitor Mode - Linux

In order to begin sniffing wireless traffic with Wireshark, your wireless card must be in monitor mode. Wireshark does not do this automatically; you have to manually configure your wireless card before starting your packet capture. However, the commands you need in order to configure the card in monitor mode can differ based on the type of wireless card and driver that you are using. This section discusses how to complete this step based on the most common wireless card and driver combination for Linux.

**TIP**

Determining the type of wireless card you have isn't always easy. While there are only a handful of manufacturers that make the wireless chipset hardware, multiple vendors re-brand the cards, thus making it difficult to identify what the actual chipset is. One resource for identifying the chipset from the card manufacturer is available at *http://linux-wless.passys.nl/*. If your specific card isn't listed here you can search using Google with the card name and keyword "chipset" (e.g., WPC55AG chipset).

# Linux Wireless Extensions Compatible Drivers

Most wireless drivers for Linux systems use the Linux Wireless Extensions interface, thus providing a consistent configuration interface for manipulating the wireless card. First, let's identify the wireless driver interface name by running the wireless card configuration utility *iwconfig* with no parameters:

```
$ iwconfig
eth0      no wireless extensions.


lo        no wireless extensions.


eth1      IEEE 802.11b  ESSID:"Beacon Wi-Fi Network"
          Mode:Managed  Frequency:2.462 GHz  Access Point: 00:02:2D:8B:70:2E
          Bit Rate:11 Mb/s   Tx-Power=20 dBm   Sensitivity=8/0
          Retry limit:7   RTS thr:off   Fragment thr:off
          Power Management:off
          Link Quality=50/100  Signal level=-71 dBm  Noise level=-86 dBm
          Rx invalid nwid:0  Rx invalid crypt:0  Rx invalid frag:0
          Tx excessive retries:0  Invalid misc:286   Missed beacon:5
```

> **NOTE**
>
> It is recommended that users take advantage of the Linux 2.6 kernel whenever possible. Most Linux distributions install their wireless tools packages for *iwconfig* and *iwpriv* by default; you will need to install these tools manually if they are not included with your default distribution. Use the package management utilities that come with your Linux distribution to search for packages with the name "wireless-tools" to identify installation options. Information specific to older Debian, SuSE, RedHat, and Mandrake distributions is available at *www.hpl.hp.com/personal/Jean_Tourrilhes/Linux/DISTRIBUTIONS.txt.*

From this output, we determine that interfaces *eth0* and *lo* do not support Linux Wireless Extensions; however, Interface *eth1* does support wireless extensions. From the output, we can see that the card is currently in managed mode and is associated with an IEEE 802.11b network with the Service Set Identifier (SSID) "Beacon Wi-Fi Network" at 2.462 GHz (channel 11).

Since we want to use this wireless interface for wireless traffic sniffing, we need to place the card in monitor mode. In order to make changes to the wireless card configuration, we need to be the *root user*. Become the root user by running the *su* command and supplying the root user password:

```
$ su
Password: enter root password
#
```

After becoming the root user, you can use the *iwconfig* utility to configure the card for monitor mode, by specifying the interface name followed by mode monitor:

```
# iwconfig eth1 mode monitor
```

After placing the card in monitor mode, run the *iwconfig* utility with the interface name as the only command-line argument, to verify the configuration change:

```
# iwconfig eth1
eth1    unassociated ESSID:off/any
        Mode:Monitor Channel=0 Access Point: 00:00:00:00:00:00
        Bit Rate:0 kb/s  Tx-Power=20 dBm  Sensitivity=8/0
        Retry limit:7  RTS thr:off  Fragment thr:off
        Encryption key:off
        Power Management:off
        Link Quality:0 Signal level:0 Noise level:0
        Rx invalid nwid:0 Rx invalid crypt:0 Rx invalid frag:0
        Tx excessive retries:0 Invalid misc:7007  Missed beacon:0
```

In this output, we see that the mode has changed from managed to monitor. At this point, the wireless card is operating in monitor mode. Next, we need to make sure the interface is in the "up" state with the *ifconfig* utility, again using the interface name as the only command-line parameter:

```
# ifconfig eth1
eth1    Link encap:UNSPEC HWaddr 00-13-CE-55-B5-EC-BC-A9-00-00-00-00-00-00-
00-00
        BROADCAST MULTICAST MTU:1500 Metric:1
        RX packets:18176 errors:0 dropped:18462 overruns:0 frame:0
        TX packets:123 errors:0 dropped:0 overruns:0 carrier:0
        collisions:0 txqueuelen:1000
        RX bytes:0 (0.0 b) TX bytes:0 (0.0 b)
        Interrupt:11 Base address:0x4000 Memory:a8401000-a8401fff
```

The first indented line of text following the interface name and hardware address (HWaddr) reports the operating flags for the interface. In this example, the interface is configured to accept broadcast and multicast traffic. The interface is not currently in the *up* state, due to the lack of the UP keyword. Modify the interface configuration by placing the interface in the *up* state, then examine the interface configuration properties as shown below:

```
# ifconfig eth1 up
# ifconfig eth1
eth1    Link encap:UNSPEC HWaddr 00-13-CE-55-B5-EC-3C-4D-00-00-00-00-00-00-
00-00
        UP BROADCAST MULTICAST MTU:1500 Metric:1
        RX packets:34604 errors:0 dropped:34583 overruns:0 frame:0
        TX packets:232 errors:0 dropped:0 overruns:0 carrier:0
        collisions:0 txqueuelen:1000
        RX bytes:18150 (17.7 Kb) TX bytes:0 (0.0 b)
        Interrupt:11 Base address:0x4000 Memory:a8401000-a8401fff
```

In this output we see that the interface is now in the *up* state and is ready to begin sniffing wireless traffic.

---

**NOTE**

Unlike the *iwconfig* tool, *ifconfig* does not understand the properties of an interface that is in monitor mode. When associated to a wireless network, the interface appears as a standard Ethernet interface; however, when in monitor mode, it appears as an unknown or unspecified link encapsulation mechanism. As a result, *ifconfig* displays a default of 16 bytes to represent the Media Access Control (MAC) address of the unspecified interface encapsulation (denoted with the string *UNSPEC*). In what appears to be a bug in the *ifconfig* tool, 8 bytes are printed to represent the MAC address, followed by 8 NULL bytes. The first 6 bytes represent the actual MAC address of the wireless card, followed by 2 bytes of uninitialized memory.

---

# MADWIFI 0.9.1 Driver Configuration

The Multiband Atheros Driver for WiFi (MADWIFI) supports wireless cards based on the popular Atheros chipsets supporting IEEE 802.11a, IEEE 802.11b, and IEEE

802.11g wireless networks. While this driver supports monitor mode access, it does not support the configuration of monitor mode access using the *iwconfig* utility. Instead, the MADWIFI developers include a custom tool for configuring wireless card properties called the *wlanconfig* utility.

The MADWIFI drivers are unique in that they support multiple interfaces on the same wireless card known as Virtual Access Points (VAPs). Each VAP appears as its own interface name with a single default VAP configured in managed mode. In order to create an interface in monitor mode, however, we need to remove all VAPs on the local system with the *wlanconfig* utility. First, examine the list of wireless devices on the system using the *iwconfig* utility with no command–line arguments:

```
# iwconfig
wifi0   no wireless extensions.

ath0    IEEE 802.11b ESSID:""
    Mode:Managed Channel:0 Access Point: 00:00:00:00:00:00
    Bit Rate:0 kb/s  Tx-Power:0 dBm  Sensitivity=0/3
    Retry:off  RTS thr:off  Fragment thr:off
    Encryption key:off
    Power Management:off
    Link Quality=0/94 Signal level=-95 dBm Noise level=-95 dBm
    Rx invalid nwid:0 Rx invalid crypt:0 Rx invalid frag:0
    Tx excessive retries:0 Invalid misc:0  Missed beacon:0
```

## NOTE

The MADWIFI drivers use a "master" interface with the naming convention *wifiX*, where *X* is *0* for the first wireless card, *1* for the second wireless card, and so on. The master interface is used to create one or more virtual interfaces with the *wlanconfig* utility. In most cases, you will only refer to the master interface when creating or destroying virtual interfaces. You will use the virtual interface for all other tasks, including sniffing wireless traffic with Wireshark, or accessing a wireless network as a station.

From this output we can see two interfaces; *wifi0* which does not support wireless extensions, and *ath0* which does. The *ath0* interface is named for the Atheros wireless chipset (*ath*) which is created by default in managed mode. In order to configure an interface in monitor mode, we must delete or "destroy" this interface using the *wlanconfig* utility:

```
# wlanconfig ath0 destroy
# iwconfig
wifi0   no wireless extensions.
```

From the output of the *iwconfig* utility, we see that the *ath0* interface is no longer present. Next, we re-create the *ath0* interface with the *wlanconfig* utility, this time indicating that the interface should be created in monitor mode, referencing the *wifi0* interface as the master interface:

```
# wlanconfig ath0 create wlandev wifi0 wlanmode monitor
ath0
# iwconfig
wifi0   no wireless extensions.

ath0    IEEE 802.11b ESSID:""
        Mode:Monitor Channel:0 Access Point: 00:00:00:00:00:00
        Bit Rate:0 kb/s  Tx-Power:0 dBm  Sensitivity=0/3
        Retry:off  RTS thr:off  Fragment thr:off
        Encryption key:off
        Power Management:off
        Link Quality=0/94 Signal level=-95 dBm Noise level=-95 dBm
        Rx invalid nwid:0 Rx invalid crypt:0 Rx invalid frag:0
        Tx excessive retries:0 Invalid misc:0  Missed beacon:0
```

Next, we must ensure the *ath0* interface is in the up state using the *ifconfig* utility, as shown below:

```
# ifconfig ath0 up
# ifconfig ath0
ath0    Link encap:UNSPEC HWaddr 00-20-A6-4F-01-40-BC-9D-00-00-00-00-00-00-
00-00
        UP BROADCAST RUNNING MULTICAST MTU:1500 Metric:1
        RX packets:0 errors:0 dropped:0 overruns:0 frame:0
        TX packets:0 errors:0 dropped:0 overruns:0 carrier:0
        collisions:0 txqueuelen:0
        RX bytes:0 (0.0 b) TX bytes:0 (0.0 b)
```

From the output of the *ifconfig* utility we see that the interface is now in the *up* state and is ready to start sniffing wireless traffic.

# Capturing Wireless Traffic - Linux

Once your wireless card in Linux has been placed in monitor mode, you are ready to start capturing wireless traffic. Recall that wireless cards can only capture traffic on a single channel at any given time. If you know the wireless channel you want to capture traffic on, configure your wireless card to listen on that channel using the *iwconfig* utility:

```
# iwconfig ath0 channel 1
# iwconfig ath0
```

Replace *ath0* with the name of your wireless interface, and the number *1* with the channel number you want to capture traffic on. As seen from the output of the *iwconfig* command, the card is currently configured to listen on 2.412 Gigahertz (GHz) (channel 1).

If you don't know the target channel number you want to use to capture traffic, you can configure your wireless card to perform channel hopping. Unfortunately, Linux doesn't come with a built-in tool for channel hopping; however, you can configure channel hopping manually with a short shell script. Enter the text found in Code 6.1 into a short shell script using your favorite text-editor. Line numbers have been added for clarity; do not enter the line numbers when creating this script.

**Code 6.1** Channel Hopping Shell Script

```
1.  #!/bin/bash
2.  IFACE=ath0
3.  IEEE80211bg="1 2 3 4 5 6 7 8 9 10 11"
4.  IEEE80211bg_intl="$IEEE80211b 12 13 14"
5.  IEEE80211a="36 40 44 48 52 56 60 64 149 153 157 161"
6.  IEEE80211bga="$IEEE80211bg $IEEE80211a"
7.  IEEE80211bga_intl="$IEEE80211bg_intl $IEEE80211a"
8.
9.  while true ; do
10.    for CHAN in $IEEE80211bg ; do
11.      echo "Switching to channel $CHAN"
12.      iwconfig $IFACE $CHAN
13.      sleep 1
14.    done
15. done
```

After saving the shell script, change the permissions on the file to make it an executable program:

```
# chmod 755 chanhop.sh
```

Change the interface name *ath0* on line 2 to reflect the name of your wireless interface. Also, change the channel designator *$IEEE802.11bg* on line 10 to reflect the channels that are supported by your wireless card. To start the channel-hopping script, run the shell script from the directory where it was created:

```
# ./chanhop.sh
Switching to channel 1
Switching to channel 2
```

When you want to stop the channel-hopping script, press **Ctrl+C**.

> **NOTE**
>
> If creating shell scripts for channel hopping isn't appealing, you can download a more sophisticated copy of this script from the Wireshark web site wiki at http://wiki.wireshark.org/CaptureSetup/WLAN.

# Starting a Packet Capture - Linux

Whether you have specified a single channel for capturing wireless traffic or are currently channel hopping, the process for capturing wireless traffic on Linux remains the same. Start Wireshark by running the *wireshark* executable with no command-line arguments as the root user, and initiate a new packet capture by pressing **Capture | Options**. This opens the "Wireshark Capture" options dialog box (see Figure 6.1).

Choose the wireless interface that has been placed in monitor mode by selecting the drop-down box labeled "Interface:" and then specify the desired capture options. Next, click **Start** to initiate the packet capture.

At this point, you've configured your system to capture wireless traffic in monitor mode. The next step is to utilize the information contained in the packets you are capturing. Fortunately, Wireshark has sophisticated analysis mechanisms that can be used for wireless traffic analysis. Let's examine the steps for configuring monitor mode support on Windows systems.

**Figure 6.1** Wireshark Capture Options Dialog Box - Linux

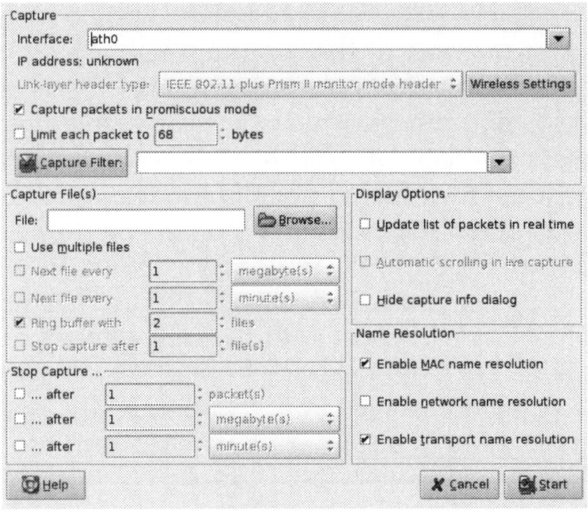

# Getting Support for Monitor Mode - Windows

Unfortunately, Windows drivers for wireless cards do not normally include support for monitor mode access, instead restricting users to operating the card in managed mode. Fortunately, through a combination of commercial and open-source software, we can overcome this limitation to use Windows hosts for wireless traffic analysis with Wireshark.

## Introducing AirPcap

In order to overcome the limitations with most wireless drivers for Windows systems, the engineers at CACE Technologies have introduced a commercial product called AirPcap. A combination of a USB IEEE 802.11b/g adapter, supporting driver software, and a client configuration utility, AirPcap provides a simple mechanism to capture wireless traffic in monitor mode on Windows workstations at a reasonable cost. AirPcap is available at *www.cacetech.com*.

After obtaining the AirPcap CD and Universal Serial Bus (USB) wireless adapter, follow the installation instructions detailed in the AirPcap User's Guide. Ensure you have installed the appropriate version (WinPcap 4.0 beta 1) of WinPcap to support the AirPcap.

**NOTE**

Unfortunately, at the time of this writing, there are no free software solutions that allow Windows users to capture wireless traffic reliably, and without violating other software license restrictions. If you need to perform wireless traffic analysis with a Windows workstation, Wireshark is an effective tool; however, you would have to purchase a driver and hardware combination that supports monitor mode.

If you want to avoid any costs associated with drivers for monitor mode packet capture, you are encouraged to use a Linux option that bundles monitor mode support with the free wireless drivers. Using a bootable Linux CD such as Backtrack from *www.remote-exploit.org*, you can create an easily accessible Linux environment by booting from the Linux CD and plugging in a supported wireless card.

**TIP**

Another option for Windows users is to use the licensed AiroPeek NX software to collect packet captures. Since Wireshark can read AiroPeek NX's *.apc* files, you can use Wireshark to augment the features you get from AiroPeek NX. Unfortunately, the demo version of AiroPeek NX does not allow you to save packet captures.

## Specifying the Capture Channel

After installing the AirPcap drivers, start the AirPcap control panel tool by navigating to **Start | All Programs | airpcap | Airpcap Control Panel** (see Figure 6.2). Using this utility, you can manipulate the following settings for the wireless capture, as described in Table 6.2.

**Figure 6.2** AirPcap Control Panel

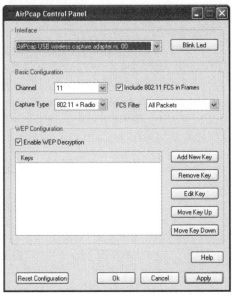

**Table 6.2** AirPcap Control Panel Settings

| Parameter | Options | Description |
|---|---|---|
| Blink LED | On, Off | Blinks the Light Emitting Diode (LED) on the Airpcap USB adapter; useful when using multiple AirPcap dongles on the same host. |
| Channel | 1–14 | Specifies the channel that Wireshark will capture traffic on with the specified AirPcap adapter. Because the AirPcap adapter is listen-only, it allows users to capture on all supported IEEE 802.11b/g channels, even those that are not permitted for use by the Federal Communications Commission (FCC). At the time of this writing, AirPcap does not include a tool to perform channel hopping during a packet capture. |
| Include 802.11 FCS in Frames | On, Off | The last 4 bytes of every packet on a wireless network is known as the Frame Check Sequence (FCS), which is a 32-bit checksum that is used to identify whether a packet was accidentally corrupted in transmission. This information is often stripped from monitor |

*Continued*

**Table 6.2 continued** AirPcap Control Panel Settings

| Parameter | Options | Description |
|---|---|---|
| | | mode packet captures on Linux systems, but can be useful to validate the integrity of a packet if present. |
| | | The recommended value is to set this option to "On" to record the FCS information in each packet. |
| Capture Type | 802.11 Only, 802.11 + Radio | Each Promiscuous Capture Library (libpcap) packet capture file or interface has a capture link type assigned to it that tells Wireshark and other sniffer tools what to expect from the sniffer. The AirPcap Control Panel allows you to specify 802.11 Only or 802.11 + Radio as the link type. The 802.11 Only link type will produce a packet capture where each packet begins with the IEEE 802.11 header contents. The 802.11 + Radio link type will prepend a header before the start of the IEEE 802.11 header, known as the *Radiotap* header. This header allows the capture to store additional information from the driver for each packet that is not part of the 802.11 header information (e.g., signal strength, signal quality, modulation type, channel type [802.11b, 802.11g], the data rate, channel number and other useful information). |
| | | The recommended value is to set this option to 802.11 + Radio to record the additional information with each packet. |
| FCS Filter | All Packets, Valid Packets, Wrong FCS Packets | Regardless of whether the Frame Check Sequence (FCS) is recorded for each frame in the packet capture, the AirPcap adapter will check the FCS of each frame to determine if it is valid or corrupted when received. AirPcap allows users to specify if they want to receive both valid and invalid packets (All Packets), only valid packets (correct FCS), or invalid packets (wrong FCS). |
| | | For most uses of AirPcap, it is recommended you select "Valid Packets," since any packets |

**Continued**

**Table 6.2 continued** AirPcap Control Panel Settings

| Parameter | Options | Description |
|---|---|---|
| | | that are invalid were likely not properly received by the station they were directed to. However, it may be useful to capture packets with a wrong FCS to determine how many packets are being corrupted in transit. |
| WEP Settings | Multiple | The AirPcap Control Panel allows users to specify static Wired Equivalent Privacy (WEP) keys to use for decrypting traffic with Wireshark. This option is also available from the Wireshark graphical user interface (GUI), and is examined later in this chapter. After selecting the desired options, press the **OK** button to activate and save your preferences. |

# Capturing Wireless Traffic - Windows

After specifying your capture preferences on the AirPcap Control Panel, start Wireshark and initiate a new packet capture by navigating to **Capture | Options**. This opens the Wireshark capture options dialog box (see Figure 6.3).

**Figure 6.3** Wireshark Capture Options - Windows

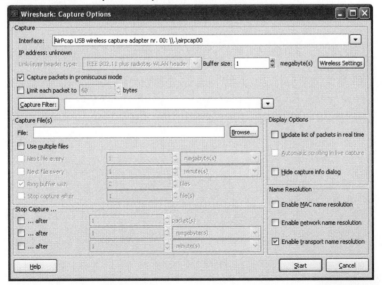

Choose the AirPcap interface by selecting the drop-down box labeled "Interface:," and then specify the desired capture options. Next, click **Start** to initiate the packet capture. Stop the capture after you have collected the desired amount of traffic by clicking on the **Stop** button, or go to **Capture | Stop** in the capture dialog box.

At this point, you are capturing wireless traffic in monitor mode on Windows. Next comes the challenging part: extracting useful information from the packet capture contents. The following section examines the many Wireshark features that make this analysis easier.

# Analyzing Wireless Traffic

Regardless of whether you are reading a packet capture from a stored file or from a live interface on a Windows or Linux host, Wireshark's analysis features are nearly identical. Wireshark offers many useful features for analyzing wireless traffic, including detailed protocol dissectors, powerful display filters, customizable display properties, and the ability to decrypt wireless traffic. Each of these features are examined in detail.

## Navigating the Packet Details Window

One of the most impressive Wireshark features is the ability to dissect the contents of traffic and present it in a collapsible "tree-like" manner. For wireless traffic, Wireshark presents the Frame Dissector window starting with frame statistics, and then the 802.11 MAC layer contents. If additional data follows for the 802.11 header, Wireshark logically divides each of the protocols that follow into a new window.

### Frame Statistics

The first group in the Packet Details window detailed summary information about the currently selected frame. The Frame window doesn't display any of the selected frame's contents, but rather general information contained in the packet capture for the selected frame (see Table 6.3).

**Table 6.3** Frame Statistical Detail

| Field Name | Description | Display Filter Reference Name |
|---|---|---|
| Arrival Time | The "Arrival Time" reflects the timestamp recorded by the station that is capturing traffic when the packet arrived. The accuracy of this field is only as accurate as the time on the receiving station. Note that packet captures from Windows systems are only represented with accuracy in seconds; no support for representing fractional seconds is available. | *frame.time* |
| Time Delta from Previous Packet | The "Time Delta" field identifies the elapsed time between the selected frame and the frame immediately before this frame. This field is updated when a display filter is applied to reflect the time from the previously displayed frame. This feature can be very useful when analyzing traffic that is transmitted with a consistent time interval (such as beacon frames) to identify interference causing dropped frames. | *frame.time_delta* |
| Time Since Reference or First Frame | The "Time Since Reference" or "First Frame" field indicates the amount of time that has elapsed since the start of the packet capture for the currently selected frame. This field is not updated when a display filter is applied. | *frame.time_relative* |
| Frame Number | The "Frame Number" field is a sequential counter starting with 1, uniquely representing the current frame. This field is useful for applying a display filter where one or more frames need to be selected or excluded from the display. | *frame.number* |
| Packet Length | The "Packet Length" reflects the actual length of the entire packet, regardless of how much of the packet was captured. By default, the entire frame is captured with Wireshark and Airodump. | *frame.pkt_len* |

**Continued**

**Table 6.3 continued** Frame Statistical Detail

| Field Name | Description | Display Filter Reference Name |
|---|---|---|
| Capture Length | The "Capture Length" reflects how much data was captured based on the specified number of bytes the user wanted to capture for each frame (known as the "snap length"). By default, Wireshark uses a snap length of 65,535 bytes to capture the entire frame contents. When an alternative snap length is specified, the capture length can be smaller if the frame size is smaller than the snap length. | *frame.cap_len* |
| Protocols in Frame | The "Protocols in Frame" field specifies all the protocols that are present, starting with the IEEE 802.11 header. | *frame.protocols* |

**TIP**

Maintaining accurate host time is important for many kinds of protocol analysis, and especially important if you want to correlate events across multiple systems. Consider using the Network Time Protocol (NTP) on you Linux or Windows clients to ensure your local system time is always accurate.

# IEEE 802.11 Header

Following the frame statistics data, Wireshark starts to dissect the protocol information for the selected packet. The IEEE 802.11 header is fairly complex; unlike a standard Ethernet header, it is between 24 and 30 bytes (compared to the standard Ethernet header of 14 bytes), has three or four addresses (compared to Ethernet's two addresses), and has many more fields to specify various pieces of information pertinent to wireless networks. What's more, wireless frames can have additional protocols appended to the end of the IEEE 802.11 header, including encryption options, Quality of Service (QoS) options, and embedded protocol identifiers (IEEE 802.2 header), all before actually getting any data to represent the upper-layer Network layer protocols.

Fortunately, Wireshark makes this analysis simple by intelligently representing this data in an easy-to-navigate form. We'll use many of these data fields when we start using display filters on wireless traffic and analyzing real-life packet captures, so it's beneficial to start with an analysis of each of the fields in the IEEE 802.11 header as shown in Table 6.4 below.

**Figure 6.4** IEEE 802.11 Header Fields

| Field Name | Description | Display Filter Reference Name |
|---|---|---|
| Type/Subtype | The Type/Subtype field value is not represented as data in the IEEE 802.11 header; rather, it is included as a convenience mechanism to uniquely identify the type and subtype combination that is included in the header of this frame. This field is commonly used in display filters. | *wlan.fc.type_subtype* |
| Frame Control | The Frame Control field is a 2-byte field that represents the first 2 bytes of the IEEE 802.11 header. Wireshark further dissects this field into four additional fields, as described below. | *wlan.fc* |
| Version | The Version field is included in the frame control header and specifies the version of the IEEE 802.11 header. At the time of this writing, this value is *0*. | *wlan.fc.version* |
| Type | The Type field is included in the frame control header and specifies the type of frame (data, management, or control). | *wlan.fc.type* |
| Subtype | The Subtype field is included in the frame control header and specifies the function for the specified frame type. For example, if the frame is a type management frame, the subtype field indicates the type of management frame (e.g., a beacon frame, authenticate request, or disassociate notice). | *wlan.fc.subtype* |
| Flags | The Flags field is a 1-byte field in the frame control header that specifies eight | *wlan.fc.flags* |

**Continued**

**Figure 6.4 continued** IEEE 802.11 Header Fields

| Field Name | Description | Display Filter Reference Name |
|---|---|---|
| | different options of the frame. Wireshark further dissects this field into each unique option, as described below. | |
| DS status | The Distribution System (DS) Status field represents the direction the frame is traveling in. Wireshark represents two unique fields as one display entry: *From DS* and *To DS*. When From DS is set to *1* and To DS is set to *0*, the frame is traveling from the AP to the wireless network. When From DS is set to *0* and To DS is set to *1*, the frame is traveling from a wireless client to the AP. | *wlan.fcds* |
| More Fragments | The More Fragments field in the flags header is used to indicate if additional fragments of a frame must be reassembled to process the entire frame. This field is not used often. | *wlan.fc.flag* |
| Retry | The Retry field in the flags header is used to indicate if the current frame is being retransmitted. The first time a frame is transmitted, the retry bit is cleared. If it is not received properly, the transmitting station retransmits the frame and sets the retry bit to indicate this status. | *wlan.fc.retry* |
| Power Management | The Power Management field in the flags header is used to indicate if the station is planning to enter a "dozing" state where they will reduce their participation in the network in an attempt to conserve power. | *wlan.fc.pwrmgmt* |
| More Data | The More Data field in the flags header is used by an AP to indicate that the station receiving frames has more packets waiting in a buffer for delivery. The More Data field is often used when a station awakens from a power-conservation mode to deliver all pending traffic. | *wlan.fc.moredata* |

**Continued**

**Figure 6.4 continued** IEEE 802.11 Header Fields

| Field Name | Description | Display Filter Reference Name |
|---|---|---|
| Protected | The Protected field in the flags header is used by an AP to indicate that an IEEE 802.11 encryption mechanism is used to encrypt the contents of the frame. At the time of this writing, the protected field indicates that the payload of the frame is encrypted with the Wired Equivalence Privacy (WEP) protocol, Temporal Key Integrity Protocol (TKIP), or the Counter Mode with Cipher Block Chaining Message Authentication Code Protocol (CCMP). | *wlan.fc.protected* |
| Order | The Order field in the flags header is used to indicate that the transmission of frames should be handled in a strict order, preventing a station from re-ordering the delivery of frames to improve performance or operational management. This field is not used often. | *wlan.fc.order* |
| Duration | The Duration field follows the frame control header and serves one of two functions. In most frames, the duration field specifies the amount of time required to complete the transmission of the frame in a quantity of microseconds. When associating to the AP, however, the duration field identifies the association identifier (i.e., a unique value assigned to each station connected to the AP). | *wlan.duration* |
| Address Fields | The IEEE 802.11 header contains one Address Field (receiver or destination address) if the type of frame is a control message, and three Address Fields for normal data or management traffic (source, destination, and basic SSID [BSSID]). Wireless LANs that bridge multiple networks together also include a fourth address. Complicating things, | *wlan.da (destination), wlan.sa (source), wlan.bssid (BSSID), wlan.ra (receiver)* |

**Continued**

**Figure 6.4 continued** IEEE 802.11 Header Fields

| Field Name | Description | Display Filter Reference Name |
|---|---|---|
| | the order of these addresses isn't consistent, and changes depending on the To DS and From DS flag settings in the frame control header. Fortunately, Wireshark correctly represents all of these fields, allowing us to apply filters using the appropriate display name. | |
| Fragment Number | The Fragment Number (FN) field is a sequential number that is used to uniquely identify a fragment of a frame, starting at 0. This field is not used often. | *wlan.frag* |
| Sequence Number | The Sequence Number (SN) field is a sequential number that is used to identify the entire frame, starting at 0. Each frame transmitted by a station should have a sequence numberthat is one greater than the previous frame, until the counter wraps at 4,095. | *wlan.seq* |

As mentioned previously, there are additional header fields that follow the IEEE 802.11 header, and Wireshark also dissects the contents of these fields. We will use our understanding of the fields in the IEEE 802.11 header in the next section, where we apply useful display filters to a traffic capture.

# Leveraging Display Filters

One of the most powerful and useful features in Wireshark is the ability to apply inclusive or exclusive display filters to a packet capture, in order to narrow down the number of packets to those containing useful data. When capturing traffic on a wireless network, it is easy to become overwhelmed by the sheer quantity of data that is captured. (At an absolute minimum, a wireless network transmits 10 frames per second, before a single station connects to the network.) Using display filters, you can exclude uninteresting traffic to reveal useful information, or search through a large packet capture for a specific set of information.

In this section, we demonstrate several useful display filters for analyzing wireless traffic. We focus on using our knowledge of the IEEE 802.11 header and frame statistic contents to apply wireless-specific filters that can be applied in real-world analysis scenarios.

# Traffic for a Specific Basic Service Set

An IEEE 802.11 wireless network with an AP providing connectivity to one or more client systems is known as a Basic Service Set (BSS). This is the most common wireless LAN implementation, and is used everywhere from corporate networks to hotspot environments and high-security government institutions.

Each wireless AP is uniquely identified by the Basic Service Set Identifier (BSSID). Recall that the BSSID is one of the addresses found in the IEEE 802.11 header, and is present in every data or management frame transmitted by a wireless station or an AP to uniquely identify the wireless LAN.

When traffic is captured in monitor mode, the wireless card reports all valid IEEE 802.11 frames for the specified channel, regardless of the BSSID or the network name being used. This can also include traffic from other nearby channels, because many wireless cards also have sufficient radio sensitivity to capture traffic from other nearby frequencies (e.g., it's not uncommon for a wireless card on channel 3 to capture traffic from channels 1, 2, 3, 4, and 5).

**TIP**

The BSSID address is often the same Medium Access Control (MAC) address as the wireless card on the AP, when there is a single network name configured. When multiple network names or virtual APs are configured, the BSSID may be similar to the MAC address of the AP's wireless card with minor variations (often in the last byte of the address).

When doing troubleshooting analysis, however, you usually want to limit the analysis to traffic to and from a specific AP that is servicing the problematic client. Using display filters, you can easily exclude traffic from nearby APs and focus the analysis on a specific AP. In this display filter, the goal is to identify all of the traffic for a single AP.

## Identify the Station MAC Address

We start by obtaining the MAC address of the station that we are troubleshooting, or any station that is connected to the target BSS. On a Windows system, we can extract this information by running the *ipconfig /all* utility from a command shell (see Figure 6.4). On a Linux system, use *ifconfig -a* to determine the MAC address (see Figure 6.5).

**Figure 6.4** Windows MAC Address Information

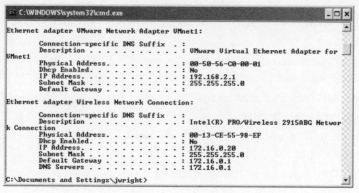

**Figure 6.5** Linux MAC Address Information

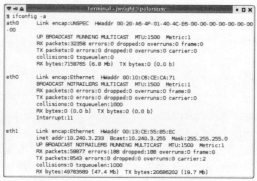

Once we have identified the correct station address, you can use it to apply a display filter to your packet capture.

## Filter for Station MAC

With the packet capture open, apply a display filter to display only traffic from the client station using the *wlan.sa* display field name. Assuming the station MAC address is *00:09:5b:e8:c4:03*, the display filter would be applied as:

```
wlan.sa eq 00:09:5b:e8:c4:03
```

A sample packet capture showing the results of this filter are shown in Figure 6.6.

From the Display Filter window, we see that 125 frames were returned from a packet capture of 1,141 total. However, when we examine the Packet Details window for the selected frame, we see that the BSSID is the broadcast address (*ff:ff:ff:ff:ff:ff*). This is because the selected frame is a *probe request* packet, which the client uses as a mechanism to discover networks in the area. We can refine our display filter to return only

**Figure 6.6** Filtering on Source MAC Address

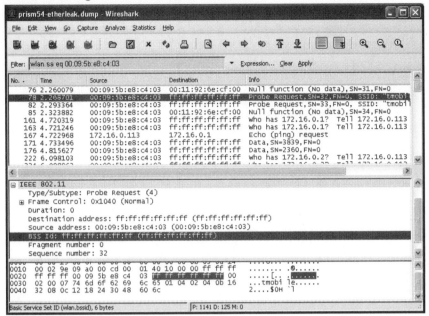

traffic destined specifically for the AP, by amending the display filter to return only
frames with our station MAC address as the source that are not destined to the broadcast BSSID. The display filter now becomes:

```
wlan.sa eq 00:09:5b:e8:c4:03 and wlan.bssid ne ff:ff:ff:ff:ff:ff
```

This updated filter is shown in Figure 6.7.

## Filter on BSSID

From the previous filter, we see that the BSSID for the station with the specified
source address is *00:11:92:6e:cf:00*. We can use this information to apply a filter for
only this BSSID, to exclude traffic from any other APs:

```
wlan.bssid eq 00:11:92:6e:cf:00
```

This final filter excludes any traffic not specifically destined to this AP, which
will allow us to focus our analysis on this specific network.

**Figure 6.7** Filtering on Source MAC Address and BSSID

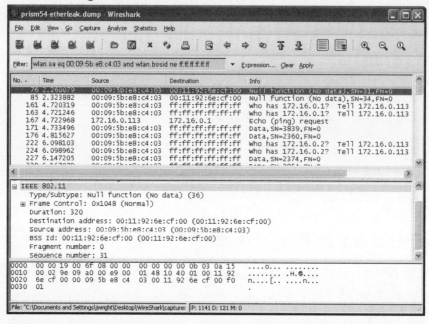

**Figure 6.8** Filtering on BSSID

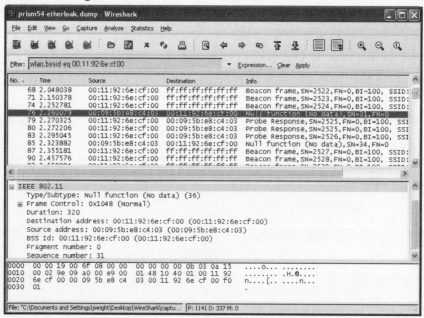

# Traffic for a Specific Extended Service Set

Filtering for a specific BSS is useful if you can narrow your troubleshooting down to a specific AP; however, initially, you may need to take a broader look at your wireless network and assess traffic for all of the APs in your capture file. Indeed, many of the problems in wireless networking have to do with roaming between APs, which forces us to assess traffic from multiple APs. Fortunately, Wireshark display filters come to the rescue.

When you configure and deploy a wireless network, each AP is configured with one or more network names (or SSIDs), also known as an Extended SSID (ESSID). When you deploy multiple APs that facilitate a client's ability to roam between APs, all of the APs with the same SSID are referred to as participating in an Extended Service Set (ESS).

In the display filter example, our goal is to identify all of the traffic for a specific ESS identified by the SSID or network name. Unfortunately, we cannot apply a filter to identify all frames for a given SSID, as many management frames and all data and control frames do not include the SSID information. Instead, we need to enumerate all the BSSIDs for a specified SSID to develop an inclusive filter.

## Filter on SSID

The first step is to apply a filter for a target SSID. As mentioned previously, this only returns management frames that include the SSID information element; however, it will present a list of all of the APs that use this SSID for additional filtering.

The SSID is included in the payload of beacon frames, probe response frames, and associate request frames. Navigate to this field by selecting any beacon frame, go to the Packet Details window, and then go to **IEEE 802.11 Wireless LAN Management Frame | Tagged Parameters | SSID Parameter Set | Tag Interpretation.** The display name for this field will be revealed as *wlan_mgt.tag.interpretation* (see Figure 6.9).

We can apply a display filter to identify all packets that includes the SSID *"NOWIRE"* as shown:

```
wlan_mgt.tag.interpretation eq "NOWIRE"
```

> ## ! WARNING
>
> All string references in Wireshark, including the SSID, are case-sensitive. When applying any filter that includes a string, ensure that you specify the proper case for a successful filter expression.

**Figure 6.9** Displaying the SSID Tagged Parameter

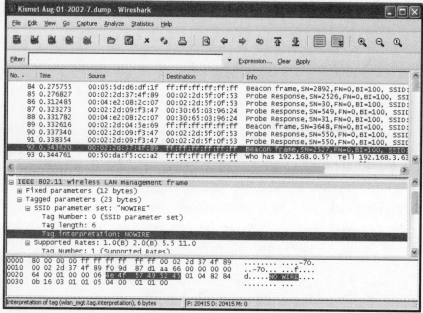

## Exclude Each BSSID

Once we have applied the filter on the SSID, the capture has been reduced to management frames (mostly beacon frames). Since our goal is to identify all of the traffic for the ESS, we need to modify this filter to identify all traffic for each BSS. Fortunately, the display filter for the SSID has revealed a list of all the APs configured with the specified SSID, which allows us to identify the BSSID for each AP.

In order to ensure that we have a complete list of all the BSSIDs, we start by applying an exclusive filter for each BSSID. Click on any beacon frame and navigate to the BSSID field by typing **IEEE 802.11 | BSS Id**. Using the display field name, *wlan.bssid*, add an exclusion display filter to the existing display filter for the given BSSID. For example, if the BSSID is *00:02:2d:37:4f:89*, our display filter becomes:

```
wlan_mgt.tag.interpretation eq "NOWIRE" and !(wlan.bssid eq 00:02:2d:37:4f:89)
```

Note that in this display filter, we are using the exclamation point as a negation operator, and testing for the BSSID equal to the specified address. This effectively returns all frames with a matching SSID except for the specified BSSID. Since our ultimate goal is to include only traffic from these BSSIDs, we negate the display filter with a leading exclamation point, which will make it easy to reverse the effect of the display filter simply by removing the exclamation point.

Next, we repeat this step for each of the remaining frames in the packet capture, selecting another BSSID and adding it to the exclusion list. For example, if the next BSSID is *00:40:05:df:93:c6*, it is added to our exclusion list:

```
wlan_mgt.tag.interpretation eq "NOWIRE" and !(wlan.bssid eq
00:02:2d:37:4f:89 or wlan.bssid eq 00:40:05:df:93:c6)
```

Repeat this process until there are no packets remaining in the capture display.

## Invert Filter

At this point, our display filter should have no packets displayed. We have effectively identified each AP in the packet capture that is associated with the specified SSID. Now, we can modify the packet capture to invert the exclusion filter on the *wlan.bssid* field to include all of the specified addresses. For example, if our packet capture looks like this:

```
wlan_mgt.tag.interpretation eq "NOWIRE" and !(wlan.bssid eq
00:02:2d:37:4f:89 or wlan.bssid eq 00:40:05:df:93:c6 or wlan.bssid eq
00:40:96:36:80:f0)
```

We can modify it by removing the filter on the *wlan_mgt.tag.interpretation* field, and the exclamation point before the list of BSSIDs:

```
(wlan.bssid eq 00:02:2d:37:4f:89 or wlan.bssid eq 00:40:05:df:93:c6 or
wlan.bssid eq 00:40:96:36:80:f0)
```

Applying this filter will return all traffic for the specified BSSIDs, effectively excluding any traffic from neighboring networks that are not part of the initially specified SSID. This allows us to focus our analysis only on traffic to and from the networks associated with the initial SSID.

> **TIP**
>
> After applying a significant display filter (as shown in this example), it is wise to save the resulting packets in a new packet capture file. This way, you can assess the results of your filter at a later time without having to repeat the filtering process. To save an extract of packets, click **File | Save As**, and then click on the **Displayed** button. Enter an appropriate filename for the results of the display filter and click on **Save**.
>
> You can also save the display filter itself by clicking **Analyze | Display Filters**. Enter a name for the display filter in the "Filter name" text box and click on **Save**. When you want to recall the filter, go to **Analyze | Display Filters** and double-click on the desired display filter name.

Even when there are no stations participating on the network, an AP will transmit at least ten packets a second to advertise the presence and capabilities of the network. These beacon frames are a vital component of any wireless network, but they can be difficult to assess a packet capture if these frames aren't particularly interesting to you.

Fortunately, we can easily apply a display filter to exclude these frames. In the Packet Details window, Wireshark identifies the type and subtype fields in the IEEE 802.11 header. By selecting a beacon frame, we can see that the type has a value of *0*, and the subtype has a value of *4* (see Figure 6.10).

**Figure 6.10** Beacon Frame Type/Subtype

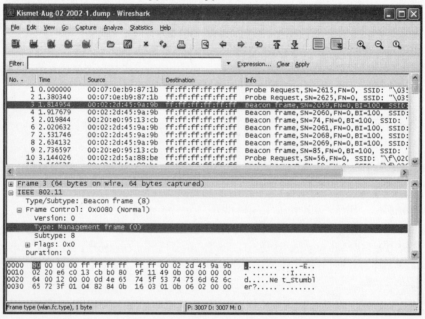

We can exclude these frames by applying a display filter as shown below:

```
!(wlan.fc.type eq 0 and wlan.fc.subtype eq 8)
```

Wireshark also gives us the "Type and Subtype Combined" field that can also be used for filtering. Instead of applying a filter on the Type and Subtype fields, we can apply a filter on the Combined Type and Subtype field as follows:

```
wlan.fc.type_subtype ne 8
```

## Tools & Traps

### Representing Wireless Frame Types

When assessing a wireless packet capture with Wireshark, it is common to apply display filters to look for or exclude certain frames based on the IEEE 802.11 frame type and frame subtype fields. If you are trying to exclude frames from a capture, it is easy to identify the Type and Subtype fields by navigating the Packet Details window and using the values for your filter. If you are looking for a specific frame type, however, you have to remember either the Frame Type and Subtype values, or the Combined Type/Subtype value assigned by Wireshark.

   Instead of expecting you to memorize the 35+ values for different frame types, we've included them here for easy reference.

| Frame Type/Subtype | Filter |
|---|---|
| Management Frames | wlan.fc.type eq 0 |
| Control Frames | wlan.fc.type eq 1 |
| Data Frames | wlan.fc.type eq 2 |
| Association Request | wlan.fc.type_subtype eq 0 |
| Association response | wlan.fc.type_subtype eq 1 |
| Reassociation Request | wlan.fc.type_subtype eq 2 |
| Reassociation Response | wlan.fc.type_subtype eq 3 |
| Probe Request | wlan.fc.type_subtype eq 4 |
| Probe Response | wlan.fc.type_subtype eq 5 |
| Beacon | wlan.fc.type_subtype eq 8 |
| Announcement Traffic Indication Map (ATIM) | wlan.fc.type_subtype eq 9 |
| Disassociate | wlan.fc.type_subtype eq 10 |
| Authentication | wlan.fc.type_subtype eq 11 |
| Deauthentication | wlan.fc.type_subtype eq 12 |
| Action Frames | wlan.fc.type_subtype eq 13 |
| Block Acknowledgement (ACK) Request | wlan.fc.type_subtype eq 24 |
| Block ACK | wlan.fc.type_subtype eq 25 |
| Power-Save Poll | wlan.fc.type_subtype eq 26 |
| Request to Send | wlan.fc.type_subtype eq 27 |

**Continued**

| Frame Type/Subtype | Filter |
|---|---|
| Clear to Send | *wlan.fc.type_subtype eq 28* |
| ACK | *wlan.fc.type_subtype eq 29* |
| Contention Free Period End | *wlan.fc.type_subtype eq 30* |
| Contention Free Period End ACK | *wlan.fc.type_subtype eq 31* |
| Data + Contention Free ACK | *wlan.fc.type_subtype eq 33* |
| Data + Contention Free Poll | *wlan.fc.type_subtype eq 34* |
| Data + Contention Free ACK + Contention Free Poll | *wlan.fc.type_subtype eq 35* |
| NULL Data | *wlan.fc.type_subtype eq 36* |
| NULL Data + Contention Free ACK | *wlan.fc.type_subtype eq 37* |
| NULL Data + Contention Free Poll | *wlan.fc.type_subtype eq 38* |
| NULL Data + Contention Free ACK + Contention Free Poll | *wlan.fc.type_subtype eq 39* |
| QoS Data | *wlan.fc.type_subtype eq 40* |
| QoS Data + Contention Free ACK | *wlan.fc.type_subtype eq 41* |
| QoS Data + Contention Free Poll | *wlan.fc.type_subtype eq 42* |
| QoS Data + Contention Free ACK + Contention Free Poll | *wlan.fc.type_subtype eq 43* |
| NULL QoS Data | *wlan.fc.type_subtype eq 44* |
| NULL QoS Data + Contention Free Poll | *wlan.fc.type_subtype eq 46* |
| NULL QoS Data + Contention Free ACK + Contention Free Poll | *wlan.fc.type_subtype eq 47* |

## Data Traffic Only

Excluding beacon frames will reduce the amount of traffic in your wireless packet capture, but it will also leave many other types of packets including other management frames, control frames, and data frames. In some cases, you may only want to examine data traffic to assess potential information disclosure risks on the network, or as a measurement of efficiency for client traffic.

The process of applying a display filter for data traffic is similar to filtering beacon frames. Navigate to a data packet and inspect the Packet Details window to inspect the packet Type and Subtype Combined field (see Figure 6.11).

**Figure 6.11** Data Frame Type/Subtype

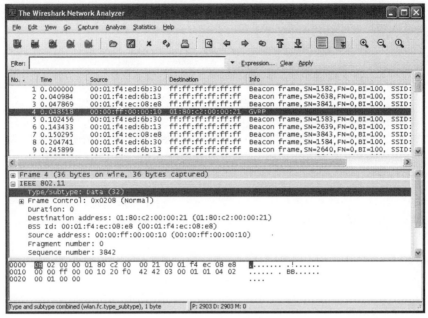

In Figure 6.11, we see that the Type and Subtype Combined field has a value of 32. We can use this field to apply a display filter that displays only this type of packet:

```
wlan.fc.type_subtype eq 32
```

While this display filter is effective at excluding traffic, it can be too restrictive for some analysis needs. Remember that that Type and Subtype Combined field is a unique identifier for both field values. When we apply a filter to display only frames with a Type and Subtype combined value of 32, we exclude other types of data frames including QoS marked wireless frames. An alternative display filter is to examine only the IEEE 802.11 type field without referencing the subtype field as well:

```
wlan.fc.type eq 2
```

A sample of this display filter is shown in Figure 6.12.

With this modified display filter, we can see all of the data frames, regardless of the Subtype field. In this example, we can see normal data traffic (such as the Internet Control Message Protocol [ICMP] request and reply frames), but we also have NULL data frames. NULL data frames are used by some APs and station cards to enter power conservation mode, or are used right before switching frequencies to

**Figure 6.12** Limiting Data Frame Type Filter

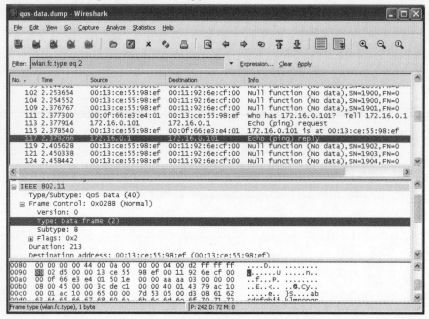

scan for other nearby networks. If NULL data frames aren't useful in your analysis, you can exclude them by modifying the display filter:

```
wlan.fc.type eq 2 and !(wlan.fc.subtype eq 4)
```

If this display filter reveals more data subtypes than are necessary for your analysis, add additional exclusion filters inside the parenthesis, separated by the *or* keyword.

# Unencrypted Data Traffic Only

Another common analysis technique is to identify wireless traffic that is not encrypted. This may be in an effort to identify misconfigured devices that could be disclosing sensitive information over the wireless network, or as part of an audit to ensure wireless traffic is encrypted, or to identify rogue APs, since most rogue devices are deployed with no encryption.

As seen in the IEEE 802.11 header analysis, one of the bits in the frame control header is known as the *protected bit* (formerly known as the WEP bit, or the privacy bit). The protected bit is set to *1* when the packet is encrypted using an IEEE 802.11 encryption mechanism such as WEP, TKIP, or CCMP; otherwise it is set to *0*. We can apply a filter using this field to identify all unencrypted wireless traffic:

```
wlan.fc.protected ne 1
```

**Figure 6.13** Excluding Encrypted Frames

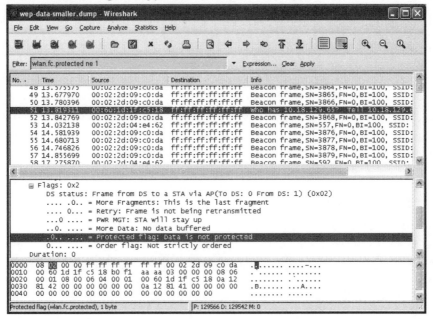

A sample packet capture with this display filter applied is shown in Figure 6.13.

While this filter shows the unencrypted wireless traffic, it is not the most effective display filter because it also reveals unencrypted management and control frames. Since these frames are always unencrypted, we can extend the display filter to identify unencrypted data frames only to get the most effective analysis:

```
wlan.fc.protected ne 1 and wlan.fc.type eq 2
```

> **NOTE**
>
> At the time of this writing, the available encryption mechanisms for IEEE 802.11 wireless networks only apply to data frames, and do not provide any confidentiality for management or control frames. However, this is slated for change with the ratification of the IEEE 802.11w amendment that was designed to extend security to management traffic as well as data traffic. The IEEE 802.11w task group is scheduled to ratify the *Protected Management Frames* amendment in April 2008.

# Identifying Hidden SSIDs

Many organizations have adopted SSID cloaking, or prevented their APs from advertising their SSIDs to anyone who asks. While this provides a minimal measure of security, it is an ineffective mechanism for controlling access to the network and should only be used in conjunction with a strong encryption and authentication mechanism.

When an AP wants to obscure the SSID of the network, it does not respond when it receives a request for the network name, and it removes the SSID advertisement from beacon frames. Because it is mandatory to include some indicator of the network name (whether legitimate or not) in beacon frames, vendors have adopted different conventions for obscuring the SSID by replacing it with one or more space characters or NULL bytes (one or more *0*s) or an SSID with a length of *0*. An example of a cloaked SSID represented by Wireshark is shown in Figure 6.14.

**Figure 6.14** Cloaked SSID Tagged Parameter

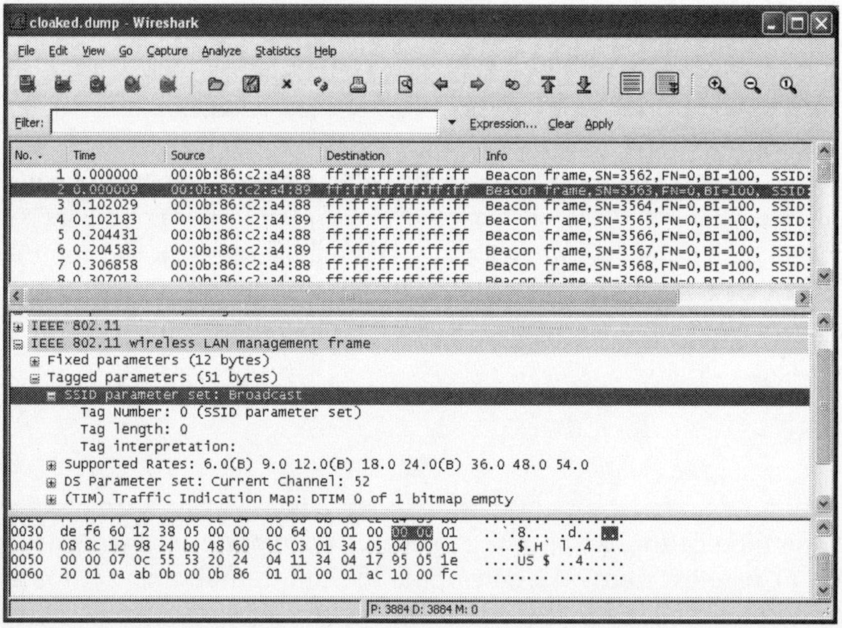

In this case, the SSID for this network has been replaced with an empty value *0* bytes in length. While this may prevent the disclosure of the SSID to the casual observer, stations will still send the SSID in plaintext over the network each time they associate to the wireless network. In this example, we see that the BSSID of the network is *00:0b:86:c2:a4:89*; we can apply a display filter for this network BSSID and associate request frames to examine the SSID name sent by the client:

```
wlan.bssid eq 00:0b:86:c2:a4:89 and wlan.fc.type_subtype eq 0
```

By applying this filter, we reveal any association requests for the specified BSSID. By clicking **IEEE 802.11 Wireless LAN Management Frame | Tagged Parameters | SSID Parameter Set**, we can see the SSID specified by the client station, revealing the SSID for the network as *guestnet* (see Figure 6.15).

**Figure 6.15** Revealed SSID on a Cloaked Network

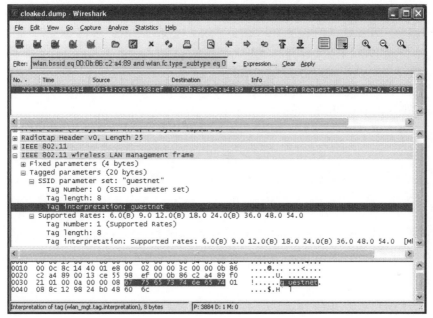

## Examining EAP Exchanges

So far, we've limited our usage of display filters to the IEEE 802.11 header and management payload data. Wireshark can also identify and apply display filters to other wireless-related protocols including the Extensible Authentication Protocol (EAP).

EAP is used in conjunction with the IEEE 802.1x network authentication mechanism to authenticate users to a wireless network by using one of several EAP methods. Common EAP methods include the Protected Extensible Authentication Protocol (PEAP), the Extensible Authentication Protocol with Transport Layer Security (EAP/TLS), Tunneled Transport Layer Security (TTLS) and the Lightweight Extensible Authentication Protocol (LEAP). By examining the exchange of EAP data with Wireshark, we can troubleshoot user authentication issues, evaluate potential security risks, and discover architecture components used by the wireless network.

To identify any EAP traffic in a capture file, apply a display filter for the EAP Over LAN protocol:

```
eapol
```

This filter will return any EAP traffic present in the capture file, including authentication requests, identity negotiation, key and encryption negotiation exchanges, and success or failure messages. Next, we examine each data exchange mechanism in the EAP exchange.

## Identifying the EAP type

If you are auditing a wireless network or trying to identify potentially misconfigured client systems, you may need to identify the EAP method used by those client systems. The EAP method is reported in an EAP exchange in the EAP type field. We can use a display filter to identify frames that report this information:

```
eap.type
```

After applying this filter, select a frame and navigate to the EAP type field by clicking **802.1x Authentication | Extensible Authentication Protocol | Type** in the Packet Details window. Wireshark will identify the numeric value for the EAP type, the name of the EAP type, and the last name of the primary author who developed the Internet Engineering Task Force (IETF) draft to describe the EAP type. In Figure 6.16, we can see that the EAP type has a value of 25, which indicates the use of the PEAP protocol.

## Evaluating Username Disclosure

EAP methods that rely on username and password authentication include PEAP, TTLS and LEAP. These methods may disclose user identity information (e.g., a username) in plaintext over the wireless network. This can be an information disclosure risk for some organizations, because it allows an attacker to enumerate valid usernames, which can be the basis for additional attacks against the wireless network.

Wireshark allows you to identify usernames that are disclosed on the network by examining the EAP Type field for a special value indicating identity information is present in the frame. This EAP mechanism uses an initial *EAP Identity Request* from the AP or the client to request the identity information, followed by an *EAP Identity Response* that contains the identify information. We can apply a display filter to return only EAP Identify Response frames by filtering on the EAP type and EAP code fields:

```
eap.type eq 1 and eap.code eq 2
```

In the sample packet capture displayed in Figure 6.17, we see that the identity information has been disclosed as the username *jwright*.

**Figure 6.16** Identifying the EAP Type

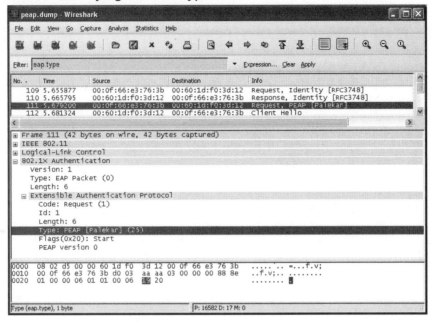

**Figure 6.17** EAP Identity Disclosure

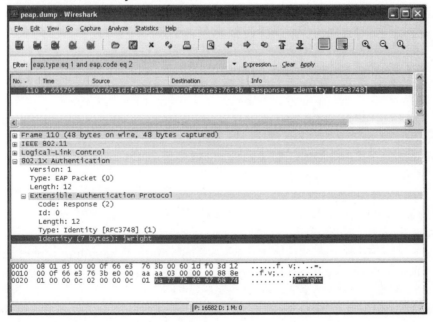

A notable exception to this rule for identifying EAP identity information is the case of non-standard EAP types; specifically, the LEAP protocol. In a LEAP exchange, identify information is not exchanged using the EAP Identity type; rather, it is included in EAP request and response frames in the data payload. We can modify our display filter to accommodate for this inconsistency by also identifying any LEAP traffic with an additional clause for the LEAP EAP type (see Figure 6.18).

**Figure 6.18** Cisco LEAP Identity Disclosure

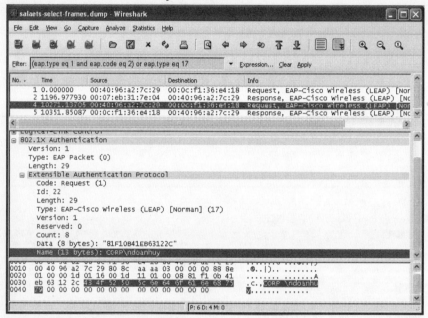

In Figure 6.18, we see that the EAP type is LEAP, and the identity information is disclosed as *CORP\ndoanhuy*. From this identity information, we can also ascertain that the target network is using a Microsoft Windows infrastructure with the domain name *CORP*.

## Identifying EAP Authentication Failures

Troubleshooting authentication problems on the wireless network can be challenging, and often requires a packet sniffer to determine if the failure is happening on the client or over the network. Wireshark can assist in providing this information by identifying EAP authentication failure messages.

The EAP code field is present in all EAP packets, and is used to indicate the content of the message that follows. Presently there are four EAP codes:

- **Code 1 – EAP Request** A value of 1 in the EAP Code field indicates that the EAP frame is requesting information from the recipient. This can be identity information, encryption negotiation content, or a response-to-challenge text.

- **Code 2 – EAP Response** A value of 2 in the EAP Code field indicates that the EAP frame is responding to an EAP Request frame.

- **Code 3 – EAP Success** A value of 3 in the EAP Code field indicates that the previous EAP Response was successful. This is primarily used as a response to authentication messages.

- **Code 4 – EAP Failure** A value of 4 in the EAP Code field indicates that the previous EAP Response failed authentication.

We can apply a display filter on the EAP Code field to identify EAP failures:

```
eap.code eq 4
```

The result of this display filter on a sample packet capture is displayed in Figure 6.19.

**Figure 6.19** EAP Failure Notification

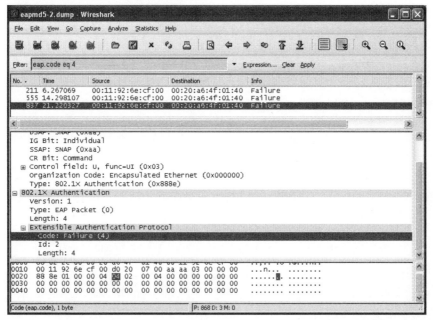

In Figure 6.19, we can see three authentication failures at approximately 8 seconds and 7 seconds apart. We can also see that the From DS bit is set in the IEEE 802.11 header, indicating that the failure message is coming from the AP. From this, we can determine that the failure message is coming from the client system, not from the network.

## Identifying Key Negotiation Properties

Some EAP methods negotiate a Transport Layer Security (TLS) tunnel before exchanging authentication information to protect weak authentication protocol data. In order to establish the TLS tunnel, at least one digital certificate is transmitted from the AP to the station. We can use Wireshark to examine this certificate information, and possibly determine other sensitive information about the network including the organization name and address.

First, apply a display filter to identify the portions of the EAP exchange that are exchanging Secure Sockets Layer (SSL) digital certificate content:

```
eap and ssl.handshake.type eq 11
```

This filter will display only EAP traffic with embedded SSL information that includes a SSL handshake exchange type that includes a digital certificate (type 11). After selecting the frame, navigate to the Packet Details window and click **802.1X Authentication | Extensible Authentication Protocol | Secure Socket Layer | TLS Record Layer: Handshake Protocol: Certificate | Handshake Protocol: Certificate | Certificate | Certificate | signedCertificate | Extensions | AuthorityKeyIdentifier | Item | directoryName | rdnSequence**. This will reveal the digital certificate content indicating the country name, state, and possibly address information and the organization name to which the certificate was issued. A sample packet capture that reveals certificate content is shown in Figure 6.20.

In Figure 6.20, we see that the certificate content reveals the organization name as *Internet Widgits Pty Ltd*, with the country identifier *AU* (Australia) and the state or province name *Some-State*.

# Identifying Wireless Encryption Mechanisms

The IT industry analysis group Gartner published a report indicating that 70 percent of successful attacks against wireless LANs will be due to the misconfiguration of APs and wireless clients. This prediction is easy to believe; many organizations deploy wireless networks without auditing their post-deployment environment with a tool like Wireshark. With the complexity of wireless APs and client systems, it is easy to

**Figure 6.20** SSL Digital Certificate Content

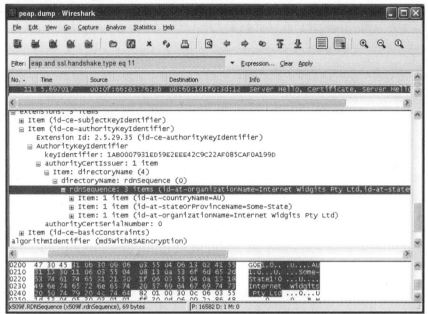

make a configuration mistake that exposes devices to weak encryption mechanisms, or no encryption.

We can assess wireless packet captures with Wireshark to identify the security mechanisms used to protect the network. We've learned how to identify the authentication mechanisms that are in place by looking for EAP traffic; we can also assess the encryption mechanism using display filters.

Common encryption mechanisms on wireless networks include standard IEEE wireless LAN encryption protocols such as WEP, TKIP and CCMP, as well as upper-layer encryption mechanisms such as Secure Internet Protocol (IPSec)/Virtual Private Network (VPN). We examine each of these mechanisms and how we can assess a packet capture to identify the encryption protocol in use.

## Identifying WEP

WEP is the most prevalent encryption mechanism used to protect wireless networks; however, it is also widely known as an insecure protocol. Wireshark uniquely identifies WEP-encrypted traffic by decoding the 4-byte WEP header that follows the IEEE 802.11 header. We can identify WEP traffic by identifying any frames that include the mandatory WEP Initialization Vector (IV):

```
wlan.wep.iv
```

A sample packet capture with this filter applied is shown in Figure 6.21. Wireshark identifies the WEP header and the IV value, along with the key index value and the WEP integrity check value (ICV).

**Figure 6.21** Identifying WEP Traffic

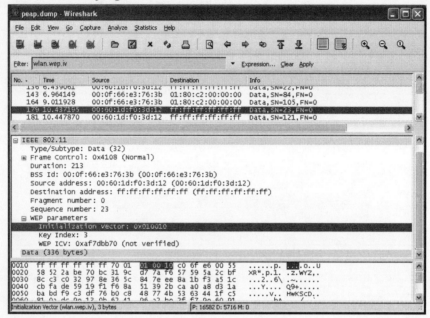

## Identifying TKIP and CCMP

TKIP is the successor to WEP, and is designed to be a software upgrade for hardware built only to support WEP. Since TKIP was designed to work on legacy WEP hardware, it retained the use of the same underlying encryption protocol, Ron's Code 4 (RC4). And while RC4 is still considered safe for current use, it is no longer an acceptable encryption mechanism for use by U.S. government agencies. Another alternative is to use the CCMP protocol, which uses the Advanced Encryption System (AES) cipher.

Like WEP, both TKIP and CCMP use an encryption protocol header that follows the IEEE 802.11 header. This header is modified from the legacy WEP header, allowing us to identify whether TKIP or CCMP are in use, but does not allow us to differentiate TKIP from CCMP; we can only determine that one or the other is currently in use by looking at this header. We can use a display filter to identify this header by filtering on the extended IV field:

```
wlan.tkip.extiv
```

Despite the use of *tkip* in this display filter, it's not possible to differentiate between TKIP or CCMP by looking at the encryption header. A sample packet capture that displays this filter and the TKIP/CCMP header is shown in Figure 6.22.

**Figure 6.22** Identifying TKIP or CCMP Traffic

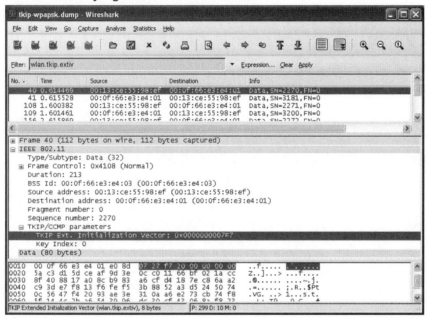

By applying this filter, we know that either TKIP or CCMP is in use for this BSS. To further differentiate whether TKIP or CCMP is in use, we need to inspect data in a beacon frame. To identify a beacon frame for this network, apply a display filter using the BSSID identified with this filter, looking for packets with the type/subtype for a beacon frame.

```
wlan.bssid eq 00:0f:66:e3:e4:03 and wlan.fc.type_subtype eq 8
```

After applying this filter, navigate to the beacon frame's tagged information element data by clicking **IEEE 802.11 Wireless LAN Management Frame | Tagged Parameters**. Look for an information element labeled "Vendor Specific: WPA" or "RSN Information." A Wi-Fi Protected Access (WPA) information element indicates that the AP has passed the testing certification program designed by the WiFi Alliance (WFA), known as WiFi Protected Access (WPA), while a RSN information element tag indicates that the AP has implemented the robust security network (RSN) standards in the IEEE 802.11i amendment. In either case, expand the information element to identify the encryption mechanism used for Unicast and multicast traffic (either AES indicating the CCMP cipher or TKIP). We can also determine the key derivation mechanism (how the dynamic keys are generated) used for the network, by examining the value next to the *auth key management suite* string; either PSK indicating a pre-shared key, or WPA indicating key derivation from a Remote Authentication Dial-In User Service (RADIUS) server over IEEE 802.1x.

A sample packet capture shown in Figure 6.23, demonstrates a beacon frame's information element indicating encryption information. In this example, we see that the "Vendor Specific: WPA" information element, which indicates both the multicast and Unicast cipher suites, are using the TKIP algorithm, with Pre-Shared Key (PSK) as the authentication key management suite mechanism.

**Figure 6.23** Identifying Multicast and Unicast Cipher Suites - Authentication Mechanism

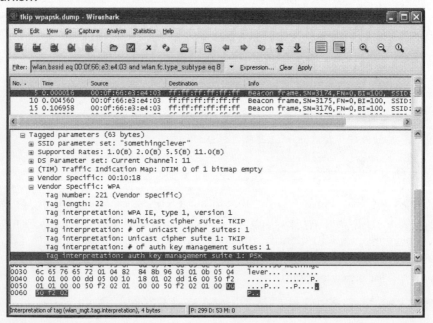

## Identifying IPSec/VPN

Some wireless networks will not use the standard IEEE 802.11 encryption mechanisms, instead opting for an upper-layer encryption mechanism such as IPSec. Wireshark can identify this type of encryption mechanism by applying a display filter for any of the associated IPSec protocols such as the Internet Security Association and Key Management Protocol (ISAKMP), the Encapsulating Security Payload (ESP), or the Authentication Header (AH) protocol. To identify IPSec traffic, apply a display filter as follows:

```
isakmp or ah or esp
```

This filter will return any of the associated IPSec protocols, as shown in Figure 6.24.

**Figure 6.24** Identifying IPSec/VPN Traffic

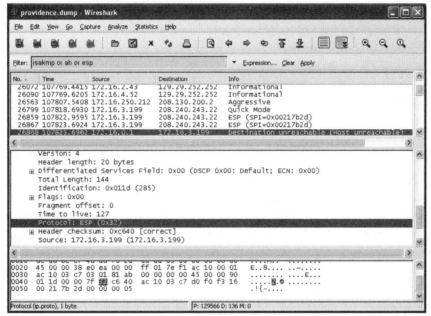

Note in Figure 6.24 that an ICMP Destination Unreachable packet is also returned. This is because Wireshark also decodes the embedded protocol within the ICMP packet, which includes ESP information.

So far, we have seen how powerful Wireshark's display filter functionality can be. The usefulness of display filters is only limited to the fields that can be identified by display name, and your creativeness in taking advantage of this powerful feature. What's more, display filters can be used for other classification and identification mechanisms as well, including the ability to colorize packets matching arbitrary display filters.

# Leveraging Colorized Packet Displays

Looking at a packet trace of any more than a handful of packets can be intimidating. If you aren't sure exactly what it is you are looking for in the packet capture, you're often left to blindly click on packets to examine the contents, or to start applying predefined display filters in the hope of identifying something useful.

In order to make it easier to examine and assess a packet capture at a glance, Wireshark allows you to customize the color of packets in the Packet List window. This often overlooked feature can be very useful for assessing a packet capture, and to simplify the process of troubleshooting a wireless connection issue when applied with useful display filters.

# Marking From DS and To DS

When examining a packet capture, it is helpful to identify if the traffic is originating from the wired network or the wireless network. For example, if you see traffic coming from a local IP address, it may not necessarily be traffic from a wireless station; it may be a wired station that is communicating with a wireless station or a wired station sending broadcast traffic.

We can determine if traffic is originating from the wireless network by examining the flags in the frame control header, looking for the From DS bit and the To DS bit set. If the From DS bit is set and the To DS bit is clear, we know that the traffic originated from the wired network (or the AP).

Applying this logic to a coloring rule that marks traffic from the wired network using one color and traffic from the wireless network using a different color allows us to determine where the traffic originated. To access the coloring rules dialog box click **View | Coloring rules.** Click **New** to create a new coloring rule with the following properties:

- **Filter Name:** Traffic from a wireless station
- **Filter String:** *wlan.fc.fromds eq 0 and wlan.fc.tods eq 1*

Next, select a foreground color and a background color to uniquely identify traffic from a wireless station. The Name and String dialog boxes will update to reflect the colors you select (see Figure 6.25).

**Figure 6.25** Color Filtering Traffic From a Wireless Station

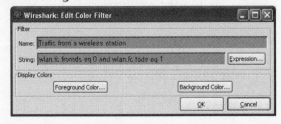

When you are happy with your selection, press **OK.**

Next, create a second coloring rule to mark traffic originating from the wired network using the following properties:

- **Filter Name:** Traffic from a wired station
- **Filter String:** *wlan.fc.fromds eq 1* and *wlan.fc.tods eq 0*

Select a foreground color and a background color to uniquely identify this traffic (see in Figure 6.26).

**Figure 6.26** Color Filtering Traffic From a Wired Station

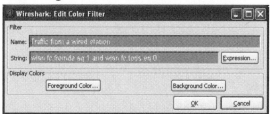

Press **OK** to accept the new filter, and then press **Apply**. If you want to save this color filter for later analysis, press **Save**; otherwise press **OK** to close the Coloring Rules dialog box. Wireshark will automatically update your packet display to apply the new coloring rules (see Figure 6.27).

**Figure 6.27** Applied Wired/Wireless Traffic Coloring Rules

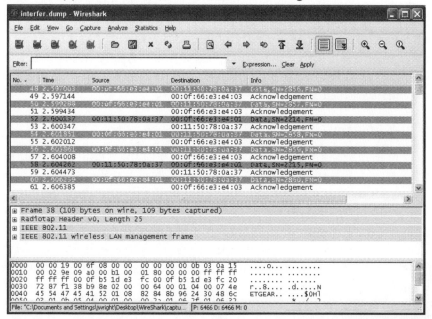

In Figure 6.27, we can identify frames 52 and 58 as traffic originating on the wireless network, and frames 48, 50, 54, 56, and 60 as originating on the wired network. The remaining frames have neither the From DS nor To DS bits set, which is appropriate for management and control frames.

## Marking Interfering Traffic

As more organizations deploy wireless networks, the amount of interference from neighboring networks grows, which can have an adverse affect on the performance of wireless LANs. While many organizations go to significant trouble to select channel plans that minimize interference for a given BSS, it's not uncommon for an AP from a neighboring organization to occupy similar frequencies and interfere with your network.

Earlier in this chapter, we learned how to create a display filter to identify all of the APs for a specific BSS. We can apply this filter to Wireshark's coloring rules using an inverse display filter, to easily identify traffic from interfering networks. Assuming our list of BSSIDs includes *00:0f:66:e3:e4:03* and *00:0f:66:e3:25:92*, create a new coloring rule with the following properties:

- **Filter Name:** Interfering networks
- **Filter String:** *!(wlan.bssid eq 00:0f:66:e3:e4:03* or *wlan.bssid eq 00:0f:66:e3:25:92*) and *!wlan.fc.type eq 1*

In this display filter, we exclude any traffic that is from one of the specified BSSIDs, as well as any control frames, since control frames do not specify a BSSID in the IEEE 802.11 header. Next, assign a foreground color and a background color to uniquely identify this coloring rule, then press **OK** and **Apply**. Wireshark will update the display to reflect the new coloring rule and allow you to identify interfering networks (see Figure 6.28).

## Marking Retries

For each data frame transmitted by a wireless station of the AP, the recipient must transmit an ACK frame to indicate the successful delivery of the packet. If the packet was not received or was received in a corrupted state, the recipient waits for the source to retransmit the packet. In all retransmitted packets, the retransmit bit in the frame control header is set.

Evidence of retransmitted frames can indicate interference on the network that is causing the initial delivery of packets to fail. We can create a coloring rule to help us identify retransmitted frames using the following properties:

**Figure 6.28** Marking Interfering Network Traffic

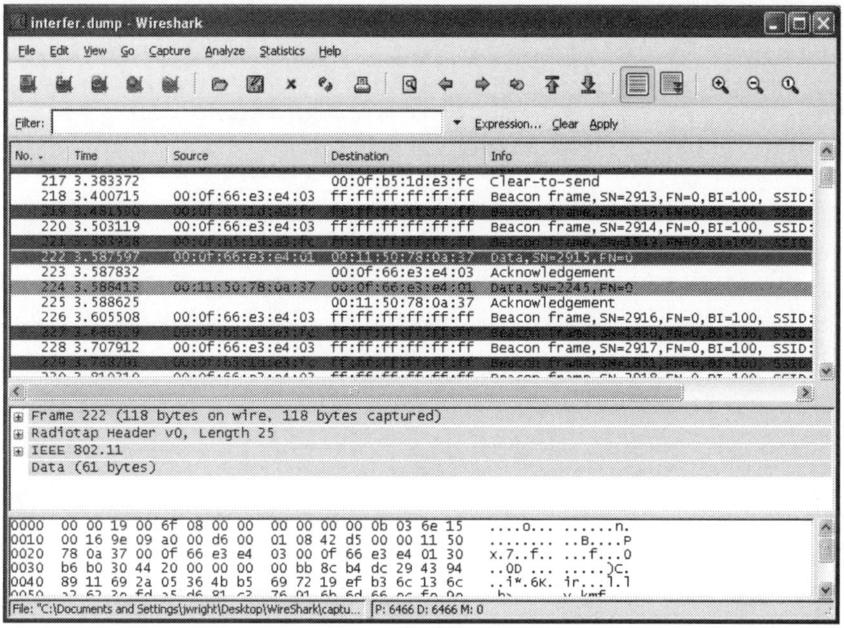

- **Filter Name:** Retransmitted frames
- **Filter String**: *wlan.fc.retry eq 1*

Once we apply this color filter, Wireshark will highlight retransmitted frames (see Figure 6.29).

In Figure 6.29, frame 503 is a retransmit of frame 502. Notice that frame 500 was sent to the station at *00:11:50:78:0a:37* and then acknowledged within $2/1000^{th}$ of a second. The frame at 502 was not positively acknowledged, or there was interference that caused the loss of the ACK frame, which then required a retransmit.

Creative use of custom coloring rules can make analyzing a packet capture much easier. Remember that you can use any Wireshark display filter to create a custom coloring rule, making this feature very flexible and effective at easily identifying important traffic characteristics.

# Adding Informative Columns

By default, Wireshark displays six columns in the Packet List window, including the frame number, time, source, destination, protocol, and information string. Wireshark allows you to customize this view, including the ability to add two additional columns that are pertinent to wireless packet captures: the IEEE 802.11 RSSI and IEEE 802.11 TX Rate columns.

**Figure 6.29** Marking Retransmitted Frames

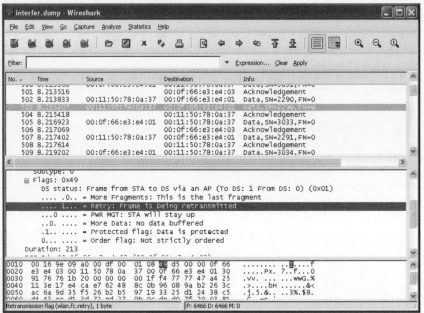

The IEEE 802.11 Received Signal Strength Indication (RSSI) column gives you an indicator as to the radio signal strength for the selected packet, while the IEEE 802.11 RX Rate column indicates the data rate that was used for transmission of this packet. Note that this information is not present in any standard IEEE 802.11 header information; rather, it is supplied in the Radiotap header information or in the Linux Prism AVS header contents. As such, this feature will not work with packet captures that do not supply this additional information, including packet captures using only the standard IEEE 802.11 link type.

To add these columns to your Packet List window, click **Edit | Preferences** and then select **Columns** under the "User Interface" menu selection. Click **New** and type **RSSI** in the "Title" text box, then click on the Format drop-down list and select the IEEE 802.11 RSSI item. Repeat this step to add the data rate column using the title "Rate," and select the IEEE 802.11 TX rate item from the Format drop-down list (see Figure 6.30).

Next, click **Save | OK**. Unlike other Wireshark preferences, adding a new column requires you to restart Wireshark in order for the change to take effect. Close Wireshark and your capture file by clicking **File | Quit**, and then restart Wireshark and open a wireless capture file. If the RSSI and TX Rate information is present in your capture file, Wireshark will populate these new columns with the appropriate information (see Figure 6.31).

**Figure 6.30** Wireshark Column Editor

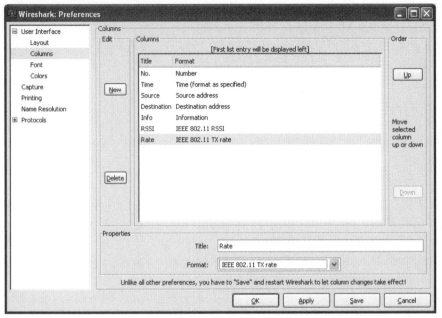

**Figure 6.31** Displaying RSSI and Rate Columns

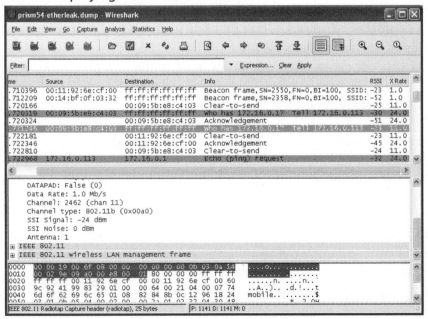

The ability to view these fields can be useful for troubleshooting and wireless intrusion detection purposes. As a station gets farther away from the AP, the TX rate for data frames drops in order to sustain connectivity to an AP. Observing a large number of stations transmitting below the optimal 11 Megabits per second (Mbps) for IEEE 802.11b networks or 54 Mbps for IEEE 802.11g or IEEE 802.11a networks, is an indicator of poor AP selection on behalf of the client (there may be a more optimal AP available), or poor deployment or configuration of APs. Inspecting the RSSI information allows you to identify drops in the signal strength for a client, which can be an indicator of interference or other Radio Frequency (RF) loss characteristics, which can also affect network performance.

# Decrypting Traffic

One of the challenges of wireless traffic analysis is the ability to inspect the contents of encrypted data frames. While Wireshark has the ability to decode many different Network layer and higher protocols, encrypted traffic limits your ability to analyze packets and troubleshoot network problems.

Fortunately, Wireshark offers some options to analyze WEP-encrypted data. When configured with the appropriate WEP key, Wireshark can automatically decrypt WEP-encrypted data and dissect the plaintext contents of these frames. This allows you to use display filters, coloring rules, and all other Wireshark features on the decrypted frame contents.

In order for Wireshark to decrypt the contents of WEP-encrypted packets, it must be given the appropriate WEP key for the network. Wireshark does not assist you in breaking WEP keys or attacking the WEP protocol. If you are the legitimate administrator of the wireless network, you can configure Wireshark with the appropriate WEP key by clicking **Edit | Preferences**, and then expanding the "Protocols" menu and selecting IEEE 802.11. In the Wireshark Preferences window, supply one or more WEP keys in hexadecimal form separated by colons (see Figure 6.32). After entering one or more WEP keys, select the **Enable Decryption** checkbox. Click **OK** when finished.

Wireshark will automatically apply the WEP key to each WEP-encrypted packet in the capture. If the packet decrypts properly, Wireshark will add a tabbed view to the Packet Bytes window, allowing you to choose between the encrypted and decrypted views. Wireshark will also dissect the contents of the unencrypted frame, allowing you to view the embedded protocol information as if the frame were unencrypted in its original state.

Unfortunately, at the time of this writing, Wireshark does not support decrypting TKIP or CCMP packets. However, you can use external tools such as the

**Figure 6.32** Specifying WEP Keys

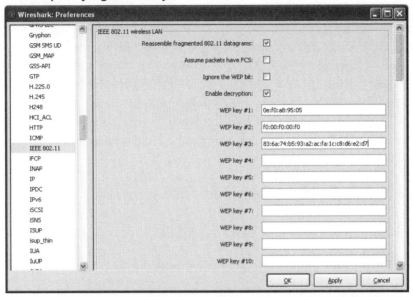

**Figure 6.33** Viewing Encrypted and Unencrypted WEP Traffic

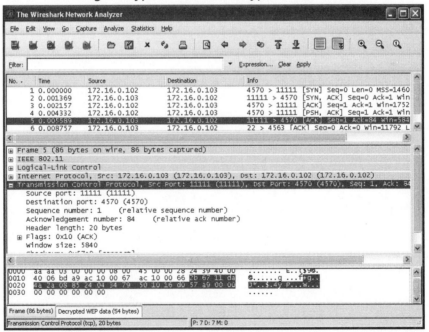

*airdecap-ng* utility (included in the open-source *Aircrack-ng* suite of tools) to rewrite a packet capture that uses the TKIP protocol. Similar to Wireshark's ability to decrypt WEP traffic, *airdecap-ng* requires you to have knowledge of either the PSK or the Pairwise Master Key (PMK) in order to decrypt TKIP traffic.

To install *airdecap-ng* on your system, you must download and complete the installation instructions for the *Aircrack-ng* tools. Download the latest version of *Aircrack-ng* from *www.aircrack-ng.org*. For Windows systems, download the *Aircrack-ng* zip file for Windows and extract it to a directory of your choosing. For Linux users, you must build the software using a C compiler, or obtain a precompiled binary from your Linux distribution vendor.

Once *Aircrack-ng* is installed, you can use the *airdecap-ng* tool to decrypt WEP or TKIP traffic, generating a new libpcap output file containing unencrypted traffic. There is no GUI interface for *airdecap-ng*, therefore, it is necessary to open a command shell and execute *airdecap-ng* from the command prompt (see Figure 6.34).

**Figure 6.34** *Airdecap-ng* Command Parameters

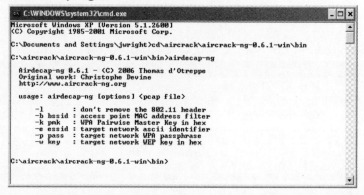

You can decrypt WEP traffic by specifying the WEP key in hexadecimal format using the -*w* flag. We'll also supply the -*l* flag to retain the IEEE 802.11 header data. By default, *airdecap-ng* strips the IEEE 802.11 header, making the traffic appear to be a wired packet capture. *Airdecap-ng* will decrypt the traffic in the identified capture file, generating a new file with -*dec* appended after the filename and before the file extension (see Figure 6.35).

Similarly, you can decrypt a TKIP packet capture using the same technique, by specifying the TKIP PMK with the -*k* parameter or by specifying the PSK with the -*p* parameter. When decrypting TKIP traffic, you must also specify the network SSID (see Figure 6.36).

In Figure 6.36, *Airdecap-ng* creates the output file *wpapsk-dec.dump*, which contains the unencrypted data frames.

**Figure 6.35** Decrypting WEP Traffic with *Airdecap-ng*

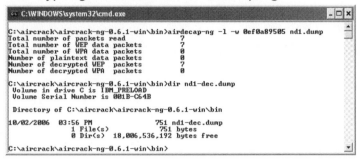

**Figure 6.36** Decrypting TKIP Traffic with *Airdecap-ng*

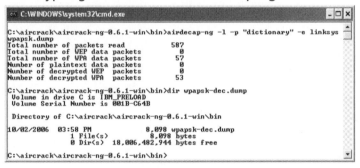

Once you have decrypted the packet captures with *airdecap-ng*, you can open and inspect the unencrypted packet contents with Wireshark.

# Real-world Wireless Traffic Captures

Now that you have learned how to leverage the wireless analysis features of Wireshark, you can examine real-world wireless traffic captures. Each of the captures reviewed in this section were selected to help reinforce the concepts learned in this chapter while demonstrating techniques that you can use to assess your own wireless network.

## Identifying a Station's Channel

### Introduction

Many administrators would agree that the wireless network configuration and management interface in Windows XP has improved steadily with each XP service pack. One of the remaining frustrations with the Windows Zero Configuration (WZC) interface for wireless networking, is the inability to report the current wireless channel that the client is operating on. This is necessary information for troubleshooting connectivity problems or intermittent performance issues on the wireless LAN.

Identifying the channel number requires you to analyze information elements transmitted by the AP. While it is possible to estimate the channel number by switching through the channels manually with the *iwconfig* utility on Linux systems, wireless cards often receive frames from off-channels. In these cases, you might configure the wireless card on channel 1 and see traffic from the wireless station; however, the station could be operating on channel 3 instead.

In this packet real-world wireless traffic capture, we examine how to identify the current channel that a target wireless station is operating on.

## Systems Affected

This traffic capture applies to all operating systems as a general analysis mechanism that is useful for network troubleshooting. The devices involved include the target wireless station and the AP. The wireless capture station will channel hop for this analysis, because it does not know which channel the target wireless station is using.

## Breakdown and Analysis

In this real-world traffic capture analysis, we reference the capture file *wireless-rwc-1.cap*. In this case, we need to identify the operating channel for the station with the MAC address *00:60:1d:1f:c5:18*.

After opening the capture file in Wireshark, apply a display filter to identify data traffic for the target station MAC address:

```
wlan.sa eq 00:60:1d:1f:c5:18 and wlan.fc.type eq 2
```

This excludes all traffic except that which originates from the target station. We apply this filter so we can examine the IEEE 802.11 protocol header information to determine the BSSID address. Click on any frame from this station and then navigate to the Packet Details window and click **IEEE 802.11 | BSS Id**. The BSSID reflects the unique identifier for this network, which we'll use to continue our analysis.

Once we know the BSSID for the network, we can clear the existing display filter and create a new filter to identify beacon frames from the AP servicing the identified station:

```
wlan.bssid eq 00:02:2d:09:c0:da and wlan.fc.type_subtype eq 8
```

Applying this filter will display beacon frames from the AP. On the summary line, we can see the source and destination address information and the summary information including the network SSID. By navigating to the Packet Details window and clicking **IEEE 802.11 Wireless LAN Management Frame | Tagged**

**Parameters | DS Parameter Set | Tag Interpretation,** we can examine the contents of this information element. This tag represents the current channel number for the AP (see Figure 6.37).

**Figure 6.37** Tagged Parameters - Current Channel

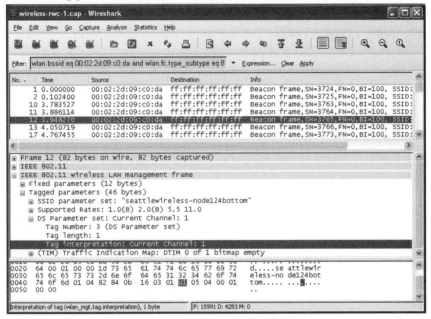

By examining this capture, we can see that the beacon contents from the AP indicate that it is operating on channel 1. By association with the BSSID, we know that the station is also on channel 1.

# Wireless Connection Failures

## Introduction

Connection problems create common troubleshooting tasks for wireless LAN administrators. Often, the errors that are observed on the wireless network don't make their way to the client system in a mechanism that allows the end user (or administrator) to identify the problem. Fortunately, Wireshark can be used to help you gain more visibility into the problems "on the air" that prevent users from establishing connectivity to the wireless network.

Because this is such an important and recurring issue for administrators, we examine three different real-world packet captures to troubleshoot an authentication issue at the IEEE 802.11 layer, and two issues at the IEEE 802.1x/EAP layer.

# Systems Affected

These traffic captures apply to all client and server operating systems that support wireless networking. One capture deals with an issue affecting a WEP-based network, and the other two captures deal with issues in LEAP networks. These principles also apply to other encryption mechanisms (e.g., TKIP, CCMP, and EAP).

# Breakdown and Analysis

## *Capture 1*

In this real-world traffic capture analysis, we reference the capture file *wireless-rwc-2a.cap*. In this case, we are responding to a Windows XP Signal Processor 2 (SP2) station that is unable to connect to the wireless network using WEP encryption. After examining standard logging mechanisms (e.g., the Windows event log) on the XP workstation, there are no apparent error messages that indicate the source of the problem. A cursory glance of the client configuration appears correct, and the WEP key was re-keyed to verify that it is correct. The Wireless Network Properties Configuration window for this network is shown in Figure 6.38.

**Figure 6.38** Station Wireless Network Configuration Properties

In an effort to troubleshoot this network, a wireless packet capture has been taken while the client was attempting to connect to the wireless network. Open the capture file *wireless-rwc-2a.cap* with Wireshark to begin analyzing the traffic.

In all wireless networks, the connection process starts with the station sending probe request frames to identify available APs in the area. The AP responds with a probe response frame (unless configured otherwise), which informs the station that the AP is available. After identifying an available AP, the station continues the connection process to authenticate and associate to the AP.

In WEP networks, the client sends an authenticate request to the AP, which elicits an authenticate response. In the case of shared-key network authentication, the AP sends a random challenge value that the client encrypted with their WEP key, and returns to the AP to verify before receiving an authenticate success or failure message. In the case of open network authentication, the AP skips the challenge/response step and issues a success message. Following authentication, the station associates to the AP by transmitting an association request packet. The AP responds with an association response message, after which the station can communicate on the wireless network.

As a logical troubleshooting step, it makes sense to verify each of these steps to identify where the connection process is failing. To reduce the number of frames displayed in the packet capture, apply the following display filter to exclude beacon frames and all control frames:

```
wlan.fc.type_subtype ne 8 and wlan.fc.type ne 1
```

The results of this display filter are shown in Figure 6.39.

**Figure 6.39** Filtering Beacons and Control Frames - Real-world Capture 2a

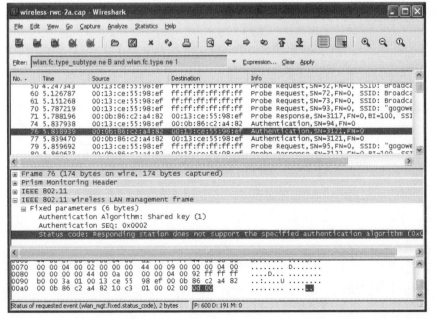

In frame 34, we see the station sending probe requests for the SSID *<No current ssid>*; another probe request in frame 35 is targeting the broadcast SSID. These repeat without response until frame 70, which probes for the *gogowepnet* SSID, gets a response from the AP in the form of a probe response frame. This is appropriate behavior, because the station needs to know the BSSID and other capability information contained in the probe response frame before connecting to the AP.

Following the probe response in frames 74, 76, and 77, we see authentication traffic. We can tell that frame 77 is a retransmit of frame 76, because the sequence number (3121) listed in the information column is the same for both packets. We start our detailed analysis with frame 74; click on this frame and expand the management parameters by clicking **IEEE 802.11 Wireless LAN Management Frame | Fixed Parameters**. This will reveal the authentication algorithm as shared key, the authentication SN, and the status code. Because this is the first packet in the authentication exchange, the status code value is irrelevant.

Now that we know the authentication algorithm information that is being requested, look at frame 77. In the management parameters information we see the authentication algorithm is still shared key, but the status code has a message indicating "Responding station does not support the specified authentication algorithm." This error is preventing the client from connecting to the AP.

As a security feature, modern APs using WEP only support open authentication with WEP encryption, because shared key authentication introduces additional vulnerabilities to the network. Since this client is requesting shared-key authentication, the AP is rejecting the request with an error. To resolve this problem, reconfigure the client system to use open authentication with WEP instead of shared authentication.

## Capture 2

In this real-world traffic capture analysis, we reference the capture file *wireless-rwc-2b.cap*. This is another example of a client that is unable to connect to the network. Open the capture file *wireless-rwc-2b.cap* and use the same display filter as in the previous capture to exclude beacon frames and control frames from the display:

```
wlan.fc.type_subtype ne 8 and wlan.fc.type ne 1
```

The result of this display filter is shown in Figure 6.40.

We can identify that the station is connecting to the AP successfully by looking at the Packet List window Information column. In frames 23 and 25, we see the probe request and response exchange, followed by two authentication frames. Clicking on frame 29 to select the second authentication frame, and clicking on **IEEE 802.11 Wireless LAN Management Frame | Fixed Parameters | Status Code** reveals that the authentication exchange was successful.

**Figure 6.40** Filtering Beacons and Control Frames - Real-world Capture 2b

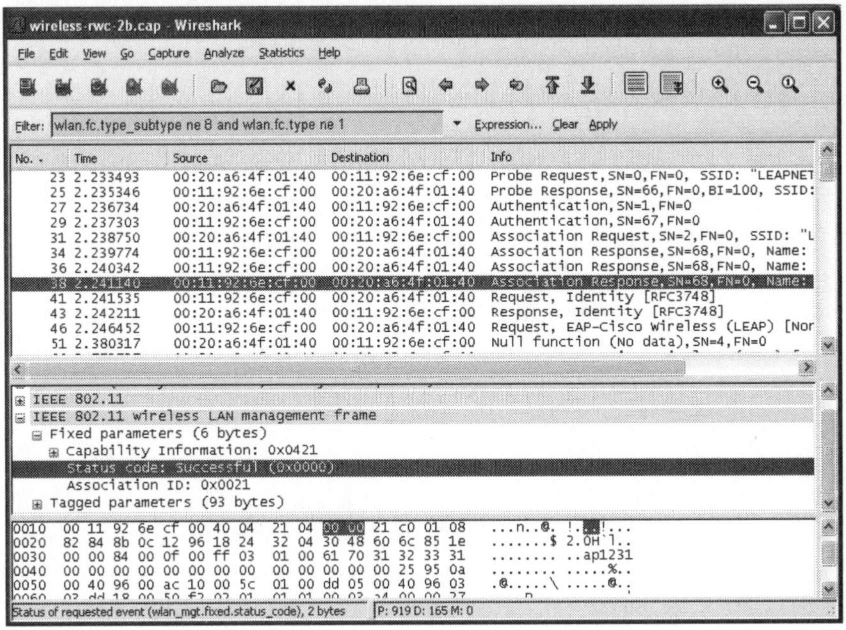

Following the authentication exchange, there is an association request in frame 31, and three authentication responses in frames 34, 36, and 38. Looking at the information column in the Packet List window for these three frames indicates that the sequence number is 68 for each packet, and that that they are retransmissions that were not properly acknowledged by the recipient. We can select frame 36 or 38 and click **IEEE 802.11 | Frame Control | Flags | Retry** to verify that these frames are retransmissions, by examining the value of the retransmit flag in the frame control header. This isn't unusual activity; however, it could indicate that some other interference source on the network is preventing the earlier frames from being received properly.

Examining the contents of the status code in the last association frame (frame number 38) by clicking **IEEE 802.11 Wireless LAN Management Frame | Fixed Parameters | Status Code**, indicates that the association was successful in completing the IEEE 802.11 authentication and association exchange.

At this point, we don't know exactly what we need to troubleshoot in this capture; therefore, it is helpful to use the coloring rules to assess the traffic capture. Apply a coloring rule to mark packets from the wired network with one color, and packets from the wireless network with a second color. This will allow you to easily assess the remainder of the frames to identify the traffic that is coming from the AP or from client systems.

Following the association response frame, we see that the beginning of the EAP authentication exchange in frame 41 is coming from the AP; this frame is requesting identity information from the station, which is returned in frame 43 with an identity response frame. In frame 46, we see a new EAP request frame indicating that the EAP type is the Cisco LEAP protocol. We can inspect the EAP details of this frame by clicking **802.1X Authentication | Extensible Authentication Protocol**. Inspecting the details of this frame, we see that the payload of the EAP packet includes an 8-byte random value and the name of the user authentication to the network. The 8-byte random value represents the challenge value that must be encrypted and returned by the authenticating station.

Frame 51 indicates a NULL data frame. This frame is not part of the EAP exchange. Rather, it is a mechanism that is used by the station to enter power-conservation mode while advertising to the AP that it should save any pending traffic for that station until it returns to the network. This can be confirmed by inspecting the power management bit in the frame control header, and by clicking **IEEE 802.11 | Frame Control | Flags | PWR MGT**. Since this value is set to *1*, we know that the station is entering power management mode. This is normal activity for some stations, especially Intel Centrino wireless cards, which are more aggressive at power conservation than other chipset manufacturers.

The station returns from power conservation mode in frame 66 with an EAP response frame. Again, we can inspect the contents of the EAP payload by clicking **802.1X Authentication | Extensible Authentication Protocol**. In the EAP payload contents, we see something labeled "Peer Challenge [8] Random Value"; this is an incorrect representation by Wireshark. Instead of being a peer challenge value, this is the actual peer response. Further, the peer response value is 24 bytes in length, not 8 bytes as indicated. This frame represents the response from the wireless station following the earlier challenge value.

Following the EAP response from the station, we would normally expect to see an EAP Success message from the AP. In this capture, we see an additional NULL data frame from the station indicating additional power management activity, followed by a multicast data frame for the Spanning Tree Protocol (STP) in frames 71 and 77, respectively. Instead of an EAP Success message, we see several deauthentication messages from the AP to the wireless client. This indicates that the LEAP authentication exchange was not successful, and that the AP is notifying the station that it has been disconnected from the network. The deauthentication frame is transmitted multiple times, because it is not properly acknowledge by the wireless station, possibly because the station is in power conservation mode.

In this packet capture, we see that the station has successfully completed the IEEE 802.11 authentication and association exchange, but was unable to complete the IEEE 802.1X authentication exchange. This failure is repeated several times by the client and the AP in the capture file, starting at frames 376 and again at frame 724. The lack of an EAP Success message indicates that there was an authentication problem that caused the EAP exchange to fail (probably the result of an incorrect password entered by the user). While Wireshark cannot confirm this, we can use other sources of information to troubleshoot this issue, including logging messages on the AP and on the RADIUS server used to perform user authentication.

## Capture 3

In this real-world traffic capture analysis, we reference the capture file *wireless-rwc-2c.cap*. This is another example of a client that is unable to connect to the network. Open the capture file *wireless-rwc-2c.cap* and use the same display filter as used in the previous capture to exclude beacon frames and control frames from the display:

```
wlan.fc.type_subtype ne 8 and wlan.fc.type ne 1
```

Also apply the coloring rules to identify traffic from the AP or from a station with different colors. The result of this display filter and coloring rule is shown in Figure 6.41.

**Figure 6.41** Filtering Beacons and Control Frames - Real-world Capture 2c

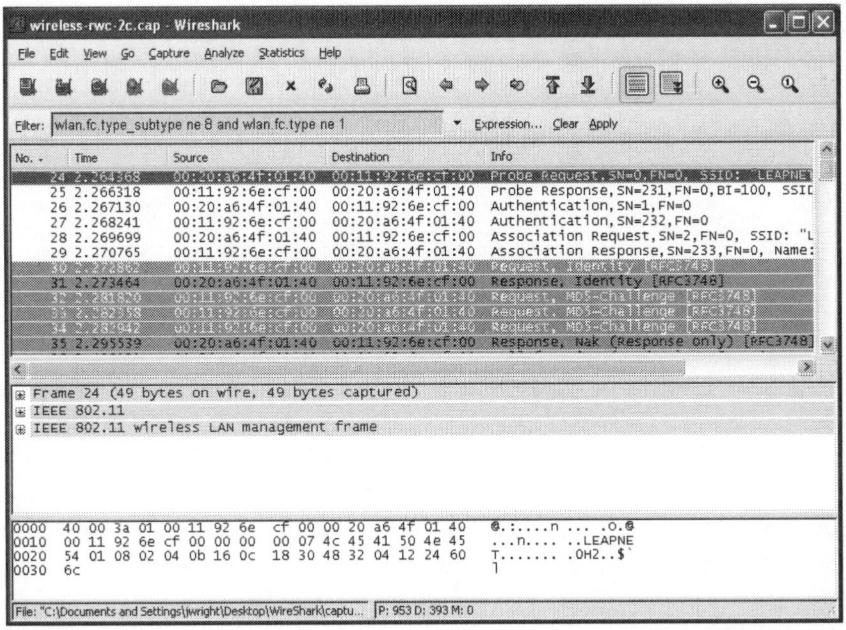

Like the previous packet capture, we determine that the station at
*00:20:a6:4f:01:40* is able to complete the IEEE 802.11 authentication and association process by examining the contents of the information column in the Packet List
window for frames 24 through 29. Following the association response frame, we see
the beginning of the EAP exchange in frame 30 with an EAP Identity Request, followed by the EAP Identity Response.

In frames 32 through 34, we see an EAP request from the AP multiple times. This is
another example of the station not immediately replying with an ACK frame, thereby
causing the AP to retransmit the frame until a response is received. In the information
column for these frames, we see the EAP type of Message Digest 5 (MD5) Challenge,
also known as EAP-MD5. This indicates that the network is configured to use EAP-
MD5 authentication on the RADIUS server, and that the AP is issuing an EAP-MD5
challenge for the station to encrypt as part of the authentication exchange.

In frame 35, we see a response from the station indicating an EAP negative
ACK or Negative Acknowledgement (NAK) response. We can view the contents of
the EAP payload for frame 35 by clicking **802.1X Authentication | Extensible
Authentication Protocol**. We can see that the EAP type is a NAK message,
which indicates that there is an error in the EAP exchange. Following the Type
field, we see that the EAP payload indicates the desired authentication type of
Cisco LEAP (see Figure 6.42).

**Figure 6.42** Identifying the EAP Type - Real-world Capture 2c

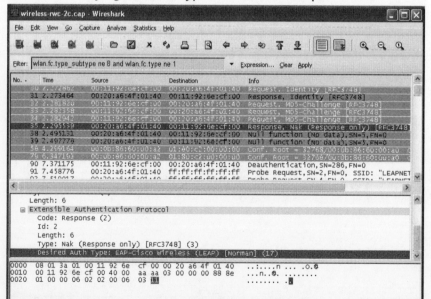

In this packet capture, the station failed to connect to the wireless network, because it was configured to use LEAP authentication when the infrastructure network was configured to use EAP-MD5 authentication. Because there was no common EAP mechanism that was acceptable to both the client and the RADIUS server, authentication failed, which resulted in the AP issuing a deauthenticate message in frame 90. Visiting the client system and reconfiguring it to use the proper authentication mechanism would solve this problem, allowing the client to successfully authenticate to the network.

# Wireless Network Probing

## Introduction

Modern wireless client software is designed to make it easier for end users to maintain a list of preferred wireless networks. Users often connect to more than one wireless network (e.g., when in the office, a user may connect a corporate wireless network called "CORPNET"; when at home, they may connect to a home wireless network called "HOMENET"). When on the road, users may connect to hotel wireless networks such as STSN or hhonors, or public hotspot networks such as PANERA or T-Mobile.

In order to simplify the process of connecting to any of these networks, most wireless clients store a list of preferred networks in a Preferred Network List (PNL). On Windows XP systems, the PNL is available by right-clicking on the wireless adapter in the Network Connections window and selecting Properties (see Figure 6.43).

**Figure 6.43** Windows XP PNL

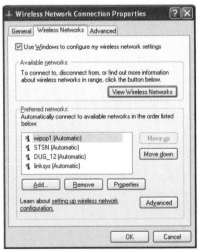

In Figure 6.43, we can see that networks *linksys*, *DUG_12*, *STSN*, and *wipop1* are all preferred networks for this client system, allowing the station to easily connect to any of these available networks without interaction from the end user.

In order to identify if the networks in the PNL are available, wireless stations regularly transmit probe request frames with the SSID specified in the payload of the frame, and wait for responses from any available networks matching the SSID. This can be a potential information disclosure threat, because it allows an attacker to monitor and identify all of the network names configured in the station's PNL, by enumerating probe request frames.

In this real-world packet capture, we examine a mechanism to enumerate the networks configured in the PNL to evaluate potential information disclosure threats, or to identify stations that are connecting to wireless networks in an unauthorized manner, by identifying suspicious SSIDs.

## Systems Affected

Both Windows and Mac OS X stations include support for PNLs, and regularly probe for all of these networks. Standard Linux systems do not include support for PNLs, although third-party applications may include support for this functionality with desktop environments such as K Desktop Environment (KDE) or GNU Network Object Model Environment (GNOME).

## Breakdown and Analysis

In this real-world traffic capture analysis, we reference the capture file *wireless-rwc-3.cap*. Open this packet capture file with Wireshark to examine the contents.

In order to identify network names from the PNL, we need to examine probe request frames coming from client systems. The packet capture file for this example has already been filtered to include only probe request frames, but we could use a display filter to identify only this frame type:

```
wlan.fc.type_subtype eq 4
```

The packet capture is displayed in Figure 6.44.

In frame 1, we see traffic from a station at *00:90:4b:1e:da:ca* sending a probe request frame to the broadcast destination address. In the information column in the Packet List window, we see that the desired SSID name for the probe request is *rogers*. In frame 2, we see another probe request, this time looking for the SSID *Rogers.* (SSID names are case sensitive.) The "Rogers" SSID is repeated until frame 8 where the SSID changes to the broadcast SSID. The broadcast SSID is indicated by

**Figure 6.44** Examining Probe Request Content - Real-world Capture 3

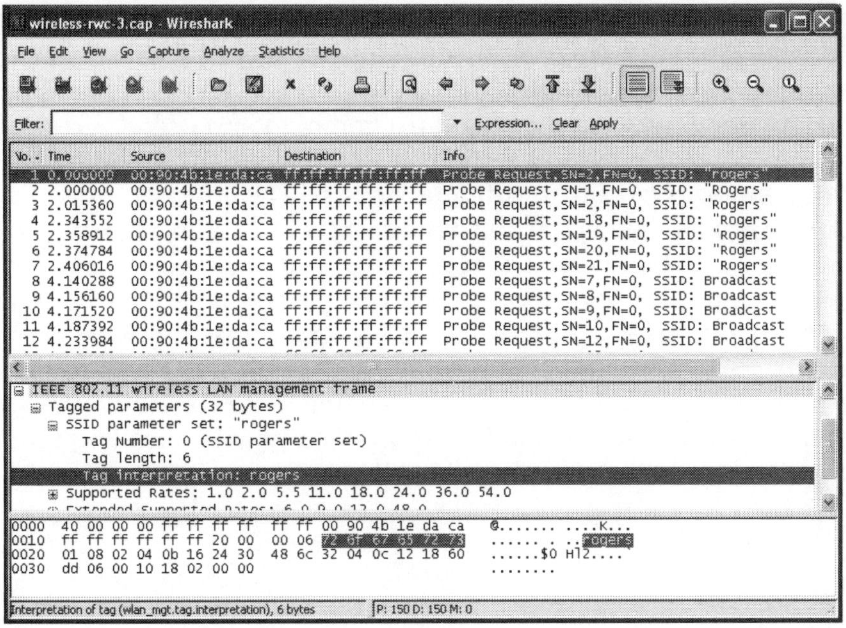

the lack of an SSID or a 0-length SSID. After selecting frame 8, we can confirm this by examining the contents of the SSID field by clicking **IEEE 802.11 Wireless LAN Management Frame | Tagged Parameters | SSID Parameter Set | Tag Length**.

We can continue to examine the SSIDs specified in the packet capture file by scrolling through the entire packet capture. Unfortunately, Wireshark display filters do not include the ability to apply a "unique" filtering mechanism where only one of each unique SSID value is specified. We can effectively get the same results from using the text-based Wireshark tool using some common UNIX text-processing utilities.

From a shell prompt, examine the contents of the *wireless-rwc-3.cap* packet capture file with the tshark tool as shown:

```
tshark -r wireless-rwc-3.cap -R "wlan.fc.type_subtype eq 4" -V
```

This syntax instructs tshark to read (*-r*) from the packet capture file using the display filter (*-R*) *wlan.fc.type_subtype eq 4* (display only probe request frames) with verbose decoding output (*-V*). Tshark processes and displays the contents of the packet capture file (see Figure 6.45).

**TIP**

UNIX operating systems are distributed with several text-processing tools that make parsing and extracting data from text-based output simple. You can download many of the most common and useful text-processing tools for Windows systems by visiting the GNU utilities for Win32 project Web site at http://unxutils.sourceforge.net. Download the *UnxUtils.zip* file and extract it to a directory in your local execution path such as *C:\WINDOWS*, or create a new directory such as *C:\BIN* for these tools and add this new directory to your system path. You can modify the system path by right-clicking on **My Computer** and then selecting **Properties | Advanced | Environment Variables**. In the System Variables section, scroll to the path variable, double-click on the value for this variable and append the new directory with a leading semi-colon to the end of the path list (e.g. *;C:\BIN*).

**Figure 6.45** TShark Output - Real-world Capture 3

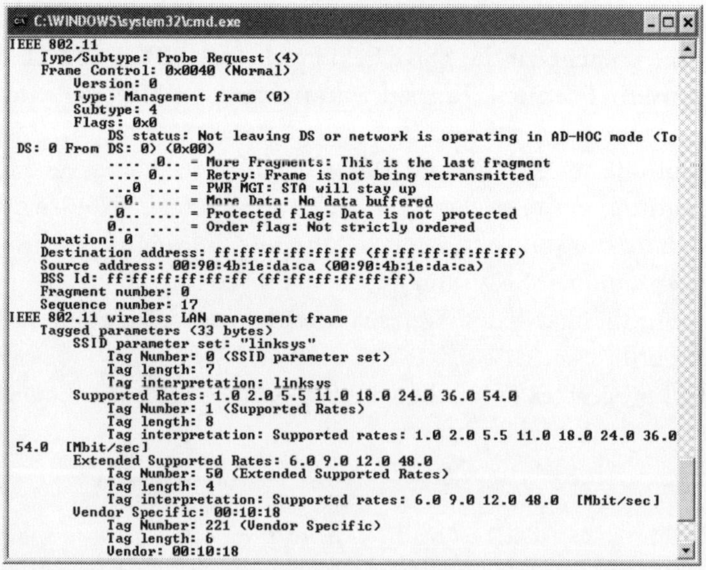

In this output, we see that the line beginning with *SSID parameter set* indicates the SSID in the probe request packet. The text processing tool *grep* can be used to filter the output from tshark to list only this line, and pass the output from *grep* into the *sort* utility. It then passes the output from *sort* to the *uniq* tool to remove dupli-cates using the following command-line argument:

```
tshark -r wireless-rwc-3.cap -R "wlan.fc.type_subtype eq 4" -V | grep "SSID
parameter set:" | sort | uniq
```

By processing the output from tshark with the *grep*, *sort*, and *uniq* tools, we can get a unique list of the SSIDs identified from probe request frames:

```
C:\wireshark>tshark -r wireless-rwc-3.cap -nV | grep "SSID parameter set:" |
sort | uniq
    SSID parameter set: "hhonors"
    SSID parameter set: "linksys"
    SSID parameter set: "matrix"
    SSID parameter set: "rogers"
    SSID parameter set: "Rogers"
    SSID parameter set: "turbonet"
    SSID parameter set: "wldurel"
    SSID parameter set: Broadcast

C:\wireshark>
```

Using this technique, you can enumerate all of the SSIDs being probed by clients for the specified capture file. If you are interested in the PNL for a specific client, modify the display filter specified with the *-R* command-line argument to specify the target client MAC address (e.g., if the client MAC address you want to assess is *00:90:4b:1e:da:ca*, modify the display filter used in the previous example:

```
wlan.fc.type_subtype eq 4 and wlan.sa eq 00:90:4b:1e:da:ca
```

This analysis can be useful for identifying misconfigured client systems that have deprecated wireless networks still listed in the PNL, or to identify stations that have possibly violated organizational policy by connecting to unauthorized networks.

# EAP Authentication Account Sharing

## Introduction

Password-based EAP types are the most popular IEEE 802.1x authentication mech-anism for wireless networks. Many of these EAP types, including PEAPv0, LEAP, and EAP-MD5, can disclose username information in plaintext as part of the authentication exchange. This can be potentially advantageous to an attacker, but is also advantageous to an administrator to assess the identities of users on the wireless network.

## Systems Affected

This analysis applies to wireless networks using IEEE 802.1x authentication for wireless networks, with an EAP type that discloses username information in plaintext as part of the authentication exchange. Examples of EAP types that disclose this information include EAP-MD5, LEAP, and PEAPv0.

## Breakdown and Analysis

In this real-world traffic capture analysis, we reference the capture file *wireless-rwc-4.cap*. Open this packet capture file with Wireshark to examine the contents.

> **NOTE**
>
> It was necessary to sanitize the *wireless-rwc-4.cap* contents before being allowed to include it as a reference for this book. Please disregard the timestamp information for each frame, as it is not valid for this analysis. Other sources of information in the capture have also been modified that do not affect the outcome of the analysis.

In order to examine username information disclosed in plaintext, we are primarily concerned with EAP traffic. Apply the following display filter to examine all EAP traffic in the capture file:

```
eap
```

The initial display after applying the filter for this packet capture is displayed in Figure 6.46.

Looking at the information column, we can see that this is a capture of Cisco LEAP (EAP-Cisco) traffic. While the first two frames in the display filter results don't disclose username information, selecting frame 12 (the third frame of the display filter results) displays the string *nthom* in the Packet Bytes window. Clicking **802.1X Authentication | Extensible Authentication Protocol | Identity** confirms that this is the username of the person at this workstation who is authenticating to the wireless network.

**Figure 6.46** Displaying EAP Traffic - Real-world Capture 4

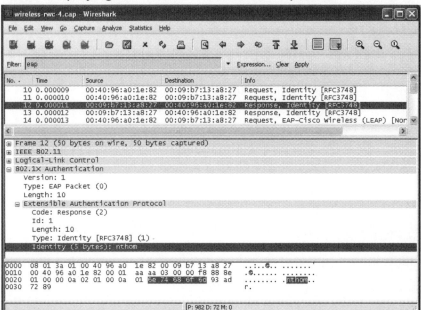

Examining the contents of the EAP header, we can reduce the number of packets returned in our display filter to include only EAP traffic of type identity and code response by applying the following display filter:

```
eap.code eq 2 and eap.type eq 1
```

The results of this updated filter allow us to focus on the usernames reported for each packet. Scrolling through each packet, we see the username *nthom* in frames 12 and 13 for the station at *00:09:b7:13:a8:27*, and the username *plynn* in frames 35 and 36 for the same station. This could indicate multiple users sharing a single work-station, or it could indicate a single user attempting to authenticate with multiple different usernames. Frequent occurrences of this type of activity or attempts for multiple usernames should be investigated for a potential security breach.

Continuing to examine the results of the display filter, we see the username *hbonn* is used from the station at *00:0a:8a:47:db:7b* in frames 77, 78, 84, 85, 101, 102, 210, and 211. Even more interesting is the reoccurrence of the username *nthom* in frame 210 from the station at *00:40:96:42:db:08*. This indicates that a single username (*nthom*) is being used from multiple stations, which is the result of multiple users sharing the same username and password. If your organization has a policy against this kind of activity, you could use this analysis to identify the offending stations and users.

# IEEE 802.11 DoS Attacks

## Introduction

IEEE 802.11 networks are vulnerable to a wide range of DoS attacks, allowing an attacker to indefinitely prevent one or more users from being able to access the medium for an indefinite amount of time. When under a DoS attack, the victim only knows that they are unable to access the wireless network and unable to identify that their loss of connectivity is the result of a malicious action or a network anomaly. Using Wireshark to analyze a traffic capture, the administrator can determine if the DoS condition is the result of malicious or non-malicious activity.

## Systems Affected

This analysis applies to any wireless network that is potentially susceptible to DoS attacks, including all wireless networks where a potential adversary can be near the physical proximity of the network.

## Breakdown and Analysis

In this real-world traffic capture analysis, we reference the capture file *wireless-rwc-5.cap*. Open this packet capture file using Wireshark to examine the contents.

After opening the packet capture, we see that the first frame is a beacon frame from the AP. By examining the packet list row for this frame, we determine that the source MAC address of the AP is *00:e0:63:82:19:c6*, and that the AP is attempting to hide or cloak the network SSID by replacing the legitimate SSID with a single space character (*0x20*). The information column for the Packet List window also gives us other information, including the packet sequence number, FN, and beacon interval (BI. Of particular interest is the sequence number information.) See Figure 6.47.

All management and data frames on an IEEE 802.11 network are transmitted with a sequence number in the 802.11 header contents. The sequence number is a 12-bit field used for fragmentation. If a transmitting station needs to fragment a large packet into multiple smaller packets, the receiving station knows which fragments belong together by the sequence number value. When an AP boots, it will start using the sequence number *0*, incremented by *1* for each packet transmitted. Once the sequence number reaches 4,095, the sequence returns to *0* and repeats.

When examining a packet capture, each packet from a single source should have a sequence number that is a positively incrementing integer value, modulo 4,095. In some cases, there may be gaps in the sequence number (usually when a transmitter goes off-channel to scan for other networks, and your capture card misses those

**Figure 6.47** Information Column Content Analysis - Real-world Capture 5

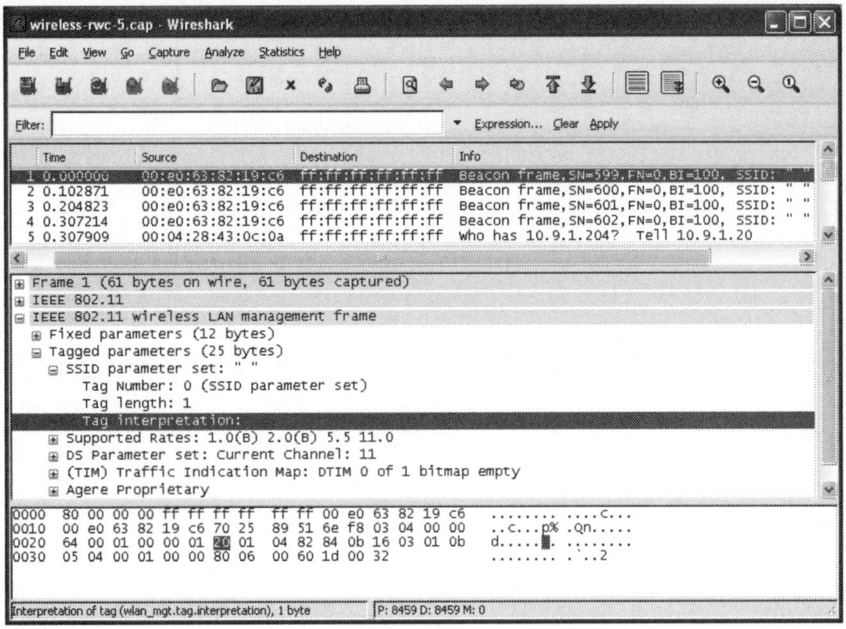

frames while remaining on a single channel), but the value should always be incremented by a positive value until it wraps. We can observe this behavior in the first several frames of this packet capture, where three beacons are transmitted sequentially, each with a new sequence number that is incremented by one (599, 600, 601).

**Tip**

The concept of monitoring the activity of SNs for a transmitter is an important characteristic of wireless Intrusion Detection Software (IDS), and is used for a variety of analysis mechanisms.

Continuing to scroll through the packets listed in the Packet List window, we see regular beacon frame activity from the AP, as well as unencrypted data frames from multiple stations, including a regular ICMP Echo Request and Response pair between the stations at *10.9.1.48* and *10.9.1.20*, respectively. At frames 45 and 46, however, we see deauthentication and disassociate frames transmitted by the AP to the broadcast address. These frames are a legitimate part of the IEEE 802.11 specification, and are used by the AP to inform stations that they have been disconnected from the network. Both deauthentication and disassociate frames include a parameter in the payload of the management frame known as the *reason code*, which identifies why the station was disconnected from the network. Selecting frame 45 and clicking **IEEE 802.11 | IEEE 802.11 Wireless LAN Management Frame | Fixed Parameter** reveals the reason code for the deauthenticate frame as *0x0002*, which indicates that the previous authentication is no longer valid. Selecting frame 46 and navigating to the reason code indicate that the station was disassociated because the AP is unable to handle all currently associated stations (*0x0005* (see Figure 6.48).

**Figure 6.48** Deauthentication and Disassociate Reason Code Analysis - Real-world Capture 5

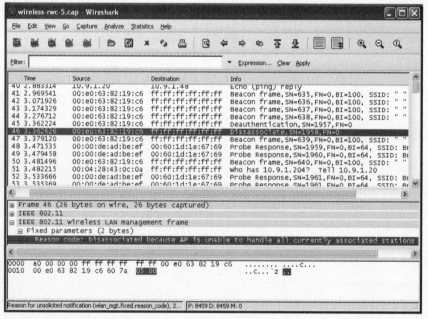

By carefully inspecting the Packet List window, we can spot several unusual conditions with this packet capture:

- A beacon in frame 47 follows the deauthentication and disassociate frames with an anomalous SN. Starting with the two beacons prior to the deauthentication frame, the sequence number pattern is 637 (beacon), 638 (beacon), 1957 (deauthentication), 1958 (disassociate), and 639 (beacon). The deauthentication and disassociate frames were transmitted with the same source MAC address as the beacon frames, but do not follow the standard convention for selection of the sequence number.

- Following frame 47, we have two probe response frames with SNs that follow the previous deauthentication and disassociate frames, but conflict with the beacon frame. This is unusual from a sequence number perspective, because we are observing probe responses without a prior probe request frame. However, it is possible that our sniffer dropped the probe request frame, which must be taken into consideration.

- The source MAC address of the probe response frames is *00:00:de:ad:be:ef*. While this is a valid MAC address, it is not the original MAC address assigned to the station that transmitted this packet.

- The SSID contents of the probe response frame are sent to the broadcast SSID (a *0*-length SSID indicates the broadcast SSID). This is also unusual, because the AP must include an SSID in the probe response frame, even if it is the cloaked SSID. (In this network, the cloaked SSID is represented with a single space character.)

These factors all point to the notion that the deauthentication and disassociate frames were spoofed and not transmitted by the legitimate source, and that the probe response frames were sent in an effort to otherwise manipulate the network to the attacker's goals.

Examining the contents of the packet capture further, we see more similar deauthentication and disassociate activity with anomalous sequence number values, as well as additional unsolicited probe responses with the unusual source MAC address. With this analysis, we can determine that any DoS conditions users are experiencing are the effect of an attack against the network, not from the result of misconfigured clients or other legitimate network anomalies.

## NOTE

The technique used in this packet capture is known as the *NULL SSID DoS* attack, where an attacker is attempting to get client stations to process malformed probe response frames in an effort to manipulate firmware on legacy wireless LAN cards. This is particularly effective as a DoS attack, because it renders the victim wireless card inoperable until the card has been power-cycled. More information on this bug is available in the Wireless Vulnerabilities and Exploits database as WVE-2006-0064 (www.wve.org/entries/show/WVE-2006-0064).

# IEEE 802.11 Spoofing Attacks

## Introduction

A significant security weakness in IEEE 802.11 networks is the lack of a cryptographically secure integrity check mechanism for traffic on the wireless network. While more modern encryption protocols such as TKIP or CCMP provide a secure integrity check over the payload of a data frame, it does not prevent at least partial analysis of a frame transmitted by an attacker with a spoofed source MAC address. This weakness exposes a wireless network to several classes of attacks, including packet spoofing attacks where an attacker impersonates a legitimate station on the network.

## Systems Affected

This analysis focuses on a vulnerability in a WEP network, but the principles of analysis for identifying spoofed traffic, apply to all IEEE 802.11 wireless networks.

## Breakdown and Analysis

In this real-world traffic capture analysis, we reference the capture file *wireless-rwc-6.cap*. Open this packet capture file with Wireshark to examine the contents.

Upon opening the packet capture, we see traffic from multiple stations and beacon frames for the *WEPNET* SSID. After examining the first few frames, you may notice an anomalous sequence number combination for the station at *00:13:ce:55:98:ef* in frames 4 (SN=2651), 8 (SN=2652), and 10 (SN=591). However, when assessing the contents of frames, it is important to examine the status of the From DS and To DS flags to determine if the frame is coming from a station on the wireless network, or if it is being retransmitted by an AP to other stations on the network. Select frame 8 and click **IEEE 802.11 | Frame Control | Flags** to examine the DS status information (see Figure 6.49).

Examining the *DS status* line, we see that the frame is being transmitted to the distribution system (To DS). This indicates that frame 8 is being transmitted by a wireless station to the AP. Selecting frame 10 and navigating to the DS status line indicates that the frame is being transmitted from the distribution system (From DS) by the AP. This is not indicative of a spoofing attack; rather, the AP is retransmitting the frame from the station to be received by other stations on the AP.

In order to inspect the sequence number patterns for signs of possible spoofing activity, we can apply a display filter to examine only traffic sent to the DS from wireless stations:

```
wlan.fc.tods eq 1 and wlan.fc.fromds eq 0
```

**Figure 6.49 sequence number** Analysis - Real-world Capture 6

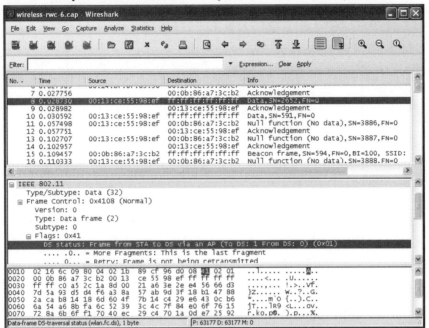

After applying this display filter, we can focus our attention on traffic from wireless stations. In the first packet, we see a NULL function frame from the wireless station with sequence number 3885. (Recall that this is often used for power management on wireless clients, to indicate to the AP that the client is entering a power-conservation state.) In frame number 4, we have a data frame with sequence number 2651 sent to a Unicast address, followed by a frame with that next sequence number in the series sent to the broadcast address. Next, we have another NULL function frame, returning to the original sequence number series.

Continuing to look at the packet capture contents, we see additional data frames sent to the broadcast address with SNs that are not part of the series used by the NULL function frames. By selecting one of these anomalous frames (e.g., frame number 11) and clicking **IEEE 802.11 | WEP Parameters**, we determine that this is a WEP-encrypted network. At this point, we have determined that there is a station that is transmitting spoofed WEP-encrypted packets sent to the broadcast address; our next task is to evaluate what the potential impact is to the network.

Wireshark can produce a simple but effective Input/Output (IO) graph to illustrate the behavior of traffic on the network. Click **Statistics | IO Graphs** to open the IO Graphs window (see Figure 6.50).

In Figure 6.50, Wireshark illustrates the characteristics of the packet capture based on our analysis preferences. By default, Wireshark plots the time on the X axis

**Figure 6.50** IO Graph Analysis - Real-world Capture 6

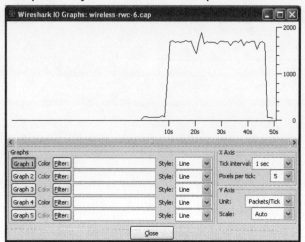

and the number of packets on the *Y* axis. This allows us to determine that there was little activity on the wireless network for the first 10 seconds of the packet capture, which increased to a rate of approximately 1,000 packets per second for approximately 38 seconds before the activity returned to a minimal level.

We can refocus the graph by modifying the *X* axis and *Y* axis values to give the best view of the network activity. Change the Tick interval on the X axis to *0.1* seconds and change the pixels per tick to *2*. This will extend the width of the graph, forcing us to scroll to see the activity of the entire capture.

> **NOTE**
>
> To obtain a better view of the graph content, you can expand the size of the IO Graphs window to any resolution supported by your video card.

By default, the IO graph illustration shows the analysis for all traffic in the capture file. We can add additional graphs to this view based on any criteria we specify with Wireshark display filters. For this example, it is useful to identify exactly how much traffic is originating from wireless stations (To the DS), and how much traffic is originating from the AP (From the DS). Click on the Graph 2 line in the Filter text box and enter the following display filter to identify all traffic from wireless stations to the DS:

```
wlan.fc.fromds eq 0 and wlan.fc.tods eq 1
```

Next, click the **Graph 2** button to update the IO illustration (see Figure 6.51).

**Figure 6.51** IO Graph/Wireless Station Traffic - Real-world Capture 6

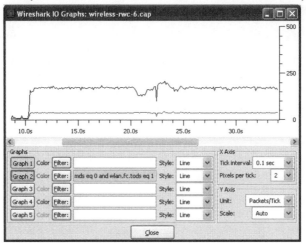

The new graph filter line illustrates the quantity and frequency of packets being transmitted from wireless stations to the DS. Approximately 30 percent of the traffic is from wireless stations; the remaining traffic is made up of traffic from the AP to the stations or management or control frames that do not set the From DS or To DS bits in the 802.11 frame control header.

In order to focus on the spoofed packets, we want to identify a pattern in the packets and apply a display filter to display only those frames. We have determined that the significant increase in activity on the network started at approximately 10 seconds into the packet capture, therefore, we can switch back to the Packet List window and scroll to this point in the capture to examine the traffic activity (see Figure 6.52).

Fortunately, this packet capture was taken with the Radiotap Link layer header information, which allows us to identify additional information about the characteristics of the traffic beyond the 802.11 header contents (e.g., the signal strength indicator is recorded with each packet that is captured, as well as the channel type and data rate information. Selecting packet 624 and clicking **Radiotap Header | SSI Signal** reveals the signal strength as 33 decibels (dB) for this NULL function packet, which is believed to be from the legitimate station. Repeating the process for frame 629 reveals the signal strength as 60 dB for the data frame that is believed to be spoofed. Sampling additional packets reveals similar information; legitimate frames have a signal level between 31 dB and 46 dB, while illegitimate (spoofed) frames have a signal level between 54 dB and 67 dB. This characteristic can be described in a display filter to display only spoofed traffic:

```
wlan.fc.tods eq 1 and wlan.fc.fromds eq 0 and wlan.sa eq 00:13:ce:55:98:ef
and radiotap.db_antsignal > 50
```

**Figure 6.52** Examining Increasing Traffic Activity - Real-world Capture 6

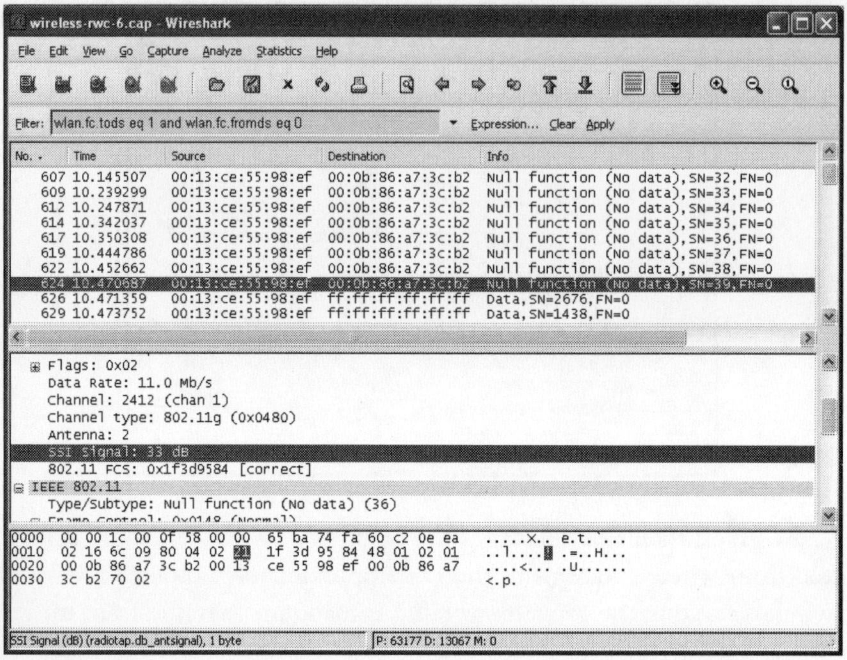

This new display filter returns 12,574 frames, all of which appear to be transmitted by an attacker through packet-spoofing techniques. While it may not be a comprehensive list of all of the spoofed frames in the packet capture (it's conceivable that some frames were transmitted with lower signal levels), it is sufficient to use for additional analysis.

With the display filter applied that only displays traffic suspected as being spoofed, we can use Wireshark's analysis and summarization features to glean additional information about this activity. Click **Statistics | Summary** to examine the summary information (see Figure 6.53).

The bottom of the Wireshark Summary window identifies several metrics regarding the traffic for all of the frames in the capture, and for packets returned with a display filter. In this case, our display filter is showing 37.5 seconds of traffic for a total of 12,574 frames at a rate of over 335 packets per second. This gives us an idea as to the rate of the attack, which appears to be aggressive based on the number of packets per second.

Returning to the IO Graphs window, we can add this new display filter and graph a third line to illustrate the traffic that is spoofed, compared to traffic sent from wireless stations. Enter the same display filter in the Filter text box for graph 3

**Figure 6.53** Frame Statistics Summary - Real-world Capture 6

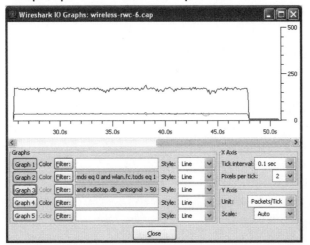

and click the **Graph 3** button. Wireshark processes the new display filter and returns a new IO graph line (see Figure 6.54).

With this new graph line, we see that nearly all of the traffic sent from the wireless network is spoofed traffic from the attacker.

**Figure 6.54** IO Graph/Spoofed Traffic Comparison - Real-world Capture 6

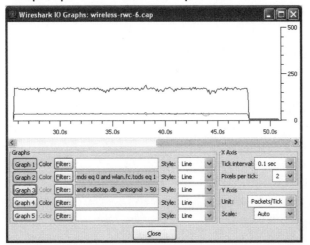

At this point in the analysis, we've determined several factors that are useful for our analysis:

- The wireless network was relatively quiet until 10 seconds into the packet capture

- An attacker started transmitting illegitimate WEP-encrypted frames into the wireless network, spoofing the source address of a legitimate station

- The attacker represents nearly 100 percent of the wireless frames sent to the DS

- The attacker is transmitting frames at approximately 335 packets per second

- In response to their spoofed traffic, the attacker's activity is generating a significant number of packets from the AP to the wireless network

With this information and some background knowledge in the weaknesses of WEP networks, we can determine that an attacker is manipulating the wireless network to accelerate the amount of traffic on the network. This is a common technique used for WEP cracking; an attacker may require several hundred-thousand packets on the wireless network to recover a WEP key. With a single station that is not regularly transmitting any encrypted traffic, it may take an attacker weeks to recover a sufficient quantity of traffic to recover the WEP key. By manipulating the network in this fashion, the attacker has increased the traffic level from a minimal number of frames to over 300 frames per second. At this rate, an attacker will have collected a sufficient number of packets (approximately 150,000 unique encrypted packets is a useful quantity for WEP cracking) in less than 10 minutes.

As the administrator of this network, you may have knowledge of the WEP key used to decrypt traffic. In this example, the WEP key for the network is *f0:00:f0:00:f0*. We can supply Wireshark with this encryption key and Wireshark will display both the encrypted and unencrypted content for each packet.

To enter the encryption key for this capture click **Edit | Preferences | Protocols | IEEE 802.11**. Type **f0:00:f0:00:f0** in an available WEP key slot, and check the **Enable decryption** checkbox (see Figure 6.55). Click **OK** when finished.

After Wireshark reloads the packet capture and decrypts each packet, any packets that are successfully decrypted with the specified WEP key include two tabs at the bottom of the Packet Bytes window labeled "Frame" and "Decrypted WEP data." With this new information, we can identify the activity that was generated by the attacker. Select frame 663 (one of the spoofed packets) and inspect the Packet Details window to identify the nature of the traffic (see Figure 6.56).

**Figure 6.55** Supplying WEP Encryption Keys - Real-world Capture 6

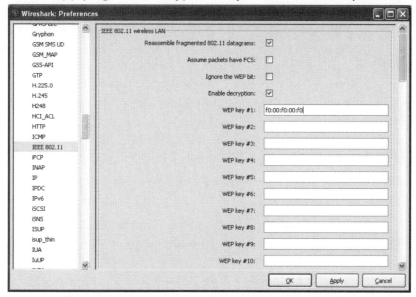

**Figure 6.56** Examining Decrypted Frame Contents - Real-world Capture 6

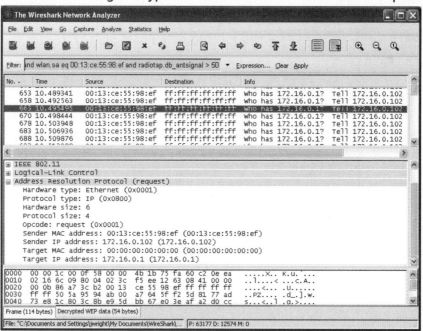

We can see that the traffic being transmitted by the attacker is a repetitive series of Address Resolution Protocol (ARP) Request packets that elicit ARP Response packets from a station on the network. This activity reinforces our analysis that the attacker is attempting to increase traffic levels on the network in order to collect enough packets to use a WEP cracking tool. We can return to the IO Graphs view and add another display filter to evaluate our earlier signal strength indicator display filter, verifying if our initial analysis of spoofed traffic matches the series of ARP request frames on the network.

Return to the IO Graphs window and add a third (and final) display filter to identify only ARP request packets in the graph 4 line:

```
wlan.fc.tods eq 1 and wlan.fc.fromds eq 0 and wlan.sa eq 00:13:ce:55:98:ef
and arp.opcode eq 1
```

Modify the line style for this graph from "Line" to "Impulse" to make the graph easier to see in context with the other graphs (see Figure 6.57).

**Figure 6.57** IO Graph/ARP Request Traffic Comparison - Real-world Capture 6

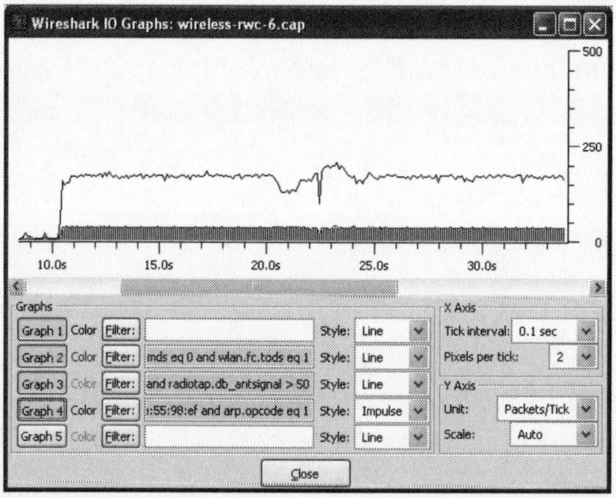

We can see that the lines from graphs 3 and 4 match very closely, indicating that our analysis of the attacker's activity based on signal strength indicators and the decrypted protocol activity are both correct.

## NOTE

This attack activity matches the mechanism implemented in the Aireplay tool that ships with the *Aircrack-ng* suite of WEP and WPA-PSK cracking tools. This attack tool is assigned the identifier WVE-2005-0015 by the Wireless Vulnerabilities and Exploits group; visit www.wve.org/entries/show/WVE-2005-0015 for additional information about this attack tool.

# Malformed Traffic Analysis

## Introduction

A recent development in the saga of wireless LAN security is the use of IEEE 802.11 protocol *fuzzing* against wireless stations to identify bugs in driver software. Fuzzing is a technique where an attacker sends malformed packets that violate the specification of a protocol to a client or a server. If the server or client software is not written to expect invalid packets, it can sometimes trigger flaws in software that can be exploited by an attacker.

### Notes from the Underground...

### IEEE 802.11 Protocol Fuzzing

A recent advancement in the list of techniques that can be used to compromise the security of a wireless network, is the use of IEEE 802.11 protocol fuzzing. Fuzzing is a technique used by security researchers and attackers to identify software weaknesses when presented with unexpected data. This technique is frequently used to identify potential security flaws in software that can be successfully exploited to the attacker's gain. Once an attacker identifies a sequence of data that causes a victim to behave in a way the target software's author did not intend, the technique is developed into an exploit that can be used repeatedly against vulnerable stations. In the case of IEEE 802.11 wireless LANs, fuzzing is being used to identify weaknesses in device driver software when presented with malformed or unexpected wireless frames. These frames can be malformed by violating the framing rules stated in the 802.11 specification or by violating the expected order and timing of otherwise legitimate packets.

**Continued**

The use of 802.11 protocol fuzzing is not necessarily a bad thing. If a researcher uses this technique to identify potential software flaws in station drivers, and uses ethical disclosure practices to communicate these flaws to the vendor, all wireless users benefit from improving the quality of otherwise buggy software. However, if the intention of the researcher is to turn them into exploits for their own gain (potentially by exploiting systems or by selling their exploits to others who will use them for ill gain), the risk to vulnerable organizations is significant.

In a wireless LAN, any attacker that gets within physical proximity of the victim network can inject packets that will be received by wireless stations, regardless of the encryption or authentication mechanisms used. If an attacker can identify a driver vulnerability in the processing of these packets, there is little that can be done to protect the vulnerable station. This is amplified because there is little security software designed to protect the integrity of client systems at the wireless LAN layer (OSI model layer 2). Most firewalls and other security tools (e.g., host-based intrusion prevention tools) start assessing traffic at layer 3 and higher, often leaving stations vulnerable and blind to any attacks at layer 2.

Fortunately, independent security researchers are actively looking for, identifying, and communicating these driver flaws to the appropriate vendors, in an effort to resolve them before they become actively exploited by attackers. Concerned organizations should take care to ensure driver software on client stations remains current, and that upper-layer analysis tools (such as intrusion detection systems) are used to identify questionable activity from compromised stations (including Internet Relay Chat [IRC] information, or signs of spyware infections and other unauthorized network use) to monitor for potentially compromised stations.

## Systems Affected

This analysis applies to all wireless LANs where an attacker can get within physical range of the wireless network.

## Breakdown and Analysis

### Capture 1

In this real-world traffic capture analysis, we reference the capture file *wireless-rwc-7.cap*. Open this packet capture file with Wireshark to examine the contents.

This packet capture includes the 4-byte FCS at the end of each frame; however, Wireshark has no way of knowing that the FCS is present. In order to successfully analyze the contents of this capture, instruct Wireshark to expect the FCS information by clicking **Edit | Preferences | Protocols | IEEE 802.11** and ensure "Assume packets have FCS" is selected. Click **OK**.

Upon opening the packet capture, we see traffic from networks with the SSIDs *Lexie* and *NETGEAR*, as well as some unencrypted data frames in the form of ICMP echo requests and responses. Scrolling through the packet capture, we notice the information column for frame 42 is labeled "Reassociation Response,SN=4027,FN=0[Malformed Packet]." This is Wireshark's mechanism to indicate that this packet does not comply with the packet framing rules of the IEEE 802.11 specification. As soon as Wireshark comes to the point in the packet where it evaluates the content as invalid, it will stop processing the remainder of the frame and insert the "Malformed Packet" label. We can navigate the Packet Details window to identify the content that caused the frame to be marked as invalid, by going to the end of the Packet Details window. In frame 42, click **IEEE 802.11 Wireless LAN Management Frame | Tagged Parameters | Reserved Tag Number**. Wireshark will attempt to decode this information, as shown in Figure 6.58:

**Figure 6.58** Assessing Malformed Frames - Real-world Capture 7

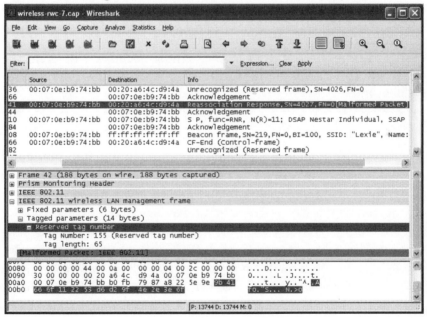

In this case, we see that the management frame payload information element is not properly evaluated by Wireshark. Each of the tagged parameters in IEEE 802.11 management packets is consistently formatted as shown below:

| Tag Type (1 byte) | Tag Length (1 byte) | Data (variable length, corresponding to tag length, between 0 and 255 bytes) |
|---|---|---|

In this example, Wireshark identifies the tag number as *155* or *0×9b* with a length is 65 bytes (*0×41*). However, only 8 bytes remain at the end of the packet before the FCS, not 65 as indicated by the frame length. This prompts Wireshark to identify the packet as malformed.

**NOTE**

Wireshark identifies this packet as malformed, because the reported tag length exceeds the number of remaining bytes in the packet, and because Wireshark knows it has received 100 percent of the bytes in the packet, as indicated by the frame packet length and capture length information. However, Wireshark also identifies this tagged parameter as using a reserved tag number.

Throughout the development of Wireshark, the authors of various dissectors maintained the software to stay current with the supported protocols and the values used in these protocols. However, over time, standards bodies such as the IEEE and IETF may allocate previously reserved values for new uses of existing protocols. As such, Wireshark doesn't assume the packet is invalid simply because it does not know how to interpret a value that it observed, such as the tag number 155 in this example.

Observing a single malformed frame does not suggest that the capture is the product of protocol fuzzing techniques or other potentially hostile activity; it is possible that this frame was accidentally corrupted when it was transmitted, or that the station that is sending this data is flawed and is sending invalid frames. We can easily determine if the first condition caused the frame to be malformed by checking the contents of the FCS field. In frame 42, click **IEEE 802.11 | Frame Check Sequence**. We see that Wireshark reports the FCS as *0×4e2e3e6f*, which it reports as correct for this packet. While it is possible that the packet could be modified by retaining a valid FCS, it is highly unlikely. As such, we can assume the packet was received in this capture exactly as it was transmitted.

The second possibility of a flawed implementation remains, which would also suggest that we would see multiple packets that shared the characteristic of the reserved tag number with a length that is longer than the number of bytes available in the capture. We can use a display filter to identify other frames that are similar to frame 42, in an attempt to prove/disprove this theory. Right-click on **Reserved**

**Tag Number** and select **Prepare a Filter | Selected**. This will place a display filter in the Filter text-box:

```
frame[174:10] == 9b:41:66:6f:11:22:53:d6:d2:9f
```

This filter instructs Wireshark to start looking at the 174-byte offer in this packet for a 10-byte sequence matching *9b:41:66:6f:11:22:53:d6:d2:9f* (note that *0×9b* is the reserved tag or 155, *0×41* is the malformed length [65], and the remaining bytes represent the actual data following this tag. Clicking **Apply** will prompt Wireshark to process this display filter and display only frames that match this characteristic. When the display filter is applied, we see that only a single frame has this characteristic, which makes the possibility of a flawed implementation generating this malformed frame less of a possibility.

Fortunately, Wireshark has a facility for performing expert information analysis in order for the packet capture to identify anomalies such as malformed frames. Instead of scrolling through the capture looking for information lines that indicate malformed frames, we can use the Expert Information feature by clicking **Analyze | Expert Info Composite**. Wireshark assesses the contents of the packet capture and opens a new window (see Figure 6.59).

**Figure 6.59** Expert Information Analysis - Real-world Capture 7

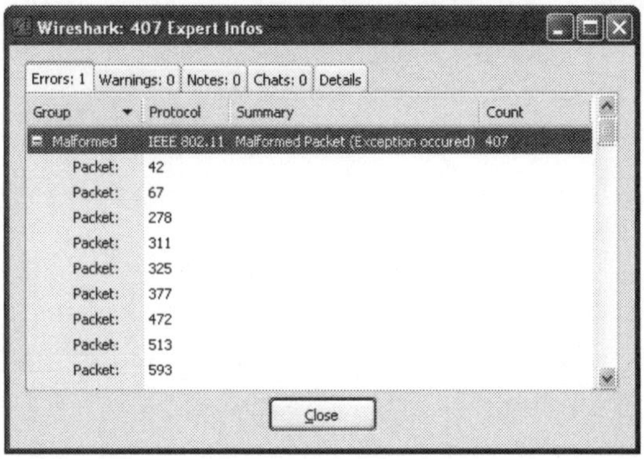

We see that Wireshark has detected 407 malformed frames in this packet capture. Expanding the list of malformed frames by clicking on the plus (+) sign in the group column, reveals the list of packets that are malformed. Clicking on any of the packet's identifiers will update the Packet List window to display the contents for the selected packet. Clicking on the Details tab will display additional information for each of the errors detected (see Figure 6.60).

**Figure 6.60** Expert Information Analysis - Detail Window - Real-world Capture 7

Here we see that each of the malformed frames has an exception in the IEEE 802.11 protocol analysis. Select frame 67 and click **IEEE 802.11 Wireless LAN Management Frame | Tagged Parameters** to view the tagged parameter list. Again, Wireshark attempts to dissect the contents of the tagged parameters, but characterizes each tag as a reserved tag number. Expanding the last tag in the management payload reveals that it is using tag number 64 with a length of 62 bytes, even though only 28 bytes are remaining in the packet payload (excluding 4 bytes for the trailing FCS).

Returning to the main Wireshark window, we can use the display filter function to display only malformed frames with the following filter:

```
malformed
```

Enter this display string in the Filter text-box and click **Apply**. Wireshark will display a list of all the frames that were identified as malformed (see Figure 6.61).

In this display we are examining only the malformed frames, which gives us some curious information about the packet capture:

- Each malformed frame has a consistent source MAC address and destination address.

- The frame types vary including reassociation response, reassociation request, probe response, action, probe requests, beacons, and so on. This is unusual because frames that should only be transmitted by an AP (beacons, reassociation response, probe response) are mixed with frames that should only be transmitted by stations (probe request, reassociation request, association request).

**Figure 6.61** Filtering on Malformed Frames - Real-world Capture 7

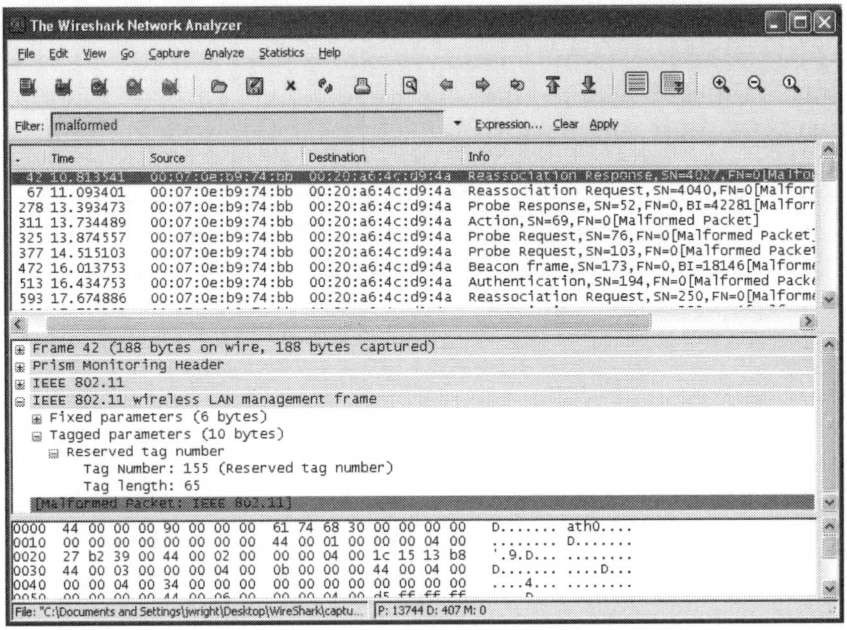

- Individual frames include values that are not reasonable; frame 278 indicates the beacon interval is 42,281 millisecond (msec) (*BI=42281*), which means the AP is transmitting beacons once every 43.3 seconds, as opposed to the standard convention of 10 times per second. Similarly, frame 472 reports a beacon interval of 18,146, or one beacon every 18.1 seconds.

Selecting individual frames reveals more anomalous activity (e.g., frame 311 is identified as an action frame, a new type of management frame designed to support the IEEE 802.11h, IEEE 802.11k, and IEEE 802.11r working groups. The Flags byte in the frame control header for this frame has the To DS bit set and the From DS bit clear, which indicates it is a wireless station and not an AP, but it also has the power management bit set (indicating the station is going to enter a power-conservation mode) and the more data bit set (indicating it is an AP which has buffered packets waiting to be delivered to a station). Further, the strict-order bit is set, which is generally not used in IEEE 802.11 implementations and should always be clear.

> **TIP**
>
> A great place to get information about upcoming IEEE 802.11 standards is the IEEE 802.11 timelines page, where each working group provides a short summary of the activity of the working group and the estimated schedule for the ratification of the standard or amendment. Linked to each task group is the project authorization request form and approval letter, which documents the intentions of the working group and the detailed status page for the activity of the working group. The IEEE 802.11 timelines page is available at http://grouper.ieee.org/groups/802/11/Reports/802.11_Timelines.htm.

Our analysis suggests evidence of IEEE 802.11 protocol fuzzing; our "malformed" display filter revealed over 400 packets that have conflicting field settings and reserved field values. However, further analysis also indicates that these 400 frames are not the only packets that appear to be the result of protocol fuzzing. Apply the following display filter to identify all frames with the consistent source and destination address we have identified for this traffic.

```
wlan.sa eq 00:07:0e:b9:74:bb and wlan.da eq 00:20:a6:4c:d9:4a
```

Applying this filter returns 4,580 frames (see Figure 6.62).

Even though many of these frames aren't recognized as malformed by Wireshark, they appear to have similar characteristics that would lead us to believe that they are also the result of IEEE 802.11 protocol fuzzing. For example, frame 55 is reported as a fragmented packet, a feature that is seldom-used in wireless LANs. However, it is also indicating that the station is going to sleep, effectively saying, "Here's the first part of a packet, now I'm going to sleep, so hold on to this for me."

From a security researcher's perspective, Wireshark is an indispensable tool for analyzing the results of protocol fuzzing activity, assisting in narrowing down the activity that caused misbehavior in the target station. From an intrusion analysis perspective, it's not likely you'll see this kind of activity on your network, because most of these packets don't elicit a response from the target station; rather, a Wireless Local Area Network (WLAN) IDS system may observe the few frames sent by the attacker to reproduce an identified vulnerability in an effort to exploit a victim system.

**Figure 6.62** Filtering on Consistent Source and Destination - Real-world Capture 7

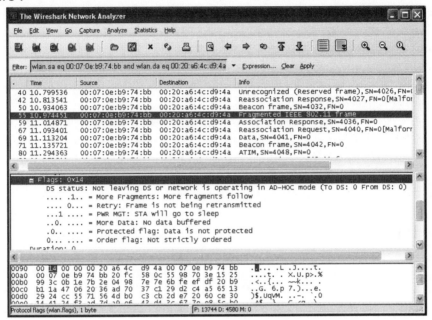

# Summary

Packet sniffing on wireless networks has unique challenges that are different than the challenges of capturing traffic on wired networks. Fortunately, many wireless cards support the ability to capture wireless traffic without needing to connect to a network with the monitor mode feature. By leveraging available tools and drivers for Windows and Linux systems, you can use a standard wireless card to capture traffic on the wireless network for analysis.

Wireshark's wireless analysis features have grown to be a very powerful tool for troubleshooting and analyzing wireless networks. Leveraging Wireshark's display filters and powerful protocol dissector features, you can sift through large quantities of wireless traffic to identify a specific condition or field value you are looking for, or exclude undesirable traffic until you are left with only a handful of traffic to assess. In this chapter, we examined several examples of display filters taken from practical analysis needs that you can apply to your own network analysis needs.

Wireshark doesn't limit itself to display filters for wireless analysis; we can also take advantage of other analysis features built into Wireshark to simplify wireless network analysis. Features like Wireshark's coloring rules allow us to leverage display filters to uniquely color-code packets in the Packet List window, which allows you to assess the contents of a packet capture by looking at the number of packets. If your packet capture includes radio signal strength information or transmission rate information, Wireshark can make that information visible as well, giving extra visibility into the health and robustness of wireless client connectivity. Finally, when configured with the appropriate encryption keys, Wireshark can decrypt traffic dynamically, to further simplify the task of network troubleshooting.

Finally, we examined several packet captures taken from production and lab wireless environments, to demonstrate Wireshark's wireless analysis and troubleshooting capabilities. Without a doubt, Wireshark is a powerful assessment and analysis tool for wireless networks that should be a part of every auditor, engineer, and consultant toolkit.

# Solutions Fast Track

## Techniques for Effective Wireless Sniffing

- ☑ Wireless cards can sniff on one channel at a time.

- ☑ Channel hopping is used to rapidly change channels and briefly capture traffic.

- ☑ Interference can result in lost traffic and incomplete packet captures.

- ☑ Locate the capture station near the station being monitored, while disabling any local transmitters and minimizing CPU utilization.

## Understanding Wireless Card Operating Modes

- ☑ Wireless card operating modes include managed, master, ad-hoc, and monitor.

- ☑ Monitor mode causes the card to passively capture wireless traffic without connecting to a network.

- ☑ Wireless cards do not normally transmit while in monitor mode.

## Configuring Linux for Wireless Sniffing

- ☑ Linux Wireless Extensions compatible drivers use the *iwconfig* utility to configure monitor mode.

- ☑ The Linux MADWIFI drivers for Atheros cards use the *wlanconfig* utility to configure monitor mode.

- ☑ Linux Wireless Extensions compatible drivers and the MADWIFI drivers use the *iwconfig* utility to specify the channel number.

## Configuring Windows for Wireless Sniffing

- ☑ Windows does not have a built-in mechanism for using a wireless driver in monitor mode.

- ☑ The commercial AirPcap drivers and USB wireless dongle can be used to capture traffic in monitor mode.

## Using Wireless Protocol Dissectors

☑ Frame statistic information is included as the first group of fields in the Packet Details window.

☑ Protocol dissectors extract and enumerate fields in the IEEE 802.11 header and payload.

☑ The IEEE 802.11 header and payload data can be very complex, but the data is easily assessed with protocol dissectors.

## Useful Wireless Display Filters

☑ Display filters can be applied to any of the fields in the IEEE 802.11 header and payload data.

☑ Complex display filters can be built by adding to a filter with *AND* or *OR* conditions.

☑ You can apply inclusive filters when looking for a specific set of data, or to remove uninteresting data from the packet list.

## Leveraging Wireshark Wireless Analysis Features

☑ Coloring rules leverage display filters to identify matching display filter conditions.

☑ Applying a handful of helpful coloring rules can make it easier to analyze large quantities of frames.

# Frequently Asked Questions

The following Frequently Asked Questions, answered by the authors of this book, are designed to both measure your understanding of the concepts presented in this chapter and to assist you with real-life implementation of these concepts. To have your questions about this chapter answered by the author, browse to **www.syngress.com/solutions** and click on the **"Ask the Author"** form.

**Q:** Can I use Wireshark for wireless intrusion analysis?

**A:** Wireshark's display filter functionality can be used to identify some attacks on wireless networks, such as deauthenticate DoS attacks (*wlan.fc.type_subtype eq 12*), FakeAP (*wlan_mgt.fixed.timestamp < "0×000000000003d070"*) and NetStumbler (*wlan.fc.type_subtype eq 32, llc.oui eq 0x00601d*, and *llc.pid eq 0x0001*), but it is not a replacement for a sophisticated WLAN IDS system.

**Q:** Can I use Wireshark to crack wireless encryption keys?

**A:** No, Wireshark does not include any key cracking functionality. Wireshark can decrypt WEP traffic, but only when configured with the correct WEP key.

**Q:** Can I use Wireshark to analyze traffic captured with Kismet?

**A:** Yes, Kismet generates several output file types including libpcap files with a *.dump* extension. Wireshark can open and assess libpcap files generated with Kismet.

**Q:** Can I use Wireshark to analyze traffic captured with NetStumbler?

**A:** No, NetStumbler does not capture traffic in monitor mode and is unable to create libpcap files for use with Wireshark.

**Q:** What is the best card to get for wireless analysis?

**A:** Wireless cards with an Atheros chipset are known to be effective at capturing wireless traffic on Linux systems, often allowing you to select between IEEE 802.11a, 802.11b and 802.11g traffic. Visit the Atheros Product Database at http://customerproducts.atheros.com/customerproducts/ResultsPageBasic.asp to identify if a card is based on an Atheros chipset. For Windows hosts, the AirPcap adapter is functional and well-supported by Wireshark, but does not yet support IEEE 802.11a channels.

**Q:** Can I use Wireshark to capture traffic while connected to an AP?

**A:** When associated to an AP, the wireless card is working in managed mode. Some drivers allow you to capture traffic in managed mode, but the data is reported as if it were coming from a standard Ethernet interface. This prevents you from seeing management frames, control frames, and data destined for other networks.

**Q:** Can Wireshark sniff IEEE 802.11a/b/g/n networks?

**A:** Wireshark isn't limited in its ability to sniff any Physical layer wireless network type, as long as the driver is compatible with libpcap/winpcap and the wireless card supports monitor mode for the desired spectrum. At the time of this writing we are just starting to see pre-802.11n networks; if your wireless card and driver support monitor mode for IEEE 802.11n modulation, Wireshark can be used to analyze the traffic.

**Q:** How can I examine signal strength information in a Wireshark capture?

**A:** Wireshark will display signal strength information in any packet capture that includes this information in the frame header contents. Some packet captures only contain the IEEE 802.11 header contents, which does not include signal strength information. When capturing traffic for a wireless network, use the Radiotap of Prism AVS link types to record signal strength information.

# Chapter 7

# Real World Packet Captures

## Solutions in this chapter:

- Scanning

- Remote Access Trojans

- Dissecting Worms

- Active Response

☑ Summary

☑ Solutions Fast Track

☑ Frequently Asked Questions

# Introduction

Now that you have learned how Wireshark works and how to use it, you are armed and ready to read real network packet captures. In this chapter we discuss real-world packet captures and traffic that you could be seeing on your network. You will learn how to read the captures, what to look for, and how to identify various types of network traffic. The Honeynet Project at http://project.honeynet.org provided some of the packet capture data in this chapter, which we have included on the accompanying CD-ROM in the /captures directory. The Honeynet Project Web site includes a great challenge called Scan of the Month that will exercise your capture analysis abilities.

# Scanning

Network scanning is used to identify available network resources. Also known as *discovery* or *enumeration*, network scanning can be used to discover available hosts, ports, or resources on the network. Once a vulnerable resource is detected, it can be exploited, and the device can be compromised. Sometimes, an actual intruder is behind the scanning, and sometimes it is a result of worm activity. In this section we focus on active intruder scanning, and worm activity is covered in a later section. Security professionals also use network scanning to assist in securing and auditing the network. In this section we use Scan1.log, which contains several different types of scans and was provided by the Honeynet Research Alliance as part of the Honeynet Project's Scan of the Month challenge. Scan1.log is located on the accompanying CD-ROM in the /captures directory.

---

**NOTE**

The Transmission Control Protocol (TCP) is connection oriented and initialized by completing a three-way handshake. The TCP three-way handshake consists of an initial packet that is sent with the SYN flag, a return packet that includes both the SYN and ACK flags, and a third packet that includes an ACK flag.

---

## TCP Connect Scan

The first scan that we will analyze is the TCP Connect scan, which is used to determine which ports are open and listening on a target device. This type of scanning is the most basic because it completes the TCP three-way handshake with open ports and immediately closes them. An intruder sends a SYN packet and analyzes the response. A response packet with the Reset (RST) and Acknowledgment (ACK) flags set indicates that the port is closed. If a SYN/ACK is received, it indicates that the port is open and listening. The intruder will then respond with an ACK to complete the connection followed by an RST/ACK to immediately close the connection. This aspect of the scan makes it easily detectable because the error messages made during attempts to connect to a port will be logged.

Figure 7.1 shows the attacker, 192.168.0.9, sending SYN packets to the target, 192.168.0.99. Most ports respond with an RST/ACK packet; however, the highlighted packets show the SYN/ACK response and the subsequent ACK followed by the RST/ACK exchange on the domain name system (DNS) port. You will also notice that the intruder's source port increases by one for each attempted connection.

**Figure 7.1** TCP Connect Scan

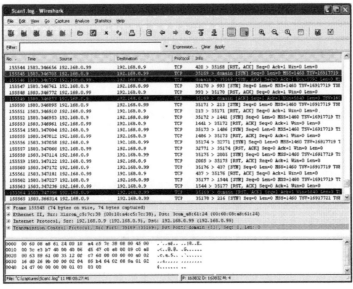

Figure 7.2 shows the active ports on the target device. You can find these by using a filter such as tcp.flags.syn==1&&tcp.flags.ack==1 or tcp.flags==18 to view packets with the SYN and ACK flags set. The filter will show multiple responses for each port because several scanning methods were used. We removed the duplicates by saving the marked packets to a file.

> **NOTE**
>
> The filter tcp.flags==18 will display packets with the SYN and ACK flags
> set because the binary value of the TCP flags field of a SYN/ACK packet is
> 00010010, which equals 18 in decimal format.

**Figure 7.2** SYN/ACK Responses

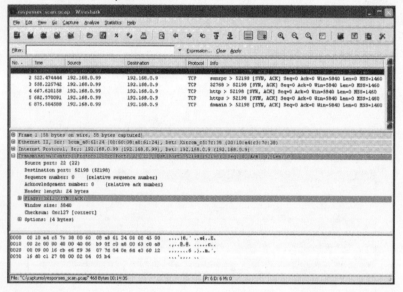

# SYN Scan

The next scan that we will analyze is a TCP SYN scan, also known as a *half-open scan* because a full TCP connection is never completed. It is used to determine which ports are open and listening on a target device. An intruder sends a SYN packet and analyzes the response. If an RST/ACK is received, it indicates that the port is closed. If a SYN/ACK is received, it indicates that the port is open and listening. The intruder will then follow with an RST to close the connection. SYN scans are known as stealth scans because few devices will notice or log them because they never create a full connection. However, many current firewalls and intrusion detection systems (IDSes) will notice this type of activity.

In Figure 7.3, the attacker, 192.168.0.9, is sending SYN packets to the target, 192.168.0.99. Most ports respond with an RST/ACK packet; however, the highlighted packets show the SYN/ACK response and the subsequent RST exchange on the https port. You will also notice that the intruder is using somewhat static source ports, 52198 and 52199.

**Figure 7.3** SYN Scan

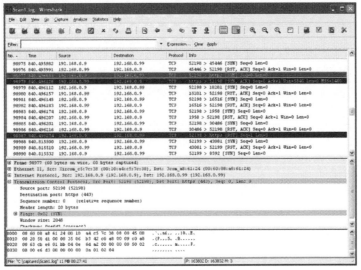

# XMAS Scan

The XMAS scan determines which ports are open by sending packets with invalid flag settings to a target device. It is considered a stealth scan because it may be able to bypass some firewalls and IDSes more easily than the SYN scans. This XMAS scan sends packets with the Finish (FIN), Push (PSH), and Urgent (URG) flags set. Closed ports will respond with an RST/ACK, and open ports will drop the packet and not respond. However, this type of scan will not work against systems running Microsoft Windows, Cisco IOS, BSDI, HP/UX, MVS, and IRIX. They will all respond with RST packets, even from open ports.

Notice that in Figure 7.4 the attacker, 192.168.0.9, is sending packets to the target, 192.168.0.99, with the FIN, PSH, and URG flags set. Most ports respond with an RST/ACK packet; however, the highlighted packet for the sunrpc port never receives a response. This lack of a response indicates that the port is open and has dropped the packet. You will also notice that the intruder is using decoy addresses of 192.168.0.1, 192.168.0.199, and 192.168.0.254. Decoy addresses are often used to obscure the real intruder's Internet Protocol (IP) address, making it harder to track down the real source of the scan. Looking closely at those packets reveals the same Media Access Control (MAC) address for all IP addresses. You will also notice that the intruder is using somewhat static source ports, 35964 and 35965.

**Figure 7.4** XMAS Scan

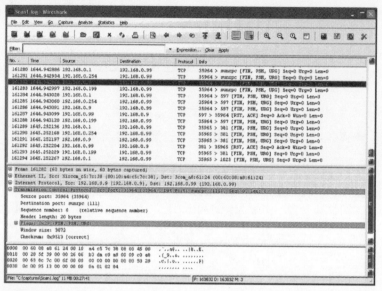

# Null Scan

The Null scan determines which ports are open by sending packets with invalid flag settings to a target device. It is considered a stealth scan because it may be able to bypass some firewalls and IDSes more easily than the SYN scans. This Null scan sends packets with all flags turned off. Closed ports will respond with an RST/ACK, and open ports will drop the packet and not respond. However, this type of scan will not work against systems running Microsoft Windows, Cisco IOS, BSDI, HP/UX, MVS, and IRIX. They will all respond with RST/ACK packets, even from open ports.

In Figure 7.5, the attacker, 192.168.0.9, is sending packets to the target, 192.168.0.99, with all flags turned off, as indicated by the empty brackets []. Most ports respond with an RST/ACK packet; however, the highlighted packet for the https port never receives a response, thereby indicating that the port is open and has dropped the packet. Notice that the intruder is using somewhat static source ports, 42294 and 42295.

# Remote Access Trojans

The term *Trojan horse* originally came from the Greek epic poem "The Odeyssey" by Homer. In the story of the Trojan War, the Greeks left a large wooden horse as an apparent peace offering to the Trojans. Once the horse was brought inside the city walls of Troy, the Greek soldiers who were hiding inside of the hollow horse emerged

**Figure 7.5** Null Scan

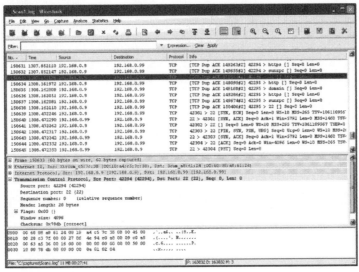

and assisted in capturing the city. In the information security field, trojans are malicious programs that are often disguised as other programs such as jokes, games, network utilities, and sometimes even the trojan removal program itself! Trojans are often used to distribute backdoor programs without the victims being aware that they are being installed. Backdoors operate in a client-server architecture and allow the intruder to have complete control of a victim's computer remotely over the network. They give an intruder access to just about every function of the computer, including logging keystrokes, activating the Webcam, logging passwords, and uploading and downloading files. They even have password protection and encryption features for intruders to protect the computers that they own! There are hundreds, maybe even thousands, of trojan programs circulating the Internet, usually with many variations of the code, making their detection with antivirus software very difficult.

In this section we will use Scan2.log, which was provided by the Honeynet Research Alliance as part of the Honeynet Project Scan of the Month challenge. Scan2.log is located on the accompanying CD-ROM in the /captures directory. We will also use our own lab-created backdoor packet captures, called subseven_log and netbus_log, also located on the accompanying CD-ROM in the /captures directory.

# SubSeven Legend

SubSeven is one of the most common Windows backdoor trojans. It is an older program, and most virus software can detect it, but there are many variations of it floating around the Internet. SubSeven is smart enough to notify the intruder, via

Internet Relay Chat (IRC), e-mail, or some other method, that the victim's computer is online. It runs over a TCP connection with a default port of 27374, although this port is configurable. SubSeven has numerous features that allow the intruder to completely control the victim's computer.

Figure 7.6 shows a packet capture of a SubSeven Legend client-server interaction. SubSeven Legend is the anniversary edition of SubSeven. The intruder is running the client on 192.168.1.1, which is connected to the server on the victim's computer at 192.168.1.200. You will notice that the server is running on the default port 27374 and that data is being pushed between the client and server.

**Figure 7.6** SubSeven Legend Backdoor Trojan

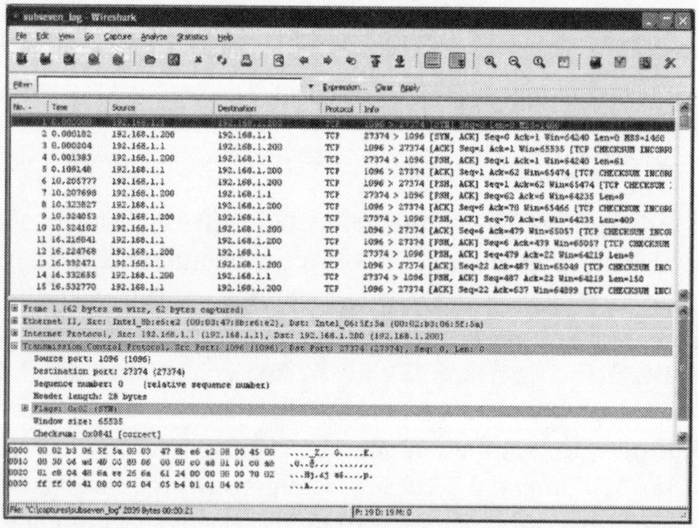

Using the Follow TCP Stream feature of Wireshark will show what is going on between the SubSeven server and client. Figure 7.7 shows the connection day and time and the version of the SubSeven server. Next, it shows that the intruder performed a directory listing of C:\ and downloaded the file secret.txt. However, the data for this file is obscured.

# NetBus

The NetBus backdoor trojan is also one of the older and more common Windows backdoor trojans. It is easily detectable using antivirus software, but like SubSeven, many variations exist. It runs over a TCP connection with default ports of 12345 and 12346, but it also is configurable. Like SubSeven it has numerous features that allow the intruder to completely control the victim's computer.

**Figure 7.7** SubSeven Client-Server Interaction

Figure 7.8 shows a packet capture of a NetBus client–server interaction. The intruder is running the client on 192.168.1.1, which is connected to the server on the victim's computer at 192.168.1.200. You will notice that the server is running on the default ports 12345 and 12346 and that data is being pushed between the client and server. The two separate source ports indicate two distinct TCP connections.

**Figure 7.8** NetBus Backdoor Trojan

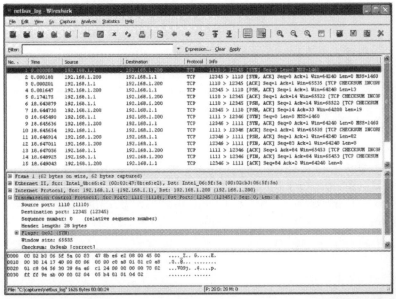

Using the Follow TCP Stream feature of Wireshark will show what is going on between the NetBus server with the port 12345 and the client. Figure 7.9 shows the version of the NetBus server and also indicates that the intruder downloaded the file C:\temp\secret.txt. Figure 7.10 shows the client revealing the contents of the downloaded file! This data means that not only the intruder but also anyone else on the line with a sniffer can read the contents of the file as it is transmitted.

**Figure 7.9** NetBus Client-Server Interaction

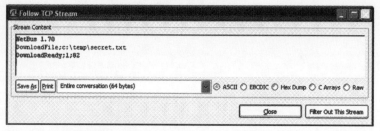

**Figure 7.10** NetBus Client-Server Content

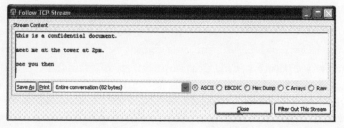

# RST.b

RST.b is a less widely used backdoor access trojan that affects various Linux platforms. The backdoor listens in promiscuous mode for User Datagram Protocol (UDP) packets to any port. To access the backdoor, the intruder sends a UDP packet containing the payload "DOM."

Figure 7.11 shows a packet capture of an intruder scanning for systems infected with the RST.b trojan. We filtered on UDP to focus on the last nine UDP packets. The intruder uses different source IP addresses and random destination ports to prevent IDSes from detecting the scan. Because the RST.b trojan listens in promiscuous mode, it will respond to UDP packets containing the "DOM" payload on any port.

**Figure 7.11** RST.b Backdoor Scan

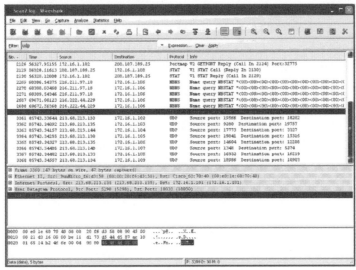

## Notes from the Underground…

### Trojan, Virus, and Worm: What's the Difference?

Many people get confused over the difference between a virus, a worm, and a trojan. The terms tend to be used interchangeably, but they are really three very distinct entities. Each uses different ways to infect computers, and each has different motivations behind its use.

A virus is a program that can infect files by attaching to them, or replacing them, without the user's knowledge. A virus can execute itself and replicate itself to other files within the system, often by attaching itself to executable files, known as host files. Viruses travel from computer to computer when users transmit infected files or share storage media, such as a floppy disk. Viruses may be benign or malicious. A benign virus does not have any destructive behavior; it presents more of an annoying or inconvenient behavior, such as displaying messages on the computer at certain times. A benign virus still consumes valuable memory, CPU time, and disk space. Malignant viruses are the most dangerous because they can cause widespread damage, such as altering software and data, removing files, or erasing the entire system. However, no viruses can physically damage your computer hardware. There are several types of viruses, including the following:

- **File infector** A virus that attaches to an executable file
- **Boot sector** A virus that places code in the disk sector of a computer so that it is executed every time the computer is booted

Continued

www.syngress.com

- **Master boot record** A virus that infects the first physical sector of all disks

- **Multi-partite** A virus that will use a number of infection methods

- **Macro** A virus that attaches itself to documents in the form of macros

A trojan is a program that is covertly hiding another potentially malicious program. The trojan is often created to appear as something fun or beneficial, such as a game or helpful utility. However, when a user executes the program, the hidden malicious program is also executed without the user's knowledge. The malicious program is then running in memory and could be controlling backdoor access for the intruder or destroying system files or data. A trojan could also contain a virus or a worm. Trojans do not replicate or propagate themselves; they are often spread by unknowing users who open an e-mail attachment to execute a file downloaded from the Internet.

A worm is a program much like a virus that has the added functionality of being able to replicate itself without the use of a host file. With a worm, you don't have to receive an infected file or use an infected floppy to become infected; the worm does this all on its own. A worm actively replicates itself and propagates itself throughout computer networks. A worm will consume not only valuable system resources but also network bandwidth while it is propagating or attempting to propagate.

# Dissecting Worms

Throughout the past few years we have seen an increase in not only worm activity but also the severity of worm attacks on systems and networks. Internet worms are becoming faster, smarter, and stealthier. Most worms attack vulnerabilities in software for which patches have been readily available for quite some time before the exploit appeared. Complex worms that can exploit several vulnerabilities and propagate in a number of different ways are beginning to emerge, making reverse engineering and defending against the worm more difficult. This section will explore three well-known worms: SQL Slammer, Code Red, and Ramen.

# SQL Slammer Worm

The SQL Slammer worm began propagating on the Internet on January 25, 2003. It exploits a vulnerability in the Resolution Service of Microsoft SQL Server 2000 and Microsoft Desktop Engine (MSDE) 2000. It is also known as the W32.Slammer worm, Sapphire worm, and W32.SQLExp.Worm. Known as the fastest-spreading worm, it infected most vulnerable systems within 10 minutes. As the worm propagated and compromised more systems, the Internet showed significant signs of degradation.

The SQL Slammer worm exploits a stack buffer overflow vulnerability that allows for the execution of arbitrary code. Once a system is compromised, the worm will attempt to propagate itself by sending 376-byte packets to randomly chosen IP addresses on UDP port 1434. All vulnerable systems that are discovered will become infected and also begin to scan for more vulnerable systems. With this type of exponential growth, it is no wonder that the worm spread so fast! This type of propagation leads to many other problems, including performance issues, crashed systems, and denial of service. Details on the SQL Slammer worm, including the patch, instructions on applying ingress and egress filtering, and recovery from a compromised system, can be found in the CERT Advisory at www.cert.org/advisories/CA-2003-04.html.

The Scan3.log file, provided by the Honeynet Research Alliance as part of the Honeynet Project Scan of the Month challenge, shows evidence of the SQL Slammer worm attempting propagation. Scan3.log is located on the accompanying CD-ROM in the /captures directory. After you open the packet capture in Wireshark, apply the UDP filter with destination port 1434, and you will see the Slammer scan traffic, as shown in Figure 7.12. You will notice that there are 55 packets from random source addresses that are sending a UDP packet to port 1434. The UDP packet also has a length of 384 bytes, which is the 376 bytes of data plus the 8-byte header. All the packets are incoming to the target 172.16.134.191, and none are going out—an indication that the system is not compromised but rather just the target of the randomly generated IP addresses on other compromised systems. You will also notice that each of the packets contains data, and although it is a

**Figure 7.12** SQL Slammer Propagation Attempt

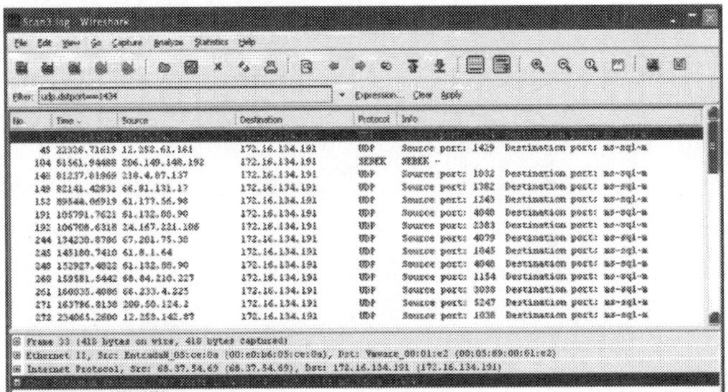

bit scrambled, you can make out the various parts of the exploit code such as ws2_32.dll, kerne32.dll, GetTickCount, socket, and send to.

## Notes from the Underground...

### Why Did Slammer Spread So Fast?

SQL Slammer has been the fastest-spreading worm to date. A detailed analysis of the spread of the SQL Slammer worm can be found at www.caida.org/analysis/security/sapphire. Several key attributes of the worm enabled it to spread at such an alarming rate:

- **Random scanning** The random scanning of the worm allowed for initial exponential growth.

- **Simple and fast scanner** The worm could scan as fast as the compromised computer could transmit packets or the network could deliver them.

- **Small size** The SQL Slammer worm was only 376 bytes.

- **UDP** The use of a single UDP packet allowed for efficient propagation because the connection does not have to wait for a response.

The propagation of the Slammer worm caused worldwide disruption in approximately 10 minutes. Fast-spreading Internet worms are a significant milestone in computer security and a reality that should be met with all available countermeasures.

## Code Red Worm

The Code Red worm was originally discovered on July 13, 2001, and since then, many variants, including Code Red II and III, have emerged. The worm infects Microsoft Windows NT, 2000, and beta versions of XP that are running ISS 4.0 and 5.0 Web servers. It exploited a vulnerability, which was discovered on June 18, 2001, by eEye Digital Security[1]. Code Red exploits a known buffer overflow vulnerability in the ISS Indexing services IDQ.DLL file. Details on the Code Red worm, including the patches, workarounds, and recovery from a compromised system, can be found in the CERT advisory CA-2001-13 [2] and CVE-2001-0500 [3].

A system infected with the Code Red worm attempts to connect to randomly generated IP addresses on port 80. If the worm discovers a Web server on the target system, it then tries to exploit the IIS buffer flow vulnerability by sending a specially crafted Hypertext Transfer Protocol (HTTP) GET request. If successful, the worm creates 100 threads of itself on the infected system. The first 99 threads are used to spread the worm, while the 100th thread is used to deface the Web. If the newly infected Web server is a U.S. English Windows NT/2000 system, the worm defaces all pages on the Web site with the message "HELLO!Welcome to www.worm.com! Hacked By Chinese!" Next, the worm performs a DOS attack on 198.137.240.91, which is the U.S. White House Web site.

The IP addresses of the target systems the worm attempts to infect are randomly generated. However, in the first version of this worm, the seed of the random number generator is a constant, resulting in all infected computers generating the same list of IP addresses to infect. Thus, the same group of infected systems is re-infected by other newly infected systems. Consequently, much network traffic is generated, resulting in an unintended DOS attack.

The first version of the worm was not as destructive as the second version of the worm. The analysis presented here is for the first version of the Code Red Worm. Both capture files, CodeRed_Stage1 and CodeRed_Stage2, are located in the /captures directory on the accompanying CD-ROM.

# Code Red Details

The Code Red worm operates in three stages, which are time sensitive: propagation, denial of service, and sleep. Although there are many variations, the general pattern of behavior is as follows:

- **Propagation mode** This stage takes place during the first 19 days of the month. An infected system will randomly generate IP addresses and attempt to connect to them on HTTP port 80. If a system is discovered and is vulnerable, the exploit code will be sent via an HTTP GET request and the Web page of the server will be defaced. The original worm defaced Web pages by displaying "HELLO! Welcome to www.worm.com! Hacked By Chinese!" However, some new variations will not deface the Web page. The worm places a file called C:\notworm on the system to signal that it has been infected. This way, if the system gets infected again, the worm will go into an infinite sleep state. If the c:\notworm file does not exist, this is the first time this system has been infected, and it will create new threads to continue the propagation scanning. This propagation activity will continue until the 20th day of the month.

- **Denial-of-service mode** This stage begins on the 20th day of the month and lasts until the 27th day. In this stage, the worm will attempt to packet-flood a specific IP address that is designated in the code by sending large amounts of data to the target's HTTP port 80. The first target was originally the White House Website at 198.137.240.91. By directing the flood to the IP address instead of the DNS host name, it was easy for whitehouse.gov system administrators to change the IP, thus making the flood ineffective.

- **Sleep mode** This stage causes the worm to enter a sleep state from the 28th day of the month until the end of the month. It will remain in memory, but it will not be active until the cycle repeats on the first day of the month.

## Code Red Capture Overview

The CodeRed_Stage1 capture (see Figure 7.13) shows the Code Red exploit and propagation in action. The Code Red capture files were provided by L. Christopher Paul and can also be downloaded from www.bofh.sh/CodeRed. This capture was lab generated to show the various Code Red stages, so time stamps may not reflect the proper dates for the various stages. The worm spreads from the system (192.168.1.1) and infects the vulnerable target (192.168.1.105). The newly compromised system then begins scanning random IP addresses for open HTTP port 80. A definite give-away in this capture is frame number 4, "GET /default.ida?NNNNNNNNN…", which is the exploit for Code Red. The random HTTP port 80 scanning beginning at frame number 12 should also alert you to something strange: this isn't typical Web surfing because none of the targets are responding.

Figure 7.14 shows the "Follow TCP Stream" output of the initial exploit. Notice the exploit in the HTTP GET request at the beginning, as well as the checking of the C:\notworm file and Web page defacement at the end.

**Figure 7.13** Code Red Stage 1 – Infection and Propagation

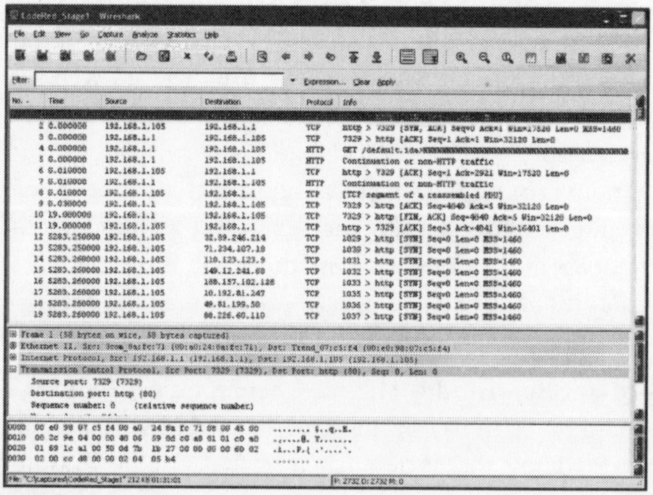

**Figure 7.14** Code Red Exploit Output

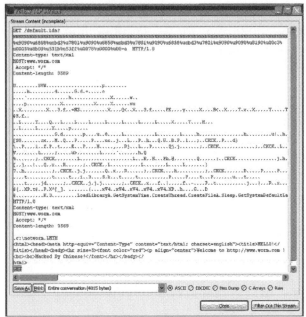

The CodeRed_Stage2 capture (see Figure 7.15) shows the denial-of-service mode of the worm. The infected server, 192.168.1.105, is attempting to flood the White House Web server at 198.137.240.91. Because this attack was performed in a lab environment, however, the actual denial of service was not accomplished.

**Figure 7.15** Code Red Stage 2: Denial of Service

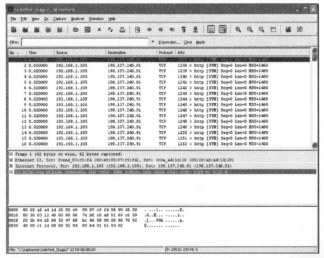

You can change the format for viewing the time stamps under the View → Time Display Format menu option.

## Detailed CodeRed_Stage1 Capture Analysis

CodeRed_Stage1 involves three systems:

- **192.168.1.1** This is the infected system that successfully attacks another server (192.168.1.105) on the network.

- **192.168.1.105** This system becomes infected by 192.168.1.1 and launches the worm propagation attack against random IP addresses.

- **192.168.1.222** This is another system on the local network. The first frame arrives at 17:51:57 of July 21, 2001. The last frame arrives at 19:22:59 of July 21, 2001.

- **Frame 1** The infected system at 192.168.1.1 sends a SYN packet to 192.168.1.105. The packet is directed to port 80 of the destination system and is from a high port 7329 of the infected system. The TTL value of the system at 192.168.1.1 is 64.

- **Frame 2** The system at 192.168.1.105, which is running a Web server at port 80, replies back with a SYN-ACK packet to the infected system. The time delay between the packets is zero because this was a lab experiment. The system 192.168.1.105 has a TTL value of 128.

- **Frame 3** The three-way handshake is completed. The computer increases its window size.

- **Frame 4** The attack starts with the worm source at 192.168.1.1, sending a crafted long GET request. The attack is on the buffer overflow vulnerability in the ida.dll of 192.168.1.105. The signature pattern of the Code Red worm is seen here. Thus, at 17:51:57 on Jul 21 2001, the successful attack began on 192.168.1.105.

- **Frames 5 to 11** The exploit code is sent from the worm source to the newly infected system. In Frame 7, the details of the HTML page, with which the Web site is defaced, can be seen. Frame 8 is where the newly infected system sends a GET packet back to the source system that infected it.

- **Frames 12 onward** The system at 192.168.1.105 has been surely infected as it attempts a series of connections to port 80 on random IP addresses. The connections are initiated from higher numbered ports in the range of 1029 to1140. Though the infected system uses port numbers that are sequentially increasing, at points there are sudden jumps in the port numbers, as shown in Table 7.1. Note the long delay between frames 11 and 12.

- **Frame 111** This frame is the last frame that has a clearly sequentially increasing port number.

- **Frame 112** This is a special point in the capture. There is a relatively huge time gap of 2.81 seconds from the time the previous packet was sent and this packet. The source port is now 1105 and is not the next number in the arithmetical progression. The time delay can be explained and is expected behavior. Frame number 112 is the 101st attempt to connect to a random IP address. After having sent the 100th packet, the worm, checks whether to branch into the Web page defacement routine. This check results in the relatively large delay. Each of the 100 destination IP addresses is now being sent a second, and then a third, TCP SYN packet. So there are three attempts to connect to port 80 on each IP address. Frame 112 is actually a retry of frame 80, and frame 212 is the third retry.

- **Frame 113 onwards** The infected host continues to retry each target system on port 80.

- **Frame 312** This is an incoming frame that came after 9.12 seconds had passed since the 100th packet was sent. The infected system's Web service is accessed by another system at 192.168.1.222, which seeks a Web page through the GET command. The packet trace does not contain all the data that was transmitted.

- **Frame 313, 314, 315, 316** In Frame 313, the infected system returns an HTTP 200 code (success) to the system at 192.168.1.222. In Frame 314, the system at 192.168.1.222 sends a GET request. In frame 315, the infected Web server returns an HTTP 304 message. The packet traces do not contain all the data that was transmitted and thus all the details of the traffic are not known.

- **Frame 317 onwards** From this frame onward, the infected computer again continues to try to infect other systems. This time, there is a new set of 100 random IP addresses. The source ports from which the packets are sent again become sequential starting from 1141. Remember, we left off at 1140 with the previous scan. Again, there are discrepancies in the sequence now and then because the numbers are not strictly in arithmetical progression, and sometimes the port numbers increase by 2. The infected system makes three attempts to connect to each new 100 IP address. Frame 417 marks the beginning of the second pass, and frame 517 marks the beginning of the third pass.

- **Frame 617 onward** From this frame onward, the infected computer again continues to try to infect a new batch of 100 systems. The source port resumes at 1253, after leaving off at 1252 in frame 416.

- **Frame 917 onward** From this frame onward, the infected computer again continues to try to infect a new batch of 100 systems. After leaving off at 1363 in frame 716, the source port resumes at 1364.

- **Frame 1218 onward** From this frame onward, the infected computer again continues to try to infect a new batch of 100 systems. After leaving off at 1471 in frame 1016, the source port resumes at 1472. Looking at the pattern, you may notice that this sequence is off by 1 frame. It should have started a new scan at frame 1217. However, another packet slipped into the traffic. Frame 1217 shows an RST packet that was sent from 192.168.1.222 to the infected system. This packet closed the connection that we saw in frames 312 to 316.

- **Frame 1518 onward** From this frame onward, the infected computer again continues to try to infect a new batch of 100 systems. After leaving off at 1585 in frame 1317, the source port resumes at 1586.

- **Frame 1818 onward** From this frame onward, the infected computer again continues to try to infect a new batch of 100 systems. After leaving off at 1695 in frame 1617, the source port resumes at 1696.

- **Frame 2133 onward** From this frame onward, the infected computer again continues to try to infect a new batch of 100 systems. After leaving off at 1807 in frame 1917, the source port resumes at 1808. According to the previous sequence, this new scan should have started at frame 2118; however, there is another connection and exchange of HTTP traffic between the system 192.168.1.122 and the infected system in frames 1918 through 1928, as we saw previously. It is still unknown what the exchange is actually doing because the entire contents of the packets were not captured. There is also a FIN/ACK packet sent from 192.168.1.1 to the infected system in frame 2129 and the associated ARP request and reply in frames 2130 and 2131.

- **Frame 2433 onward** From this frame onward, the infected computer again continues to try to infect a new batch of 100 systems. After leaving off at 1919 in frame 2232, the source port resumes at 1920. This is the last propagation attempt, and the scanning (and the capture file) ends at frame 2732.

There are some interesting patterns in the numbers associated with the worm. One interesting pattern is in the port numbers used by the infected system, as shown in Table 7.1.

**Table 7.1** Pattern in Source Port Numbers in Frames 12 to 112

| Frame Number | Port Number | Frame Number | Port Number |
|---|---|---|---|
| 12 | 1029 | 53-57 | Sequentially Increases |
| 13 | 1030 | 58 | Jumps by 2 to 1081 |
| 14-16 | Sequentially Increases | 58-63 | Sequentially Increases |
| 17 | Jumps by 2 to 1035 | 64 | Jumps by 2 to 1088 |
| 17-22 | Sequentially Increases | 64-75 | Sequentially Increases |
| 23 | Jumps by 2 to 1042 | 76 | Jumps by 2 to 1101 |
| 23-34 | Sequentially Increases | 76-87 | Sequentially Increases |
| 35 | Jumps by 2 to 1055 | 88 | Jumps by 2 to 1114 |
| 35-46 | Sequentially Increases | 88-93 | Sequentially Increases |
| 47 | Jumps by 2 to 1068 | 94 | Jumps by 2 to 1121 |
| 47-52 | Sequentially Increases | 94-97 | Sequentially Increases |
| 53 | Jumps by 2 to 1075 | 98 | Jumps by 3 to 1127 |
| | | 98-111 | Sequentially Increases |
| | | 112 | Resets to 1105 |

Another pattern is in the time flow. After the 100th frame there is always a delay since the worm begins retrying the connection attempts to the 100 random IP addresses or attempting to scan a new set of random 100 IP addresses. Table 7.2 provides the frame numbers of the 101st packet being sent at various points in the flow and the time delay between sending the 100th and 101st frames. Across different sets of 100 packets there is also a pattern, which can be approximated as 3-, 6-, and 12-second delays. Thus, the approximate pattern of 3-6-12 second delays can be seen running through the Delay column of Table 7.2. The shorter delays are when the same IP addresses are scanned for the second and third time. The longest delay is when the scanning begins on a new set of 100 random IP addresses.

**NOTE**

To search for all frames that were sent, for example, three seconds after their preceding frame, use the **Edit → Find Packet** search feature.

Choose **string** and search for **"Time delta from previous packet: 3"** in **packet details**. This will search for frames with 3.x.x delay. You must continue to choose **Find Next** (Ctrl-N) to locate all matching packets. Before this step, ensure that the **View → Time Display Format** is selected to be **Seconds Since Previous Packet**. You may also use the **frame.time_delta** filter to search for various time deltas.

**Table 7.2** Delay between the 100th and 101st Frames

| Frame Number of 101st packet | Delay (Seconds) | Frame Number of 101st packet | Delay (Seconds) |
| --- | --- | --- | --- |
| 112 | 2.81 | 1418 | 5.81 |
| 212 | 5.9 | 1518 | 11.92 |
| 317 | 2.66 | 1618 | 2.69 |
| 417 | 2.77 | 1718 | 5.71 |
| 517 | 5.8 | 1818 | 11.82 |
| 617 | 11.9 | 1918 | 2.03 |
| 717 | 2.77 | 2029 | 5.71 |
| 817 | 5.8 | 2133 | 11.48 |
| 917 | 11.91 | 2233 | 2.69 |
| 1017 | 2.79 | 2333 | 5.71 |
| 1117 | 5.8 | 2433 | 11.83 |
| 1218 | 5.75 | 2533 | 2.5 |
| 1318 | 2.78 | 2633 | 5.51 |

Viewing the packet capture source port information also reveals interesting patterns. To understand the source ports better, click on the **Info** column in the Packet List frame. This will sort the frames according to the **Info** field, which by default contains the source port first. This sort will show the lowest source port to highest source port in sequential order. You can see the lowest and highest source port numbers used and the pattern of three attempts to each port. Table 7.3 represents the frames and source port sequence numbers. The pattern represented goes on similarly for the rest of the packets.

**Figure 7.3** Source port patterns

| Packet Number | Frame Number | Source Port Range | |
|---|---|---|---|
| | | **In approximate sequence** | **Not in sequence** |
| 0 | 12 | 1029-1140 | |
| 100 | 111 | | |
| 0 | 112 | | 1029-1140 |
| 100 | 211 | | |
| 0 | 212 | | 1029-1140 |
| 100 | 311 | | |
| 0 | 317 | 1141-1252 | |
| 100 | 416 | | |
| 0 | 417 | | 1141-1252 |
| 100 | 516 | | |
| 0 | 517 | | 1141-1252 |
| 100 | 616 | | |
| 0 | 617 | 1253-1363 | |
| 100 | 716 | | |
| 0 | 717 | | 1253-1363 |
| 100 | 816 | | |
| 0 | 817 | | 1253-1363 |
| 100 | 916 | | |

# Detailed CodeRed_Stage2 Capture Analysis

This packet capture file covers the second stage of the Code Red worm's activity. In this stage the worm attempts a denial-of-service attack against the IP address 198.137.240.91, which was reportedly the IP address of the White House Web site and is now registered to the Executive Office of the President of the United States.

In this capture file the infected system packet floods SYN packets to the IP address 198.137.240.91. The capture file contains 299 frames. The infected system starts sending the packets from port 1237 and sequentially increases the port number to 1335 in frame 99. There is a relatively large delay between sending the 99th and the 100th packet and between the 199th and the 200th frames. This is when the worm restarts the synflood a second and third time. You may verify this by applying the tcp.srcport filter and searching on the various source ports. Each should occur three times.

We would like to thank Deapesh Misra for contributing this detailed, frame-by-frame analysis and insightful pattern detection.

# References

[1] eEye Digital security Advisory al 20010717
http://www.eeye.com/html/research/advisories/AL20010717.html
[2] Cert advisory CA-2001-13. http://www.cert.org/advisories/CA-2001-13.html
[3] CVE-2001-0500. http://cve.mitre.org/cgi-bin/cvename.cgi?name=CAN-2001-0500

# Ramen Worm

The Ramen worm is a collection of tools that can exploit several known vulnerabilities and can self-propagate. The original CERT Incident Note, posted on January 18, 2001, can be found at www.cert.org/incident_notes/IN-2001-01.html. Ramen targets Red Hat Linux 6.2 and Red Hat Linux 7.0 servers with vulnerable versions of the following:

- **wu–ftpd** This program runs on TCP port 21, and vulnerable versions contain a format string input validation error in the site_exec() function.

- **rpc.statd** This program runs on UDP port 111, and vulnerable versions contain format string input validation errors in the syslog() function.

- **Lprng** This program runs on TCP port 515, and vulnerable versions contain format string input validation errors in the syslog() function.

Once a host is compromised, the Ramen tools are copied into a directory called /usr/src/.poop. They are started and controlled by a series of shell scripts. Some of the important characteristics of the Ramen worm include the following:

- The Web page is defaced by replacing the index.HTML file. The new Web page consists of the phrase "Hackers loooooooooooooooooove noodles" and a picture of a package of Ramen noodles.

- E-mail is sent to gb31337@yahoo.com and gb31337@hotmail.com with the text "Eat Your Ramen!"

- The tcpwrappers access control list (ACL) is disabled by removing the /etc/hosts.deny file.

- The file /usr/src/.poop/myip contains the IP address of the local system.

- The file /etc/rc.d/rc.sysinit is modified to include a startup script that initiates scanning and exploitation.

- A new program called *asp* is added, which creates a listener on TCP port 27374. This port is used to send the ramen.tgz toolkit file to other compromised systems. SubSeven also uses this port. Coincidence? It is unclear why the author would want to use an already well-known port because most IDSes should have been configured to alert activity on that port.

- The user names *ftp* and *anonymous* are added to /etc/ftpusers to disable anonymous FTP (File Transfer Protocol). By disabling anonymous FTP, this part of the worm code is actually fixing the vulnerability that it used to exploit the system!

- The rpd.statd and rpc.rstatd services are terminated, and the /sbin/rpc.statd and /usr/sbin/rpc.statd files are deleted. However, there is no service called rpc.rstatd.

- The lpd service is terminated and the /usr/sbin/lpd system file is deleted.

Once the system has been modified, the Ramen worm begins scanning and exploiting the vulnerable systems that it finds. The worm generates random class B IP addresses to scan. It will then send packets with the SYN and FIN flags set and with a source and destination port of 21. Once a vulnerable system is compromised, the following actions occur:

- The /usr/src/.poop directory is created on the victim.

- The ramen.tgz toolkit is copied to the new directory and to the /tmp directory. The /tmp directory is where the toolkit is stored so that it can be copied out to new vulnerable systems.

- The ramen.tgz toolkit is unarchived in the /usr/src/.poop directory, and the initial shell script is started. The system is now fully compromised and will begin scanning for new vulnerable systems.

The ramenattack.gz packet capture was downloaded from www.ouah.org/ramenworm.htm. Here, you will find a very detailed analysis of the Ramen worm by Max Vision, called "Ramen Internet Worm Analysis" as well as the ramen.tgz source code. The ramen attack.gz capture file is also located on the accompanying CD-ROM in the /captures directory. Wireshark will automatically uncompress the file when you open it.

We will step through the various parts of the packet capture to show how the Ramen worm works.

1. In Figure 7.16, the infected system 192.168.0.23 is performing a SYN/FIN scan on the 10.0.0.0/24 Class B network. It receives a SYN/ACK from the target system at 10.0.0.23.

**Figure 7.16** Ramen Work Propagation Scanning

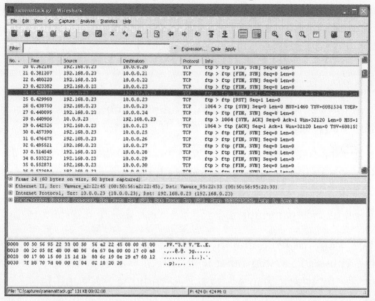

2. Next, in packet 26, the worm connects to the system to grab the FTP banner and determine if the system is a Red Hat 6.2 or 7.0 server. The banner that the Red Hat 6.2 server returns is as follows:

```
220 test2.whitehats.com FTP server (Version wu-2.6.0(1) Mon Feb 28
10:30:36 EST 2000) ready.
221 You could at least say goodbye.
```

3. Next, the wu-ftp and rpc.statd exploits are launched against the potential target. The wu-ftp attempt begins at packet 137 and is unsuccessful, but the rpc.statd exploit succeeds. Figure 7.17 shows the payload of the rpc.statd exploit. Notice the padding of "90 90 90 90…" and the trailing "/bin/sh" that will execute a command shell. You will also notice in packet 289 that once the SYN/FIN scan is finished scanning the target 10.0.0.0/24 range, it sends a SYN/FIN packet to 10.9.9.9 from port 31337. This represents the packet that is sent to www.microsoft.de when the scan is complete. Because the worm was activated and analyzed in a lab environment, 10.9.9.9 was chosen to represent www.microsoft.de.

**Figure 7.17** Ramen Worm rpc.statd Exploit

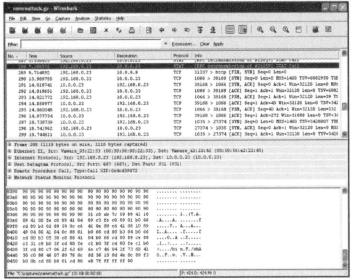

4. You will also notice in packet 290 that a connection is made with the port 39168 on the target system. The rpc.statd exploit created a backdoor on the victim's computer on this port, and it is now used to initiate the transfer of the worm and execute it. It also sends an e-mail to accounts at Hotmail and Yahoo. The output from this transfer is shown in Figure 7.18.

**Figure 7.18** Ramen Worm Execution

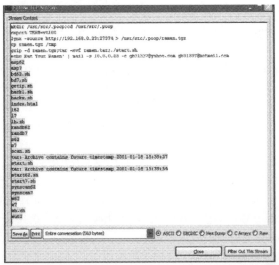

5.  The last connection you will see, beginning in packet 297 in Figure 7.17, is the actual transfer of the Ramen toolkit that was initiated in previous script. The new compromised system connects back to the attacker at port 27374 to download a copy of the worm.

6.  The worm is now executing on the victim and will begin scanning for new vulnerable hosts.

Overall, the Ramen worm is easy to detect, especially since it uses a well-known trojan port for the worm transfer. It contains unexplained and inefficient code and makes no attempt to be stealthy. There are also several places where its functionality could be optimized. However, this worm exploits several different vulnerabilities and self-propagates, so you should be on the lookout for more versions of this worm.

**NOTE**

A day-zero attack is an exploit on a vulnerability that is not yet known about and for which there is no patch.

# Active Response

Both the Snort Intrusion Detection System (IDS) and the Netfilter firewall in the Linux kernel offer the ability to send TCP RST packets to forcibly close TCP sessions. These RST packets are generated in response to a rule match on specific criteria such as malicious application layer data within one of the TCP packets in an established TCP stream. However, the mechanisms used by Snort and Netfilter to build RST packets are quite distinct, resulting in RST packets that also exhibit many differences under Wireshark's gaze. An attacker may also be able to analyze these variations to identify the type of active response solution you are using. This real-world packet capture examines the RST packets that emanate from the flexresp and flexresp2 detection plugins in Snort, as well as from the REJECT target in Netfilter, after detecting a simplistic client attempt to view the /etc/passwd file through a Web server (note that we are dissecting a response technology here as opposed to presenting a new exploit). In all of the following examples we execute the command *echo "/etc/passwd" | nc webserver 80* to put the string /etc/passwd within a TCP session with a Web server (with hostname "webserver"). The Wireshark screen shots display the resulting RST packets from Snort and from the Netfilter REJECT target.

> **NOTE**
>
> Netfilter is a kernel level packet filtering framework that offers application layer inspection with its string match extension. It is located at www.netfilter.org.

Because Netfilter is specific to the Linux kernel, the TCP RST packets generated by the Netfilter REJECT target can come from only a Linux system. Snort has been ported to many platforms, so there is no such restriction on RST packets sent by the flexresp or flexresp2 detection plugins.

First, we examine the RST packet that the flexresp plugin in Snort sends when we try to view the /etc/passwd file from a Web server. To accomplish this, we need to add a basic rule to Snort that interfaces with the flexresp plugin to send an RST. Note the use of the resp keyword with an argument of rst_all, which instructs Snort to send RST packets to both the client and server sides of the TCP connection:

```
alert tcp any any -> any 80 (msg:"WEB /etc/passwd attempt";
content:"/etc/passwd"; sid:100226; rev:1; resp:rst_all;)
```

Upon sending the string /etc/passwd across a TCP session with a Web server and capturing the traffic, we see the RST packet in Wireshark as shown in Figure 7.19. Notice that the RST packet exhibits several characteristics, including a Time To Live (TTL) of 81 in the IP header. Both the RST and ACK flags are set, and the TCP Window value is set to zero. The flexresp plugin sets the TTL value randomly between 64 and 255, but always sets the TCP Window value to zero (these details can be verified by examining the file snort-2.6.0/src/detection-plugins/sp_respond.c in the Snort-2.6.0 sources).

**Figure 7.19** Flexresp RST Packet

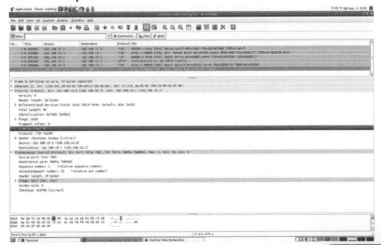

The flexresp2 plugin uses a different strategy to close a TCP connection by blasting several RST packets with slightly different sequence and acknowledgment numbers in an attempt to throw a connection into an unusable state. The syntax for the resp keyword is slightly different for the flexresp2 plugin than for the flexresp plugin. The reset_both argument again instructs Snort to send a RST packet to both sides of the TCP connection:

```
alert tcp any any -> any 80 (msg:"WEB /etc/passwd attempt";
content:"/etc/passwd"; sid:100226; rev:1; resp:reset_both;)
```

Figure 7.20 shows the flexresp2 plugin in action. In this case, we see that five RST packets have been sent back to the client (these have been spoofed by Snort as though the server generated them). With the exception of the TCP sequence and acknowledgment numbers, each of these packets is identical with the TTL value set at 128, both the RST and ACK flags are set, the TCP Window size is 184 (scaled). The flexresp2 plugin calculates the TTL and TCP Window sizes based on the values of the packet that matches the Snort rule. For more information, see the file snort-2.6.0/src/detection-plugins/sp_respond2.c in the Snort-2.6.0 sources).

**Figure 7.20** Flexresp2 RST Packet

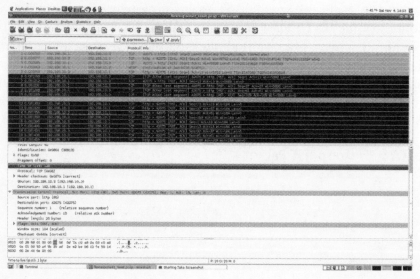

Finally, we examine an RST packet that is generated by the Netfilter REJECT target from within the Linux kernel. To have Netfilter send an RST when our Web client tries to grab the /etc/passwd file, we execute the following iptables command on the Web server:

```
# iptables -I INPUT 1 -p tcp --dport 80 -m string --string "/etc/passwd" --
algo bm -j REJECT --reject-with tcp-reset
```

Now, when we connect to the Web server and attempt to view the /etc/passwd file, the RST packet looks like the one shown in Figure 7.21. This time, there is only one RST packet so the REJECT target is similar to the flexresp plugin. However, one significant difference (not displayed here because the packet trace is captured on the client system) is that the REJECT target can generate the RST packet only to the source IP address of the packet that matches the string match rule; it cannot also send an RST packet to the destination IP address (in this case the server IP). Initially, this would seem to be a fairly severe limitation because the client system could simply filter the incoming RST packet before it hits the local TCP stack so that the connection would not be shut down (Netfilter on the client side could be used to accomplish this). However, the Netfilter REJECT target also drops the matching packet (in this case the packet that contains the /etc/passwd string) so that the TCP connection would never progress beyond the point where /etc/passwd is sent because the server would never receive it. The ability to drop the packet stems from the fact the Netfilter is a firewall and is therefore by definition inline to network traffic. Snort cannot drop packets unless it is deployed in inline mode.

**Figure 7.21** Netfilter REJECT target RST Packet

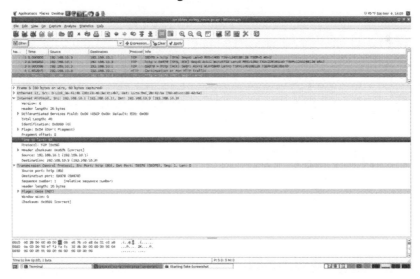

Finally, the TCP Window size is set to zero, and although the TTL value here is 64, all versions of the Linux kernel before 2.6.16 used the value 255. These values are assigned within the REJECT sources located in the file linux/net/ipv4/net-filter/ipt_REJECT.c in the Linux kernel sources.

This real-world packet capture was contributed by Mike Rash. We thank him for his keen insight and expert analysis.

# Summary

Analyzing real-world packet captures is both a science and an art. A high-traffic network segment can present the analyzer with thousands of packets containing hundreds of connections, sessions, and protocols. Wireshark's built-in features, such as TCP session reconstruction, display filters, and packet colorization, help simplify the process of analyzing data. However, as with honing any skill, you must practice, practice, practice. Constantly analyzing network data will help you quickly assess what is normal and what is unusual behavior. If you don't have the ability to analyze your own network traffic data, participate in the Honeynet Project Scan of the Month challenge. These challenges cover network traffic analysis, as well as malicious code, exploits, and methodology.

You should also become familiar with reading and interpreting hexadecimal output. This experience will come in handy when you are analyzing day-zero attacks, and you may have to implement your own custom signature. Intrusion detection systems often match a signature on the content of a packet in hexadecimal format.

In this chapter we presented several different types of packet captures and the processes used to analyze the data. You should have an understanding of the types of activity to look for in a packet capture and how to identify various types of network traffic. Combining this skill with the network troubleshooting methodology presented in Chapter 2 will help you to detect, analyze, and respond quickly to the next major worm outbreak.

# Solutions Fast Track

## Scanning

- ☑ Network scanning is used to detect open ports and services on systems.
- ☑ A TCP Connect scan completes the TCP three-way handshake and is easily logged and detected.
- ☑ SYN scans were once used as stealthy scanning techniques; however, most firewalls and IDSes can now detect these types of scans.

☑ XMAS scans are ineffective against Microsoft operating systems because they will respond with an RST from all ports, even if they are open.

☑ A Null scan sends packets with all flags turned off. Closed ports will respond with an RST/ACK, and open ports will just drop the packet.

# Remote Access Trojans

☑ Remote access backdoor programs are often delivered to unsuspecting users within a trojan program.

☑ Remote access backdoors operate in a client-server architecture, allowing the intruder complete control over the compromised system.

☑ SubSeven can notify the intruder—via IRC, e-mail, or some other method—that the victim's computer is online.

☑ NetBus is an older Windows backdoor trojan that is easily detected by antivirus software, but like SubSeven, many variations exist.

☑ The RST.b trojan listens in promiscuous mode and will respond to UDP packets containing the "DOM" payload on any port.

# Dissecting Worms

☑ Internet worms are becoming increasingly fast and complex.

☑ The SQL Slammer worm uses UDP to accomplish its fast propagation.

☑ The original Code Red worm operated in three stages: propagation, denial of service, and sleep.

☑ The Ramen worm is a collection of tools that can exploit several known vulnerabilities in the wu-ftpd, rpc.statd, and lprng utilities.

# Active Response

☑ Both Snort and Netfilter perform active response by terminating a TCP session with a TCP RST.

☑ An attacker may be able to identify the active response solution based on the characteristics in the TCP RST packets.

☑ TCP RST packets from Snort flexresp, Snort flexresp2, and Netfilter are each very distinct.

# Frequently Asked Questions

The following Frequently Asked Questions, answered by the authors of this book, are designed to both measure your understanding of the concepts presented in this chapter and to assist you with real-life implementation of these concepts. To have your questions about this chapter answered by the author, browse to **www.syngress.com/solutions** and click on the **"Ask the Author"** form.

**Q:** Why is it that when I right-click on some of my packets, the "Follow TCP Stream" option is grayed out?

**A:** The underlying protocol that you are trying to reconstruct does not use TCP for its connection method. It may use the connectionless UDP method for its transmission.

**Q:** Can I use Wireshark to discover a trojan that is being sent to someone on my network?

**A:** No, Wireshark can be used to discover only the active use of the backdoor access program that the trojan installs. To Wireshark or any network analyzer, the transmission of the trojan will appear to be a regular executable file.

**Q:** Can I use Wireshark to discover a virus that is being sent to someone on my network?

**A:** No, like a trojan, the transmission of a virus will look like a regular executable or some other type of file. Wireshark will not be able to tell that the file is infected.

**Q:** Are there network activities that will falsely resemble network scan attacks?

**A:** Yes, there are lots of activities that will resemble network scans. A client program that is automatically searching for a server at startup may continue to send TCP SYN packets to the target address. Often multiple and rapid TCP connections that are associated with FTP and HTTP downloads also resemble network scan attacks and trigger alarms.

# Chapter 8

# Developing Wireshark

## Solutions in this chapter:

- **Prerequisites for Developing Wireshark**
- **Wireshark Design**
- **Developing a Dissector**
- **Running a Dissector**
- **Advanced Topics**

☑ **Summary**

☑ **Solutions Fast Track**

☑ **Frequently Asked Questions**

# Introduction

Because Wireshark is open-source code software that is distributed under the General Public License (GPL), many developers throughout the world are able to contribute to the Wireshark project. This collaboration by many different individuals has made Wireshark a viable tool for many organizations.

Wireshark developers have contributed new features to the growing number of tools in the Wireshark distribution, including the console-based version of Wireshark named, Tshark, as well as a number of other tools that are part of the Wireshark distribution.

The main Wireshark application is a Graphical User Interface (GUI) application that utilizes components of GNU's Not UNIX (GNU) Image Manipulation Program (GIMP). The latest version of the GIMP Toolkit is called GTK+, and is maintained as a separate entity at www.gtk.org. Wireshark uses the GTK library for its GUI implementation, and new features often require modifications to the GUI (e.g., new menu items or modifications to existing menu selections). The core of this application includes the main window, menus, utility functions, and so forth.

The components of Wireshark that dissect packet structures are called *protocol dissectors*. These components are individual source code modules that instruct the main Wireshark application on how to dissect a specific type of protocol. The dissector can be complex or simple, based on the protocol that is being dissected. Most of the contributions to the Wireshark project are either new dissectors or enhancements to existing ones.

By utilizing the concepts within this chapter, you will learn the basic steps to become a contributor to the Wireshark project. Many users and developers worldwide will benefit from your efforts and welcome your contribution.

---

## Notes from the Underground…

### Development Note

Because of the wide range of development on the Wireshark project, there may already be work in progress on a specific feature or protocol dissector. The Wireshark developer mailing list (wireshark-dev@wireshark.org) is a good way to stay abreast of any work being done in a specific area. Questions can also be posted to the *wireshark-dev* mailing list, or you can consult the Wireshark Web site for more information at www.wireshark.org.

# Prerequisites for Developing Wireshark

The first step in the development process is to acquire the Wireshark source code. You can download many different distributions from the Wireshark Web site, such as the currently released source code or the last nightly backup of the source code. You can also utilize the Subversion (SVN) repository to keep up to date throughout the development process. SVN is the most risky compared to released versions of Wireshark, because with SVN you are compiling code that hasn't been fully tested. Generally, however, the SVN code is of high quality.

If you have an issue with the current SVN code, you can usually get a member of the Wireshark mailing list (wireshark-dev@wireshark.org) to help resolve the issue. SVN gives you access to code changes as they are checked into the master build. It is the most up-to-date, but can contain unidentified bugs. Keep in mind that the SVN distribution is routinely updated; you might develop code using the current SVN code base and then find out that a specific function you are working with has changed. Instructions for utilizing the latest builds and the SVN repository can be found at www.wireshark.org.

Before you can add to or modify Wireshark, you must be able to build the application from source code. To build from source code, you need additional libraries and tools. Wireshark is a multi-platform application (i.e., runs on many different operating systems); you need to be able to successfully build on the particular operating system that you will be developing on.

It is important to understand that Wireshark was developed and built using a number of different programming languages, including many Uniplexed Information and Computing System (UNIX)-based programs and shell scripts (e.g., several modules within Wireshark are written in Python and Perl). Although it may not be necessary for you to be proficient in each programming language, you might find times where you need to understand just enough of the language to make a simple change. A majority of the code base for Wireshark is American National Standards Institute (ANSI)-C. The requirement for ANSI-C is due to the portability of the code to multiple operating system platforms. When writing in C, special care must be taken to use only those functions that are defined as ANSI-C and are portable. You should be able to use most C compilers with the Wireshark source code, including GNU C Compiler (GCC) on Linux and Microsoft Visual C++ on Windows.

> ### Damage & Defense
>
> ## Portability
>
> Before starting any work, read the Portability section 1.1.1 of the *README.developer* document contained in the *.doc* directory of the source code distribution. The word *portability* is used in reference to the steps a developer should take to ensure that Wireshark source code can be compiled on all of the supported operating systems (e.g., you don't want to use a function that only exists on a win32 platform). This would cause the Wireshark source code to not compile or build correctly on the other supported operating systems. *Porting* is when a program is written to one operating system platform and then made to run on a different platform.

# Skills

To build a new dissector or modify the main application, you must be able to program in C. However, keep in mind that modifications to existing dissectors may also require that you be knowledgeable in another language.

Modifications to the Wireshark GUI requires some knowledge of GTK. To obtain online and downloadable tutorials for programming in GTK, go to www.gtk.org.

Contributions to the Wireshark project come from many different levels of developers. Some are novices while others are experts. However, the overall Wireshark project is maintained by a single group of highly experienced developers. New contributions are reviewed by this group and then, following any necessary changes, incorporated into the source code distribution. In some cases, the individual reviewing the changes may make a recommendation for a specific change; in other cases, the individual may actually make the changes.

# Tools/Libraries

In most cases, you need the developer kit for access to the necessary libraries. A developer kit is different from a normal binary distribution. Generally, the developer package includes the compiled binaries for the operating system it was built for (e.g., because Wireshark utilizes the GTK libraries for its GUI implementation, you must have the developer kit for GTK). You also need to download the correct developer kit for the operating system that you are going to develop on. If possible, use the latest released version of the developer kit. Although you might be able to build Wireshark with an older set of libraries, the results might not be as expected. However, in some cases, this might not be an option. Some operating systems only support certain versions of support libraries. In general, you can consult the Wireshark developer mailing list or the developer section of the www.wireshark.org Web site.

The Win32 ports of the required libraries are not necessarily located at their respective project sites (e.g., the win32 port for the promiscuous capture library (libpcap) is called WinPcap). The Web page anonsvn.wireshark.org/wireshark-win32-libs/trunk/packages/ contains most of what you need, but if you want to build with an additional library package that is not listed on the Wireshark site, refer to the respective organization's Web page to locate the correct Win32 ports.

When building Wireshark, you need the GTK library and the General Language for Instrument Behavior (GLIB) library. Wireshark can be built using either the older GTK v1.2, v1.3 or the newer GTK v2.*x* versions. The newer v2.*x* version adds more font control and has a better look and feel; it can be downloaded from www.gtk.org. The "Installation" section of this book identifies some of these issues when installing on Solaris and Red Hat distributions.

The console version of Wireshark, called Tshark, only requires the GLIB libraries. If you are just building the Tshark application, you do not need GTK.

If you are going to build with packet capture support in Wireshark or Tshark, you need to have the libpcap libraries found at www.tcpdump.org. Without packet capture support, users of the compiled program can only view packet trace files; they will not be able to perform new packet captures. Win32 developers need the WinPcap libraries, which can be downloaded from winpcap.polito.it/.

UNIX/Linux operating systems detect installed libraries using the *automake* process, which identifies the library packages that can be included when building Wireshark. Additionally, you can enable/disable optional library components during the configure process. For example:

```
mylinuxbox:/home/user1/wireshark $ ./autogen.sh
mylinuxbox:/home/user1/wireshark $ ./configure –without-net-snmp –with-ucd-snmp –with-ssl
```

On Win32-based computers, the *config.nmake* file should be modified to define what libraries you want to include in the build process. These libraries are added to the final binary during the linker process of the build. On Windows, the developer kits are required to build the Wireshark binaries. However, if you decide to build a binary distribution package, the normal support library binary packages are also required, because the Win32 binary distribution copies the dynamically linked libraries (DLLs) to the */Program Files/Wireshark* directory for use when the application is executed.

The following is a list of the libraries needed to build Wireshark. Remember that you need to download the developer kit to acquire the necessary libraries for your operating system. Some packages are optional and can be linked to add additional features.

The following library packages are required when building the Wireshark binaries:

- **glib** Low-level core library for GTK.

- **gettext** GNU language conversion.

- **libiconv** Character set conversion library.

- **GTK** GIMP toolkit for creating Wireshark.

The following library packages are optional and can be linked to provide multiple features. On UNIX/Linux use the **–with** and **–without** command-line switches with the configure process. On Win32, comment and uncomment the respective lines in the *config.nmake* file.

- **libpcap** Packet capture library for UNIX/Linux-based operating systems (UNIX/Linux).

- **WinPcap** Packet capture library for Win32-based operating systems (Win32).

- **ADNS GNU** Advanced Domain Name Server (ADNS) client library. Adds DNS lookup support (All).

- **GNUTLS TLS** Library for decryption of Secure Sockets Layer (SSL) and other encrypted protocols (All).

- **libgcrypt** Cryptographic libraries for decryption of encrypted packets (All)

- **GTK_Wimp** GTK theme for Windows. Adds Windows XP-type look and feel to Wireshark (Win32).

- **Lua** A powerful lightweight programming language library. Enables Lua scripting support (All). www.lua.org

- **net-snmp** Simple Network Management Protocol (SNMP) library. Adds SNMP Management Information Base (MIB) support (ALL).

- **ucd-snmp** Alternative SNMP library for UNIX/Linux operating systems (UNIX/Linux).

- **nettle** A low-level encryption library. Adds Kerberos decryption support (All).

- **Perl Compatible Regular Expressions (PCRE) Library** Adds Perl regular expression filters (All).

- **zlib** File compression library. Adds compressed file support (All).

If you are building with GTK version 1.2 or 1.3, no additional libraries are needed. Otherwise, when building with GTK 2.*x,* you need the following additional libraries:

- **atk**  Accessibility toolkit (All).
- **pango**  Internalization of text (All).

Windows users must choose to either attempt to build from within cygwin using GCC, or with a Win32-based compiler such as Microsoft's Visual C++ (MSVC++). Windows users must also download a number of additional libraries. The default location specified in the Wireshark distribution for the libraries on a Win32 workstation is *C:\wireshark-win32-libs.* Download and extract each required library to this location. Wireshark's scripts will then locate the libraries at build time. Otherwise, you will have to modify the *config.nmake* file located in the main distribution directory to point to the correct location for each library.

## Notes from the Underground...

### Win32 Development Note

Most, if not all, of the necessary Win32 development packages have been placed in the Wireshark repository. Win32 developers can execute a switch with *nmake* to download these packages automatically.

```
nmake -f Makefile.nmake setup
```

The nmake process will download and extract the necessary library packages as configured in the config.nmake file in the root directory of the distribution. The directory \wireshark-win32-libs will be created on the local boot drive if it doesn't exist. Once a package has been downloaded and decompressed, the original compressed file is removed from the system. If all configured libraries can be downloaded and installed a message will be displayed to indicate that wireshark is ready to build.

In order for this option to work with *nmake*, Win32 developers must make sure that they have Cygwin, the Wireshark source code, and the appropriate C compiler installed. Refer to the Wireshark wiki site at wiki.wireshark.org for more information.

Each tool is specific to the operating system it runs on. The Wireshark compile and build process utilizes script files that require a number of tools to run successfully.

Most of the tools have roots in the UNIX/Linux operating systems. To compile and build Wireshark on non-UNIX-based operating systems, you need to have access to similar tools.

Windows users need to install Cygwin, which is a Linux-like environment for Windows-based computers. It gives both a Linux Application Program Interface (API) emulator and a set of Linux-based tools. These tools allow the scripts utilized by Wireshark during the build process to work on Windows-based computers. Cygwin can be downloaded and installed from www.cygwin.com.

Windows users must use Python, the native Windows package can be downloaded and installed from www.python.org. But Python from the Cygwin distribution can be used and is the preferred method based on the comments in the config.nmake configuration file.

Most UNIX and Linux-based operating systems include a C compiler and many of the required tools needed to build Wireshark.

The following is a list of the tools needed to compile and build Wireshark:

- **Cygwin** Provides UNIX/Linux tools for Win32 developers. This is not needed for UNIX/Linux.

- **Perl** Needed for all operating systems.

- **pod2man** Part of Perl.

- **pod2html** Part of Perl.

- **Python** Needed for all operating systems.

- **Flex** Needed for all operating systems.

- **Bison** Needed for all operating systems.

- **Nullsoft Scriptable Install System (NSIS) (Win32 only)** This optional package allows developers to build Win32 distribution packages. You do not need this tool on Win32 if you do not plan on building a distribution package.

- **Doxygen** Optional tool for all operating systems. Builds off-line documentation.

- **Hand-held Computer (HHC)** Win32 only. Adds compressed Windows-based Help files (*.chm*)

## Tools & Traps…

### Building on UNIX- and Linux-based Operating Systems

Detailed instructions for building the Wireshark binary code from source code are included in the *.install* file located in the main source directory. Chapter 3 of this book also outlines the build process on Red Hat Linux.

It is important to understand the implications of building binary Red Hat Package Manager (RPM) packages for distribution to a diverse user base (e.g., when building with a feature such as SSL decryption). You should require your user base to have the required library components installed prior to the installation of your new Wireshark RPM. The SSL decryption libraries that are required for SSL decryption support are part of the *gnutls* and *gcrypt* library packages. Unless you are running the same version of UNIX/Linux as your development system, you may find it difficult to locate the correct dependency packages. When building an RPM to be distributed to a wide range of users, you may choose to limit the feature set of Wireshark to the basic functionality.

### Building on Windows-based Operating Systems

Detailed instructions for building the Wireshark binaries from source code are included in the *README.win32* file located in the main source code directory. This file includes instructions for building on both MSVC++ and cygwin. It is also important to use the **cmd.exe** command (not **command.com**) when attempting to build Wireshark. The **cmd.exe** command provides many file-naming conventions, whereas the older **command.com** is limited to 8.3 file-naming conventions. Wireshark's source code contains many file-naming conventions and is not supported with **command.com**.

Windows users may need to update or change the default environment variables in order for their compiler to locate additional support libraries (e.g., when building Wireshark, the wiretap source code must include header files for Windows Sockets (winsock) support. It is important that the build process can locate the correct "include" files. Validate that the following user environment variables are defined correctly:

- Include
- Lib

It's also important to make sure that cygwin is located in the user-path environment variable in order to locate the necessary cygwin executables during the build process. These executables are the Windows equivalent of UNIX/Linux binaries (e.g., **bison.exe** is the equivalent of its UNIX/Linux counterpart **bison**.

**Continued**

> If you are developing with MSVC++ and need to change the environ-ment to include the cygwin paths, make sure that you always append the path to the end. Otherwise, during the compile or link process, you may retrieve a cygwin-based include or library component instead of the desired MSVC++ component.

# Other Developer Resources

The Wireshark Web site hosts several different pages to assist in the development process. They include a bug database (Bugzilla) at bugs.wireshark.org/bugzilla, a wiki section for developer comments, information, and details at wiki.wireshark.org, and a Wish List page located on the Wireshark wiki at wiki.wireshark.org/WishList. These online resources can be utilized by developers for additional information.

Bugzilla is the online bug report database. Any Wireshark user can submit a bug report, which should contain the following information.

- Copy and paste the version information from the Wireshark's "about" box.

```
Version 0.99.4 (SVN 20061028081818)

Copyright 1998-2006 Gerald Combs <gerald@wireshark.org> and contributors.
This is free software; see the source for copying conditions. There is NO
warranty; not even for MERCHANTABILITY or FITNESS FOR A PARTICULAR PURPOSE.

Compiled with GTK+ 2.6.8, with GLib 2.6.5, with WinPcap (version unknown),
with libz 1.2.3, with libpcre 6.3, with Net-SNMP 5.2.1.2, with ADNS,
without Lua.

Running with WinPcap version 3.1 (packet.dll version 3, 1, 0, 27), based on
libpcap version 0.9[.x] on Windows XP S, build 2600.
```

- Describe the bug in as much detail as possible.
- Include steps to duplicate the bug.
- Attach any screenshots, sample packet traces, and so on.

# The Wireshark Wiki

The wiki page contains a lot of information, including user and developer resources, protocol information, and developer notes. The Developer Guide and the User

Guide are also located on the Wireshark wiki. This site should be reviewed if you have any questions about a specific feature or resource.

# The Wireshark Wish List

The Wireshark Wish List is a list of the top feature requests made by users and developers, and is a good place to go to when beginning the Wireshark development process.

# The Wireshark Mailing List

In addition to the newer resources for developers and users, the Wireshark mailing lists are your lifeline to the Wireshark community. If you can't find the information you need from the documentation included in the Wireshark distribution or the online resources, you can subscribe to the wireshark-dev mailing list and submit questions, patches, and so forth.

# Wireshark Design

The Wireshark source code distribution includes a main source code directory and several subdirectories. The main source code directory contains the following important source code files:

- *autogen.sh* Wireshark configuration script for UNIX/Linux autogen utility.
- *config.nmake* Instructs Wireshark where to locate libraries during the build with *nmake* on Win32.
- *Makefile.nmake* The instructions for *nmake* to build the Wireshark binaries on Win32.
- *Makefile.am* Automake configuration file for UNIX/Linux.
- *Makefile.common* Common *makefile* definitions for both *make* and *nmake*.
- *cleanbld.bat* Removes some generated files so that the build system is not confused when switching between UNIX and Win32 builds in the same tree.
- *configure* File for UNIX/Linux build and install.
- *INSTALL* UNIX/Linux installation instructions.
- *make-xxx* Script files to build support modules.

- **README.xxx** Associated *readme* files for multiple platforms.

- **tap-xxx** Protocol TAPs.

- **xxxx** Remaining files contain utility functions for Wireshark's Tshark.

In Figure 8.1, you can see a breakdown of the directories contained in the Wireshark distribution.

**Figure 8.1** Main Directory

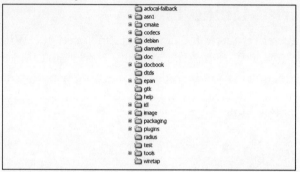

## .svn

The hidden *.svn* directory contains configuration information for the SVN client.

## aclocal-fallback and autom4te.cache

The *aclocal-fallback* and *aclocal-missing* directories are used to store the information used by automake on UNIX/Linux-based systems.

## ASN1 Directory

If a protocol has an ASN1 specification, the "asn2wrs" utility that is shipped with Wireshark allows developers to create a dissector based on the actual specification. The associated files are stored in the *ASN1* directory. To use the asn2wrs compiler you must have the following four input files:

- ASN1 protocol specification

- *xxx.cnf* configuration

- *packet-xxx-template.h*

- *packet-xxx-template.c*

For details and examples of each type of required file, consult the Wireshark wiki site at .wiki.wireshark.org.

# *Debian* Directory

The *Debian* directory is used for compatibility with Debian Linux-based operating systems. These files are not located under packaging, because the Debian tools require that the *Debian* directory be at the top-level directory of a source code package.

# *Diameter* Directory

This directory contains the eXtensible Markup Language (XML) protocol specification files for the diameter protocol dissector.

# *doc* Directory

Contained within the *doc* directory are text documents to assist you in the development process. They are:

- **README.*binarytrees*** Provides information for utilizing binary trees within a protocol dissector.

- **README.*capture*** Provides information on the capture interface to XML/Packet Capture (*pcap*) libraries.

- **README.*design*** Provides some useful information on the core structure of Wireshark.

- **README.*developer*** The main document to assist in the development of new protocol dissectors. Also included are helpful design pointers, a sample template, and potential problems.

- **README.*idl2wrs*** Refer to this document when you want to build a dissector from an IDL file.

- **README.*malloc*** Outlines the new memory management API of Wireshark.

- **README.*packaging*** Gives information on the redistribution of Wireshark.

- **README.*plug-ins*** Documentation for utilizing the plug-in interface of Wireshark.

- **README.*regression*** Steps for testing and regressing new dissectors. This file provides a template that you can use to test for regressions in packet decodes. The file is structured as a *makefile* that can be utilized after modifying the core Wireshark code or a dissector to ensure that Wireshark operates correctly.

- **README.stats_tree** The stats tree is a generic GUI that gives developers the ability to add specific Terminal Access Controller (TAC) information to their protocol dissectors without having to learn GTK or programming in the Wireshark GUI. This document outlines the process of using the stats tree.

- **README.tapping** Detailed information on the tapping system built into Wireshark.

- **README.xml-output** Tshark provides a mechanism to output data in XML/Packet Details Markup Language (PDML) format. This document outlines what this capability provides.

- **xxx.html** A number of html files are also included in the *doc* directory. These files are the basic manual pages for each standalone binary included in the Wireshark distribution.

# DocBook

The Wireshark user's guide and developer's guide are included in the Wireshark source code, to allow developers to add these files to their distribution. To utilize the DocBook features, you have to install the DocBook application within cygwin (on win32). Refer to the *README.txt* file in this directory for more information.

# dtds Definition

This directory contains the Document Type Definition (DTD) files used by the XML dissector. The XML dissector uses these files to dissect specific XML data that is being transported by Hypertext Transfer Protocol (HTTP), Session Initiation Protocol (SIP), and other protocols. For information on the structure of the DTD files, refer to the XML section of the Wireshark wiki.

# *epan* Directory

The *Ethernet Protocol Analyzer (EPAN)* directory contains the protocol dissectors and most of the utility and global functions used within dissectors. The subdirectory *dfilter* contains source code for display filter functionality. Dissectors contains all of the non-plug-in protocol dissectors. The *ftypes* subdirectory contains source code that defines the different data types that are utilized in the data type logic (see Figure 8.2).

**Figure 8.2** *EPAN* Directory

# *gtk* Directory

Contained within the *gtk* directory are the source code files for the main Wireshark application, which includes the main GUI as well as the menu, toolbar, conversations statistics, endpoints statistics, and so on. Basically, the Wireshark source code needed to access the GUI resides within this directory.

# *gtk2.tmp* Directory

When building with GTK+ 2.x, the *make* process creates the *gtk2.tmp* directory. It copies the *gtk* directory source code files and then compiles them. These files should not be edited, because they will be deleted/refreshed the next time a build is performed. The modification of files should be done in the *gtk* directory.

# *Help* Directory

The *Help* directory holds the source code files that are used to build the content for the Help menu dialogs. These are built during compile time and linked to the Wireshark binary file.

# *IDL* Directory

The *IDL* directory contains the IDL definitions for protocol dissectors developed using the *idl2wrs* application. For more information, consult the Wireshark wiki.

# *Image* Directory

The icons and bitmaps linked to the Wireshark binary are stored in the *image* directory (see Figure 8.3). The custom icons are stored in the toolbar subdirectory and are in X PixMap (XPM) format. The XPM file format is used to create icons and bitmaps for X-Windows-based operating systems.

**Figure 8.3** *Image* Directory

# *Packaging* Directory

The *packaging* directory contains the necessary scripts and files to generate a binary distribution (see Figure 8.4). Currently supported distributions include the Nullsoft Scriptable Installation System (NSIS) to generate a Windows installation package, or the RPM and System V Release 4 (SVR4) to generate Linux and UNIX installation packages.

**Figure 8.4** *Packaging* Directory

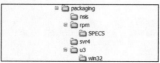

# Plug-ins

A number of dissectors have been written to interface with Wireshark through the plug-in interface (see Figure 8.5). For detailed information on how to create a plug-in, refer to the *README.plugins* document in the *doc* directory.

**Figure 8.5 Plug-ins Interface**

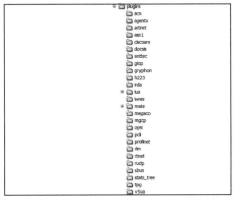

# *Radius* Directory

Located in the *radius* directory are the dictionary files that define the different vendor specifications for the Radius dissector. Please refer to the Wireshark wiki for more information.

# *Test* Directory

The *test* directory is a combination of scripts that are used to test the command line interface of the Tshark applications.

# *Tools* Directory

Wireshark's source code distribution contains several tools in the *tools* directory. The *WiresharkXML.py* file is a Python script used to read Tshark-generated PDML files. The *lemon* directory contains the *Lemon* tool, which generates C source code files based on a supplied template (see Figure 8.6). Lemon is a parser generator for C and C++ that does the same job as Bison and Yet Another Compiler-Compiler (Yacc); however, Lemon provides more flexibility and does a better job of eliminating common errors. It also runs much faster than the other tools and is reentrant and thread-safe.

**Figure 8.6** *Lemon* Directory

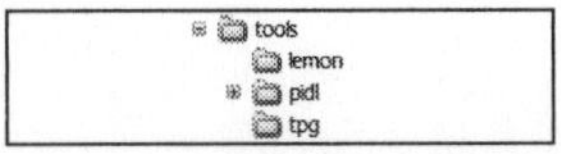

## *Wiretap* Directory

The *wiretap* directory is the core capture file support library, which provides the support to read and write different capture file formats. For information on how to add or modify the capture file types supported by Wireshark, refer to the *README.developer* document located in the *wiretap* directory.

# Developing a Dissector

A protocol dissector is commonly written in C, although there are components of Wireshark that build C source code from Python scripts, IDL files, and Perl scripts. These files are named after the protocol they dissect (e.g., a protocol dissector for a protocol called *myprot* would be named *packet-myprot.c*). These files are located off of the main source code directory in the *EPAN/dissectors* directory . Some dissectors have been implemented as plug-ins. The advantage of a plug-in is that it does not require a complete recompile of the whole Wireshark source code during development. However, even a plug-in starts out as a *packet-xxx.c* source code file. This section discusses the necessary steps for creating a standard *packet-xxx.c* dissector.

## Notes from the Underground…

### Before You Start

Before you start work on your dissector, open the *README.developer* file in the *doc* directory. Cut and paste the sample template, which provides enough of a skeleton to get you started.

## Tools & Traps...

### Source Code Editor Considerations

It is important that your editor save files in the proper format. Wireshark source code is composed of UNIX-style files. The source code file should not contain lines that end in carriage return, line feeds (CR/LF). Lines of text should be terminated only by the line feed character. If you are programming on non-UNIX-based computers, you need to make sure that your editor supplies the correct end-of-line formatting. Otherwise, you will have to reformat the source code files prior to submitting them back to the *wireshark-dev* mailing list.

# Step 1 Copy the Template

There are several steps that must be completed in order to integrate a new dissector into Wireshark. The first step is the comments, as seen in the following code. Remember that Wireshark is open-source code, so the main comment identifies not only that you created the dissector, but also includes information on the original contributor of Wireshark and the GPL.

```
/* packet-PROTOABBREV.c
 * Routines for PROTONAME dissection
 * Copyright 2000, YOUR_NAME <YOUR_EMAIL_ADDRESS>
 *
 * $Id: README.developer,v 1.86 2003/11/14 19:20:24 guy Exp $
 *
 * Wireshark - Network traffic analyzer
 * By Gerald Combs <gerald@wireshark.org>
 * Copyright 1998 Gerald Combs
 *
 * Copied from WHATEVER_FILE_YOU_USED (where "WHATEVER_FILE_YOU_USED"
 * is a dissector file; if you just copied this from README.developer,
 * don't bother with the "Copied from" - you don't even need to put
 * in a "Copied from" if you copied an existing dissector, especially
 * if the bulk of the code in the new dissector is your code)
 *
 * This program is free software; you can redistribute it and/or
 * modify it under the terms of the GNU General Public License
```

```
* as published by the Free Software Foundation; either version 2
* of the License, or (at your option) any later version.
*
* This program is distributed in the hope that it will be useful,
* but WITHOUT ANY WARRANTY; without even the implied warranty of
* MERCHANTABILITY or FITNESS FOR A PARTICULAR PURPOSE. See the
* GNU General Public License for more details.
*
* You should have received a copy of the GNU General Public License
* along with this program; if not, write to the Free Software
* Foundation, Inc., 59 Temple Place - Suite 330, Boston, MA 02111-1307, USA.
*/
```

When working with the template, you need to replace certain text with your information. For example, for line 1, you would replace *packet-PROTOABBREV.c* with *packet-myprot.c*. Change line 2 (PROTONAME) to indicate the protocol your dissector is meant to decode. Line 3 should be modified with the copyright date, your name, and your e-mail address. Note that since Wireshark is open-source code, this is your claim to ownership of the submitted code. This doesn't keep other developers from modifying your code, but it limits other people from taking ownership of your work. Once you contribute your code to the Wireshark project, it becomes part of the GPL and you are added to the growing list of Wireshark contributors. Line 5 of the comment is important to the SVN system, as it identifies the current file intrusion detection (ID) and revision. This line is modified when source code is checked in and out of the SVN system; make sure you do not remove this line. Finally, line 11 should be modified to document the source code of your information used to build the dissector. If this information is not available or cannot be disclosed, this section can be omitted. The rest of the comments should remain intact to reflect the original author (Gerald Combs) and the GPL information.

# Step 2 Define the Includes

As seen in the following code, the next portion of the template defines the includes for this source code program. Includes are needed for global functions that this dissector calls. Wireshark defines a number of global functions that can be used within your protocol dissector. You may need to include standard header files from your compiler or standard library (e.g., *string.h* is a standard header file for string functions).

```
#ifdef HAVE_CONFIG_H
# include "config.h"
#endif
```

```
#include <stdio.h>
#include <stdlib.h>
#include <string.h>

#include <glib.h>

#ifdef NEED_SNPRINTF_H
# include "snprintf.h"
#endif

#include <epan/packet.h>
#include "packet-PROTOABBREV.h"
```

Output variables are set or passed to the C pre-processor to determine specific includes that may be needed to perform the build under specific conditions (e.g., the *HAVE_CONFIG_H* include is only processed by *make* if this value is true). On Linux-based operating systems, *autoconf* generates output variables that may define additional output variables based on the build environment. Please refer to www.gnu.org/software/autoconf for more information.

## Notes from the Underground…

### Global Functions

Wireshark includes a large number of functions that can be used within your protocol dissector. To use these functions, you must include the header file for the source code that contains the defined function. One of the hardest parts in utilizing the global functions provided by Wireshark is identifying those available for use. Say that you have an Internet Protocol (IP) address that you want to display. You could manually format a display string or you could use the built-in global function. But where is the global function? The following list displays some of the most common includes that define the global functions that might be needed by your dissector:

- *prefs.h* Structure and functions for manipulating system preferences.
- *reassemble.h* Structure and functions for reassembly of packet fragments.
- *tap.h* Functions for utilizing the built-in TAP interface.

**Continued**

- *epan/column-utils* Functions for manipulating the Summary window column data.

- *epan/conversation.h* Functions for tracking conversations (Request to Reply).

- *epan/int-64bit.h* Functions for manipulating 64-bit integers.

- *epan/plugins.h* Functions for plug-in support.

- *epan/resolve.h* Functions for resolving addresses to names.

- *epan/strutil.h* Common string functions.

- *epan/to_str.h* Functions for string conversion.

- *epan/tvbuff.h* Testy Virtual Buffer (*tvbuff*). A method used by dissectors to access packet data.

- *epan/value_string.h* Functions to locate strings based on numeric values.

The following structures may contain information important for your dissector.

- *epan/column-info.h* Structure of Summary window column data.

- *epan/framedata.h* Structure of frame data.

- *epan/packet-info.h* Structure of packet information.

- *epan/expert.h* Structure and functions to call the expert TAP.

There are many more functions and structures defined in the Wireshark source code. In some cases, you will need to research available functions by analyzing other *packet-xxx.c* dissectors. Most of the utility functions you will need are located in the epan directory.

## Damage & Defense

### Static Functions

It is strongly recommended that the functions you create within your dissector be declared *static*. This will limit their scope to the current dissector and not conflict with any other functions that may be defined in another dissector or program. For example, if you create a function called *dissect_my_protocol*, you should create a function prototype as:

```
static void dissect_my_protocol();
```

**Continued**

How does Wireshark know how to call your protocol dissector if the functions are declared static? Part of the build process includes a Python script, which processes each defined protocol dissector. During this process, the required functions are automatically registered with the main Wireshark application. In the next step, we look further into the registration of a protocol dissector.

# Step 3 Create the Function to Register

This step in the development of a protocol dissector is to create the function to register your dissector with Wireshark.

```
/* Register the protocol with Wireshark

/* this format is required because a script is used to build the C function
   that calls all the protocol registration.
*/

void
proto_register_PROTOABBREV(void)
{

/* Setup list of header fields  See Section 1.6.1 for details */
     static hf_register_info hf[] = {
          { &hf_PROTOABBREV_FIELDABBREV,
              { "FIELDNAME",                 "PROTOABBREV.FIELDABBREV",
                FIELDTYPE, FIELDBASE, FIELDCONVERT, BITMASK,
                "FIELDDESCR" }
          },
     };

/* Setup protocol subtree array */
     static gint *ett[] = {
          &ett_PROTOABBREV,
     };

/* Register the protocol name and description */
     proto_PROTOABBREV = proto_register_protocol("PROTONAME",
          "PROTOSHORTNAME", "PROTOABBREV");
```

```
/* Required function calls to register the header fields and subtree used */
    proto_register_field_array(proto_PROTOABBREV, hf, array_length(hf));
    proto_register_subtree_array(ett, array_length(ett));
```

It is important that the *proto_register_xxx* function is left-justified, as shown in the template. The scripts used to register protocol dissectors are *make-reg-dotc* and *make-reg-dotc.py*. These scripts parse all of the *packet-xxx* files to build a list of all dissectors to be registered with the Wireshark engine. If this function does not meet the proper syntax requirements, the scripts will fail to register your new dissector. The file that is generated by the scripts is called *register.c* and is located in the *epan/dissectors* directory. This file should not be edited manually, because it is recreated each time you compile and build Wireshark.

The first part of the *proto_register_myprot* function sets up the *hf* array fields of the dissection. Although these are not required for packet dissection, they are recommended to take advantage of the full-featured display filter capabilities of Wireshark. Each item that is defined within the *hf* array will be an individual item that can be filtered within Wireshark (e.g., *ip.src* is an element within the *packet-ip* dissector). You can enter a display filter of *ip.src==10.10.0.1*. If the *ip.src* element was not defined, this would be an invalid filter.

```
{ &hf_ip_src,
{ "Source", "ip.src", FT_IPv4, BASE_NONE, NULL, 0x0,
    "", HFILL }},
```

## Tools & Traps...

### *hf* Element Items

For a detailed description of each component of an element within the *hf* array, refer to the *README.developer* document located in the *doc* directory.

The next part of the registration process is to define the array for the subtree called *ett*. The *ett* variables keep track of the state of the tree branch in the GUI protocol tree (e.g., whether the tree branch is open [expanded] or closed). The protocol is registered with both short and long naming conventions with Wireshark by calling the *proto_register_protocol* function (this causes the protocol to be displayed in the Enabled Protocols window). The final step is to register the *hf* and *ett* arrays with the *proto_register_field_arry* and the *proto_register_subtree_array*.

How would Wireshark know when to pass the data stream from a specific type of packet to this new dissector? Wireshark requires that each dissector instructs Wireshark when it should be called. For example, suppose you are writing a dissector to decode packets that are being transported on top of Transmission Control Protocol (TCP) with a port of 250. You need to instruct Wireshark to pass all packets that meet this criteria to your new dissector.

# Step 4 Instruct Wireshark

```
void
proto_reg_handoff_PROTOABBREV(void)
{
    dissector_handle_t PROTOABBREV_handle;

    PROTOABBREV_handle = create_dissector_handle(dissect_PROTOABBREV,
        proto_PROTOABBREV);
    dissector_add("PARENT_SUBFIELD", ID_VALUE, PROTOABBREV_handle);
```

The *proto_reg_handoff_xxx* function is used to instruct Wireshark on when to call your dissector. The *create_dissector_handle* function passes the function that Wireshark will call to dissect the packets and the *proto_xxx* value that was registered as the protocol in the *proto_register_protocol* function. The *dissector_add* function allows you to specify the criteria that will trigger Wireshark to pass the packet to your dissector. The *PARENT_SUBFIELD* function allows you to specify the element within the parent dissector that you will trigger off of (e.g., for TCP port 250, you would set this value to *tcp.port*. You would then set the *ID_VALUE* to 250). Wireshark then automatically passes data to your dissector by calling the function defined in *create_dissector_handle* if the value of *tcp.port* equals 250.

Also note that *PARENT_SUBFIELDs* are named similar to *hf* fields, but they are not the same. The *PARENT_SUBFIELDS* are values that are exported by parent dissectors to allow linking with the next dissector (e.g., there is a value *ethertype* that is a *PARENT_SUBFIELD*, but it does not follow the pattern of being named after an *hf* field.

```
void
proto_reg_handoff_myprot(void)
{
    dissector_handle_t myprot_handle;

    myprot_handle = create_dissector_handle(dissect_myprot,
```

```
        proto_myprot);
    dissector_add("tcp.port", 250, myprot_handle);
}
```

# Step 5 Create the Dissector

The next step is to create your dissector. You need to create the function that was registered with Wireshark for your packet dissection. In this example, this function is called *dissect_myprot*. Wireshark passes three data structures to this function: *tvb*, *pinfo*, and *tree*. The *tvb* structure is used to extract and decode the data contained in each element of the packet. The *pinfo* structure provides specific information about the packet, based on information that was previously dissected by other processes (e.g., the *pinfo* structure tells you which packet number this packet relates to). It also contains flags for processing fragmented packets or multiple dissections. Finally, the tree structure provides a pointer to the location in memory of the protocol tree data. For this example, the pointer points to a memory location that represents the data just below the TCP protocol, and is the starting point for where your dissected data is displayed in the Decode window by the Wireshark GUI (see Figure 8.7).

**Figure 8.7** Dissector Data Displayed in the Decode Window

```
⊞ Frame 11 (62 bytes on wire, 62 bytes captured)
⊞ Ethernet II, Src: 44:45:53:54:42:00, Dst: 00:00:66:61:6b:65
⊞ Internet Protocol, Src Addr: 164.99.192.69 (164.99.192.69), Dst Addr: 137.65.80.178 (137.65.80.178)
⊞ Transmission Control Protocol, Src Port: cma (1050), Dst Port: ncp (524), Seq: 4077633585, Ack: 0, Len: 0
```

Your decode data will start immediately after the TCP section. In some cases, you may want to put information from the data stream into a local variable so that you can make logical decisions based on its value. To acquire data from the packet, we used *tvb_get_xxx* functions. For example, let's assume that the first byte in the packet is an unsigned integer that contains the value *0* for a request packet, or a value of *1* for a reply packet. First define your variable and then use a *tvb_get_guint8* function to get the data from the packet.

```
guint request_reply;
request_reply = tvb_get_guint8(tvb, 0);
```

The variable *request_reply* now contains the value of the first byte in the data stream. The parameters passed to the *tvb_get_xxx* functions vary, but all will take the pointer to your local *tvb* and an offset. In many cases, it makes sense to create a variable for the offset value and then increment that variable after making each *tvb* call.

```
guint request_reply, offset = 0;
request_reply = tvb_get_guint8(tvb, offset);
```

## Notes from the Underground…

### Variable and Function Name Syntax

Wireshark utilizes a lower-case format for all syntax. The C language is case-sensitive and the variable *RequestReply* is a different variable than one named *requestreply*. The preferred syntax when writing source code for Wireshark is to use all lower-case characters and to separate words with the underscore (_) character. For our example, *request_reply* was used. It is strongly recommended that you follow this requirement, because it allows all of the Wireshark code to have the same look and feel.

### Endianness

Wikipedia (www.wikipedia.com) defines endianess as:
In computing, **endianness** generally refers to sequencing methods used in a one-dimensional system (such as writing on computer memory). The two main types of endianness are known as **big-endian** (big units first) and **little-endian** (little units first). Systems which exhibit aspects of both conventions are often described as **middle-endian**. When specifically talking about bytes in computing, endianness is also referred to as **byte order** or **byte sex**.

There seems to be no significant advantage in using one method of endianness over the other, and both have remained common in terms of the number of different architectures that use them. However, because little-endian Intel x86 based processors (and their clones) are used in most personal computers and laptops, the vast majority of desktop computers in the world today are little-endian. This is sometimes called "Intel format". Networks generally use big-endian numbers as addresses; this is historically because this allowed the routing to be decided as a telephone number was dialed.

### Motorola *tvb_get* Functions

There are a number of *tvb_get_xxx* functions that allow you to retrieve data from the packet data stream based on the type of data you want to acquire. For example, you may need *x* number of bytes or you may need a 4-byte value. You may also find that the data in the data stream is in the wrong order. For example, you are expecting a value to be returned as 0001 from the packet data stream, but instead it is returned as 1000. There are two types of *tvb_get_xxx* functions that allow you to obtain the data from the data stream in the endianess you need. Refer to the *README.tvbuff* and the *README.developer* documents located in the *doc* directory.

**Continued**

## Value Types

Wireshark utilizes a number of common value definitions that are defined in the *README.tvbuff* and the *README.developer* documents located in the *doc* directory. Different development environments refer to value types by different names. Wireshark provides a common set of value types to allow for easier portability between operating systems. The following is a brief listing of the most common:

- **guint8**  1-byte value
- **guint16**  2-byte value
- **guint32**  4-byte value
- **guint64**  8-byte value
- **guint8***  pointer to a byte value
- **gchar***  pointer to a character string

Now, we want to display whether this is a request or reply packet. This is done with the *proto_tree_add_xxx* functions. In our example, we only want to display a message indicating if this is a request or reply packet.

```
if (request_reply==0)
     proto_tree_add_text(tree, tvb, offset, 1, "Request-(%d)",
         request_reply);
else
     proto_tree_add_text(tree, tvb, offset, 1, "Reply-(%d)",
         request_reply);
```

The *proto_tree_add_text* function requires the following parameters.

- *tree*  Pointer to the protocol tree.
- *tvb*  The *tvbuff* to mark as the source code data.
- *offset*  The offset in the *tvb* where the data is located.
- *1*  The length of the value (in bytes) in the *tvb*.
- *Request Packet (%d)*  The *printf* type format for displaying the data.
- *request_reply*  The data value to be displayed via the *printf* format.

## Notes from the Underground…

### proto_tree_add_xxx

You might wonder why the *tvbuff* information gets passed to the *proto_tree_add_xxx* function. We have already extracted the information into the variable *request_reply*. The *tvbuff* parameters tell Wireshark the portion of the data in the hex display window to highlight when this value is selected in the Decode window. Also note that the *tvbuff* starts at the beginning of the data passed to your dissector (e.g., getting data from the *tvbuff* with an offset of 0 is the first byte of the packet data that is related to your protocol). The previous packet data that was decoded by a higher-level dissector is not accessible. This ensures that the data seen by your dissector only pertains to the protocol dissection you are attempting to accomplish.

There is one problem with this example. If we utilize the *proto_tree_add_text* function, this value is not a filterable element. Therefore, if a user wanted to create a filter for all request packets in your dissector, they would not be able to. You could rewrite the example to utilize the *hf* array and make the *request_reply* value a filterable item.

```
if (request_reply==0)
      proto_tree_add_item(tree, hf_request, tvb, offset, 1, FALSE);
else
      proto_tree_add_item(tree, hf_reply, tvb, offset, 1, FALSE);
```

Although this example allows users to filter on the request or reply condition, this is not the most efficient use of the *proto_tree_add_xxx* functions. Because the value is already stored, there is no reason to force the dissector to reread the data. The *proto_tree_add_uint* function can be used to display the data already stored in the *request_reply* variable. If the value had not already been stored in a variable, the *proto_tree_add_item* function would be the most efficient to use.

```
if (request_reply==0)
            proto_tree_add_uint(tree, hf_request, tvb, offset, 1,
               request_reply);
else
            proto_tree_add_uint(tree, hf_reply, tvb, offset, 1,
               request_reply);
```

If we change the *proto_tree_add_text* to *proto_tree_add_xxx*, we utilize an *hf* element for displaying the data in the Decode window. Now we need to add the *hf_request* and *hf_reply* variables to the *hf* array.

You must first declare the *hf* variables at the top of the source code file after your include statements.

```
static int hf_request = -1;
static int hf_reply = -1;
```

Now, we add the element information to the *hf* array.

```
{ &hf_request,
  { "Request Packet", "myprot.request",
  FT_UINT8, BASE_DEC, NULL, 0x0,
  "", HFILL }},

{ &hf_reply,
  { "Reply Packet", "myprot.reply",
  FT_UINT8, BASE_DEC, NULL, 0x0,
  "", HFILL }},
```

With these changes, if the user wants to filter on all request packets in the *myprot* dissector, they enter the *myprot.request* filter. Any packet that meets the *request_reply* value of 0 will contain an array element of *myprot.request*. Reply packets contain an element of *myprot.reply*. Figure 8.8 shows an example of how a user might enter a display filter to force Wireshark to only display the packets for the new dissector.

**Figure 8.8** Sample Display Filter

Filter: | myprot.request or myprot.reply

**NOTE**

It is important to understand that the example above is not the most efficient way to complete this activity. It would be much easier to define a value string (covered later in this chapter) to identify the request/reply values. The values could then be passed to a single *hf* item, which would display the proper information to the user based on the actual value contained in the packet. For example:

```
static const value_string myprot_packet_types[] = {
    { 0x00000000, "Request" },
    { 0x00000001, "Reply" },
    { 0,          NULL }
};


/* inside our dissection code */
my_prot_packet_type = tvb_get_ntohl(tvb, foffset);
proto_tree_add_uint(my_prot_tree, hf_my_prot_packet_type, tvb, foffset, 4,
my_prot_packet_type);


/* defined in the hf array */
        { &hf_my_prot_packet_type,
        { "Packet Type",    "my_prot.packet_type",
          FT_UINT32,    BASE_HEX,    VALS(my_prot_packet_types),    0x0,
          "Packet Type", HFILL }},
```

With this modified example, you can filter just request packets by entering the filter *myprot.packet_type==0* for request packets or *myprot.packet_type==1* for replies. If you want to enter a filter to just locate all packets of the protocol *myprot*, you could enter a *myprot* filter.

## Notes from the Underground...

### *proto_tree* Functions

There are many variations of the *proto_tree_add_xxx* functions. The *proto_tree_add_item* is the most versatile, because it allows the format of the data to be defined in the *hf* array. If you attempt to pass the wrong data types to any of the *proto_tree_add_xxx* functions, a runtime error will be displayed and Wireshark will halt. This error processing allows Wireshark to trap for errors instead of allowing memory to be overrun or corrupted. It is good practice to utilize the *hf* array even if you do not want end users to be able to filter on a specific item in the decode. For these conditions, you can specify that the element be hidden so that the end users will not know of its definition. For detailed information on all of the different *proto_tee_add_xxx* types and the format of the *hf* array, refer to the *README.developer* document in the *doc* directory.

The real work of the dissector begins here. You must go through the logic of each type of packet that the dissector decodes. You should utilize the *tvb_get_xxx* functions to obtain the data you need to evaluate as well as the *proto_tree_add_xxx* functions to display information in the Decode window.

The Summary window (see Figure 8.9) allows you to browse quickly through the packet trace without having to look at each packet decode. It also allows you to display brief, but important, information relative to the packet. Typically, most developers provide summary data on request packets and error information on reply packets. The *col_set_str* function allows you to set the value of the data within any of the displayed Summary window columns.

**Figure 8.9** Summary Window

| No.. | Time | Source | Destination | Protocol | Info |
|------|------|--------|-------------|----------|------|
| 11 | 22.720221 | 164.99.192.69 | 137.65.80.178 | TCP | 1050 > 524 [SYN] Seq=0 Ack=0 Win=16384 Len=0 MSS=1370 |
| 12 | 22.724357 | 137.65.80.178 | 164.99.192.69 | TCP | 524 > 1050 [SYN, ACK] Seq=0 Ack=1 Win=6144 Len=0 MSS=1370 |
| 13 | 22.724372 | 164.99.192.69 | 137.65.80.178 | TCP | 1050 > 524 [ACK] Seq=1 Ack=1 Win=16440 Len=0 |
| 14 | 22.724704 | 164.99.192.69 | 137.65.80.178 | NCP | C Create Connection Service |
| 15 | 22.729828 | 137.65.80.178 | 164.99.192.69 | NCP | R OK |
| 16 | 22.729856 | 164.99.192.69 | 137.65.80.178 | NCP | C Get Big Max Packet Size - 65535 |
| 17 | 22.734531 | 137.65.80.178 | 164.99.192.69 | NCP | R OK |

The following code shows the *check_col()* and *col_set_str()* functions, which are a subset of the column functions available.

```
if (check_col(pinfo->cinfo, COL_PROTOCOL))
    col_set_str(pinfo->cinfo, COL_PROTOCOL, "MYPROT");
```

Note that the first thing we do is to evaluate whether the column data exists. If not, we cannot write to the column data structure. This is an important step, because without this check you could potentially write to undefined memory. We then make the *col_set_str* function call to set the value of the protocol column *COL_PRO-TOCOL* to our protocol name *MYPROT*.

```
if (request_reply==0)
{


    if (check_col(pinfo->cinfo, COL_INFO))
        col_set_str(pinfo->cinfo, COL_INFO, "Request");
}
else
{


    if (check_col(pinfo->cinfo, COLINFO))
```

```
        col_set_str(pinfo->cinfo, COL_INFO, "Reply");
}
```

Now we want to set the summary column to reflect if this is a request or reply packet. This is done by using the *col_set_str* function. Note that we still perform the check to validate that the column information is valid. Later in our dissector, we can append information to the info column by using the *col_append_str* function.

## Notes from the Underground…

### Column Functions

Wireshark includes a number of column functions that allow you to clear, set, and append to existing column data. These functions are defined in the *epan/column-utils.h* file and the *README.developer* document in the *doc* directory.

# Step 6 Pass Payloads

The final thing a dissector should do is pass on any payload remaining to be dissected by additional dissectors. This handoff of the payload data is what each of the lower-level dissectors performs to allow entry points for further dissection (e.g., the TCP dissector decodes the TCP header information but the remaining payload is dissected by different higher-level dissectors). In some cases, you may not need to pass on payload data, but it is recommended that your dissector look at the remaining data in the packet and pass it on if there is anything else to dissect. In some cases, your dissector may contain a data payload that can't be dissected. In this case, if you have remaining data in the packet structure that needs to be decoded by another dissector or as payload information. The remaining data should be displayed in some manner. The passing of the remaining payload back to Wireshark will automatically be displayed as [Data] if no further dissection can be performed (e.g., there is no defined lower-level dissector to handle the decoding of the remaining data). If the remaining data is payload for your dissector, utilize the *proto_tree_add_item* and pass a *-1* as the length parameter. Wireshark will then mark all of the remaining data in the packet as the defined *proto_tree_add_item*. The following information is extracted from the *README.developer* document located in the *doc* directory.

An example from *packet-ipx.c* –

```
void
dissect_ipx(tvbuff_t *tvb, packet_info *pinfo, proto_tree *tree)
{
    tvbuff_t         *next_tvb;
    int              reported_length, available_length;

    /* Make the next tvbuff */
    next_tvb = tvb_new_subset(tvb, IPX_HEADER_LEN, -1, -1);

/* call the next dissector */
    dissector_next(next_tvb, pinfo, tree);
```

The information contained in this portion of the chapter allows you to create a simple dissector. In the next section, we discuss how to modify the files used to build Wireshark so that it can be compiled into the rest of the project. Before you start major work on your dissector, you should make sure that the build process will complete with your new dissector included. This will also validate that your registration is working and that Wireshark passes the packet data to your dissector as expected. In the "Advanced Topics" section of this chapter, we explore some of the more complex issues you may encounter when creating a protocol dissector.

# Running a Dissector

To add a new dissector to the Wireshark project you need to modify the *Makefile.common* file located in the *epan/dissectors* directory.

```
DISSECTOR_SRC = \
    packet-aarp.c \
    packet-acap.c \
    packet-afp.c  \
    packet-afs.c  \
```

Add your dissector to the *DISSECTOR_SRC* section of the file. When you build Wireshark, this section is parsed and each dissector is compiled and linked into the main Wireshark binary.

In the *Makefile.common* file you will also find an additional section to define any includes you may have for your dissector.

```
DISSECTOR_INCLUDES =        \
      $(PIDL_DISSECTOR_INCLUDES)          \
```

```
format-oid.h        \
packet-acp133.h       \
packet-acse.h       \
```

Add your dissector includes to the *DISSECTOR_INCLUDES* section of the file. As with the dissector source code definition, the section will be parsed and included during the compile and link process.

Once you have successfully built Wireshark with your modifications, go back and analyze your code in places where you have not made comments. This allows you to look at the code at a later date to determine what that particular section is doing. Also make note of any warnings reported by your compiler and try to resolve them. This might be improper data type casts or unused variable definitions.

After you have finished cleaning up of the code and are satisfied with its functionality, please contribute your changes to the Wireshark project by sending a patch to the *wireshark-dev* mailing list. For changes to existing files, it is recommended that the changes be sent as a patch to the existing file in SVN. It is also important to consult with the proper individuals before submitting any proprietary information back to the Wireshark distribution. Remember that Wireshark is released under GPL and your submissions will automatically be under the same license agreement.

If you are working with a SVN distribution you can perform an update by issuing the following command:

```
svn up
```

or

```
svn update
```

Then you should generate a patch based on the full source code with the command:

```
svn diff | gzip > my_patch.gz
```

Or, for an individual file, you can specify the filename.

```
svn diff my_prot.c | gzip > my_prot.c.diff.gz
```

If the file you need to send is a new dissector, you should send the complete source code file *packet-myprot.c*, any includes, and a patch to the file *Makefile.common*. Attempting to create an SVN patch on your new dissector will not generate any information if your source code does not exist in the SVN repository. Your initial contribution should be a complete copy of the new source code and patch files for any modified files that already exist in the current repository. Future modifications should be submitted in patch form by generating a SVN unified patch file. An SVN unified patch file is sometimes referred to as a diff file or differential file.

# The Dissection Process

When does your dissector get called? When Wireshark reads a packet via the wiretap library it performs the following steps:

1. The frame data is passed to the *epan_dissect_run()* function.

2. The *epan_dissect_run()* function defines the frame, column, and data pointers and calls the function *dissect_packet()*.

3. The *dissect_packet()* function creates the topmost *tvbuff* and then calls the *dissect_frame()* function.

4. The *dissect_frame()* function dissects the frame data and displays it in the Decode window of the GUI (e.g., arrival time, frame number, frame length).

5. The *dissect_frame()* function then calls the *dissector_try_port()* to see if there are any protocol dissectors to dissect the next part of the *tvbuff*. In Figure 8.7, we can see in the Decode window that we were passed to the Ethernet packet type dissector; this is the *dissect_eth_common()* function.

6. The *dissect_eth_common()* function then decodes and displays the Ethernet header in the Decode window of the Wireshark GUI. Several different functions can be called at this point based on the Ethernet frame type. However, once the Ethernet frame type has been decoded, the remaining *tvbuff* is passed to the core Wireshark function *dissector_try_port()* again.

7. The *dissector_try_port()* function again looks to see if there is another dissector registered for the remaining *tvbuff*.

8. This process of decoding each layer of the packet continues, header-by-header, until you reach your protocol dissector. Wireshark calls each dissector, each dissector processes its data, and then the dissector creates a new *tvbuff* and sends it back to *dissector_try_port()*. In our example, we saw that *myprot* would eventually be the payload of a TCP packet, and that Wireshark would continue each dissection until the TCP dissector was processed. At this point, *dissector_try_port()* would see that we are registered for TCP port 250.

9. Finally, the *dissector_try_port()* function calls the dissector *myprot*.

10. Once the dissector has completed its work, it passes any remaining *tvbuff* back again. The process continues until there is no more data or no more registered dissectors for the remaining data. Once this happens, the next frame is read from the packet trace file.

## Notes from the Underground…

### When Wireshark Calls Your Dissector

It is important to know that your dissector can be called multiple times. Every time a display or color filter is applied to a packet trace, Wireshark re-dissects the data. When a user clicks on an item in the Decode window, the dissector is called again to dissect that specific packet. Your dissector should evaluate the *fd.flags.visited* flag in the *pinfo* data structure to determine if it needs to perform additional work. Otherwise, you might overwrite data that is necessary to properly decode your packets (e.g., adding new conversations into an existing conversation list). Construct your dissector to take into consideration whether or not the initial dissection has already been completed.

# Advanced Topics

The previous section discussed the information necessary to create a basic dissector. However, as your dissector becomes more complex you will need to implement more advanced features. Wireshark provides many different mechanisms to assist you in making your dissector display and decode packet data into a more informative manner. In this section, we look at some of the more complex tasks that you may want to incorporate into your *packet-xxx* dissector.

We also look at modifying the Wireshark GUI. This process requires that you have some knowledge of GTK features and mechanisms. Since Wireshark's GUI is generated using the GTK libraries, it makes calls to functions that are not included in the Wireshark distribution. These functions are part of the GTK binaries that you downloaded in the GTK developer kit. Documentation on these functions is available at the GTK Web site at www.gtk.org.

Finally, this section includes a short description of the TAP and plug-in implementations in Wireshark. TAPs allow you to build tools that acquire real-time data from Wireshark. The plug-in interface allows you to convert a *packet-xxx* dissector into a plug-in that can be loaded and unloaded.

# Dissector Considerations

When composing a dissector you need to consider the following factors:

- If the protocol that needs dissection runs on top of a connection-oriented protocol, you may need to track the request reply packets to ensure that they match.

- Connection-oriented protocols generally guarantee delivery.

- The underlying protocol retransmits packets if they are not acknowledged by their peer.

- Your dissector may need to handle payloads that exceed the maximum packet size.

- The actual payload may span several packets that your dissector needs to defragment.

- There are situations where you might want to store information either in the form of a memory value or across loading of the application.

You will probably encounter at least one of these conditions. The following section provides some advanced topics to help you develop ways to handle these situations.

# Creating Subtrees

Most of the time, decoded data should be branched to a separate subtree. This practice allows you to see important summary information in the Decode window and allows you to expand specific sections of the Decode window to see more detail (e.g., you might want to branch at a sub-level or a particular item that contains more data or attributes than would normally be displayed (see Figure 8.10 and Figure 8.11).

**Figure 8.10** Closed Item in Decode Window

```
⊞ Communications Transports: 2
⊞ Tree Walker Transport Type: 2
```

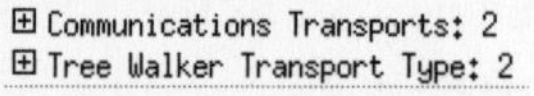

**Figure 8.11** Expanded Item in Decode Window

```
⊟ Communications Transports: 2
      (TCP Protocol)
      (IPX Protocol)
⊟ Tree Walker Transport Type: 2
      (TCP Protocol)
      (IPX Protocol)
```

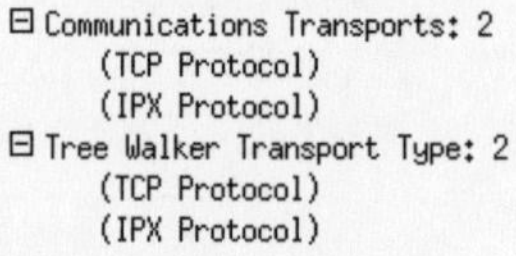

You can click on the **Entry Information** field within the Decode window to expand the item and get more detailed information. Subtrees are easily implemented with the *proto_tree* functions.

```
proto_item          *subitem;
proto_tree          *subtree;


subitem = proto_tree_add_text(tree, tvb, offset, -1, "Some Description");
subtree = proto_item_add_subtree(subitem, ett_myprot);
proto_tree_add_item(subtree, hf_myvalue, tvb, offset, 4, FALSE);
proto_item_set_end(subitem, tvb, offset+4);
```

The first step is to declare the *proto_item* and *proto_tree* variables. The *proto_tree_add_text* function allows you to create a label. This is only one of many uses of the *proto_tree_add_text* function. In this example, we pass the tree pointer that was given to us when our dissector was called. We also pass the *tvb*, offset, and length of the function so that when you highlight the label in the Decode window, the remaining packet data will be highlighted. The *-1* tells *proto_tree_add_text* that the function is comprised of all remaining data starting from the beginning offset. Finally, the label is passed to the function to describe what the subtree actually contains. You can branch from an actual element within the Decode window and create a label. To do this you could replace the *proto_tree_add_text* with a different *proto_tree_add* function. Once the label has been created in the original tree a new item pointer is returned in the sub-item variable.

The *proto_item_add_subtree* function sets up the subtree in the display. It creates the subtree so that when you perform another *proto_tree_add* function, you can reference the new subtree pointer.

The next call is to the *proto_tree_add_item* function, which is where the pointer for the new subtree is passed to. This places the new element beneath the expandable label that was created. The value is not viewable in the Decode window until the subtree label is clicked on and expanded.

The final step in this example is to set the overall length of the *proto_tree_add_item* with the *proto_item_set_end* function. This is used when the length of the value being set is unknown. If you are working with items of known length, this function call is not necessary.

There will be times when you want to create several branches of subtrees. To do this, create multiple *proto_items* and *proto_tree* pointers. You would create subtree 1 and then subtree 2, but reference subtree 1 as the source code tree. A visual display of the multi-level tree view can be seen in Figure 8.12.

```
item1 = proto_tree_add_text(tree, tvb, offset, -1,
    "Selector Option");
tree1 = proto_item_add_subtree(item1, ett_myprot);
number_of_items = tvb_get_ntohl(tvb, offset);
proto_tree_add_uint(tree, hf_num_objects, tvb, offset, 4,
    number_of_items);
foffset += 4;
for (i = 1 ; i <= number_of_items; i++ )
{
    item2 = proto_tree_add_text(tree1, tvb, offset, -1,
        "Option - %u", i);
    tree2 = proto_item_add_subtree(item2, ett_myprot);
}
```

**Figure 8.12** Visual Display of Multi-level Tree View

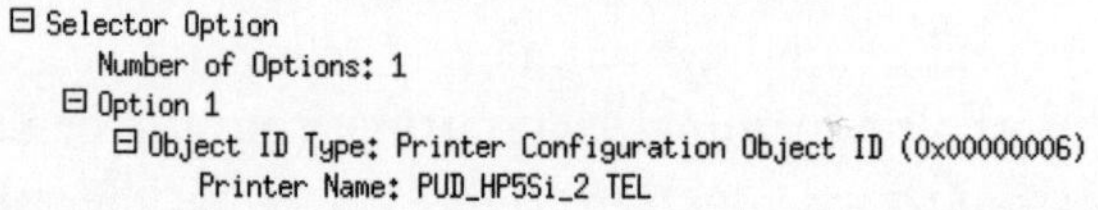

```
⊟ Selector Option
    Number of Options: 1
⊟ Option 1
    ⊟ Object ID Type: Printer Configuration Object ID (0x00000006)
        Printer Name: PUD_HP5Si_2 TEL
```

# Bitfields

In some cases, you may have a value that represents specific information based on what bits are set within the value. Bitfields give you a visual display of each bit and whether they are enabled within the value (see Figure 8.13).

**Figure 8.13** Visual Display of Bits

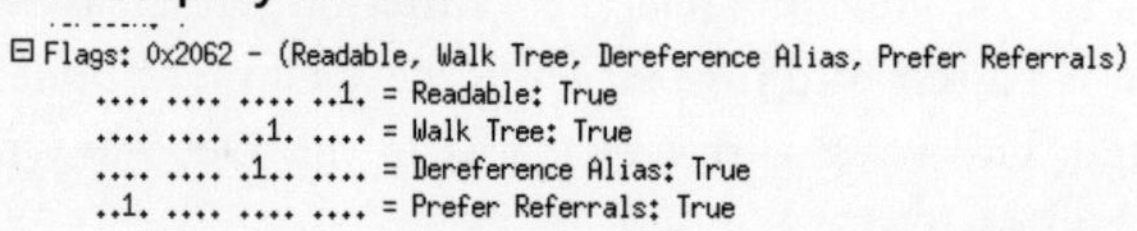

```
⊟ Flags: 0x2062 - (Readable, Walk Tree, Dereference Alias, Prefer Referrals)
    .... .... ..1. = Readable: True
    .... .... ..1. .... = Walk Tree: True
    .... .... .1.. .... = Dereference Alias: True
    ..1. .... .... .... = Prefer Referrals: True
```

Bitfields are implemented using the *hf* array elements. The following code is an example of the calling function that builds the subtree and summary data:

```
#define FLAG1 0x01
#define FLAG2 0x02

flags = tvb_get_guint8(tvb, offset);
strcpy(flags_str, "");
sep = " (";
```

```
if (flags & FLAG1) {
    strcat(flags_str, sep);
    strcat(flags_str, "Flag 1");
    sep = ",";
}
if (flags & FLAG2) {
    strcat(flags_str, sep);
    strcat(flags_str, "Flag 2");
    sep = ",";
}
if (flags_str[0] != '\0')
    strcat(flags_str, ")");
ti = proto_tree_add_uint_format(tree, hf_flags,
        tvb, offset, 1, flags, "Flags: 0x%04x%s", flags,
        flags_str);
flags_tree = proto_item_add_subtree(ti, ett_myprot);
```

The first step is to acquire the value from the *tvbuff* into the value flags. Next, you build the initial string and compare the value of flags with your defined flag bits. If they match, you combine the string with the flag information. Once your summary string has been built, you can create a subtree and display the data. You now have to display each of the valid bits in a bit view:

```
proto_tree_add_item(flags_tree, hf_flag_1,
        tvb, offset, 1, FALSE);
proto_tree_add_item(flags_tree, hf_flag_2,
        tvb, offset, 1, FALSE);

{ &hf_flag_1,
    { "Flag 1", "myprot.flag.1",
      FT_BOOLEAN, 8, NULL, FLAG1,
      "Is Flag one set? ", HFILL }},
{ &hf_flag_2,
    { "Flag 2", "myprot.flag.2",
      FT_BOOLEAN, 8, NULL, FLAG2,
      "Is Flag two set? ", HFILL }},
```

The bitfields are displayed by calling the *proto_tree_add_item* function with reference to the new subtree and the bitfield *hf* element names. Then, in the *hf* array, we define our new values. The key here is parameters 3, 4, and 6. Parameter 3 defines this as a Boolean value, which means that it will evaluate this as a true or false condition. Parameter 4 defines that we will display 8 bits. Parameter 6 defines the actual value of the bitmask. As seen in our example, this value can be substituted with the explicit mask or a variable.

# Unicode Strings

There will be times when you run into situations where the actual data contained in the packet contains Unicode data. Unicode data is normally seen in the Hex Data window as a 2-byte value. For example you might see:

```
57 00 6f 00 72 00 6b 00 73 00 74 00 61 00 74 00 69 00 6f 00 6e 00
W    o    r    k    s    t    a    t    i    o    n
```

When processing the data, most string conversion utilities see the second byte of the multi-byte character as a terminating null. You may find that you need to parse the string to acquire single-byte character strings. Many of the main string functions within Wireshark perform this process for you, but you may have a situation that requires you to manually perform the conversion. Several dissectors include functions to convert multi-byte character strings to single-byte strings. The following code is an example extracted from *packet-ncp2222.inc*:

```
static void
uni_to_string(char * data, guint32 str_length, char *dest_buf)
{
        guint32 i;
        guint16 c_char;
        guint32 length_remaining = 0;

        length_remaining = str_length;
        dest_buf[0] = '\0';
        if(str_length == 0)
        {
            return;
        }
        for ( i = 0; i < str_length; i++ )
        {
            c_char = data[i];
            if (c_char<0x20 || c_char>0x7e)
            {
                    if (c_char != 0x00)
```

```
                    {
                            c_char = '.';
                            dest_buf[i] = c_char & 0xff;
                    }
                    else
                    {
                            i--;
                            str_length--;
                    }
            }
            else
            {
                    dest_buf[i] = c_char & 0xff;
            }
            length_remaining--;

            if(length_remaining==0)
            {
                    dest_buf[i+1] = '\0';
                    return;
            }
    }
    dest_buf[i] = '\0';
    return;
}
```

## Conversations

Wireshark conversations are a key component of many protocol dissectors. Each dissector that needs to track conversations defines and maintains their own conversation table, which gives the dissector the ability to track request and reply packets. You might ask why you would need to track the conversation. What if there is no information contained in the reply packets that identifies which request the reply is for? In this case, you would store the original request packet in memory so that when the reply packet is found it can be decoded. (e.g., the NetWare Core Protocol (NCP) only defines a sequence number on the request packet; each request reply sequence is a unique session. Running on top of TCP or Internetwork Packet Exchange (IPX), the request packet is made from a specific address with a unique port/socket. If you match these conversation components you can logically assume that the reply packet is a response to the original request. Unfortunately, these may not come in the proper order in a packet trace. The conversation list saves each request conversation within your conversation list. When you encounter a reply packet, you should perform a lookup in the conversation list to determine which request the reply matches. If no originating request packet is found, display a message in the Decode window that the packet could not be decoded due to no request packet being found. Section 2.2 of the *README.developer* document located in the *doc* directory provides basic skeleton code and associated information necessary to set up a conversation table.

Important steps should not be missed when using conversations lists, including the *initialization function* and the *cleanup function,* which have to be placed in the protocol register routine. Many dissectors include conversation lists. If, after reviewing the section in the *README.developer* document, you still need a clearer example, refer to other dissectors that utilize this capability.

## Packet Retransmissions

Packet retransmissions are common on busy networks. Your dissector should be able to handle such an occurrence if it is going to attempt to handle fragmented packets. If your dissector or protocol does not process fragmented packets, it can treat these packets as normal packets. In most cases, a simple conversation list can check for the occurrence of a request packet; however, if nothing triggers your dissector, it might be a duplicate entry. You may also find that you need to manage another memory table to track a retransmitted packet. However, in other cases, the lower-level protocol might have already detected the retransmissions.

The packet information structure, *pinfo*, provides information for the status of the current packet being decoded. TCP and Sequenced Packet Exchange (SPX) are both connection-oriented protocols that retransmit data if acknowledgments are not received. Since TCP handles both the retransmission and fragmentation of packets, your higher-level dissector only has to be concerned with the real data. However, in the case of SPX, the higher-level dissector has to trap for retransmissions if it is handling packet fragmentation. The next section discusses how the SPX dissector passes this information to the higher-level dissectors. It is important to understand that a retransmission is a common occurrence on many networks. Your dissector should be able to determine if a packet is a retransmission or a normal packet. In some cases, you may choose not to dissect retransmitted packets and just identify the original packet. Remember that a retransmission can occur at any time, and may consist of a complete packet or an individual fragment.

# Passing Data Between Dissectors

The *pinfo->private_data* element can be used to pass a pointer to a memory table with information regarding the specific packet being decoded. You should first define a structure in your lower-level dissector that will hold the information. The following information was extracted from *packet-ipx.h* and *packet-ipx.c*:

```
/*
 * Structure passed to SPX subdissectors, containing information from
 * the SPX header that might be useful to the subdissector.
 */
typedef struct {
        gboolean eom;                 /* end-of-message flag in SPX header */
        guint8 datastream_type;       * datastream type from SPX header */
} spx_info;
```

We then update the structure and save it to *pinfo*:

```
static void
dissect_spx(tvbuff_t *tvb, packet_info *pinfo, proto_tree *tree)
{
      spx_info      spx_info;


              /*
              * Pass information to subdissectors.
              */
              spx_info.eom = conn_ctrl & SPX_EOM;
              spx_info.datastream_type = datastream_type;
              pinfo->private_data = &spx_info;
```

Now, you can retrieve this information in the higher-level dissector. The following information was extracted from the source code file *packet-ndps.c*:

```
static void
ndps_defrag(tvbuff_t *tvb, packet_info *pinfo, proto_tree *tree)
{
    spx_info             *spx_info;


    /* Get SPX info from SPX dissector */
    spx_info = pinfo->private_data;
```

The higher-level dissector can now utilize the information from the lower-level dissector to perform logical operations on the packet data.

# Saving Preference Settings

It is important to determine how the protocol dissector might handle specific features of your dissector (e.g., the packet fragmentation code can be enabled or disabled under the protocol preferences dialog). To implement a user-configurable setting that will either be used during runtime or saved across multiple loads of Wireshark, you should add the ability to utilize the system preference file.

```
ldap_module = prefs_register_protocol(proto_ldap, NULL);
prefs_register_bool_preference(ldap_module, "desegment_tcp",
    "Desegment all LDAP messages spanning multiple TCP segments",
    "Whether the LDAP dissector should desegment message",
    &ldap_desegment);
```

This code goes into the *proto_register_xxx* routine and creates a new entry in the preference files with the value of the referenced variable *myprot_desegment*. The following is an example of the entry created in the preference file. Figure 8.14 is an example of how the value will look when you go to the preferences option in Wireshark and select your protocol. We used the Lightweight Directory Access Protocol (LDAP) protocol dissector for our example.

```
# Whether the LDAP dissector should desegment messages
# TRUE or FALSE (case-insensitive).
ldap.desegment: TRUE
```

**Figure 8.14** Example of a LDAP Preference

Desegment all LDAP messages spanning multiple TCP segments:  [X]

# Packet Fragmentation

Packet fragmentation can be handled at many different protocol layers. TCP already includes packet reassembly. If your dissector needs to do additional packet reassembly, you can utilize the reassembly functions defined in Wireshark. A good example of how to handle packet reassembly by TCP is located in section 2.7 of the *README.developer* document in the *doc* directory. It covers how to handle packet reassembly when your dissector is running on top of TCP and User Datagram Protocol (UDP).

The *packet-ncp2222.inc, packet-atalk.c,* and *packet-clnp.c* files give examples of how to defragment messages that are fragmented within the protocol you are dissecting. The logic involved in defragmented packets can be complicated. You will find yourself spending many hours troubleshooting and fine-tuning the defragmentation function.

# Value Strings

There will be times when you read a specific value from the packet datastream that could be defined by many different descriptions based on that value. You should present a string to the user indicating what the value actually means (e.g., an error return value in a reply packet). The numerical value indicates which error is being returned. Section 1.7.1 in the *README.developer* document located in the *doc* directory lists the *match_strval* and the *val_to_str* functions. The first step is to create the array of values:

```
static const value_string my_values[] = {
        { 0x00000000, "Value 1" ),
        { 0x00000001, "Value 2" },
        { 0x00000002, "Value 3" },
        { 0, NULL }
};
```

It is important to note that the final line in the value string {0, NULL}. This is the termination record for the *value_string* function. If this is omitted, Wireshark will continually scan memory and possibly generate a bounds error.

You can now utilize the *match_strval* or *val_to_str* functions to process the value:

```
valuestr = match_strval(value2, my_values);
```

This process can be simplified even further by utilizing the values (VALS) capability of the *hf* array:

```
{ &hf_valuestr,
{ "This is my value", "myprot.valuestr",
  FT_UINT8, BASE_DEC, VALS(my_values), 0x0,
  "My value string", HFILL }}
```

This way, you can just utilize the simple *tvb_get* and *proto_tree_add* functions:

```
value2 = tvb_get_guint8(tvb, 1);
proto_tree_add_uint(tree, hf_valuestr, tvb, 1, 1, value2);
```

The same feature can be utilized to display true or false value strings in the Decode window of the GUI (e.g., if you want to display "Yes" or "No" based on a true or false value).

```
    typedef struct true_false_string {
        char    *true_string;
        char    *false_string;
    } true_false_string;
```

Value strings are important for processing return values that might contain a large number of error codes. The value string gives you the ability to process all of the possible values and return a specific string to identify the actual error. Without this information, end users are forced to research and locate the return value. In some cases, the value may not really indicate a problem; however, by providing the string to the end user you will eliminate much frustration and make your dissector even more valuable. Figure 8.15 shows an example of data displayed in the Decode window when utilizing a value string to return a string based on the return value.

**Figure 8.15** Example of a Value String

```
NDS Completion Code: 0xfffffda5, (-603) No Such Attribute
```

# The Expert TAP

One of the newer features of Wireshark is the expert TAP. This TAP is an important addition to building a dissector. The expert TAP has the ability to display expert information to end users. There are a number of conditions that can be defined as well as a wide range of parameters. More developers are choosing to add the expert TAP to their dissectors. It is recommended that advanced expert information be configurable via the protocol preferences, so that users can enable or disable the echoing of statistical information to the expert TAP (e.g., you may choose to have your dissector echo a message to the expert TAP each time it detects a specific condition). This information might be very valuable to some users, but clutter up the statistical information for others. If your protocol dissector allows users to disable the feature, those not wanting the information can turn it off:

To enable the expert TAP you have to include the expert header file *epan/expert.h*:

```
#include <epan/expert.h>
```

We now need to make *global proto item* and value parameters to pass to the expert TAP.

```
/* global item and value for passing expert data */
static proto_item   *expert_item;
static guint32      expert_status;
```

Finally, we build our expert data and call the *expert_add_info_format* function to pass the data to the expert TAP. Note that the example function looks to see if the return value is non-0. If it is, we call the expert TAP with the required parameters:

```
expert_status = tvb_get_ntohl(tvb, foffset);
expert_item = proto_tree_add_item(my_tree, hf_my_return_code, tvb,
foffset, 4, FALSE);
    if (expert_status != 0) {
        expert_add_info_format(pinfo, expert_item, PI_RESPONSE_CODE,
            PI_ERROR, "Fault: %s", val_to_str(expert_status,
        my_error_types, "Unknown Error (0x%08x)"));
    }
```

Note that the *expert_add_info_format* will process strings in the typical *printf* style format.

The expert TAP utilizes the following defined severity values from the *epan/proto.h* file:

```
/* expert severities */
#define PI_SEVERITY_MASK
#define PI_CHAT
#define PI_NOTE
#define PI_WARN
#define PI_ERROR

/* expert "event groups" */
#define PI_GROUP_MASK
#define PI_CHECKSUM
#define PI_SEQUENCE
#define PI_RESPONSE_CODE
#define PI_REQUEST_CODE
#define PI_UNDECODED
#define PI_REASSEMBLE
#define PI_MALFORMED
#define PI_DEBUG
```

The expert TAP is processed during the initial decoding of Wireshark to colorize the Decode window (e.g., the following colors are defined for the expert TAP):

- **Errors:** Red
- **Warnings:** Yellow
- **Notes:** Cyan
- **Chat:** Grey

The process of colorizing decoded data to display the item passed by the expert TAP, allows dissectors to identify certain conditions and then relay that information directly to the user through a visual display. Without this feature, users would be required to develop color filters to identify these types of packets in the Summary window.

The expert TAP data is also available via the menu items *expert Info* and *expert Info Composite* from the "Analyze" menu.

## Notes from the Underground...

### Development Note

The expert TAP does not require you to pass a *proto* item. You can construct the *expert_add_info_format()* function in a more simplified manner if you just want to pass some informational data. For example:

```
expert_add_info_format(pinfo, NULL,
            PI_RESPONSE_CODE, PI_ERROR, "Fault in my
            protocol");
```

In this example we are only passing the message "Fault in my protocol" to the expert TAP.

### IMPORTANT

If you do not pass a *proto* item with the expert info, the item will not be filterable from the composite expert info dialog. The composite expert info statistic will use the *proto* item passed to build a display filter when selected by the user.

# Debugging Your Dissector

There are a number of ways to debug Wireshark or a protocol dissector. The easiest method is to utilize a live debugger (e.g., on Windows you can use the Microsoft Visual Studio to step through your protocol dissector). There are a number of real time debuggers available from proprietary software vendors as well as open-source code solutions.

Another solution might be to add debug messages to a file or the console. An example of this type of debugging is included in the protocol dissector for SSL called */epan/dissectors/packet-ssl.c*:

```
ssl_debug_printf("ssl_association_add port %d ctport %d info %s handle
    %p\n", port, ctport, info, assoc->handle);
```

One other method implemented by several components of Wireshark is the use of a simple dialog message. This is a GTK Message window that displays an icon, some text, and an OK button. During the development process, you may decide to display a simple message to the user, or even to yourself, to aid in the further development of your code.

```
#include "simple_dialog.h"
simple_dialog(ESD_TYPE_ERROR, ESD_BTN_OK, error_string->str);
```

UNIX developers can utilize the standard *printf* function, which will echo to the console program. A newer *proto_tree_xxx* function added to Wireshark called *proto_tree_add_debug_text* can also be utilized instead of generating a pop-up window like the *simple_dialog* function does. Most developers have their own preferred method of debugging. It can be a combination of methods, but not all will agree on what is the best for all situations. Depending on the OS on which you are debugging, there may be times that certain methods work better then others. Wireshark gives you flexibility in debugging by providing several different ways to achieve the same results.

# The Wireshark GUI

The Wireshark GUI is created through calls to the GTK library. When you develop for the Wireshark GUI, you must consider compatibility issues for other builds of Wireshark. This means that you must program for GTK versions 1.2 and 2.*x*. Some GTK functions work in both versions, but others need to be programmed specifically for the version that Wireshark is built with. As a reference, you can use the GTK Web site at www.gtk.org as well as other GUI code located in the *gtk* directory.

## The Item Factory

The main menu for Wireshark is created via a GTK item factory. The following information is extracted from the *gtk/menu.c* source file included in the Wireshark source code distribution:

```
/* This is the GtkItemFactoryEntry structure used to generate new menus.
        Item 1: The menu path. The letter after the underscore indicates an
            accelerator key once the menu is open.
```

```
            Item 2: The accelerator key for the entry
            Item 3: The callback function.
            Item 4: The callback action.  This changes the parameters with
                    which the function is called.  The default is 0.
            Item 5: The item type, used to define what kind of an item it is.
                    Here are the possible values:

                    NULL                    -> "<Item>"
                    ""                      -> "<Item>"
                    "<Title>"               -> create a title item
                    "<Item>"                -> create a simple item
                    "<ImageItem>"           -> create an item holding an image (gtk2)
                    "<StockItem>"   -> create an item holding a stock image (gtk2)
                    "<CheckItem>"           -> create a check item
                    "<ToggleItem>"          -> create a toggle item
                    "<RadioItem>"           -> create a radio item
                    <path>                  -> path of a radio item to link against
                    "<Separator>"           -> create a separator
                    "<Tearoff>"             -> create a tearoff separator (gtk2)
                    "<Branch>"              -> create an item to hold sub items
(optional)
                    "<LastBranch>"      -> create a right justified branch
        Item 6: extra data needed for ImageItem and StockItem (gtk2)
    */
    ITEM_FACTORY_ENTRY("/Copy", NULL, copy_selected_plist_cb, 0, NULL, NULL),
    ITEM_FACTORY_ENTRY("/<separator>", NULL, NULL, 0, "<Separator>", NULL),


    ITEM_FACTORY_ENTRY("/Expand Subtrees", NULL, expand_tree_cb, 0, NULL,
NULL),
    ITEM_FACTORY_ENTRY("/Expand All", NULL, expand_all_cb, 0, NULL, NULL),
    ITEM_FACTORY_ENTRY("/Collapse All", NULL, collapse_all_cb, 0, NULL,
NULL),
```

When the item factory option is selected, the function listed in Item 3 is called. In GTK, callback functions are called when an item is selected.

The *set_menu_sensitivity* function enables and disables the availability of menu items based on a specified condition:

```
    /* make parent menu item sensitive only, if we have any valid files in
the list */
    set_menu_sensitivity(main_menu_factory, MENU_RECENT_FILES_PATH, cnt);
```

Generally, you only need to modify the Wireshark menu if you are creating a tool or making a change to some other portion of the GUI.

# Using GTK

When an item is selected, GTK passes a handle to the active selection, which are called *widgets*.

```
void
my_widget(GtkWidget *w _U_, gpointer d _U_)
{
    GtkWidget      *main_vb
    GtkTooltips    *tooltips;
#if GTK_MAJOR_VERSION < 2
    GtkAccelGroup *accel_group;
#endif
```

## Notes from the Underground…

### Development Note

Note the _U_ value being defined in the *my_widget* function. The _U_ represents an undefined parameter. These values are not used within the function. The process of defining them as _U_ allows the compiler to not issue a warning on the function due to undefined variables.

### Function Names

It is important to understand that the GTK functions used within the Wireshark GUI code are not always the original GTK function name. Most GTK functions are globally defined within the Wireshark source code include file *gtk/compat_macros.h*. It may sometimes be necessary to consult this file prior to looking up specific information on the GTK Web site.

When our menu item is selected, GTK passes the GTK widget pointer and data structure to us. We then create a new GTK widget for our window.

The *GtkTooltips* is a structure that allows you to store information about a widget that is displayed when the user places his or her mouse pointer over the GTK item. For example, suppose you have a button on our window that (when clicked) changes the current display filter to one of our choosing. Although the size of the button only allows us to label it "Filter," we can define a tool tip that provides a more detailed description of the button's function.

The *GtkAccelGroup* is necessary for GTK version 1.2. It allows for accelerator keys to be used on the keyboard to access menu items:

```
/* First check to see if the window already exists. If so make it active. */
  if (mywindow_w != NULL) {
    /* There's already a "My Window" dialog box; reactivate it. */
    reactivate_window(mywindow_w);
    return;
  }
  /* Create our new window */
  mywindow = dlg_window_new("Wireshark: My Window");
  /* Register our callback function to clean up memory if the window is
     closed */
  SIGNAL_CONNECT(mywindow_w, "destroy", mywindow_destroy_cb, NULL);
  /* Start the tooltips */
  tooltips = gtk_tooltips_new ();


#if GTK_MAJOR_VERSION < 2
  /* Accelerator group for the accelerators (or, as they're called in
     Windows and, I think, in Motif, "mnemonics"; Alt+<key> is a mnemonic,
     Ctrl+<key> is an accelerator). */
  accel_group = gtk_accel_group_new();
  gtk_window_add_accel_group(GTK_WINDOW(mywindow_w), accel_group);
#endif
```

We first check to make sure the window is not already open. If it is, we reactivate it. If it is not, we create a new dialog window. When creating the new window, you should create a callback handler to take care of the window being closed, by the user clicking the **EXIT** button in the upper right-hand corner of the dialog box. The *SIGNAL_CONNECT* function tells GTK what to do when the specified signal occurs. In this case, we are trapping for the destroy signal.

Finally, we initialize the *tooltips*. Notice that we only perform the accelerator group for GTK versions older then GTK 2.*x*. Accelerator keys in GTK 2.*x* are defined when creating the item:

```
/* Container for each row of widgets */
  main_vb = gtk_vbox_new(FALSE, 3);
  gtk_container_border_width(GTK_CONTAINER(main_vb), 5);
```

```
gtk_container_add(GTK_CONTAINER(mywindow_w), main_vb);
gtk_widget_show(main_vb);
```

The first step is to create our main window. Next, we create a box on the new window. The *gtk_vbox_new* creates the new box that we will add to our window. The *gtk_container_border_width* defines the border for our window. The *gtk_container_add* now adds our new box to the main window. Finally, the *gtk_widget_show* forces GTK to paint the information to the screen. The following demonstrates the creation of an **OK** button on the *main_vb* window.

```
/* Button row: OK button */
bbox = gtk_hbutton_box_new();
gtk_button_box_set_layout (GTK_BUTTON_BOX (bbox), GTK_BUTTONBOX_END);
gtk_button_box_set_spacing(GTK_BUTTON_BOX(bbox), 5);
gtk_container_add(GTK_CONTAINER(main_vb), bbox);
gtk_widget_show(bbox);


#if GTK_MAJOR_VERSION < 2
  ok_bt = gtk_button_new_with_label ("OK");
#else
  ok_bt = gtk_button_new_from_stock(GTK_STOCK_OK);
#endif
  SIGNAL_CONNECT(ok_bt, "clicked", capture_prep_ok_cb, cap_open_w);
  GTK_WIDGET_SET_FLAGS(ok_bt, GTK_CAN_DEFAULT);
  gtk_box_pack_start (GTK_BOX (bbox), ok_bt, TRUE, TRUE, 0);
  gtk_widget_grab_default(ok_bt);
  gtk_widget_show(ok_bt);
```

The first section of this code creates a new horizontal button box, adds it to the *main_vb* window, and forces GTK to paint the new box.

We then check the GTK version and create the new button depending on the version of GTK. Note that GTK version 2.*x* allows us to specify the icon used for this button. This is how you create custom icons and incorporate them into Wireshark. We register the callback function for GTK to use when the button is clicked, register the button as the default button, and paint the button on the screen. Note that it is not necessary to force GTK to draw each time the window is updated or a new item is added. You can build your dialog window and then call *gtk_widget_show()* to have GTK draw the window and all of it's attached components.

You can also register widget data to a widget so that when it is selected, the data associated to the widget is passed to the calling function (e.g., in the *gtk/find_dlg.c* file, a number of defines are set to identify the buttons within the find window):

```
/* Capture callback data keys */
#define E_FIND_FILT_KEY          "find_filter_te"
#define E_FIND_BACKWARD_KEY   "find_backward"
```

Next, the keys are registered as data to the dialog with the *object_set_data* function.

```
OBJECT_SET_DATA(find_frame_w, E_FIND_FILT_KEY, filter_text_box);
OBJECT_SET_DATA(find_frame_w, E_FIND_BACKWARD_KEY, backward_rb);
```

Finally, when the *find_frame_w* is selected, the callback function can access the values of the attached buttons by calling the *object_get_data* function:

```
filter_te = (GtkWidget *)OBJECT_GET_DATA(parent_w, E_FIND_FILT_KEY);
backward_rb = (GtkWidget *)OBJECT_GET_DATA(parent_w, E_FIND_BACKWARD_KEY);
```

The GTK Web site contains many examples and a window builder tool that you can download and experiment with. To program in GTK, you must know the static defines for predefined items like *GTK_STOCK_XXX* and *GTK_CAN_DEFAULT*.

# TAPs

*Wireshark* implements a TAP system to allow for real-time statistics during packet captures. These can also be used by statistical information tools that register to the TAP interface and command Wireshark to re-dissect a saved packet capture file. Examples of this type of use of the TAP system include conversation lists, endpoints, expert TAP, and so on. The TAP system is documented in the *README.tapping* document located in the *doc* directory. Also in the main source code directory you will find a number of *tap-xxx* files that you can use for a reference on the TAP interface. The *gtk/endpoint_talkers_table.c* file can be used as an example of how to implement a TAP inside of an included statistics menu option.

The TAP interface is implemented in two steps. The first step is to install the TAP into the protocol dissector you want to get information from. The second step is to add the TAP listener to your new application. Many of the protocol dissectors included in Wireshark already contain TAPs. Most likely you will only need to create your TAP listener and perform the work you need to do. If you find that a TAP is not installed in the protocol you need, adding the TAP is simple through the use of a few lines of code. Refer to the *README.tapping* for more information.

Some of the most common TAPs used today in protocol dissectors are:

- Expert
- Conversations
- Endpoints
- SRT

There are a number of examples for each of these types of TAPs. Protocol dissectors define and register the TAPs that they will be providing information too. To register a TAP, the following process must be added to your dissectors *proto_register_xxx* function:

```
my_srt_tap=register_tap("my_srt");
```

Inside of the protocol dissection process you should call the *tap_queue_packet* function with the necessary information needed by the TAP:

```
tap_queue_packet(my_srt_tap, pinfo, pointer_to_my_tap_data);
```

Note that *pointer_to_my_tap_data* can be a pointer to any data that you want to pass to your specific TAP implementation. However, it is important when adding TAPs for already established interfaces like, conversations, endpoints, and so on, that you verify that your new TAP will pass a pointer to the correct information required by that TAP interface.

Now that the protocol dissector is registering the TAP, you can create a conversation, endpoint, or SRT statistic option to use the information the TAP provides. The first step in writing the code to manage the information is to create a new file in the *gtk* directory for the specific TAP data type. The file naming convention used for each type of statistic source code file is:

- *gtk/conversations_myprot* Conversations
- *gtk/myprot_stat* SRTs
- *hostlist_myprot* Endpoints

Note that the TAP modules for Tshark are located in the *root* directory of the source code distribution. These files are typically named *tap-myprot*.

First we create the standard header and includes. We will need different includes depending on the type of statistic we are processing. In this example we are using the SRT statistics:

```
/* mysrt_stat.c
 * mysrt_stat   2006 My_Name
 *
```

```
 * $Id: mysrt_stat.c 00000 2006-01-01 00:00:00Z xxx $
 *
 * Wireshark - Network traffic analyzer
 * By Gerald Combs <gerald@wireshark.org>
 * Copyright 1998 Gerald Combs
 *
 * This program is free software; you can redistribute it and/or
 * modify it under the terms of the GNU General Public License
 * as published by the Free Software Foundation; either version 2
 * of the License, or (at your option) any later version.
 *
 * This program is distributed in the hope that it will be useful,
 * but WITHOUT ANY WARRANTY; without even the implied warranty of
 * MERCHANTABILITY or FITNESS FOR A PARTICULAR PURPOSE.  See the
 * GNU General Public License for more details.
 *
 * You should have received a copy of the GNU General Public License
 * along with this program; if not, write to the Free Software
 * Foundation, Inc., 59 Temple Place - Suite 330, Boston, MA  02111-1307, USA.
 */

#ifdef HAVE_CONFIG_H
# include "config.h"
#endif

#ifdef HAVE_SYS_TYPES_H
# include <sys/types.h>
#endif

#include <string.h>
#include <gtk/gtk.h>
#include <epan/packet_info.h>
#include <epan/epan.h>
#include <epan/value_string.h>
#include <epan/tap.h>
#include "service_response_time_table.h"
#include "../stat_menu.h"
#include "../tap_dfilter_dlg.h"
#include "gtkglobals.h"
```

We now need a structure to store our SRT statistics in:

```
/* used to keep track of the statistics for an entire program interface */
typedef struct _mysrtstat_t {
        GtkWidget *win;
        srt_stat_table my_srt_table;
} mysrtstat_t;
```

We must register our new SRT statistics option with Wireshark. This registration process will add the new option to the SRT statistical menu and add this statistic as a sub-option of the SRT menu item or as a tab in the tabbed/notebook view:

```
static tap_dfilter_dlg mysrt_stat_dlg = {
        "My Protocol SRT Statistics",
        "mysrt,srt",
        gtk_mysrtstat_init,
        -1
};


void
register_tap_listener_gtkmysrtstat(void)
{
        register_dfilter_stat(&mysrt_stat_dlg, "MYSRT",
             REGISTER_STAT_GROUP_RESPONSE_TIME);

}
```

The main registration function (*register_dfilter_stat()*) passes the parameters, points to the function to call when a user selects the item (*mysrt_stat_dlg*), and names the display in the menu (*MYSRT*) and the statistical menu item we are adding this item too (*REGISTER_STAT_GROUP_RESPONSE_TIME*).

The function called when the user selects the new SRT menu option (*mysrt_stat_dlg()*) passes the information to the initialization function (*gtk_mysrtstat_init*).

The first process in the initialization function (*gtk_mysrtstat_init*) is to create the GTK window that will hold our statistical information.

```
static void
gtk_mysrtstat_init(const char *optarg, void *userdata _U_)
{
        /* Define a pointer to our structure */
        mysrtstat_t *ss;
        const char *filter=NULL;
```

```
/* Allocate memory for our table */
ss=g_malloc(sizeof(mysrtstat_t));

/* Get the current filter passed */
if(!strncmp(optarg,"mysrt,srt,",8)){
        filter=optarg+8;
} else {
        filter=NULL;
}

/* Create the main window */
ss->win=window_new(GTK_WINDOW_TOPLEVEL, "mysrt-stat");
gtk_window_set_default_size(GTK_WINDOW(ss->win), 300, 400);
vbox=gtk_vbox_new(FALSE, 3);
gtk_container_add(GTK_CONTAINER(ss->win), vbox);
gtk_container_set_border_width(GTK_CONTAINER(vbox), 12);

/* Print a label on the menu to describe this statistic */
label=gtk_label_new("My Protocol Service Response Time Statistics");
gtk_box_pack_start(GTK_BOX(vbox), label, TRUE, TRUE, 0);

/* Display the current display filter */
g_snprintf(filter_string,255,"Filter:%s",filter?filter:"");
label=gtk_label_new(filter_string);
gtk_box_pack_start(GTK_BOX(vbox), label, FALSE, FALSE, 0);

/* Let's create a notebook view */
main_nb = gtk_notebook_new();
gtk_box_pack_start(GTK_BOX(vbox), main_nb, TRUE, TRUE, 0);
temp_page = gtk_vbox_new(FALSE, 6);
label = gtk_label_new("Groups");
gtk_notebook_append_page(GTK_NOTEBOOK(main_nb), temp_page, label);

/* Create a Close button row. */
bbox = dlg_button_row_new(GTK_STOCK_CLOSE, NULL);
gtk_box_pack_end(GTK_BOX(vbox), bbox, FALSE, FALSE, 0);

close_bt = OBJECT_GET_DATA(bbox, GTK_STOCK_CLOSE);
window_set_cancel_button(ss->win, close_bt, window_cancel_button_cb);
```

```
    /* Tell GTK what functions to call when a delete or destroy is
detected */
    SIGNAL_CONNECT(ss->win, "delete_event", window_delete_event_cb, NULL);
    SIGNAL_CONNECT(ss->win, "destroy", win_destroy_cb, ss);


    gtk_widget_show_all(ss->win);
    window_present(ss->win);
```

Inside the initialization function, after creating the window for the data, we must register a listener for the TAP information.

```
/* Register the tap listener */
    error_string=register_tap_listener("my_srt", ss, filter,
            mysrt_reset, mysrt_packet, mysrt_draw);
    if(error_string){
        simple_dialog(ESD_TYPE_ERROR, ESD_BTN_OK, error_string->str);
        g_string_free(error_string, TRUE);
        g_free(ss);
        return;
    }
```

When you register the TAP listener, you pass the TAP name as parameters (*my_srt*), the pointer to the local *srt_stat_table* variable/structure (*SS*), the current filter (if used; otherwise pass NULL), the function to call when a reset signal is detected by GTK (*mysrt_reset*), the function to call when a new packet/event is detected (*mysrt_packet*), and the function to call when GTK performs a refresh (*mysrt_draw*).

At this point, most of the TAP listener applications will initiate a retap/redissect process so that the information will again be passed to the TAP channel. There are two methods available to initiate this process:

```
cf_redissect_packets(&cfile);
```

or

```
cf_retap_packets(&cfile, FALSE);
```

The main difference between these two calls is that the *cf_redissect_packets* forces Wireshark to do a complete reload and dissection of the current trace, including recreation of the GUI items, whereas, the *cf_retap_packets* forces Wireshark to reload and rescan the packet data. The *retap* function is preferred, if possible, because it takes less time for Wireshark to complete and is less intensive. However, in cases where dissector information requires a re-dissection process including the GUI items, you may need to perform the *cf_redissect_packets* instead. Developers should weigh the benefit vs. cost prior to implementing a full re-dissection of the packet trace.

The remaining code for handling conversations, endpoints, or SRT statistics, varies depending on the implementation. In our example, we now need to compose our functions to handle the reset, packet, and draw conditions:

```
static void
mysrtstat_reset(void *pss)
{
        mysrtstat_t *ss=(mysrtstat_t *)pss;
        /* Call the global SRT function to reset the table data */
        reset_srt_table_data(&ss->my_srt_table);
}


static int
mysrtstat_packet(void *pss, packet_info *pinfo, epan_dissect_t *edt _U_,
const void *prv)
{
        mysrtstat_t *ss=(mysrtstat_t *)pss;
        const my_dissectors_tap_data_type *request_val=prv;

        /* if we haven't seen the request, just ignore it */
        if(!request_val){
                return 0;
        }
        /* Call the global SRT function to add the new packet data */
        add_srt_table_data(&ss->my_srt_table, request_val->command,
                &request_val->req_time, pinfo);

        return 1;
}


static void
mysrtstat_draw(void *pss)
{
        mysrtstat_t *ss=(mysrtstat_t *)pss;
        /* Call the global SRT function to draw the window */
        draw_srt_table_data(&ss->my_srt_table);
}
```

It is also important to remember to clean up the memory when your application ends. Therefore, we also need to define our cleanup function if the window is just closed by the user:

```
void protect_thread_critical_region(void);
void unprotect_thread_critical_region(void);
static void
win_destroy_cb(GtkWindow *win _U_, gpointer data)
{
        mysrtstat_t *ss=(mysrtstat_t *)data;

        protect_thread_critical_region();
        remove_tap_listener(ss);
        unprotect_thread_critical_region();

        free_srt_table_data(&ss->my_srt_table);
        g_free(ss);
}
```

It is recommended that you utilize one or more of the currently available sources for any new additions. Inside the *gtk* directory are a number of examples for all of the defined types of TAPs. Although our example was for the service response time statistics, the coding for conversations and endpoints are basically the same.

## Notes from the Underground...

### Development Note

It is important to note that even though the expert info is a TAP, you do not have to implement any type of utility code to process the expert info as you do with conversations, SRT, and endpoints statistics. As mentioned previously, you modify your dissector to call the expert TAP directly.

# Plug-ins

Wireshark also supports the implementation of protocol dissectors as plug-ins. Plug-ins are preferred by some developers, because they can be developed and debugged without having to rebuild the whole Wireshark distribution. Another reason that some developers utilize the plug-in option for their dissector, is to protect proprietary information. When releasing a protocol dissector in Wireshark, your code is checked and automatically becomes subject to the rules defined in the GPL; however, a plug-in can be distributed in binary form, and, therefore, the GPL will not apply to the specific plug-in.

You can compile and build your plug-in and then copy the binary to the plug-ins directory under the name of your plug-in. Wireshark ships with a number of plug-ins and each can be loaded or unloaded depending on whether they are installed prior to launching Wireshark. The plug-in interface mimics the dissector interface. In fact, plug-ins are first developed as a normal dissector. Then, additional code is added to make the dissector a plug-in. This procedure changed starting with Ethereal version 0.10.10. Making your *packet-xxx* protocol dissector a plug-in is a multi-step process, which includes the creation of a source code directory to house the plug-in and it's support files, as well as modifications to the *makefiles* in the root of the source code distribution. The *README.plugins* file located in the *doc* directory outlines the steps you need to take to generate a plug-in dissector for Wireshark.

# Summary

This chapter outlined some of the most important parts of developing in Wireshark. There are several components that can contributed:

- Protocol dissectors
- Plug-ins
- The Wireshark GUI
- Tools

This chapter went into great detail documenting the proper steps to take when creating a dissector. By consulting the *README.developer* document in the *doc* directory, you can cut and paste a template to help you get started. However, the document does not clearly define each step necessary in the development process. This chapter attempts to provide these steps in a logical order. First, modify the header and the *include* statements. Next, register the protocol dissector. Finally, create the dissector code to decode the data. The important factor in the decode section is to utilize the *hf* array in the register function so that elements can be filtered upon.

This chapter also covered several advanced topics including a basic guide to GTK programming. Many of the topics covered will be experienced by someone creating a protocol dissector. Handling advanced topic issues correctly can eliminate many hours of unnecessary work and research. After debugging your work, make sure you go back and clean up as much of the code as possible. Insert comments to make the code clear. In addition, make sure you remove unused variable definitions. If possible, clean up any remaining warnings displayed in the compile process by your compiler. Finally, contribute your modifications back to the Wireshark project by e-mailing a patch to the *wireshark-dev* mailing list. Again, make sure that any information that you contribute back to Wireshark is not going to violate any proprietary claims. Wireshark is released under the GPL and all contributions should be consistent with this licensing agreement.

# Solutions Fast Track

## Prerequisites for Developing Wireshark

☑ The Wireshark source code must be obtained before you can start any new development. You have the option of downloading different types of download packages. The Wireshark Web site (www.wireshark.org) contains links to download previous versions, the current release version, nightly backups, and SVN code.

☑ The requirements for Windows-based computers are different from UNIX/Linux-based computers. Windows-based computers require additional tools to emulate the UNIX/Linux environment.

☑ To build Wireshark, a number of libraries and tools are needed. There are several libraries that are optional depending on whether you decide to add a specific feature.

☑ Wireshark can be compiled and run on a number of operating systems. For this reason, you must ensure that you program in ANSI C for portability between all of the supported platforms.

☑ Before you start any work on Wireshark, make sure you can compile and link Wireshark into its executable binary form.

☑ The Wireshark Web site contains a number of additional resources for developers, including Bugzilla, wiki, and the Wish List.

## Wireshark Design

☑ The main directory of the source code distribution is the primary location of the configuration files used by the compiler to build the Wireshark binaries.

☑ The GTK directory is used to store the GUI source code used in Wireshark. You will find the main application as well as the toolbar, menu, conversations, endpoints, SRT statistics, and other GTK source code in this directory.

☑ Most of the utility functions for Wireshark are located in the EPAN directory. These functions include conversion functions as well as *tvb* and column functions.

☑ The *doc* directory of the distribution is where you will locate most of the documentation that is shipped with the Wireshark source code. This is a great resource for anyone wanting to develop in Wireshark.

# Developing a Dissector

☑ Before you start any Wireshark development, make sure you can build the Wireshark executable.

☑ The first step in developing a dissector is to utilize the template provided in the *README.developer* document.

☑ It is important to consider the GPL and other factors when modifying the header comments from the template. Note that this is where you need to add your personal information so that you can receive credit for your work.

☑ Global Wireshark functions are provided to ease the development of dissectors.

☑ Registering your protocol dissector is a necessary process so that Wireshark knows when to pass packet data on to your dissector.

☑ The *hf* array provides the mechanism to incorporate display and color filters. By utilizing the *proto_tree_add_item()* functions, the *hf* array defines the data type to be used to convert specific data into the proper string representations in the Decode window.

☑ Use *tvb_get_xxx* functions to access data from the frame. The data passed to your dissector does not include the data that has already been decoded by other dissectors.

☑ Using the *proto_tree* functions allow you to print to the Decode window of the Wireshark GUI.

☑ One of the most important steps a dissector should do is to pass any remaining packet data back to Wireshark. This way, future dissectors can be written to dissect the remaining packet data.

# Advanced Topics

☑ Creating subtrees allows you to display data in a more informative way in the Decode window of the GUI. Users needing more detailed information can expand the item to view the details.

☑ Wireshark provides a mechanism to display bitfields in a graphical view. This allows the user to see from the bit display what the actual fields represent.

☑ Many dissectors must be able to handle Unicode strings. Unicode strings present a challenge to normal string processing, because of their 2-byte width.

☑ There are situations that require you to have the ability to track request and reply packet pairs. Wireshark provides the conversations list functions to keep specific information of a source code packet so that it can be matched to a reply packet.

☑ Packet retransmissions are a normal occurrence on most networks. It is important that Wireshark protocol dissectors can handle this type of condition. The use of conversation lists can help in this process.

☑ Users should have the ability to configure different components in Wireshark, including the ability to turn a feature on or off within your protocol dissector. The preference files give you a place to store values so that your dissector can retrieve them the next time Wireshark is active.

☑ During the processing of data within a packet, you may need to know certain information from another dissector. Wireshark provides a mechanism to pass data between dissectors with the *pinfo->private_data* pointer.

☑ Fragmentation occurs when the payload of a packet exceeds the actual size of the packet. The protocol breaks the payload into pieces and then sends each one within a fragment. The destination device then collects all of the fragments and reassembles the original payload. Dissectors need to have the ability to process these packet fragments. Wireshark utilizes several defragment functions to track and reassemble fragmented data.

☑ There are many times within the packet data that number should be displayed as a user-friendly string to define the value. Most error codes are returned as numerical values, but the number itself means little to end users. Value strings give you the ability to convert numerical values to a meaningful message.

☑ Wireshark's GUI utilizes the GTK item factory for creating and manipulating its menu items. Adding a new menu item is a quick process by adding new items to the item factory.

☑ If you plan to develop or modify any of the Wireshark GUI, you need to become familiar with GTK programming and it's rich set of functions. The GTK Web (www.gtk.org) site provides documentation and examples on the proper ways of writing to the GTK library.

☑ Wireshark provides a mechanism to receive real-time data. Tools can utilize the TAP system to gather information from a live capture or from an existing packet trace. Examples of tools that utilize the Wireshark TAP interface are conversations, endpoints, SRTs, and the expert.

☑ Programming to the expert TAP only requires modification to the protocol dissector, whereas other TAPs require a more extensive work to process the TAP information and extend the Wireshark menu.

☑ Packet dissectors do not have to be compiled into the Wireshark source code. The plug-in interface provides a mechanism to convert your dissector from *packet-xxx* type source code to a plug-in. Plug-ins can be compiled quicker and can also be added and removed prior to launching the Wireshark executable.

# Frequently Asked Questions

The following Frequently Asked Questions, answered by the authors of this book, are designed to both measure your understanding of the concepts presented in this chapter and to assist you with real-life implementation of these concepts. To have your questions about this chapter answered by the author, browse to **www.syngress.com/solutions** and click on the **"Ask the Author"** form.

**Q:** How does Wireshark know when a dissector should be called?

**A:** The *dissector_add* function defines the condition in which the dissector should be called.

**Q:** Where do I locate the design document for developing Wireshark?

**A:** There really isn't a design document, but the *README.developer* document and the other documents contained in the *doc* directory contain useful information. A developer's guide is being constructed on the Wireshark wiki site as well.

**Q:** How do you pass information from one dissector to another?

**A:** By using the *pinfo->private_data* to pass a pointer to the other dissectors data.

**Q:** How do I know what functions are provided by Wireshark?

**A:** We have tried to list many of the common functions within this chapter, but for a complete listing you should look at the header files of the source code for all *exports*. Exports are the mechanism that allows you to define the public functions that will be available to the rest of the application. Functions that are not exported are limited in visibility to the module in which they are defined. However, although they may be limited in their visibility, it is important that you do not create a function within your dissector that might conflict with a public function that has been exported. This is one of the reasons why you should declare your private functions as static unless you plan to export the function to use with other Wireshark modules. Note that exports are ignored by some operating systems but used in others (e.g., Windows uses exports to define global application functions as described above).

**Q:** Can I build Wireshark with Microsoft Visual C++?

**A:** Yes. You need to make sure you have all of the required libraries and tools. It is important to realize that building under Microsoft Visual C++ does not include using the visual studio environment. Building Wireshark utilizes the command-line interface and you build Wireshark.exe with *nmake.exe*. Wireshark does not include any visual studio workspace or configuration files to be used with the visual studio GUI. To build Wireshark under Microsoft Visual C++, open a command (CMD) window and navigate to the main source code directory of Wireshark. Finally, execute *nmake* with the syntax *nmake –f makefile.nmake*.

**Q:** Where can I find more information on programming the GUI?

**A:** The GTK Web site has development tutorials and examples at www.gtk.org.

**Q:** I built an Wireshark Red Hat Package Manager (RPM) with SSL decryption, but some of my users complain that they can't find the dependency file *libgcrypt.so.11*.

**A:** When building with features like SSL decryption, the actual decryption is performed by decryption libraries *gnutls* and *libgcrypt*. Many systems may have a newer version of these modules. For systems with newer packages, you can perform the following.

- Create a softlink to the newer library package (*/usr/lib/ # ln -s libgcrypt.so.12 libgcrypt.so.11*).

- Then you need to update the system configuration (*/usr/lib/ # ldconfig*).

For systems running older versions of the failing dependency package, it is recommended that users upgrade to a newer version. If none are available, it is recommended that you build another RPM without this feature.

# Chapter 9

# Other Programs Packaged with Wireshark

## Solutions in this chapter:

- TShark
- editcap
- mergecap
- text2pcap
- capinfos
- dumpcap

☑ Summary

☑ Solutions Fast Track

☑ Frequently Asked Questions

# Introduction

Most people familiar with Wireshark tend to use the Wireshark graphical user interface (GUI). However, when Wireshark is installed, it also comes with several other supporting programs: the command-line version of Wireshark, called *TShark*, and five other programs to assist you in manipulating, assessing, and creating capture files—editcap, mergecap, text2pcap capinfos and dumpcap. These supporting programs can be used together to provide very powerful capture file manipulation. For example, files can be captured with TShark, edited with editcap, and merged into a single packet capture file with mergecap. They can then be viewed with TShark or Wireshark. As you read this chapter, you will see the vast capabilities and the granular control these supporting programs give you when manipulating capture files.

# TShark

TShark is the command-line version of Wireshark. It can be used to capture, decode, and print to screen live packets from the wire or to read saved capture files. Some of the same features apply to both TShark and Wireshark, as they use the same capture library, libpcap, and most of the same code. TShark can read all the same packet capture formats as Wireshark, and will automatically determine the type. If TShark is compiled with the zlib library, it can automatically uncompress and read files that have been compressed with gzip. The advantage to using TShark is that it is highly scriptable.

The following information is the usage output for the TShark program. Notice the various types of formats in which TShark can save files by using the −F option:

```
$ tshark -h
TShark 0.99.4 (SVN Rev 19507)
Dump and analyze network traffic.
See http://www.wireshark.org for more information


Copyright 1998-2006 Gerald Combs <gerald@wireshark.org> and contributors.
This is free software; see the source for copying conditions. There is NO
warranty; not even for MERCHANTABILITY or FITNESS FOR A PARTICULAR PURPOSE.


Usage: tshark [options] ...


Capture interface:
  -i <interface>           name or idx of interface (def: first non-loopback)
  -f <capture filter>      packet filter in libpcap filter syntax
```

```
  -s <snaplen>            packet snapshot length (def: 65535)
  -p                      don't capture in promiscuous mode
  -y <link type>          link layer type (def: first appropriate)
  -D                      print list of interfaces and exit
  -L                      print list of link-layer types of iface and exit

Capture stop conditions:
  -c <packet count>       stop after n packets (def: infinite)
  -a <autostop cond.> ... duration:NUM - stop after NUM seconds
                          filesize:NUM - stop this file after NUM KB
                              files:NUM - stop after NUM files
Capture output:
  -b <ringbuffer opt.> ... duration:NUM - switch to next file after NUM secs
                          filesize:NUM - switch to next file after NUM KB
                              files:NUM - ringbuffer: replace after NUM files
Input file:
  -r <infile>             set the filename to read from (no pipes or stdin!)

Processing:
  -R <read filter>        packet filter in Wireshark display filter syntax
  -n                       disable all name resolutions (def: all enabled)
  -N <name resolve flags>  enable specific name resolution(s): "mntC"
  -d <layer_type>==<selector>,<decode_as_protocol> ...
                          "Decode As", see the man page for details
                          Example: tcp.port==8888,http
Output:
  -w <outfile|->          set the output filename (or '-' for stdout)
  -F <output file type>   set the output file type, default is libpcap
                          an empty "-F" option will list the file types
  -V                      add output of packet tree       (Packet Details)
  -x                      add output of hex and ASCII dump (Packet Bytes)
  -T pdml|ps|psml|text    output format of text output (def: text)
  -t ad|a|r|d             output format of time stamps (def: r: rel. to
first)
  -l                      flush output after each packet
  -q                      be more quiet on stdout (e.g. when using
statistics)
  -X <key>:<value>        eXtension options, see the man page for details
  -z <statistics>         various statistics, see the man page for details
```

```
Miscellaneous:
  -h                        display this help and exit
  -v                        display version info and exit
  -o <name>:<value> ...     override preference setting
```

The following command-line options are used to control TShark's data capture and output:

- Capture Interface Options

  - **−i** *interface* Specifies the interface you want to use to capture data. The −D option can be used to find out the names of your network interfaces. You can use the number or the name as a parameter to the **−i** option. If you run TShark without the −i option, it will search the list of interfaces and choose the first non-loopback interface it finds. If it doesn't find any non-loopback interfaces, it will use the first loopback interface. If this doesn't exist, TShark will exit with an error.

  - **−f** *capture filter expression* Allows you to set the filter expression to use when capturing data. For example, **tshark −f tcp port 80** will only capture incoming and outgoing HTTP packets.

  - **−s** *snaplen* Allows you to set the default snapshot length to use when capturing data. The parameter *snaplen* specifies the length, in bytes, of each network packet that will be read or saved to disk. The default *snaplen* is 65535 bytes, which should be large enough to capture the entire frame contents for all data link types.

  - **−p** Tells TShark to not put the interface in promiscuous mode. This will cause TShark to only read traffic sent to and from the system on which TShark is running, broadcast traffic, and multicast traffic.

  - **−y** *type* Allows you to set the data link type to use while capturing packets. You can use the **−L** option to lists the data link types that are supported by an interface.

  - **−D** Instructs TShark to print a list of available interfaces on the system. It will print the interface number, name, and description and then return to the command prompt. You can then supply the number or the name to the **−i** flag to specify an interface on which to capture data. Specifying this option causes TShark to open and attempt to capture on each interface it finds. It will only display the interfaces on which this was successful. Also, if you need to be logged in as root to run TShark but are not, this option will not display any available interfaces.

- ■ **–L** Lists the data link types that are supported by an interface and then exits. You can specify an interface to use, or TShark will choose the first one it finds as stated in the **–i** option information.

- Capture Stop Options

  - ■ **–c** *count* Sets the default number of packets to read when capturing data. For example, if you only want to capture 100 packets you would specify **–c 100**.

  - ■ **–a** *test:value* Used when capturing to a file. It specifies to TShark when to stop writing to the file. The criterion is in the form *test:value*, where test is either *duration* or *file size*. Duration will stop writing to a file when the specified number of seconds have elapsed, and file size will stop writing to a file after a size of *value* kilobytes has been reached.

- Capture Output Option

  - ■ **–b** *number of ring buffer files [:duration]* Used with the **–a** option, and causes TShark to continue capturing data to successive files. This is known as *ring buffer* mode and will keep saving files up to the number specified within the option. When the first file reaches the maximum size, as specified with the **–a** option, TShark will begin writing to the next file. When all files are full, it will continue to write new files as it removes the older ones. However, if the *number of files* is specified as 0, the number of files TShark writes to will be unlimited, and will only be restricted to the size of the hard disk. An optional duration parameter can also be specified so TShark will switch to the next file when the instructed number of seconds has elapsed. This will happen even if the current file is not yet full. The filenames created are based on the number of the file and the creation date and time. You can only save files in the libpcap format when this option is used.

- Capture Input Option

  - ■ **–r** *file* Reads and processes a saved capture file.

- Capture Processing Options

  - **–R** *filter* Causes a read filter to be applied before displaying or writing the packets to a file. Packets that do not match the filter will be discarded.

  - **–n** Used to disable network object name resolution, such as host names and port names.

  - **–N** *resolving flags* Used to enable name resolving for specified address types and port numbers. The **m** flag enables MAC address resolution, the **n** flag enables network address resolution, and the **t** flag enables transport-layer port number resolution. The **C** flag enables concurrent (asynchronous) Domain Name System (DNS) lookups if TShark is compiled with Asynchronous DNS (ADNS). The **–N** option overrides the **–n** option.

  - **–d** *layer type==selector, decode-as protocol* Allows you to specify the way in which traffic is decoded. The parameters denote that if the layer type has a specified value, packets should be decoded as the specified protocol. For example, **–d tcp.port==8080, http** would decode all traffic to and from Transmission Control Protocol (TCP) port 8080 as HyperText Transfer Protocol (HTTP) traffic. This is valuable for applications that allow you to run services on nonstandard ports.

  - **–B** *buffer size* Available only on Windows systems, causing TShark to allocate a buffer size in MB (default is 1MB) to use for storing packet data during a capture before writing to the disk. This option is useful if your packet capture is dropping frames due to the overhead associated with writing to the disk.

- Capture Output Options

  - **–w** *file* Writes the packets to the filename specified following the option. If the option specified is -, standard output is used. This option suppresses the packet display decoding unless the **S** option is also specified.

  - **–F** *type* Used to set the format of the output of the capture file. For example, if you want to save a file in the Sun snoop format so snoop can read the capture file, you would use the **–F snoop** option.

- **–V** Displays the capture in protocol tree form instead of the default summary packet form.

- **–S** Decodes and displays the contents of packets even when writing to a file.

- **–x** Displays the capture in a hexadecimal and ASCII dump format along with the summary or protocol tree view.

- **–T pdml | ps | text** Allows you to set the display format to use when viewing packet data. When using the Packet Details Markup Language (PDML) option, the protocol data tree is always displayed. If the desired format is omitted, "text" is used as the default.

- **–t format** Allows you to set the format of the packet timestamp that is displayed on the summary line. The format parameter will specify the method used to display the data. Relative time is specified by the **r** parameter and displays the time elapsed between the first packet and the current packet. Absolute time is specified by the **a** parameter and is the actual time the packet was captured. The absolute date and time are specified by the **ad** parameter and are the actual time and date the packet was captured. The delta time is specified by the **d** parameter and displays the time since the previous packet was captured. By default, the time is specified as relative.

- **–l** Flushes the standard output buffer after each packet is printed instead of waiting until it fills up. It is normally used when piping a capture to a script so that the output for each packet is sent as soon as it is read and dissected.

- **–q** Allows you to turn off the packet count when capturing network packets to a file. The count will still be displayed at the end of the capture. On some systems, such as various BSD systems, that support the SIGINFO signal, typing **control-T** will cause the current count status to be displayed.

- **–X** Allows the user to specify an option that will be passed to a TShark module. Currently, this option is used to specify additional analysis functionality using Lua scripts with the syntax **lua_script:*filename***.

- **–z *statistics*** Causes TShark to collect various types of statistics about the data being captured. The results will be displayed after reading the capture file.

- Miscellaneous Options

  - **–h** Prints the version of TShark and the help options and then exits.

  - **–v** Prints the TShark version information and then exits.

  - **–o** *prefname:value* Allows you to set a preference value that will override any default value or value read from a preference file. The parameter to this option is in the format of *prefname:value*, where *prefname* is the name of the preference as it would appear in the preference file, and *value* is the value to which it should be set.

By default, TShark will display packets to the screen in summary line form. These are the same lines that are displayed in the Wireshark summary pane. However, it does not print the *frame number* field when capturing and displaying real time. The **–V** option can be used to print detailed information about the packets instead of just a summary. TShark can also read saved data capture files, and print the information in either summary (default) or detailed form (**–V**). This method will display the frame numbers with the saved packets. Finally, the **–x** command will cause TShark to print a hexadecimal and ASCII dump of the packet data with either the summary line or detailed protocol tree. TShark has a very strong display filter language and can use the TCPDump filter syntax as well. These can be used to narrow the type of traffic you want to capture.

When using TShark to write a capture to a file, the file will be written in libpcap format by default. It will write all the packets and all the detail about the packets to the output file; thus, the **–V** and the **–x** options aren't necessary. Since TShark and Wireshark are compatible with many other sniffers, you can also write the output in several different formats. The **–F** option can be used to specify a format in which to write the file.

The following is a basic example of using TShark to perform a capture and display the output in a protocol tree view along with the associated hexadecimal and ASCII output.

```
C:\Program Files\Wireshark>tshark -V -x
Capturing on \Device\NPF_{A302C81E-256D-4C92-8A72-866F2E1ED55F}
Frame 1 (114 bytes on wire, 114 bytes captured)
    Arrival Time: Nov 28, 2003 22:14:16.221349000
    Time delta from previous packet: 0.000000000 seconds
    Time since reference or first frame: 0.000000000 seconds
    Frame Number: 1
    Packet Length: 114 bytes
    Capture Length: 114 bytes
```

```
IEEE 802.3 Ethernet
    Destination: ff:ff:ff:ff:ff:ff (Broadcast)
    Source: 00:05:5d:ee:7e:53 (D-Link_ee:7e:53)
    Length: 100
Logical-Link Control
    DSAP: NetWare (0xe0)
    IG Bit: Individual
    SSAP: NetWare (0xe0)
    CR Bit: Command
    Control field: U, func = UI (0x03)
        000. 00.. = Unnumbered Information
        .... ..11 = Unnumbered frame
Internetwork Packet eXchange
    Checksum: 0xffff
    Length: 96 bytes
    Transport Control: 0 hops
    Packet Type: PEP (0x04)
    Destination Network: 0x00000000 (00000000)
    Destination Node: ff:ff:ff:ff:ff:ff (Broadcast)
    Destination Socket: SAP (0x0452)
    Source Network: 0x00000000 (00000000)
    Source Node: 00:05:5d:ee:7e:53 (D-Link_ee:7e:53)
    Source Socket: Unknown (0x4008)
Service Advertisement Protocol
    General Response
    Server Name: TARGET1!!!!!!!!A5569B20ABE511CE9CA400004C762832
        Server Type: Microsoft Internet Information Server (0x064E)
        Network: 00 00 00 00
        Node: 00:05:5d:ee:7e:53
        Socket: Unknown (0x4000)
        Intermediate Networks: 1
0000   ff ff ff ff ff ff 00 05 5d ee 7e 53 00 64 e0 e0   ........].~S.d..
0010   03 ff ff 00 60 00 04 00 00 00 00 ff ff ff ff ff   ....`..........
0020   ff 04 52 00 00 00 00 00 05 5d ee 7e 53 40 08 00   ..R......].~S@..
0030   02 06 4e 54 41 52 47 45 54 31 21 21 21 21 21 21   ..NTARGET1!!!!!!
0040   21 21 41 35 35 36 39 42 32 30 41 42 45 35 31 31   !!A5569B20ABE511
0050   43 45 39 43 41 34 30 30 30 30 34 43 37 36 32 38   CE9CA400004C7628
0060   33 32 00 00 00 00 00 00 05 5d ee 7e 53 40 00 00   32.......].~S@..
0070   01 01
```

The following is an example of using TShark to capture traffic on interface 4 and output the data to a file called *output*. The output files will have a maximum file size of 5 kilobytes each, and when they are full, a new output file will be created. This will continue to a maximum of 10 output files. The following example is the command used to perform this capture.

```
C:\Program Files\Wireshark>tshark -i4 -a filesize:5 -b 10 -w output
```

The output files generated are appended with the file number, date, and times-tamp. You will see the following 10 output files start at number 43 because they have begun to drop the oldest file as they create new files, so a maximum of 10 files exists at all times.

```
output_00043_20031128212900
output_00044_20031128212900
output_00045_20031128212900
output_00046_20031128212900
output_00047_20031128212901
output_00048_20031128212903
output_00049_20031128212958
output_00050_20031128213045
output_00051_20031128213211
output_00052_20031128213316
```

The following is an example of using a TShark capture filter to capture all traffic except packets to and from HTTP port 80.

```
C:\Program Files\Wireshark>tshark -f "tcp port !80"
Capturing on \Device\NPF_{A302C81E-256D-4C92-8A72-866F2E1ED55F}
  0.000000 D-Link_ed:3b:c6 -> Broadcast    ARP Who has 192.168.100.40?  Tell
192.168.100.5
  0.000026 D-Link_ee:7e:53 -> D-Link_ed:3b:c6 ARP 192.168.100.40 is at
00:05:5d:ee:7e:53
  0.000066 D-Link_ee:7e:53 -> D-Link_ed:3b:c6 ARP 192.168.100.40 is at
00:05:5d:ee:7e:53
 10.089720 00000000.00055dee7e53 -> 00000000.ffffffffffff IPX SAP General
Response
 10.089763 00000000.00055dee7e53 -> 00000000.ffffffffffff IPX SAP General
Response
```

The following is an example of using a TShark read filter to output the Telnet data packets from a file called *capture*.

```
C:\Program Files\Wireshark>TShark -r capture -R "telnet"
   7  10.071157 192.168.100.122 -> 192.168.100.132 TELNET Telnet Data ...
   8  10.071464 192.168.100.132 -> 192.168.100.122 TELNET Telnet Data ...
   9  10.071515 192.168.100.132 -> 192.168.100.122 TELNET Telnet Data ...
  11  10.076114 192.168.100.132 -> 192.168.100.122 TELNET Telnet Data ...
  12  10.076155 192.168.100.132 -> 192.168.100.122 TELNET Telnet Data ...
  14  10.089546 192.168.100.122 -> 192.168.100.132 TELNET Telnet Data ...
  15  10.089672 192.168.100.132 -> 192.168.100.122 TELNET Telnet Data ...
```

The following is an example of using TShark to read a libpcap capture file called *capture2* and output it to a file called *netmon_output* in the Microsoft Network Monitor 2.*x* format; this command generates no output. Note that the *editcap* command can also be used to perform this function, as we'll see later in this chapter.

```
C:\Program Files\Wireshark>tshark -r capture2 -w netmon_output -F netmon2
```

# TShark Statistics

Whether troubleshooting network activity, identifying potential attacks, or performance-tuning network links, a common task in analyzing traffic is to identify statistical information. Using this statistical data, we can narrow our focus on specific protocols or data exchanges, instead of trying to assess a larger set of packets.

Fortunately, TShark can collect and display statistical information for live or stored packet captures, supplying basic analysis information and detailed protocol information. By specifying the **z** flag with TShark, you can specify one or more of several supported statistics reporting options. The format of the statistics reporting options uses the following convention:

   *-z major name, minor name, option(s), filter*

In this example where **-z** is the command-line option to TShark, instructing it to expect a statistics reporting option, and *major* and *minor name* are one of several available statistics reporting options. Following the minor statistics reporting name are one or more options specific for the selected statistics option. At the end of each statistics reporting option, you can specify a filter string that will cause the statistics reporting to be applied only to the packets matching the specified filter. As of Wireshark 0.99.4, 30 unique statistics reporting options are available. We've provided detailed explanations of several of the most commonly used statistics reporting options in the following section.

**TIP**

By default, TShark will print a one-line summary for each packet received. When examining statistical information by using the **-z** option, you may want to suppress this information and show only the statistics reporting by adding the **-q** option as well.

## Protocol Hierarchy Statistics

**Syntax:** `-z io,phs[,filter]`

**Description:** The protocol hierarchy statistics (PHS) option reports a summary of the protocols identified in the packet capture, and the number of packets and bytes for each protocol. Optionally, specify a display filter to report protocol hierarchy and traffic statistics for an identified group of frames.

**Example:** The following is an example of using the TShark statistics function to display a report of all bytes and frames for each protocol detected during a live capture on the first available interface, disabling name resolution and the packet summary output, and reporting the collected statistics after ending the capture by typing **Ctrl + C**.

```
C:\Program Files\Wireshark>tshark –nqz io,phs
<cntrl-c>

===================================================================
Protocol Hierarchy Statistics
Filter: frame
frame                                 frames:560 bytes:115233
  eth                                 frames:560 bytes:115233
    ip                                frames:558 bytes:115005
      udp                             frames:53 bytes:10383
        dns                           frames:21 bytes:3215
        data                          frames:8 bytes:496
        isakmp                        frames:24 bytes:6672
      tcp                             frames:505 bytes:104622
        http                          frames:107 bytes:81798
    llc                               frames:2 bytes:228
      ipx                             frames:2 bytes:228
        ipxsap                        frames:2 bytes:228

===================================================================
```

# Protocol Statistics by Interval

**Syntax:** `-z io,stat,interval[,filter][,filter][,filter]...`

**Description:** The protocol statistics by interval option reports a summary of the number of frames and bytes recorded in the capture file for each specified interval duration. The interval must be specified in a duration of seconds as a whole or a fractional number of seconds. The output of the statistics reporting will contain one or more columns; by default, with no display filter specified, the first column will indicate the statistics for the entire contents of the packet capture. If one or more display filters are specified, the results of each will be displayed in the first and successive columns. This allows you the quickly examine the nature of traffic for the entire packet capture, and the results of one or more display filters.

The protocol statistics by interval option can also report statistics based on calculations, including `COUNT()`, `SUM()`, `MIN()`, `MAX()`, and `AVG()` using the following convention in the place of a display filter:

`[COUNT|SUM|MIN|MAX|AVG](<field>)<filter>`

where `<field>` is the name of a display field you wish to apply the calculations on, and `<filter>` is a display filter that includes the specified field name. Note that you can only perform the calculations on fields that are integers or relative time fields, and the display filter must include the named field in the filter syntax.

**Example:** The following example demonstrates TShark statistics by interval reporting while reading from a stored packet capture file named Kismet-Sep-06-2005.dump in five-minute (300 second) intervals for both the entire capture file (denoted with the globally matching display filter `frame`) and the results of the display filter `ip.addr eq 10.18.129.130`, while suppressing the standard display output.

```
C:\>tshark -r Kismet-Sep-06-2005.dump -z io,stat,300,"frame","ip.addr eq
10.18.129.130" -q


====================================================================
IO Statistics
Interval: 300.000 secs
Column #0: frame
Column #1: ip.addr eq 10.18.129.130
                 |   Column #0    |    Column #1
Time             |frames|  bytes  |frames|   bytes
000.000-300.000       82    5874       0          0
300.000-600.000      248   18104       8        928
```

| | | | | |
|---|---|---|---|---|
| 600.000-900.000 | 1171 | 86793 | 9 | 1044 |
| 900.000-1200.000 | 1247 | 93774 | 10 | 1160 |
| 1200.000-1500.000 | 1377 | 102314 | 6 | 696 |
| 1500.000-1800.000 | 2128 | 819636 | 4 | 464 |
| 1800.000-2100.000 | 1357 | 102840 | 8 | 928 |
| 2100.000-2400.000 | 1587 | 116295 | 10 | 1160 |
| 2400.000-2700.000 | 1565 | 179061 | 2 | 232 |
| 2700.000-3000.000 | 1450 | 98959 | 7 | 812 |
| 3000.000-3300.000 | 1436 | 101291 | 4 | 464 |
| 3300.000-3600.000 | 1826 | 218948 | 7 | 812 |
| 3600.000-3900.000 | 517 | 48140 | 0 | 0 |

===================================================================

**Tip**

When specifying display filters using command-line tools, use the alphabetic comparison operators (eq, ne, lt, gt). This will prevent your shell from interpreting meta-characters such as the exclamation mark.

The next example of statistics interval reporting reports the average frame size (using the display filter frame.pkt_len), the smallest frame size, and the maximum frame size in five-minute intervals.

```
C:\>tshark -r wireless-rwc-1.cap -qz
io,stat,300,AVG(frame.pkt_len)frame.pkt_len,MIN(frame.pkt_len
)frame.pkt_len,MAX(frame.pkt_len)frame.pkt_len
```

```
===================================================================
IO Statistics
Interval: 300.000 secs
Column #0: AVG(frame.pkt_len)frame.pkt_len
Column #1: MIN(frame.pkt_len)frame.pkt_len
Column #2: MAX(frame.pkt_len)frame.pkt_len
```

| Time | Column #0 AVG | Column #1 MIN | Column #2 MAX |
|---|---|---|---|
| 000.000-300.000 | 71 | 58 | 82 |
| 300.000-600.000 | 73 | 58 | 116 |
| 600.000-900.000 | 74 | 54 | 608 |

| | | | |
|---|---|---|---|
| 900.000-1200.000 | 75 | 58 | 388 |
| 1200.000-1500.000 | 74 | 58 | 132 |
| 1500.000-1800.000 | 385 | 58 | 1532 |
| 1800.000-2100.000 | 75 | 58 | 1432 |
| 2100.000-2400.000 | 73 | 58 | 388 |
| 2400.000-2700.000 | 114 | 58 | 1532 |
| 2700.000-3000.000 | 68 | 58 | 116 |
| 3000.000-3300.000 | 70 | 58 | 360 |
| 3300.000-3600.000 | 119 | 52 | 1532 |
| 3600.000-3900.000 | 93 | 58 | 336 |

```
===================================================================
```

# Conversation Statistics

**Syntax:** `-z conv,type[,filter]`

**Description:** The conversation statistics reporting option will display the conversations between stations in the capture file of the specified type, matching the specified display filter or all traffic if the display filter is omitted. Currently supported conversation types are:

- `eth` Ethernet
- `fc` Fiber channel
- `fddi` FDDI
- `ip` IP addresses
- `ipx` IPX addresses
- `tcp` TCP/IP socket pairs
- `tr` Token ring
- `udp` UDP/IP socket pairs

This option is useful to assess the conversations between stations on the network. This is a common technique for analyzing traffic for signs of worm activity, since an infected station will often scan large quantities of hosts to look for additional infection targets, as opposed to stations that are not infected, which typically restrict their conversations to a small number of hosts.

**Example:** This example reads from the capture file defcon.dump and collects statistics for IP conversations, using the display filter `ip.addr eq 216.250.64.68`, which will restrict the statistics to conversations from this host (output of this command has been trimmed for space).

```
$ tshark -r defcon.dump -nqz conv,ip,"ip.addr eq 216.250.64.68"
================================================================================
IPv4 Conversations
Filter:ip.addr eq 216.250.64.68
```

| | <- | | | -> | | | Total | |
|---|---|---|---|---|---|---|---|---|
| | Frames | Bytes | | Frames | Bytes | | Frames | Bytes |
| 216.250.64.68 <-> 192.168.2.215 | 85 | 8887 | | 98 | 19007 | | 183 | 27894 |
| 216.250.64.68 <-> 192.168.2.237 | 69 | 7076 | | 42 | 8555 | | 111 | 15631 |
| 216.250.64.68 <-> 192.168.2.23 | 60 | 6064 | | 4 | 795 | | 64 | 6859 |
| 216.250.64.68 <-> 192.168.2.212 | 51 | 4687 | | 2 | 453 | | 53 | 5140 |
| 216.250.64.68 <-> 192.168.0.173 | 35 | 3859 | | 16 | 3099 | | 51 | 6958 |
| 216.250.64.68 <-> 192.168.2.149 | 19 | 1791 | | 26 | 4493 | | 45 | 6284 |
| 216.250.64.68 <-> 192.168.2.102 | 18 | 2933 | | 20 | 3852 | | 38 | 6785 |
| 216.250.64.68 <-> 192.168.1.120 | 29 | 2657 | | 9 | 1257 | | 38 | 3914 |
| 216.250.64.68 <-> 192.168.2.72 | 9 | 864 | | 22 | 5472 | | 31 | 6336 |
| 216.250.64.68 <-> 192.168.0.153 | 20 | 1871 | | 9 | 3658 | | 29 | 5529 |
| 216.250.64.68 <-> 192.168.41.150 | 25 | 2348 | | 3 | 348 | | 28 | 2696 |
| 216.250.64.68 <-> 192.168.2.248 | 12 | 2370 | | 15 | 3459 | | 27 | 5829 |
| 216.250.64.68 <-> 192.168.2.192 | 14 | 1454 | | 13 | 2460 | | 27 | 3914 |
| 216.250.64.68 <-> 192.168.2.185 | 10 | 1087 | | 17 | 5907 | | 27 | 6994 |
| 216.250.64.68 <-> 192.168.2.103 | 16 | 1690 | | 10 | 1759 | | 26 | 3449 |
| 216.250.64.68 <-> 192.168.3.2 | 19 | 1735 | | 6 | 1973 | | 25 | 3708 |
| 216.250.64.68 <-> 192.168.2.7 | 13 | 1208 | | 11 | 4155 | | 24 | 5363 |
| 216.250.64.68 <-> 192.168.0.127 | 11 | 1123 | | 12 | 2094 | | 23 | 3217 |
| 216.250.64.68 <-> 192.168.2.121 | 18 | 1752 | | 5 | 1150 | | 23 | 2902 |

# Packet Length Distribution

**Syntax:** -z plen,tree[,*filter*]

**Description:** The packet length distribution reporting option will identify the distribution of frames in the capture file by 20-byte increments, identifying the rate and percentage of each packet length group. This feature can be helpful in network troubleshooting, where large quantities of small packets can place additional burden on networking equipment that leads to reduced throughput.

**Example:** The following example reads from the dc11.dump capture file and reports the distribution of packet sizes. This particular capture has an unusually large quantity of frames between 40 and 79 bytes in length, which might warrant further analysis.

```
C:\>tshark -r dc11.dump -nqz plen,tree
```

=================================================================

| Packet Length | value | rate | percent |
|---|---|---|---|
| Packet Length | 664070 | 0.001293 | |
| 0-19 | 0 | 0.000000 | 0.00% |
| 20-39 | 0 | 0.000000 | 0.00% |
| 40-79 | 494456 | 0.000962 | 74.46% |
| 80-159 | 114463 | 0.000223 | 17.24% |
| 160-319 | 16117 | 0.000031 | 2.43% |
| 320-639 | 13583 | 0.000026 | 2.05% |
| 640-1279 | 3597 | 0.000007 | 0.54% |
| 1280-2559 | 21854 | 0.000043 | 3.29% |
| 2560-5119 | 0 | 0.000000 | 0.00% |
| 5120- | 0 | 0.000000 | 0.00% |

=================================================================

# Destinations Tree

**Syntax:** -z dests,tree,*filter*

**Description:** The Destinations Tree statistics option identifies the number of frames, data rate, and transport-layer protocol information for the specified capture file. This report allows you to quickly assess the activity in the capture file, characterizing the nature of traffic to destination hosts.

**Example:** The following example reads from the http.cap capture file and identifies the destination addresses, transport protocol, and the percentage of network activity by destination address.

```
C:\>tshark -r http.cap -nqz dests,tree
```

=================================================================

| Destinations | value | rate | percent |
|---|---|---|---|
| Destinations | 43 | 0.001415 | |
| 145.254.160.237 | 20 | 0.000658 | 46.51% |
| TCP | 19 | 0.000625 | 95.00% |
| 80 | 19 | 0.000625 | 100.00% |
| UDP | 1 | 0.000033 | 5.00% |

| | | | |
|---|---|---|---|
| 53 | 1 | 0.000033 | 100.00% |
| 65.208.228.223 | 18 | 0.000592 | 41.86% |
| TCP | 18 | 0.000592 | 100.00% |
| 3372 | 18 | 0.000592 | 100.00% |
| 145.253.2.203 | 1 | 0.000033 | 2.33% |
| UDP | 1 | 0.000033 | 100.00% |
| 3009 | 1 | 0.000033 | 100.00% |
| 216.239.59.99 | 4 | 0.000132 | 9.30% |
| TCP | 4 | 0.000132 | 100.00% |
| 3371 | 4 | 0.000132 | 100.00% |

```
=====================================================================
```

# Packet Summary Columns

**Syntax:** -z proto,colinfo,*filter*,*field*

**Description:** The packet summary columns statistics option allows you to add any Wireshark protocol field to the one-line display output. By default, TShark will display several fields in the one-line display output when processing a packet capture. If you require additional fields to be reported, you can specify additional fields to be reported as well, giving us tremendous reporting flexibility that can be sent to other scripting tools to extract and use the reported data. This parameter can be specified multiple times on the command line to add an arbitrary number of additional columns. Note that it is necessary to include the field you wish to append to the packet summary output in the display filter string.

**Example:** The following example reads from the http.cap capture file and reports the standard summary output.

```
C:\>tshark -r http.cap -n
  1    0.000000 145.254.160.237 -> 65.208.228.223 3372 > 80 [SYN] Seq=0 Len=0
MSS=1460
  2    0.911310 65.208.228.223 -> 145.254.160.237 80 > 3372 [SYN, ACK] Seq=0
Ack=1 Win=5840 Len=0 MSS=1380
  3    0.911310 145.254.160.237 -> 65.208.228.223 3372 > 80 [ACK] Seq=1 Ack=1
Win=9660 Len=0
```

The next example uses the packet summary columns feature to add the IP identification and time-to-live values to the summary output.

```
C:\>tshark -r http.cap -nz proto,colinfo,ip.ttl,ip.ttl -z
proto,colinfo,ip.id,ip.id
```

```
  1    0.000000 145.254.160.237 -> 65.208.228.223 3372 > 80 [SYN] Seq=0 Len=0
MSS=1460  ip.id == 0x0f41  ip.ttl == 128

  2    0.911310 65.208.228.223 -> 145.254.160.237 80 > 3372 [SYN, ACK] Seq=0
Ack=1 Win=5840 Len=0 MSS=1380  ip.id == 0x0000  ip.ttl == 47

  3    0.911310 145.254.160.237 -> 65.208.228.223 3372 > 80 [ACK] Seq=1 Ack=1
Win=9660 Len=0  ip.id == 0x0f44  ip.ttl == 128
```

# SIP Statistics

**Syntax:** `-z sip,stat,filter`

**Description:** The Session Initialization Protocol (SIP) statistics reporting option will identify all the SIP traffic in the capture and report the number of sent and re-sent messages, the status codes from SIP responses, and the observed SIP messages. This reporting option is helpful to assess the activity on voice over IP (VoIP) networks that use the SIP protocol for call setup and teardown. By default, statistics are reported on all SIP activity in the capture; note that you can supply a display filter to limit the statistics reporting to a single host (such as `ip.addr eq 192.168.1.1`).

**Example:** The following example reads from the sip1.dump stored capture file and reports the observed SIP statistics for all hosts:

```
C:\>tshark -r sip1.dump -nqz sip,stat


======================================================================
SIP Statistics

Number of SIP messages: 37
Number of resent SIP messages: 0


* SIP Status Codes in reply packets
  SIP 407 Proxy Authentication Required :     1 Packets
  SIP 200 OK                 :     10 Packets
  SIP 100 Trying             :      4 Packets
  SIP 180 Ringing            :      2 Packets


* List of SIP Request methods
  INVITE          :      9 Packets
  BYE             :      2 Packets
  ACK             :      9 Packets
```

# H.225 Counters

**Syntax:** `-z h225,counter[,filter]`

**Description:** VoIP networks using H.323 also use the H.225 protocol for call establishment and control (signaling) and registration, admission and status functions (RAS). The H.225 counters statistics will count H.225 messages in the capture and the reason codes associated with the messages. By default, all H.225 messages will be used for reporting, but you may optionally supply a display filter to restrict the analysis to a specified group of packets.

**Example:** The following example reads from the specified compressed capture file and reports observed H.225 statistics.

```
C:\>tshark -r rtp_example.raw.gz -nqz h225,counter
================== H225 Message and Reason Counter ==================
RAS-Messages:
Call Signalling:
  setup : 1
  callProceeding : 1
  connect : 1
  alerting : 1

====================================================================
```

# H.225 Service Response Time

**Syntax:** `-z h225,srt[,filter]`

**Description:** Another H.225 statistics reporting mechanism, the H.225 Service Response Time (SRT) statistics option reports the RAS message type; minimum, maximum, and average SRT metrics; the number of open requests (that have not yet received a response); discarded requests; and duplicate messages. Each of these statistics can be useful for analyzing activity on VoIP networks to identify traffic patterns and metrics that could negatively influence VoIP service.

# Media Gateway Control Protocol Round Trip Delay

**Syntax:** `-z mgcp,rtd[,filter]`

**Description:** The Media Gateway Control Protocol (MGCP) is used in VoIP networks as an intermediary between traditional telephone circuits and data packets. Using this statistics reporting option, you can identify the response time delay (RTD) between stations and the MGCP server, and duplicate requests and responses, requests to unresponsive servers, and responses that do not match any requests.

# SMB Round Trip Data

**Syntax:** `-z smb,rtt[,filter]`

**Description:** The Server Message Blocks (SMB) protocol is a mechanism used for networked file systems, predominately used for Microsoft Windows clients. Using the SMB Round Trip Data (RTD) statistics reporting option, we can assess the responsiveness of Windows file-sharing servers and other SMB resources (including some networked printers) to identify the responsiveness of server resources.

**Example:** In this example, the packet capture file rtl-fileshare.dump is read using TShark to report SMB RTT statistics. Note that the Max RTT for the SMB Trans request in this output may indicate a burdened server resource that is unable to respond to the request sooner.

```
$ tshark -r rtl-fileshare.dump -nqz smb,rtt
```

```
===================================================================
SMB RTT Statistics:
Filter:
Commands                  Calls   Min RTT    Max RTT    Avg RTT
Open                          1   0.00186    0.00186    0.00186
Close                         4   0.00023    0.00176    0.00066
Trans                         5   0.00190   13.69178    2.76430
Open AndX                     1   0.00450    0.00450    0.00450
Read AndX                   309   0.00025    0.01865    0.00412
Tree Disconnect               7   0.00117    0.14601    0.02324
Negotiate Protocol            8   0.00026    0.07451    0.02226
Session Setup AndX           16   0.00028    0.01928    0.00578
Logoff AndX                  12   0.00074    0.00872    0.00258
Tree Connect AndX             7   0.00081    0.00399    0.00190
NT Create AndX                4   0.00029    0.00270    0.00132

Transaction2 Commands     Calls   Min RTT    Max RTT    Avg RTT
FIND_FIRST2                   1   0.19993    0.19993    0.19993
QUERY_FS_INFO                 2   0.00023    0.00248    0.00135
QUERY_FILE_INFO               2   0.00040    0.00551    0.00296

NT Transaction Commands   Calls   Min RTT    Max RTT    Avg RTT
===================================================================
```

# SMB Security Identifier Name Snooping

**Syntax:** `-z smb,sids`

**Description:** Another SMB analysis feature is the capability to use security identifier (SID) snooping techniques to identify potentially sensitive SIDs and their associated account names. This feature can be useful when performing a security audit of traffic captured from a Windows network, representing information that is valuable to an attacker for impersonating a legitimate user.

Because of the sensitive nature of this feature, the SMB SID snooping feature is not enabled by default. To use this statistics reporting option on the command line, you must also enable the Snoop SID preference in Wireshark by clicking **Edit | Preferences | Protocols | SMB | Snoop SID to name mappings**, or specify the preference on the command line with `-o smb.sid_name_snooping:TRUE`.

# BOOTP Statistics

**Syntax:** `-z bootp,stat,[filter]`

**Description:** TShark can report statistics for the BOOTP protocol used by DHCP, including the DHCP message and the number of packets for each type. This can be helpful to troubleshoot DHCP server problems, or to diagnose rogue (e.g., unauthorized) DHCP servers that may exist on your network.

**Example:** The following example reads from a stored capture file and identifies the BOOTP statistics in the file, identifying the DHCP server message types and packet counts. Note that the tailing comma after the *stat* keyword is required, even though a display filter is not specified in this example.

```
$ tshark -nqr rtl-fileshare.dump  -z bootp,stat,


======================================================================
BOOTP Statistics with filter
BOOTP Option 53: DHCP Messages Types:
DHCP Message Type      Packets nb
            Inform 74
               ACK 275
           Release 10
               NAK 82
           Decline 25
           Request 1255
          Discover 1811
             Offer 279

======================================================================
```

# HTTP Statistics

**Syntax:** `-z http,stat,[filter]`

**Description:** TShark can report statistics for the HTTP transactions, identifying the status response codes and request methods observed in the capture file. This feature can be useful to quickly identify how a particular Web server is being used, identifying errors being returned from the server.

**Example:** The following example reads from a stored capture file and identifies the observed HTTP statistics. Note that the tailing comma after the *stat* keyword is required, even though a display filter is not specified in this example.

```
$ tshark -r Kismet-Aug-01-2002-2.dump -nqz http,stat,


===================================================================
HTTP Statistics
* HTTP Status Codes in reply packets
    HTTP 408 Request Time-out
    HTTP 301 Moved Permanently
    HTTP 302 Moved Temporarily
    HTTP 304 Not Modified
    HTTP 200 OK
    HTTP 206 Partial Content
    HTTP 100 Continue
    HTTP 403 Forbidden
    HTTP 404 Not Found
* List of HTTP Request methods
      SEARCH   336
         GET   1447
        POST   8
        HEAD   2
===================================================================
```

# HTTP Tree Statistics

**Syntax:** `-z http,tree[,filter]`

**Description:** In addition to the HTTP statistics reporting feature, TShark can also present a tree-like view of HTTP activity, identifying the types of request and response packets, the quantities of each type, data rates, and overall percentages of all request and response types. This feature is also helpful at identifying how a Web server is being used, and can even identify potentially malicious activity with unsupported or broken HTTP requests or responses.

**Example:** The following example reads from a stored capture file and reports HTTP statistics in the tree-like view.

```
C:\>tshark -r Kismet-Aug-01-2002-2.dump -nqz http,tree
```

```
===================================================================
HTTP/Packet Counter          value          rate          percent
-------------------------------------------------------------------
Total HTTP Packets           8067       0.001504
 HTTP Request Packets        1793       0.000334          22.23%
  SEARCH                      336        0.000063          18.74%
  GET                         1447       0.000270          80.70%
  POST                        8          0.000001           0.45%
  HEAD                        2          0.000000           0.11%
 HTTP Response Packets       1296       0.000242          16.07%
  ???: broken                 0          0.000000           0.00%
  1xx: Informational          121        0.000023           9.34%
   100 Continue               121        0.000023         100.00%
  2xx: Success                689        0.000128          53.16%
   200 OK                     685        0.000128          99.42%
   206 Partial Content        4          0.000001           0.58%
  3xx: Redirection            479        0.000089          36.96%
   304 Not Modified           452        0.000084          94.36%
   302 Found                  24         0.000004           5.01%
   301 Moved Permanently      3          0.000001           0.63%
  4xx: Client Error           7          0.000001           0.54%
   408 Request Time-out       4          0.000001          57.14%
   404 Not Found              1          0.000000          14.29%
   403 Forbidden              2          0.000000          28.57%
  5xx: Server Error           0          0.000000           0.00%
 Other HTTP Packets          4978       0.000928          61.71%


===================================================================
```

# HTTP Request Statistics

**Syntax:** `-z http_req,tree[,filter]`

**Description:** If you wish to get more detailed reporting of activity with an HTTP server, you can use TShark's HTTP Request statistics reporting option, which will identify all the HTTP request URLs for each HTTP server in the packet capture, including the number of frames, data rate, and request percentage. This is useful to identify popular requests for a specific server (the HTTP requests that are most popular will have the highest percentage values for each server). This option is often used with a display filter to assess the activity for one or more hosts, but can also be used without a display filter to identify the servers and URLs requests by client systems within your organization.

**Example:** The following example reads from a stored capture file and reports HTTP request statistics in the tree-like format, limiting the analysis to traffic to or from the host at 66.207.160.150.

```
C:\>tshark -r Kismet-Aug-01-2002-2.dump -nqz http_req,tree,"ip.addr eq
66.207.60.150"
```

```
===========================================================
HTTP/Requests                     value      rate        percent
-----------------------------------------------------------
HTTP Requests by HTTP Host         35      0.000757
 www.megatokyo.com                 35      0.000757      100.00%
  /parts/mt2-head-top.gif           3      0.000065        8.57%
  /parts/mt2-merchandise.gif        2      0.000043        5.71%
  /parts/mt-shadow-right.gif        8      0.000173       22.86%
  /parts/mt-glow-top.gif            4      0.000087       11.43%
  /parts/mt-blk_bar-credits.gif    14      0.000303       40.00%
  /parts/pix-dark.gif               1      0.000022        2.86%
  /parts/mt-bottom-prev.gif         2      0.000043        5.71%
  /parts/mt-glow-bottom.gif         1      0.000022        2.86%


===========================================================
```

## Notes from the Underground...

### XML Compatible Protocol Dissection

A new feature to TShark in version 0.10.0 is the ability to display output in PDML format by using the **–T pdml** option. The Politecnico Di Torino group, known for Analyzer and WinPcap, created the PDML specification. PDML is a simple language to format information related to packet decodes. The PDML data TShark produces differs slightly from the specification and is not readable by Analyzer. The TShark PDML output contains the following flags:

- **<pdml>** This PDML file is delimited by the <pdml> and </pdml> tags. This tag does not have any attributes.
  Example: <pdml version="0" creator="Wireshark/0.10.0">

- **<packet>** A PDML file can contain multiple packets by using the <packet> element. This tag does not have any attributes.

- **<proto>** A packet can contain multiple protocols, designated by the <proto> element. The <proto> tag can have the following attributes:

  - **name** The display filter name for the protocol.

  - **showname** The label used to describe this protocol in the protocol tree.

  - **pos** The starting offset within the packet data where this protocol starts.

  - **size** The number of octets in the packet data this protocol covers.
    Example: <proto name="ip" showname="Internet Protocol, Src Addr: 192.168.100.132

    (192.168.100.132), Dst Addr: 192.168.129.201 (192.168.129.201)" size="20" pos="14">

- **<field>** A protocol can contain multiple fields, designated by the <field> element. The <field> tag can have the following attributes:

  - **name** The display filter name for the field.

  - **showname** The label used to describe this field in the protocol tree.

  - **pos** The starting offset within the packet data where this field starts.

**Continued**

- **size** The number of octets in the packet data this field covers.
- **value** The actual packet data, in hex, this field covers.
- **show** The representation of the packet data as it appears in a display filter.

Example: <field name="ip.version" showname="Version: 4" size="1"

pos="14" show="4" value="45"/>

Two tools are provided in the Wireshark-0.10.0a/tools directory to assist with PDML output parsing. WiresharkXML.py is a Python module used to read a PDML file and call a specified callback function. msnchat is a sample program that uses WiresharkXML to parse PDML output for MSN chat conversations. It takes one or more capture files as input, invokes TShark with a specified read filter, and produces HTML output of the conversations. The usage output for msnchat is as follows:

```
[root@localhost tools]# ./msnchat -h
msnchat [OPTIONS] CAPTURE_FILE [...]
  -o FILE        name of output file
  -t TSHARK   location of TShark binary
  -u USER        name for unknown user
```

The following command can be used to read and parse a saved capture file called msn_test1.

```
[root@localhost tools]# ./msnchat -o outfile msn_test1
```

When viewed with a Web browser, the HTML outfile looks like this:

```
---- New Conversation @ Dec 30, 2003 14:21:08 ----
(14:21:08) Luke: hello
(14:21:22) Unknown: how are you?
(14:21:53) Luke: are we meeting at noon?
(14:22:03) Unknown: yes, at the secret location.
(14:22:11) Luke: great, see you then
(14:22:17) Unknown: ok
(14:22:18) Unknown: bye
```

You can add a name for the Unknown user by typing the command:

```
[root@localhost tools]# ./msnchat -o outfile -u Leia msn_test1
```

The HTML output would then look like this:

**Continued**

```
---- New Conversation @ Dec 30, 2003 14:21:08 ----

(14:21:08) Luke: hello

(14:21:22) Leia: how are you?

(14:21:53) Luke: are we meeting at noon?

(14:22:03) Leia: yes, at the secret location.

(14:22:11) Luke: great, see you then

(14:22:17) Leia: ok

(14:22:18) Leia: bye
```

The msnchat code will give you a good idea of how to write your own scripts to parse capture files, manipulate the PDML data, and print the output in HTML format.

# editcap

editcap is a program used to remove or select packets from a file and to translate the format of captured files. It doesn't capture live traffic; it only reads data from a saved capture file and then saves some or all of the packets to a new capture file. editcap can read all of the same types of files Wireshark can, and by default writes to libpcap format. editcap can also write captures to standard and modified versions of libpcap, Sun snoop, Novell LANalyzer, Networks Associate's Sniffer, Microsoft Network Monitor, Visual Network traffic capture, Accellent 5Views capture, and Network Instruments Observer version 9 captures. editcap can determine the file type it is reading, and is capable of reading files that are compressed with gzip.

By default, editcap writes all of the packets in the capture file to the output file. If you specify a list of packet numbers on the command line, those packets will *not* be written to the output capture file. If the **–r** option is specified, it will reverse the default configuration and write only the specified packets to the output capture file. You can also specify a range of packets to include or exclude in the output capture file.

The following information is the usage output for the editcap program.

```
C:\Program Files\Wireshark>editcap
Usage: editcap [-r] [-h] [-v] [-T <encap type>] [-E <probability>]
               [-F <capture type>] [-s <snaplen>] [-t <time adjustment>]
               [-c <packets per file>]
               <infile> <outfile> [ <record#>[-<record#>] ... ]
    where
        -c <packets per file> If given splits the output to different files
```

```
     -E <probability> specifies the probability (between 0 and 1)
          that a particular byte will have an error.
-F <capture type> specifies the capture file type to write:
          libpcap - libpcap (tcpdump, Ethereal, etc.)
          rh6_1libpcap - RedHat Linux 6.1 libpcap (tcpdump)
          suse6_3libpcap - SuSE Linux 6.3 libpcap (tcpdump)
          modlibpcap - modified libpcap (tcpdump)
          nokialibpcap - Nokia libpcap (tcpdump)
          nseclibpcap - Nanosecond libpcap (Ethereal)
          lanalyzer - Novell LANalyzer
          ngsniffer - Network Associates Sniffer (DOS-based)
          snoop - Sun snoop
          netmon1 - Microsoft Network Monitor 1.x
          netmon2 - Microsoft Network Monitor 2.x
          ngwsniffer_1_1 - Network Associates Sniffer (Windows-based) 1.1
          ngwsniffer_2_0 - Network Associates Sniffer (Windows-based) 2.00x
          nettl - HP-UX nettl trace
          visual - Visual Networks traffic capture
          5views - Accellent 5Views capture
          niobserverv9 - Network Instruments Observer version 9
          rf5 - Tektronix K12xx 32-bit .rf5 format
          default is libpcap
     -h produces this help listing.
     -r specifies that the records specified should be kept, not deleted,
                    default is to delete
     -s <snaplen> specifies that packets should be truncated to
          <snaplen> bytes of data
     -t <time adjustment> specifies the time adjustment
          to be applied to selected packets
     -T <encap type> specifies the encapsulation type to use:
          ether - Ethernet
          tr - Token Ring
          slip - SLIP
          ppp - PPP
          fddi - FDDI
          fddi-swapped - FDDI with bit-swapped MAC addresses
          rawip - Raw IP
          arcnet - ARCNET
```

```
arcnet_linux - Linux ARCNET
atm-rfc1483 - RFC 1483 ATM
linux-atm-clip - Linux ATM CLIP
lapb - LAPB
atm-pdus - ATM PDUs
atm-pdus-untruncated - ATM PDUs - untruncated
null - NULL
ascend - Lucent/Ascend access equipment
isdn - ISDN
ip-over-fc - RFC 2625 IP-over-Fibre Channel
ppp-with-direction - PPP with Directional Info
ieee-802-11 - IEEE 802.11 Wireless LAN
prism - IEEE 802.11 plus Prism II monitor mode header
ieee-802-11-radio - IEEE 802.11 Wireless LAN with radio
information
ieee-802-11-radiotap - IEEE 802.11 plus radiotap WLAN header
ieee-802-11-avs - IEEE 802.11 plus AVS WLAN header
linux-sll - Linux cooked-mode capture
frelay - Frame Relay
frelay-with-direction - Frame Relay with Directional Info
chdlc - Cisco HDLC
ios - Cisco IOS internal
ltalk - Localtalk
pflog-old - OpenBSD PF Firewall logs, pre-3.4
hhdlc - HiPath HDLC
docsis - Data Over Cable Service Interface Specification
cosine - CoSine L2 debug log
whdlc - Wellfleet HDLC
sdlc - SDLC
tzsp - Tazmen sniffer protocol
enc - OpenBSD enc(4) encapsulating interface
pflog - OpenBSD PF Firewall logs
chdlc-with-direction - Cisco HDLC with Directional Info
bluetooth-h4 - Bluetooth H4
mtp2 - SS7 MTP2
mtp3 - SS7 MTP3
irda - IrDA
user0 - USER 0
```

```
user1 - USER 1
user2 - USER 2
user3 - USER 3
user4 - USER 4
user5 - USER 5
user6 - USER 6
user7 - USER 7
user8 - USER 8
user9 - USER 9
user10 - USER 10
user11 - USER 11
user12 - USER 12
user13 - USER 13
user14 - USER 14
user15 - USER 15
symantec - Symantec Enterprise Firewall
ap1394 - Apple IP-over-IEEE 1394
bacnet-ms-tp - BACnet MS/TP
raw-icmp-nettl - Raw ICMP with nettl headers
raw-icmpv6-nettl - Raw ICMPv6 with nettl headers
gprs-llc - GPRS LLC
juniper-atm1 - Juniper ATM1
juniper-atm2 - Juniper ATM2
redback - Redback SmartEdge
rawip-nettl - Raw IP with nettl headers
ether-nettl - Ethernet with nettl headers
tr-nettl - Token Ring with nettl headers
fddi-nettl - FDDI with nettl headers
unknown-nettl - Unknown link-layer type with nettl headers
mtp2-with-phdr - MTP2 with pseudoheader
juniper-pppoe - Juniper PPPoE
gcom-tie1 - GCOM TIE1
gcom-serial - GCOM Serial
x25-nettl - X25 with nettl headers
juniper-mlppp - Juniper MLPPP
juniper-mlfr - Juniper MLFR
juniper-ether - Juniper Ethernet
juniper-ppp - Juniper PPP
```

```
juniper-frelay - Juniper Frame-Relay
juniper-chdlc - Juniper C-HDLC
default is the same as the input file
-v specifies verbose operation, default is silent


A range of records can be specified as well
```

The following command-line options are used to control editcap's data translation and output.

- **–F** *type* Used to set the format of the output capture file. For example, if you want to save a file in the Sun snoop format so snoop can read the capture file, you would use the **–F snoop** option.

- **–h** Prints the help options of editcap, and then exits.

- **–r** Causes the packets whose numbers are specified on the command line to be written to the output capture file. This is opposite of the default action, which is to remove the packets that are specified on the command line. Packets can only be specified as a consecutive range in the *start-end* format, or individually; they cannot be comma delimited.

- **–s** *snaplen* Sets the snapshot length to use when writing the data to the output capture file. Packets that are larger than the *snaplen* will be truncated. This option is helpful if you only want to save the packet headers, or if the program you will be importing the capture file into can only read packets of a certain size.

- **–t [-]***seconds[.fractional seconds]* Allows you to specify a time adjustment to apply to selected frames in the output capture file. The time adjustment is specified in seconds and fractions of seconds. An option of **–t 3600** will advance the timestamp on the selected frames by one hour, while the option of **–t –3600** will reduce the timestamp on the selected frames by one hour. This option is useful when you need to synchronize packet traces with other logs from different devices.

- **–T** *type* Sets the packet encapsulation type of the output capture file. The default type is the same encapsulation type as the input file. This option forces the encapsulation type of the output capture file to be a specified type; however, the packet headers will remain the same encapsulation type as the input capture file. This is because the encapsulation type is stored as meta-data, outside of the packet data. The encapsulation type is a single variable that is changed, thus allowing the packet data and headers of the original packet to remain unchanged.

- **–v** Causes editcap to print various messages to the screen while it is processing files.

The following is an example of using editcap to translate the first five packets, and packets 10, 15, and 17 from a TShark libpcap capture file called *capture* to a Sun snoop output file called *capture_snoop*.

```
C:\Program Files\Wireshark>editcap -r -v -F snoop capture capture_snoop 1-5
10 15 17
File capture is a libpcap (tcpdump, Wireshark, etc.) capture file.
Add_Selected: 1-5
Inclusive ... 1, 5
Add_Selected: 10
Not inclusive ... 10
Add_Selected: 15
Not inclusive ... 15
Add_Selected: 17
Not inclusive ... 17
Record: 1
Record: 2
Record: 3
Record: 4
Record: 5
Record: 10
Record: 15
Record: 17
```

The next example uses editcap to copy all packets, except packets 5 through 120, from a libpcap capture file called *capture* to a libpcap output file called *capture_out*.

```
C:\Program Files\Wireshark>editcap -v capture capture_out 5-120
File capture is a libpcap (tcpdump, Wireshark, etc.) capture file.
Add_Selected: 5-120
Inclusive ... 5, 120
Record: 1
Record: 2
Record: 3
```

```
Record: 4
Record: 121
Record: 122
```

The next example uses editcap to adjust the timestamp forward by five and a half seconds on all packets. It uses an NAI Sniffer capture file called *capture.dump* as input and saves the output to a Novell LANalyzer file called *capture_out*.

```
C:\Program Files\Wireshark>editcap -v -F lanalyzer -t 5.5 capture.dump
capture_out
File capture is a libpcap (tcpdump, Wireshark, etc.) capture file.
Record: 1
Record: 2
Record: 3
Record: 4
Record: 5
Record: 6
Record: 7
Record: 8
Record: 9
Record: 10
output removed
```

The next example uses editcap to save the first 35 bytes of the input capture file called *capture* to the output capture file called *capture_out*. This will include the full Ethernet and IP headers in the output file.

```
C:\Program Files\Wireshark>editcap -v -s 35 capture capture_out
File capture is a libpcap (tcpdump, Wireshark, etc.) capture file.
Record: 1
Record: 2
Record: 3
Record: 4
Record: 5
Record: 6
Record: 7
Record: 8
Record: 9
Record: 10
output removed
```

The next example uses editcap to translate the input capture file called *capture* to the output capture file called *capture_out* with an encapsulation type of IEEE 802.11 Wireless LAN.

```
C:\Program Files\Wireshark>editcap -v -T ieee-802-11 capture capture_out
File capture is a libpcap (tcpdump, Wireshark, etc.) capture file.
Record: 1
Record: 2
Record: 3
Record: 4
Record: 5
Record: 6
Record: 7
Record: 8
Record: 9
Record: 10
output removed
```

# mergecap

mergecap is used to combine multiple saved capture files into a single output file. mergecap can read all of the same types of files Wireshark can, and by default writes to libpcap format. mergecap can also write the output capture file to standard and modified versions of libpcap, Sun snoop, Novel LANalyzer, NAI Sniffer, Microsoft Network Monitor, Visual Network traffic capture, Accellent 5Views capture, and Network Instruments Observer version 9 captures. mergecap can determine the file type it is reading, and is capable of reading files that are compressed with gzip. By default, the packets from the input files are merged in chronological order based on each packet's timestamp. If the **–a** option is specified, packets will be copied directly from each input file to the output file regardless of timestamp.

The following command-line options are used to control editcap's data translation and output.

- **–a** Ignores the timestamps in the input capture files and merges the capture files one after the other. When this option is omitted, the packets in the input files are merged in chronological order based on the packet timestamps.

- **–F type** Used to set the format of the output capture file. For example, if you want to merge capture files and save them in the Sun snoop format so snoop can read the output file, you would use the **–F** snoop option.

- **−h** Prints the help options of mergecap, and then exits.

- **−s** *snaplen* Sets the snapshot length to use when writing the data to the output capture file. Packets larger than the *snaplen* will be truncated. This option is helpful if you only want to save the packet headers, or if the program you will be importing the capture file into can only read packets of a certain size.

- **−T** *type* Sets the packet encapsulation type of the output capture file. The default type is the same encapsulation type as the input files, if they are all the same. If the input files do not all have the same encapsulation type, the encapsulation type of the output file will be set to WTAP_ENCAP_PER_PACKET. However, libpcap and other capture formats do not support this type of encapsulation. The **−T** option forces the encapsulation type of the output capture file to be a specified type; however, the packet headers will remain the same encapsulation type as the input capture file.

- **−v** Causes mergecap to print various messages to the screen while it is processing files.

- **−w** *file* Writes the packets to the filename specified following the option. This option is required for mergecap to merge files.

The following is an example of using mergecap to merge the first 35 bytes of each of the four capture files (*capture1*, *capture2*, *capture3*, and *capture4*) into a single Sun snoop output file called *merge_snoop* in chronological order by packet timestamp; it will keep reading packets until the end of the last file is reached.

```
C:\Program Files\Wireshark>mergecap -s 35 -v -F snoop -w merge_snoop
capture1 capture2 capture3 capture4
mergecap: capture1 is type libpcap (tcpdump, Wireshark, etc.).
mergecap: capture2 is type libpcap (tcpdump, Wireshark, etc.).
mergecap: capture3 is type libpcap (tcpdump, Wireshark, etc.).
mergecap: capture4 is type libpcap (tcpdump, Wireshark, etc.).
mergecap: opened 4 of 4 input files
mergecap: selected frame_type Ethernet (ether)
Record: 1
Record: 2
Record: 3
Record: 4
Record: 5
Record: 6
```

```
Record: 7
Record: 8
Record: 9
Record: 10
output removed
```

The following is an example of using mergecap to merge four capture files (*capture1, capture2, capture3,* and *capture4*) into a single output file called *merge_file* regardless of packet timestamp; it will write all of the packets of capture1, followed by capture 2, and so on.

```
C:\Program Files\Wireshark>mergecap -v -a -w merge_file capture1 capture2
capture3 capture4
mergecap: capture1 is type libpcap (tcpdump, Wireshark, etc.).
mergecap: capture2 is type libpcap (tcpdump, Wireshark, etc.).
mergecap: capture3 is type libpcap (tcpdump, Wireshark, etc.).
mergecap: capture4 is type libpcap (tcpdump, Wireshark, etc.).
mergecap: opened 4 of 4 input files
mergecap: selected frame_type Ethernet (ether)
Record: 1
Record: 2
Record: 3
Record: 4
Record: 5
Record: 6
Record: 7
Record: 8
Record: 9
Record: 10
output removed
```

The following is an example of an attempt to use mergecap to merge three capture files with different encapsulation types (*capture1, capture2,* and *capture3*) into a single output file called *merge_encap* The merge will attempt to set the default encapsulation type and then report an error because libpcap does not understand that type of encapsulation.

```
C:\Program Files\Wireshark>mergecap -v -w merge_encap capture1 capture2
capture3
mergecap: capture1 is type libpcap (tcpdump, Wireshark, etc.).
mergecap: capture2 is type libpcap (tcpdump, Wireshark, etc.).
mergecap: capture3 is type libpcap (tcpdump, Wireshark, etc.).
```

```
mergecap: opened 3 of 3 input files
mergecap: multiple frame encapsulation types detected
          defaulting to WTAP_ENCAP_PER_PACKET
          capture1 had type (null) ((null))
          capture2 had type Ethernet (ether)
mergecap: selected frame_type (null) ((null))
mergecap: Can't open/create merge_encap:
          That file format doesn't support per-packet encapsulations
```

The following is an example of an attempt to use mergecap to merge three capture files with different encapsulation types (*capture1*, *capture2*, and *capture3*) into a single output file called *merge_encap*; the **–T** option is used to force an Ethernet encapsulation type for the output file.

```
C:\Program Files\Wireshark>mergecap -v -T ether -w merge_encap capture1
capture2 capture3
mergecap: capture1 is type libpcap (tcpdump, Wireshark, etc.).
mergecap: capture2 is type libpcap (tcpdump, Wireshark, etc.).
mergecap: capture3 is type libpcap (tcpdump, Wireshark, etc.).
mergecap: opened 3 of 3 input files
Record: 1
Record: 2
Record: 3
Record: 4
Record: 5
Record: 6
Record: 7
Record: 8
Record: 9
Record: 10
output removed
```

# text2pcap

text2pcap generates capture files by reading ASCII hexadecimal dump captures and writing the data to a libpcap output file. It is capable of reading a hexdump of single or multiple packets, and building capture files from it. text2pcap can also read hexdumps of application-level data only, by creating dummy Ethernet, IP, and User Datagram Protocol (UDP) or TCP headers so Wireshark and other sniffers can read the full data. The user can specify which headers to add.

text2pcap uses the octal dump (od) format of hexadecimal output. Octal dump is a UNIX command used to output a file or standard input to a specified form, such as octal, decimal, or hexadecimal format. The format is specified by the parameters given to the **–t** option. The command **od –t x1** will generate output text2pcap can understand (the **x1** describes the format of hexadecimal). The following is an example of the type of hexadecimal dump text2pcap can read.

```
0000   00 05 5d ee 7e 53 08 00 20 cf 5b 39 08 00 45 00    ..].~S.. .[9..E.
0010   00 9a 13 9e 40 00 3c 06 e0 70 c0 a8 64 7a c0 a8    ....@.<..p..dz..
0020   64 84 00 17 05 49 0e a9 91 43 8e d8 e3 6a 50 18    d....I...C...jP.
0030   c1 e8 ba 7b 00 00 4c 61 73 74 20 6c 6f 67 69 6e    ...{..Last login
0040   3a 20 53 75 6e 20 4e 6f 76 20 20 32 20 31 37 3a    : Sun Nov  2 17:
0050   30 36 3a 35 33 20 66 72 6f 6d 20 31 39 32 2e 31    06:53 from 192.1
0060   36 38 2e 31 30 30 2e 31 33 32 0d 0a 53 75 6e 20    68.100.132..Sun
0070   4d 69 63 72 6f 73 79 73 74 65 6d 73 20 49 6e 63    Microsystems Inc
0080   2e 20 20 20 53 75 6e 4f 53 20 35 2e 39 20 20 20    .   SunOS 5.9
0090   20 20 20 20 47 65 6e 65 72 69 63 20 4d 61 79 20       Generic May
00a0   32 30 30 32 0d 0a 23 20                            2002..#
```

The beginning of each line has an offset of more than two hexadecimal, or octal, digits that is used to track the bytes in the output. If the offset is 0, this indicates the beginning of a new packet. If there are multiple packets in a file, they will be output to the packet capture file with one second between each packet. If a line doesn't have this offset, it is ignored. The text output at the end of the line is also ignored. Text files can also contain comments that begin with the # character. text2pcap has the capability to support commands and options by using the **#TEXT2PCAP** command at the beginning of the line. text2pcap currently doesn't have any commands and options supported, but future development could incorporate methods to control the way the hexadecimal dump is processed.

The following command-line options are used to control text2pcap's data processing and output.

- **–h** Prints the help options of text2pcap, and then exits.
- **–d** Displays debugging information during the processing. Like verbose options, it can be used several times for more information.
- **–q** Causes text2pcap to be quiet while processing.
- **–o h|o** Specifies either hexadecimal or octal formats for the offset of the output. The default is hexadecimal.

- **−l *typenum*** Lets you specify the data link layer type of encapsulation for the packet. This option is used when your hexdump is a complete, encapsulated packet. The encapsulation type is specified as a number using the *typenum* parameter. A complete list of encapsulation types and their associated numbers can be found in the /libpcap-0.7.2/bpf/net/bpf.h file included in the libpcap source distribution. For example, Point-to-Point Protocol (PPP) is encapsulation type 9. The default is Ethernet, encapsulation type 1.

- **−e *l3pid*** Allows you to include a dummy Ethernet header for each packet. You would use this option when your dump file has any type of Layer 3 header, such as IP, but no Layer 2 information.

- **−i *proto*** Allows you to include a dummy IP header for each packet. The *proto* parameter allows you to specify the IP protocol in decimal format. You would use this option when your dump file has complete Layer 4 information, but no Layer 3 IP information. This option will also include the necessary Ethernet information. For example, **−i 88** will set the set the protocol to Enhanced Interior Gateway Routing Protocol (EIGRP).

- **−m *max-packet*** Allows you to set the maximum packet length with the *max-packet* parameter. The default is 64000.

- **−u *srcport, destport*** Allows you to include a dummy UDP header for each packet. The *srcport* and *destport* parameters allow you to specify the source and destination UDP ports in decimal format. You would use this option when your dump file does not contain any UDP Layer 4 or below information. This option will also include the necessary IP and Ethernet information.

- **−T *srcport, destport*** Allows you to include a dummy TCP header for each packet. The *srcport* and *destport* parameters allow you to specify the source and destination TCP ports in decimal format. You would use this option when your dump file does not contain any TCP Layer 4 or below information. This option will also include the necessary IP and Ethernet information.

- **−s *srcport, destport, tag*** Allows you to include a dummy Stream Control Transmission Protocol (SCTP) header for each packet. The *srcport* and *destport* parameters allow you to specify the source and destination SCTP ports in decimal format. The *tag* parameter allows you to specify a verification tag. You would use this option when your dump file does not contain any SCTP Layer 4 or below information. This option will also include the necessary IP, Ethernet, and CRC32C checksum information.

- **–S** *srcport, destport, ppi* Allows you to include a dummy SCTP header for each packet. The *srcport* and *destport* parameters allow you to specify the source and destination SCTP ports in decimal format. The *ppi* parameter allows you to specify a payload protocol identifier for a dummy SCTP DATA chunk header. The verification tag will automatically be set to 0. You would use this option when your dump file does not contain any SCTP Layer 4 or below information. This option will also include the necessary IP, Ethernet, and CRC32C checksum information.

- **–t** *timefmt* Allows you to specify a time format for the text before the packet. The *timefmt* parameter follows the format of strptime(3), such as "%H:%M:%S.", which converts a character string to a time value.

The following is an example of using text2pcap to read a hexadecimal dump, *hex_sample.txt*, and output it to the *libpcap_output* file.

```
C:\Program Files\Wireshark>text2pcap hex_sample.txt libpcap_output
Input from: hex_sample.txt
Output to: libpcap_output
Wrote packet of 168 bytes at 0
Read 1 potential packets, wrote 1 packets
```

The next example uses text2pcap to read a file with multiple hexadecimal packets, *hex_sample2.txt*, and output the format as Telnet/TCP packets to the *libpcap_output2* file.

```
C:\Program Files\Wireshark>text2pcap -T 1297,23 hex_sample2.txt
libpcap_output2
Input from: hex_sample2.txt
Output to: libpcap_output2
Generate dummy Ethernet header: Protocol: 0x800
Generate dummy IP header: Protocol: 6
Generate dummy TCP header: Source port: 1297. Dest port: 23
Wrote packet of 62 bytes at 0
Wrote packet of 62 bytes at 62
Wrote packet of 60 bytes at 124
Wrote packet of 69 bytes at 184
output removed
Read 76 potential packets, wrote 76 packets
```

The od command can also be piped into the text2pcap program. text2pcap will then read the output of the od command as standard input. The next example uses text2pcap to read a data stream as input, and output the format as HTTP/TCP packets to the output.pcap file. The **−Ax** parameter to the od command prints the offsets as hexadecimal. The **−m1460** parameter to text2pcap specifies a maximum packet size of 1460 bytes. The maximum Ethernet packet size is 1500 bytes, minus the 20 bytes for the IP and TCP headers, leaves 1460 bytes for the data. By default, the **−T** parameter will create TCP, IP, and Ethernet dummy headers. The following shows the command and associated output.

```
[root@localhost root]# od -Ax -tx1 input | text2pcap -m1460 -T1234,80 -
output.pcap
Input from: Standard input
Output to: output.pcap
Generate dummy Ethernet header: Protocol: 0x800
Generate dummy IP header: Protocol: 6
Generate dummy TCP header: Source port: 1234. Dest port: 80
Wrote packet of 1460 bytes at 0
Wrote packet of 1460 bytes at 1460
Wrote packet of 1460 bytes at 2920
Wrote packet of 788 bytes at 4380
Read 4 potential packets, wrote 4 packets
```

# capinfos

capinfos is a new command-line tool included with Wireshark that examines a stored capture file and reports statistics related to the number of packets, packet sizes, and timing information. Unlike other statistics reporting mechanisms in other Wireshark tools, capinfos does not report on the contents of traffic, instead giving a quick summary of the capture file contents.

The following command-line options are used to control capinfos' output.

- **−h** Prints the help options of capinfos, and then exits.

- **−t** Displays the capture file type as one of the supported Wireshark capture file formats, regardless of the filename extension.

- **−c** Displays the number of packets in the capture file.

- **−d** Displays the total length of all the packets in the file as a number of bytes.

- **−u** Displays the capture file duration in seconds.

- **−a** Displays the capture start time.

- **−e** Displays the capture end time.

- **–y** Displays the average data rate in bytes per second.

- **–i** Displays the average data rate in bits per second.

- **–h** Displays the average packet size in bytes.

capinfos can be run with only a filename as a command-line parameter, and will display all the available statistics, as shown here:

```
C:\>capinfos all-ml.dump
File name: all-ml.dump
File type: libpcap (tcpdump, Ethereal, etc.)
Number of packets: 282905
File size: 41418290 bytes
Data size: 56143385 bytes
Capture duration: 7579.713771 seconds
Start time: Mon Sep 15 09:44:53 2003
End time: Mon Sep 15 11:51:13 2003
Data rate: 7407.06 bytes/s
Data rate: 59256.47 bits/s
Average packet size: 198.45 bytes
```

# dumpcap

The dumpcap utility is used to capture traffic from a live interface and save to a libpcap file. This utility includes a subset of the functions available in TShark, but does not include the vast library of protocol decoders. This gives dumpcap a significantly smaller footprint, which can be beneficial on low-memory systems capturing traffic with multiple processes.

The following command-line options are used to control dumpcap's data processing and output.

- **–a** *test:value* Instructs dumpcap to stop writing to a file when it meets the specified test condition and value. This option mirrors the functionality of **–a** in TShark.

- **–b** *number of ring buffer files [:duration]* Used with the **–a** option, causes dumpcap to continue capturing data to successive files. This option mirrors the functionality of **–b** in TShark.

- **–B** *buffer size* Available only on Windows systems, causes dumpcap to allocate a buffer for storing packet data during a capture before writing to the disk. This option mirrors the functionality of **–B** in TShark.

- **–c** *count* Sets the default number of packets to read when capturing data. This option mirrors the functionality of **–c** in TShark.

- **–D** Instructs dumpcap to print a list of available interfaces on the system, mirroring the functionality of **–D** in TShark.

- **–f** *capture filter expression* Allows you to set the filter expression to use when capturing data, mirroring the functionality of **–f** in TShark.

- **–h** Prints the version of dumpcap and the help options, and then exits.

- **–i** *interface* Specifies the interface you want to use to capture data, mirroring the functionality of **–i** in TShark.

- **–L** Lists the data link types that are supported by an interface and then exits, mirroring the functionality of **–L** in TShark.

- **–p** Tells dumpcap to not put the interface in promiscuous mode, mirroring the functionality of **–p** in TShark.

- **–s** *snaplen* Allows you to set the default snapshot length to use when capturing data, mirroring the functionality of **–s** in TShark.

- **–v** Prints the dumpcap version information and exits.

- **–w** *file* Writes the packets to the filename specified following the option, mirroring the functionality of **–w** in TShark.

- **–y** *type* Allows you to set the data link type to use while capturing packets, mirroring the functionality of **–y** in TShark.

Run with no command-line arguments, dumpcap will select the first available network interface and start capturing traffic, saving the contents to a libpcap file with a randomly selected filename.

dumpcap can be useful to leverage the flexibility of capture autostop conditions and ringbuffer output files, without the overhead associated with the Wireshark GUI or the memory and CPU requirements of TShark. For example, dumpcap can collect traffic for five minutes before stopping, saving the contents to the named libpcap file, as shown here:

```
C:\>dumpcap -i 2 -a duration:300 -w eventcollection.cap
```

# Summary

As shown in this chapter, Wireshark is more than the GUI; it is a suite of programs that provide command-line capturing, formatting, and manipulating capabilities. The programs can be used together to provide even more processing capabilities, while output from one program can be piped as input to another. Since these programs are command line, they also provide powerful scripting capabilities.

TShark provides just about all the same processing capabilities as Wireshark, minus the GUI. editcap, although used primarily for removing packets from a capture file, can also be used to translate capture files into various formats. mergecap provides the capability to merge various capture files, even from different network analyzers. This is a great resource when performing audits or incident response and you need to combine captures from various sources such as sniffers, IDSs, and logs. text2pcap allows you to translate hexadecimal data streams to sniffer readable packet captures. You can even add dummy Layer 2–4 data when you only have an application output stream. capinfos provides summary information about the contents of a capture file, and dumpcap can be used as an attractive alternative to TShark for automating traffic capture tasks.

# Solutions Fast Track

## TShark

☑ TShark can read packets from the network or from a packet capture file.

☑ TShark can decode and print the captured packets to screen or save them to a file.

☑ One of the best advantages of using TShark is that it is highly scriptable.

☑ TShark can apply both capture and display filters to the packet captures.

☑ TShark can collect various types of statistics about the data being captured.

☑ Like editcap, TShark can be used to translate capture file formats.

## editcap

☑ editcap can be used to remove packets from a capture file or translate the format of capture files.

☑ The **–t** option in editcap is used to apply a time adjustment to the timestamps of the packets.

☑ The snapshot length can be specified with the **–s** option to decrease the size of each packet.

☑ editcap can specify an encapsulation type for the packets in the output file with the **–T** option.

## mergecap

☑ mergecap can merge several packet capture files into a single output file.

☑ mergecap can read capture files of various formats and output them to a single format.

☑ By default, the packets from the input files are merged in chronological order based on each packet's timestamp; however, if the **–a** option is specified, packets will be copied directly from each input file to the output file regardless of timestamp.

☑ mergecap can merge capture files with different encapsulation types into a single output file by using the **–T** option to force the output encapsulation type.

# text2pcap

- ☑ text2pcap reads ASCII hexadecimal dump captures and writes the data to a libpcap output file.
- ☑ text2pcap can inserts dummy Ethernet, IP, and UDP or TCP headers.
- ☑ The command **od −t x1** will generate output text2pcap can understand.
- ☑ An offset of 0 indicates the beginning of a new packet.
- ☑ text2pcap options give you a lot of control over the dummy headers, timestamps, and encapsulation type for each packet.

# Capinfos

- ☑ capinfos provides summary statistics about a specified packet capture file.
- ☑ capinfos calculates and reports the average packet size data rate in the capture file.
- ☑ You can selectively enable one or more reporting features using command-line parameters.

# dumpcap

- ☑ dumpcap reads from a live network interface and saves the contents to one or more libpcap files.
- ☑ dumpcap has several of the capture features in TShark, but requires less memory per dumpcap instance.
- ☑ dumpcap will select the first available interface and store packets in a randomly selected filename when no arguments are specified.

# Frequently Asked Questions

The following Frequently Asked Questions, answered by the authors of this book, are designed to both measure your understanding of the concepts presented in this chapter and to assist you with real-life implementation of these concepts. To have your questions about this chapter answered by the author, browse to **www.syngress.com/solutions** and click on the **"Ask the Author"** form.

**Q:** What is the difference between using TShark and editcap to translate the format of capture files?

**A:** Nothing—they both perform the same function. However, editcap would be a more efficient method of converting files because TShark contains a lot of code for protocol dissection, whereas editcap is a smaller program with only a few functions. You can also use the Wireshark GUI to do the same thing by choosing **Save As** from the **File** menu.

**Q:** Can mergecap combine gzipped files?

**A:** Yes, mergecap can automatically uncompress, read, and merge gzip files.

**Q:** What types of things can I do to make scripting with TShark faster?

**A:** One way to make scripting faster with TShark is to use the **–l** option to flush the standard output after each packet is printed instead of waiting until it fills up. This way, each packet is sent as soon as it is read and dissected. You can also use the **–n** option to disable network object name resolution to make the process faster.

**Q:** Can I use filters to specify what packets to remove with editcap?

**A:** No, editcap does not have the capability to use filters. You must know the packet numbers you want to include or exclude from the output capture file. You can use TShark to read a capture file, apply filters, and output the results to a new capture file.

# Index

# E

e-mail
  batching mailing list, in daily
    digest, 65–66
  protecting, 44
  protocols, 20
EAP (Extensible Authentication
    Protocol)
  authentication account sharing,
    341–343
  exchanges, analyzing, 307–312
eavesdropping, 2, 6
Edit Capture Filter List dialog box,
    177–178
Edit Display Filter List dialog box,
    180–183
Edit menu, options, 153–155
editcap program, 68–69, 502–509,
    520, 522
editing color filters, 162–164
Enabled Protocols dialog box,
    184–185
encryption
  Digital Signature Algorithm
    (DSA), 43
  identifying wireless mechanisms,
    312–317
  for IEEE 802.11 wireless
    networks, 305
  opportunistic, 50
  and sniffer protection, 42, 90–91
endianness, 431
enumeration (network scanning),
    372
Ethernet
  protocol described, 10–11

protocols used by, 22–25
  securing, 83
Ethernet Protocol Analyzer
    (EPAN), 418–419
EtherPeek network analyzer, 9
Ettercap sniffer, 9, 87
Expert Info, Expert Info
    Composite menu options,
    189
expert TAP, 452–454
expressions in display filters,
    238–241
Extended Service Set (ESS), 297
Extensible Authentication Protocol
    (EAP), 307–312, 341–343

# F

Fedora Core platform, 102
File menu, options, 144–145
files, formats for saving, 147–148
filesnarf utility, 87
Filter Bar feature, 142–144
filters
  command-line options, 215–216
  debugging, 125
  display, using for analysis,
    292–324
  IP display, 61–63
  Wireshark's capture and display,
    60–61
  writing capture, 222–237
  writing display, 237–254
Find Packet dialog box, 155–156
*Find Packet* function, 83
Fink, installing Wireshark on
    MacOSX using, 122–123

# X

# Y

# Z

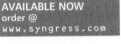

# Syngress: *The Definition of a Serious Security Library*

**Syn·gress** (sin-gres): *noun, sing.* Freedom from risk or danger; safety. See *security*.

# Syngress: *The Definition of a Serious Security Library*

**Syn·gress** (sin–gres): *noun, sing.* Freedom from risk or danger; safety. See *security*.

## Hacking the Code: ASP.NET Web Application Security

Mark Burnett

Are Your Web Applications Really Secure? This unique book walks you through the many threats to your web application code, from managing and authorizing users and encrypting private data to filtering user input and securing XML. For every defined threat, it provides a menu of solutions and coding considerations. And, it offers coding examples and a set of security policies for each of the corresponding threats.

ISBN: 1-93226-665-8

Price: $49.95 US   $69.95 CAN

## Nessus, Snort, & Ethereal Power Tools: Customizing Open Source Security Applications

Brian Caswell, Gilbert Ramirez, Jay Beale, Noam Rathaus, Neil Archibald

If you have Snort, Nessus, and Ethereal up and running and now you're ready to customize, code, and torque these tools to their fullest potential, this book is for you. The authors of this book provide the inside scoop on coding the most effective and efficient Snort rules, Nessus plug-ins with NASL, and Ethereal capture and display filters. When done with this book, you will be a master at coding your own tools to detect malicious traffic, scan for vulnerabilities, and capture only the packets YOU really care about.

ISBN: 1-59749-020-2

Price: $39.95 US   $55.95 CAN

## Hack the Stack: Using Snort and Ethereal to Master the 8 Layers of An Insecure Network

Michael Gregg

Remember the first time someone told you about the OSI model and described the various layers? It's probably something you never forgot.  This book takes that same layered approach but applies it to network security in a new and refreshing way. It guides readers step-by-step through the stack starting with physical security and working its way up through each of the seven OSI layers. Each chapter focuses on one layer of the stack along with the attacks, vulnerabilities, and exploits that can be found at that layer. The book even includes a chapter on the mythical eighth layer. It's called the people layer. It's included because security is not just about technology it also requires interaction with people, policy and office politics.

ISBN: 1-59749-109-8

Price: $49.95 U.S.   $64.95 CAN

SYNGRESS®

# Syngress: *The Definition of a Serious Security Library*

**Syn·gress** (sin–gres): *noun, sing.* Freedom from risk or danger; safety. See *security.*

# Syngress: *The Definition of a Serious Security Library*

**Syn·gress** (sin–gres): *noun, sing.* Freedom from risk or danger; safety. See *security*.

## Syngress IT Security Project Management Handbook
Susan Snedaker

The definitive work for IT professionals responsible for the management of the design, configuration, deployment and maintenance of enterprise-wide security projects. Provides specialized coverage of key project areas including Penetration Testing, Intrusion Detection and Prevention Systems, and Access Control Systems.

ISBN: 1-59749-076-8

Price: $59.95 US   $77.95 CAN

## Combating Spyware in the Enterprise
Paul Piccard

Combating Spyware in the Enterprise is the first book published on defending enterprise networks from increasingly sophisticated and malicious spyware. System administrators and security professionals responsible for administering and securing networks ranging in size from SOHO networks up the largest enterprise networks will learn to use a combination of free and commercial anti-spyware software, firewalls, intrusion detection systems, intrusion prevention systems, and host integrity monitoring applications to prevent the installation of spyware, and to limit the damage caused by spyware that does in fact infiltrate their networks.

ISBN: 1-59749-064-4

Price: $49.95 US   $64.95 CAN

## Practical VoIP Security
Thomas Porter

After struggling for years, you finally think you've got your network secured from malicious hackers and obnoxious spammers. Just when you think it's safe to go back into the water, VoIP finally catches on. Now your newly converged network is vulnerable to DoS attacks, hacked gateways leading to unauthorized free calls, call eavesdropping, malicious call redirection, and spam over Internet Telephony (SPIT). This book details both VoIP attacks and defense techniques and tools.

ISBN: 1-59749-060-1

Price: $49.95 U.S.   $69.95 CAN

**SYNGRESS®**

# Syngress: *The Definition of a Serious Security Library*

**Syn·gress** (sin-gres): *noun, sing.* Freedom from risk or danger; safety. See *security*.

## Cyber Spying: Tracking Your Family's (Sometimes) Secret Online Lives

Dr. Eric Cole, Michael Nordfelt, Sandra Ring, and Ted Fair

Have you ever wondered about that friend your spouse e-mails, or who they spend hours chatting online with? Are you curious about what your children are doing online, whom they meet, and what they talk about? Do you worry about them finding drugs and other illegal items online, and wonder what they look at? This book shows you how to monitor and analyze your family's online behavior.

ISBN: 1-93183-641-8

Price: $39.95 US   $57.95 CAN

## Stealing the Network: How to Own an Identity

Timothy Mullen, Ryan Russell, Riley (Caezar) Eller, Jeff Moss, Jay Beale, Johnny Long, Chris Hurley, Tom Parker, Brian Hatch
The first two books in this series "Stealing the Network: How to Own the Box" and "Stealing the Network: How to Own a Continent" have become classics in the Hacker and Infosec communities because of their chillingly realistic depictions of criminal hacking techniques. In this third installment, the all-star cast of authors tackle one of the fastest-growing crimes in the world: Identity Theft. Now, the criminal hackers readers have grown to both love and hate try to cover their tracks and vanish into thin air...

ISBN: 1-59749-006-7

Price: $39.95 US   $55.95 CAN

## Software Piracy Exposed

Paul Craig, Ron Honick

For every $2 worth of software purchased legally, $1 worth of software is pirated illegally. For the first time ever, the dark underground of how software is stolen and traded over the Internet is revealed. The technical detail provided will open the eyes of software users and manufacturers worldwide! This book is a tell-it-like-it-is exposé of how tens of billions of dollars worth of software is stolen every year.

ISBN: 1-93226-698-4

Price: $39.95 U.S.   $55.95 CAN

**SYNGRESS®**

# Syngress: *The Definition of a Serious Security Library*

**Syn·gress** (sin–gres): *noun, sing.* Freedom from risk or danger; safety. See *security*.

## Phishing Exposed

Lance James, Secure Science Corporation,
Joe Stewart (Foreword)

If you have ever received a phish, become a victim of a phish, or manage the security of a major e-commerce or financial site, then you need to read this book. The author of this book delivers the unconcealed techniques of phishers including their evolving patterns, and how to gain the upper hand against the ever-accelerating attacks they deploy. Filled with elaborate and unprecedented forensics, Phishing Exposed details techniques that system administrators, law enforcement, and fraud investigators can exercise and learn more about their attacker and their specific attack methods, enabling risk mitigation in many cases before the attack occurs.

ISBN: 1-59749-030-X

Price: $49.95 US  $69.95 CAN

## Penetration Tester's Open Source Toolkit

Johnny Long, Chris Hurley, SensePost,
Mark Wolfgang, Mike Petruzzi

This is the first fully integrated Penetration Testing book and bootable Linux CD containing the "Auditor Security Collection," which includes over 300 of the most effective and commonly used open source attack and penetration testing tools. This powerful tool kit and authoritative reference is written by the security industry's foremost penetration testers including HD Moore, Jay Beale, and SensePost. This unique package provides you with a completely portable and bootable Linux attack distribution and authoritative reference to the toolset included and the required methodology.

ISBN: 1-59749-021-0

Price: $59.95 US  $83.95 CAN

## Google Hacking for Penetration Testers

Johnny Long, Foreword by Ed Skoudis

Google has been a strong force in Internet culture since its 1998 upstart. Since then, the engine has evolved from a simple search instrument to an innovative authority of information. As the sophistication of Google grows, so do the hacking hazards that the engine entertains. Approaches to hacking are forever changing, and this book covers the risks and precautions that administrators need to be aware of during this explosive phase of Google Hacking.

ISBN: 1-93183-636-1

Price: $44.95 U.S.  $65.95 CAN

SYNGRESS®

# Syngress: *The Definition of a Serious Security Library*

**Syn·gress** (sin-gres): *noun, sing.* Freedom from risk or danger; safety. See *security*.

# Syngress: *The Definition of a Serious Security Library*

**Syn·gress** (sin-gres): *noun, sing.* Freedom from risk or danger; safety. See *security.*

## How to Cheat at Designing Security for a Windows Server 2003 Network

Neil Ruston, Chris Peiris

While considering the security needs of your organiztion, you need to balance the human and the technical in order to create the best security design for your organization. Securing a Windows Server 2003 enterprise network is hardly a small undertaking, but it becomes quite manageable if you approach it in an organized and systematic way. This includes configuring software, services, and protocols to meet an organization's security needs.

ISBN: 1-59749-243-4
Price: $39.95 US   $55.95 CAN

## How to Cheat at Designing a Windows Server 2003 Active Directory Infrastructure

Melissa Craft, Michael Cross, Hal Kurz, Brian Barber
The book will start off by teaching readers to create the conceptual design of their Active Directory infrastructure by gathering and analyzing business and technical requirements. Next, readers will create the logical design for an Active Directory infrastructure. Here the book starts to drill deeper and focus on aspects such as group policy design. Finally, readers will learn to create the physical design for an active directory and network Infrastructure including DNS server placement; DC and GC placements and Flexible Single Master Operations (FSMO) role placement.

ISBN: 1-59749-058-X
Price: $39.95 US   $55.95 CAN

## How to Cheat at Configuring ISA Server 2004

Dr. Thomas W. Shinder, Debra Littlejohn Shinder

If deploying and managing ISA Server 2004 is just one of a hundred responsibilities you have as a System Administrator, "How to Cheat at Configuring ISA Server 2004" is the perfect book for you. Written by Microsoft MVP Dr. Tom Shinder, this is a concise, accurate, enterprise tested method for the successful deployment of ISA Server.

ISBN: 1-59749-057-1
Price: $34.95 U.S.   $55.95 CAN

SYNGRESS®

# GNU GENERAL PUBLIC LICENSE

Version 2, June 1991

Copyright (C) 1989, 1991 Free Software Foundation, Inc.

59 Temple Place - Suite 330, Boston, MA 02111-1307, USA

## Preamble

The licenses for most software are designed to take away your freedom to share and change it. By contrast, the GNU General Public License is intended to guarantee your freedom to share and change free software—to make sure the software is free for all its users. This General Public License applies to most of the Free Software Foundation's software and to any other program whose authors commit to using it. (Some other Free Software Foundation software is covered by the GNU Library General Public License instead.) You can apply it to your programs, too.

When we speak of free software, we are referring to freedom, not price. Our General Public Licenses are designed to make sure that you have the freedom to distribute copies of free software (and charge for this service if you wish), that you receive source code or can get it if you want it, that you can change the software or use pieces of it in new free programs; and that you know you can do these things.

To protect your rights, we need to make restrictions that forbid anyone to deny you these rights or to ask you to surrender the rights. These restrictions translate to certain responsibilities for you if you distribute copies of the software, or if you modify it.

For example, if you distribute copies of such a program, whether gratis or for a fee, you must give the recipients all the rights that you have. You must make sure that they, too, receive or can get the source code. And you must show them these terms so they know their rights.

We protect your rights with two steps: (1) copyright the software, and (2) offer you this license which gives you legal permission to copy, distribute and/or modify the software.

Also, for each author's protection and ours, we want to make certain that everyone understands that there is no warranty for this free software. If the software is modified by someone else and passed on, we want its recipients to know that what they have is not the original, so that any problems introduced by others will not reflect on the original authors' reputations.

Finally, any free program is threatened constantly by software patents. We wish to avoid the danger that redistributors of a free program will individually obtain patent licenses, in effect making the program proprietary. To prevent this, we have made it clear that any patent must be licensed for everyone's free use or not licensed at all.

The precise terms and conditions for copying, distribution and modification follow.

## TERMS AND CONDITIONS FOR COPYING, DISTRIBUTION AND MODIFICATION

**0.** This License applies to any program or other work which contains a notice placed by the copyright holder saying it may be distributed under the terms of this General Public License. The "Program", below, refers to any such program or work, and a "work based on the Program" means either the Program or any derivative work under copyright law: that is to say, a work containing the Program or a portion of it, either verbatim or with modifications and/or translated into another language. (Hereinafter, translation is included without limitation in the term "modification".) Each licensee is addressed as "you".

Activities other than copying, distribution and modification are not covered by this License; they are outside its scope. The act of running the Program is not restricted, and the output from the Program is covered only if its contents constitute a work based on the Program (independent of having been made by running the Program). Whether that is true depends on what the Program does.

**1.** You may copy and distribute verbatim copies of the Program's source code as you receive it, in any medium, provided that you conspicuously and appropriately publish on each copy an appropriate copyright notice and disclaimer of warranty; keep intact all the notices that refer to this License and to the absence of any warranty; and give any other recipients of the Program a copy of this License along with the Program.

You may charge a fee for the physical act of transferring a copy, and you may at your option offer warranty protection in exchange for a fee.

**2.** You may modify your copy or copies of the Program or any portion of it, thus forming a work based on the Program, and copy and distribute such modifications or work under the terms of Section 1 above, provided that you also meet all of these conditions:

**a)** You must cause the modified files to carry prominent notices stating that you changed the files and the date of any change.

**b)** You must cause any work that you distribute or publish, that in whole or in part contains or is derived from the Program or any part thereof, to be licensed as a whole at no charge to all third parties under the terms of this License.

**c)** If the modified program normally reads commands interactively when run, you must cause it, when started running for such interactive use in the most ordinary way, to print or display an announcement including an appropriate copyright notice and a notice that there is no warranty (or else, saying that you provide a warranty) and that users may redistribute the program under these conditions, and telling the user how to view a copy of this License. (Exception: if the Program itself is interactive but does not normally print such an announcement, your work based on the Program is not required to print an announcement.)

These requirements apply to the modified work as a whole. If identifiable sections of that work are not derived from the Program, and can be reasonably considered independent and separate works in themselves, then this License, and its terms, do not apply to those sections when you distribute them as separate works. But when you distribute the same sections as part of a whole which is a work based on the Program, the distribution of the whole must be on the terms of this License, whose permissions for other licensees extend to the entire whole, and thus to each and every part regardless of who wrote it.

Thus, it is not the intent of this section to claim rights or contest your rights to work written entirely by you; rather, the intent is to exercise the right to control the distribution of derivative or collective works based on the Program.

In addition, mere aggregation of another work not based on the Program with the Program (or with a work based on the Program) on a volume of a storage or distribution medium does not bring the other work under the scope of this License.

**3.** You may copy and distribute the Program (or a work based on it, under Section 2) in object code or executable form under the terms of Sections 1 and 2 above provided that you also do one of the following:

**a)** Accompany it with the complete corresponding machine-readable source code, which must be distributed under the terms of Sections 1 and 2 above on a medium customarily used for software interchange; or,

**b)** Accompany it with a written offer, valid for at least three years, to give any third party, for a charge no more than your cost of physically performing source distribution, a complete machine-readable copy of the corresponding source code, to be distributed under the terms of Sections 1 and 2 above on a medium customarily used for software interchange; or,

**c)** Accompany it with the information you received as to the offer to distribute corresponding source code. (This alternative is allowed only for noncommercial distribution and only if you received the program in object code or executable form with such an offer, in accord with Subsection b above.)

The source code for a work means the preferred form of the work for making modifications to it. For an executable work, complete source code means all the source code for all modules it contains, plus any associated interface definition files, plus the scripts used to control compilation and installation of the executable. However, as a special exception, the source code distributed need not include anything that is normally distributed (in either source or binary form) with the major components (compiler, kernel, and so on) of the operating system on which the executable runs, unless that component itself accompanies the executable.

If distribution of executable or object code is made by offering access to copy from a designated place, then offering equivalent access to copy the source code from the same place counts as distribution of the source code, even though third parties are not compelled to copy the source along with the object code.

**4.** You may not copy, modify, sublicense, or distribute the Program except as expressly provided under this License. Any attempt otherwise to copy, modify, sublicense or distribute the Program is void, and will automatically terminate your rights under this License. However, parties who have received copies, or rights, from you under this License will not have their licenses terminated so long as such parties remain in full compliance.

**5.** You are not required to accept this License, since you have not signed it. However, nothing else grants you permission to modify or distribute the Program or its derivative works. These actions are prohibited by law if you do not accept this License. Therefore, by modifying or distributing the Program (or any work based on the Program), you indicate your acceptance of this License to do so, and all its terms and conditions for copying, distributing or modifying the Program or works based on it.

**6.** Each time you redistribute the Program (or any work based on the Program), the recipient automatically receives a license from the original licensor to copy, distribute or modify the Program subject to these terms and conditions. You may not impose any further restrictions on the recipients' exercise of the rights granted herein. You are not responsible for enforcing compliance by third parties to this License.

**7.** If, as a consequence of a court judgment or allegation of patent infringement or for any other reason (not limited to patent issues), conditions are imposed on you (whether by court order, agreement or otherwise) that contradict the conditions of this License, they do not excuse you from the conditions of this License. If you cannot distribute so as to satisfy simultaneously your obligations under this License and any other pertinent obligations, then as a consequence you may not distribute the Program at all. For example, if a patent license would not permit royalty-free redistribution of the Program by all those who receive copies directly or indirectly through you, then the only way you could satisfy both it and this License would be to refrain entirely from distribution of the Program.

If any portion of this section is held invalid or unenforceable under any particular circumstance, the balance of the section is intended to apply and the section as a whole is intended to apply in other circumstances.

It is not the purpose of this section to induce you to infringe any patents or other property right claims or to contest validity of any such claims; this section has the sole purpose of protecting the integrity of the free software distribution system, which is implemented by public license practices. Many people have made generous contributions to the wide range of software distributed through that system in reliance on consistent application of that system; it is up to the author/donor to decide if he or she is willing to distribute software through any other system and a licensee cannot impose that choice.

This section is intended to make thoroughly clear what is believed to be a consequence of the rest of this License.

**8.** If the distribution and/or use of the Program is restricted in certain countries either by patents or by copyrighted interfaces, the original copyright holder who places the Program under this License may add an explicit geographical distribution limitation excluding those countries, so that distribution is permitted only in or among countries not thus excluded. In such case, this License incorporates the limitation as if written in the body of this License.

**9.** The Free Software Foundation may publish revised and/or new versions of the General Public License from time to time. Such new versions will be similar in spirit to the present version, but may differ in detail to address new problems or concerns.

Each version is given a distinguishing version number. If the Program specifies a version number of this License which applies to it and "any later version", you have the option of following the terms and conditions either of that version or of any later version published by the Free Software Foundation. If the Program does not specify a version number of this License, you may choose any version ever published by the Free Software Foundation.

**10.** If you wish to incorporate parts of the Program into other free programs whose distribution conditions are different, write to the author to ask for permission. For software which is copyrighted by the Free Software Foundation, write to the Free Software Foundation; we sometimes make exceptions for this. Our decision will be guided by the two goals of preserving the free status of all derivatives of our free software and of promoting the sharing and reuse of software generally.

**NO WARRANTY**

**11.** BECAUSE THE PROGRAM IS LICENSED FREE OF CHARGE, THERE IS NO WARRANTY FOR THE PROGRAM, TO THE EXTENT PERMITTED BY APPLICABLE LAW. EXCEPT WHEN OTHERWISE STATED IN WRITING THE COPYRIGHT HOLDERS AND/OR OTHER PARTIES PROVIDE THE PROGRAM "AS IS" WITHOUT WARRANTY OF ANY KIND, EITHER EXPRESSED OR IMPLIED, INCLUDING, BUT NOT LIMITED TO, THE IMPLIED WARRANTIES OF MERCHANTABILITY AND FITNESS FOR A PARTICULAR PURPOSE. THE ENTIRE RISK AS TO THE QUALITY AND PERFORMANCE OF THE PROGRAM IS WITH YOU. SHOULD THE PROGRAM PROVE DEFECTIVE, YOU ASSUME THE COST OF ALL NECESSARY SERVICING, REPAIR OR CORRECTION.

**12.** IN NO EVENT UNLESS REQUIRED BY APPLICABLE LAW OR AGREED TO IN WRITING WILL ANY COPYRIGHT HOLDER, OR ANY OTHER PARTY WHO MAY MODIFY AND/OR REDISTRIBUTE THE PROGRAM AS PERMITTED ABOVE, BE LIABLE TO YOU FOR DAMAGES, INCLUDING ANY GENERAL, SPECIAL, INCIDENTAL OR CONSEQUENTIAL DAMAGES ARISING OUT OF THE USE OR INABILITY TO USE THE PROGRAM (INCLUDING BUT NOT LIMITED TO LOSS OF DATA OR DATA BEING RENDERED INACCURATE OR LOSSES SUSTAINED BY YOU OR THIRD PARTIES OR A FAILURE OF THE PROGRAM TO OPERATE WITH ANY OTHER PROGRAMS), EVEN IF SUCH HOLDER OR OTHER PARTY HAS BEEN ADVISED OF THE POSSIBILITY OF SUCH DAMAGES.

**END OF TERMS AND CONDITIONS**

How to Apply These Terms to Your New Programs

If you develop a new program, and you want it to be of the greatest possible use to the public, the best way to achieve this is to make it free software which everyone can redistribute and change under these terms.

To do so, attach the following notices to the program. It is safest to attach them to the start of each source file to most effectively convey the exclusion of warranty; and each file should have at least the "copyright" line and a pointer to where the full notice is found.

*one line to give the program's name and an idea of what it does.*

Copyright (C) *yyyy   name of author*


This program is free software; you can redistribute it and/or
modify it under the terms of the GNU General Public License
as published by the Free Software Foundation; either version 2
of the License, or (at your option) any later version.


This program is distributed in the hope that it will be useful,
but WITHOUT ANY WARRANTY; without even the implied warranty of
MERCHANTABILITY or FITNESS FOR A PARTICULAR PURPOSE.  See the
GNU General Public License for more details.

You should have received a copy of the GNU General Public License

along with this program; if not, write to the Free Software

Foundation, Inc., 59 Temple Place - Suite 330, Boston, MA 02111-1307, USA.

Also add information on how to contact you by electronic and paper mail.

If the program is interactive, make it output a short notice like this when it starts in an interactive mode:

Gnomovision version 69, Copyright (C) *year name of author*

Gnomovision comes with ABSOLUTELY NO WARRANTY; for details

type `show w'. This is free software, and you are welcome

to redistribute it under certain conditions; type `show c'

for details.

The hypothetical commands 'show w' and 'show c' should show the appropriate parts of the General Public License. Of course, the commands you use may be called something other than 'show w' and 'show c'; they could even be mouse-clicks or menu items—whatever suits your program.

You should also get your employer (if you work as a programmer) or your school, if any, to sign a "copyright disclaimer" for the program, if necessary. Here is a sample; alter the names:

Yoyodyne, Inc., hereby disclaims all copyright

interest in the program `Gnomovision'

(which makes passes at compilers) written

by James Hacker.

*signature of Ty Coon*, 1 April 1989

Ty Coon, President of Vice

This General Public License does not permit incorporating your program into proprietary programs. If your program is a subroutine library, you may consider it more useful to permit linking proprietary applications with the library. If this is what you want to do, use the GNU Library General Public License instead of this License.

## SYNGRESS PUBLISHING LICENSE AGREEMENT

THIS PRODUCT (THE "PRODUCT") CONTAINS PROPRIETARY SOFTWARE, DATA AND INFORMATION (INCLUDING DOCUMENTATION) OWNED BY SYNGRESS PUBLISHING, INC. ("SYNGRESS") AND ITS LICENSORS. YOUR RIGHT TO USE THE PRODUCT IS GOVERNED BY THE TERMS AND CONDITIONS OF THIS AGREEMENT.

**LICENSE:** Throughout this License Agreement, "you" shall mean either the individual or the entity whose agent opens this package. You are granted a limited, non-exclusive and non-transferable license to use the Product subject to the following terms:

(i) If you have licensed a single user version of the Product, the Product may only be used on a single computer (i.e., a single CPU). If you licensed and paid the fee applicable to a local area network or wide area network version of the Product, you are subject to the terms of the following subparagraph (ii).

(ii) If you have licensed a local area network version, you may use the Product on unlimited workstations located in one single building selected by you that is served by such local area network. If you have licensed a wide area network version, you may use the Product on unlimited workstations located in multiple buildings on the same site selected by you that is served by such wide area network; provided, however, that any building will not be considered located in the same site if it is more than five (5) miles away from any building included in such site. In addition, you may only use a local area or wide area network version of the Product on one single server. If you wish to use the Product on more than one server, you must obtain written authorization from Syngress and pay additional fees.

(iii) You may make one copy of the Product for back-up purposes only and you must maintain an accurate record as to the location of the back-up at all times.

**PROPRIETARY RIGHTS; RESTRICTIONS ON USE AND TRANSFER:** All rights (including patent and copyright) in and to the Product are owned by Syngress and its licensors. You are the owner of the enclosed disc on which the Product is recorded. You may not use, copy, decompile, disassemble, reverse engineer, modify, reproduce, create derivative works, transmit, distribute, sublicense, store in a database or retrieval system of any kind, rent or transfer the Product, or any portion thereof, in any form or by any means (including electronically or otherwise) except as expressly provided for in this License Agreement. You must reproduce the copyright